Contents of the Companion CD-ROM

This free CD-ROM contains several tools you'll find invaluable. The disk contains the following software:

- Information Access Company's Computer Select Trial Edition (©1995 Information Access Company). The trial edition contains a full year of article text and abstracts from over 100 leading publications, over 10,000 company profiles, specifications for over 75,000 hardware and software products, and nearly 20,000 computer term definitions.
- ITI's DispBind (v1.00 ©1994–1995 ITI). This public domain software displays account information for logged-in users.
- Montauk Software's Netalk (v1.5 ©1995 Montauk Software, Inc.). This freeware package allows users to chat with each other more easily than NetWare's SEND command.
- NETMan's NET-ALERT (v2.2 ©1994 NETMan). The demonstration version of this utility monitors up to three file servers and notifies up to three pagers with a numeric message when one of the servers goes down.
- K.F. Soft's Nice Capture (v1.2a ©1994 K.F. Soft). This utility provides users with a full-screen DOS interface for capturing print jobs in NetWare 3.11.
- K.F. Soft's Nice Login (v1.8 ©1994 K.F. Soft). This utility provides a full-screen DOS interface for logging into servers and provides better prompting and error messages than NetWare's LOGIN command.
- Sexwax Software's LOG.EXE (v1 ©1994 Sexwax Software). This freeware program records account names, connection numbers, network addresses, dates, and times as users log into the network.

See the inside back cover for installation instructions.

INTRODUCING NETWORK PRESS™

Welcome to Network Press, the new and expanded successor to **Sybex's** acclaimed **Novell Press**® book series. This book represents a significant change in how you will access the best networking knowledge in the future. Readers who value Sybex's Novell Press books now have an independent source in Network Press for unbiased information on Novell, Microsoft, and other network environments.

Network Press, building upon Sybex's twenty-year history of technical and publishing excellence, is dedicated to expanding the range and depth of publications available to you. You'll find the same dedication to quality, contents, and timeliness that you have come to expect from Sybex. Look to Network Press for a truly comprehensive body of knowledge on the complete spectrum of networks and networking issues.

With striking new covers, emblematic of networks that form the natural world, and completely updated contents, you'll soon find that the book you need looks a lot like this one. To be assured of unparalleled quality in your computer book selections, look for the Sybex logo.

All previously released Novell Press titles remain available from Sybex. New editions will be released as part of the expanding Network Press family of titles.

In addition to this outstanding title, the Network Press library includes:

The CNE Study Guide, by David James Clarke, IV
The CNA Study Guide, by David James Clarke, IV
The Network Press Dictionary of Networking, by Peter Dyson
The Complete Guide to NetWare 4.1, by James E. Gaskin
Introduction to Local Area Networks, by Robert M. Thomas

For more information, please contact:
Sybex Inc.
2021 Challenger Drive
Alameda, CA 94501
Tel: (510) 523-8233/(800) 227-2346
Fax: (510) 523-2373

Managing an Inherited NetWare® Network

Michael Joseph Miller

San Francisco ▪ Paris ▪ Düsseldorf ▪ Soest

Acquisitions Manager: Kristine Plachy
Developmental Editor: Guy Hart-Davis
Editor: Nancy Crumpton
Project Editors: Emily Smith, Valerie Potter
Technical Editor: Deni Connor
Book Designer: Seventeenth Street Studios
Technical Artist: Cuong Le
Desktop Publishers: Deborah Maizels, Stephanie Hollier
Proofreader/Production Assistant: Renée Avalos
Indexer: Matthew Spence
Cover Designer: Archer Design
Cover Photographer: Darrell Gulin

Library of Congress Card Number: 95-69861
ISBN: 0-7821-1745-7

Manufactured in the United States of America
10 9 8 7 6 5 4 3 2 1

Warranty

SYBEX WARRANTS THE enclosed CD-ROM to be free of physical defects for a period of ninety (90) days after purchase. If you discover a defect in the CD during this warranty period, you can obtain a replacement CD at no charge by sending the defective CD, postage prepaid, with proof of purchase to:

Sybex Inc.
Customer Service Department
2021 Challenger Drive
Alameda, CA 94501
(800) 227-2346
Fax: (510) 523-2373

After the 90-day period, you can obtain a replacement CD by sending us the defective CD, proof of purchase, and a check or money order for $10, payable to Sybex.

Disclaimer

SYBEX MAKES NO warranty or representation, either express or implied, with respect to this medium or its contents, its quality, performance, merchantability, or fitness for a particular purpose. In no event will Sybex, its distributors, or dealers be liable for direct, indirect, special, incidental, or consequential damages arising out of the use of or inability to use the software even if advised of the possibility of such damage.

The exclusion of implied warranties is not permitted by some states. Therefore, the above exclusion may not apply to you. This warranty provides you with specific legal rights; there may be other rights that you may have that vary from state to state.

Copy Protection

NONE OF THE programs on the CD is copy-protected. However, in all cases, reselling or making copies of these programs without authorization is expressly forbidden.

Acknowledgments

I'D LIKE TO buy a round of drinks for those who helped bring this book to life:

A bottle of scotch to Jim Sumser, without whom this book would still be a germ in the back of my mind.

One liter of vodka to Gary Ellis, who first gave me the opportunity to make and play with a production network.

Shots of tequila to Tom Esber, who provided a network to inherit, to Jeff Bauman, who remains my personal networking guru, and to Kevin McCarthy, my 26-hour workday tag-teammate.

Finger-numbing pints to Guy Hart-Davis, Emily Smith, and Val Potter at Sybex for their guidance and nimble work with the cattle prod.

Tumblers of gin straight up to the Sybex production team of Renée Avalos, Deborah Maizels, and Stephanie Hollier for their patience, perseverance, and skills.

A split of champagne to Nancy Crumpton for her outstanding editing and appreciation of dry wit.

And a glass of wine in toast to the memory of Sandy Jackson, whose friendship and support made so many projects more bearable.

Contents at a Glance

Table of Contents

Introduction

SO YOU FIND yourself in the middle of the Age of Ubiquitous Networking, and you figure network management might be a pretty steady gig with cool toys to play with, a decent salary, and maybe some professional prestige.

You're not put off by the potential for long hours, the irritation of dealing with angry users, and the frustration of reporting to managers who don't appreciate the magnitude of the minor miracles you work each day to keep their production systems running.

Networking is pervasive, and the network operating system with the largest following is Novell's NetWare, so opportunity abounds. And thanks to Novell's training and certification program, as well as to the teeming throngs of books, videos, and courses that can help you learn about the operating system itself, there are many ways to become proficient with NetWare.

There are markedly fewer opportunities to learn how to manage a real-world network. If you can become part of a team of experienced network professionals, or if you find that rare position running a network that doesn't need much attention, you can probably learn enough on the job to absorb the required knowledge at your own pace and in your own way.

In most circumstances, a network administration job doesn't give you the luxury of learning about the network haphazardly. The demands of a production-oriented network environment, with real users experiencing real problems, leaves little time for random poking and prodding.

Who Should Read This Book

IF YOU'RE STARTING or anticipating starting a job managing a network that consists primarily of NetWare servers and users, this book is intended for you. If you're already managing a network and are finding that it has evolved to the point that you're not familiar with it, this book can help you sort out the most important issues and give you the power to assert yourself in the network administrator's role. And if you are hiring new network management staff members, consider reading this book before passing it on to the new folks. Take the opportunity to acquaint yourself with the issues your support staff will be struggling with.

What This Book Will Do for You

LOOK AROUND AT the other books on the shelves in the networking section of your bookstore. Check out the books offered by your club. If you want to know how to use NetWare utilities, pass NetWare certification exams, or create programs for NetWare networks, you'll find plenty of resources.

Most of us aren't simply faced with the task of using a particular tool or learning about a certain technology. As network administrators, we are called upon to repair, nurture, and expand a dynamic infrastructure. We are required to balance the advantages and risks of new technologies. We need to be identifying the business goals that are most important to our organizations so we can improve performance and reliability in these areas. They don't call it network *management* for nothing; business concerns should be shaping the technology.

This book takes an organized approach to discovering what your network is like, making changes that are immediately necessary, and preparing for ongoing management and development. At each stage, we discuss ways in which you can increase your knowledge about the work being done on the network so that you can make changes to support current needs and make plans to support new business processes as they develop.

How This Book Works

THE BOOK IS organized into four sections. In the first five chapters, you look over the network as it currently exists. You identify network equipment and structures, network operating systems and protocols, client station configurations, and the division of business functions on the network. You also update and verify important disaster recovery measures.

In the next five chapters, you begin to take charge of the network. You ascertain production needs and identify production system problems. You begin to assert yourself in the network administrator's role. Then you resolve network security issues, eliminate useless network baggage, and document your stabilized, secured, and streamlined network.

In the third group of five chapters, you begin your maintenance and ongoing care routines. You identify and resolve network problems, implement important network upgrades, develop and automate network checkup routines, make use of network administration tools, and work with in-house staff, value-added resellers, and professional associations to improve your knowledge and clout.

In the last five-chapter section, you prepare for future development. You learn to anticipate future networking demands, consider some hardware and software upgrades that may be advantageous, tap sources of information about emerging technologies, and work to gain and maintain management support.

In each chapter, there's a quick description of the main information and tasks discussed. You can use these lists to check your progress as you work through the most important aspects of inherited network management. And throughout the book, a process-oriented approach is emphasized. The Appendix contains a brief description of the NetWare commands that are discussed throughout the book. If you encounter unfamiliar terms, consult the Glossary.

But Wait, Don't Answer Yet...

THERE'S A LOT of information here, but there are also some goodies. On the CD-ROM included with this book, you'll find several freeware and shareware utilities, along with a full trial edition of the Computer Select product. This invaluable information resource includes a year's worth of articles from the leading computer and technical publications as well as an enormous glossary and guides to computer hardware, software, and companies.

That's the book in a nutshell. Now it's time to roll up your sleeves and get into the good stuff!

Taking Stock of the Network

Surveying Your Spread: Looking Over the Physical Layout

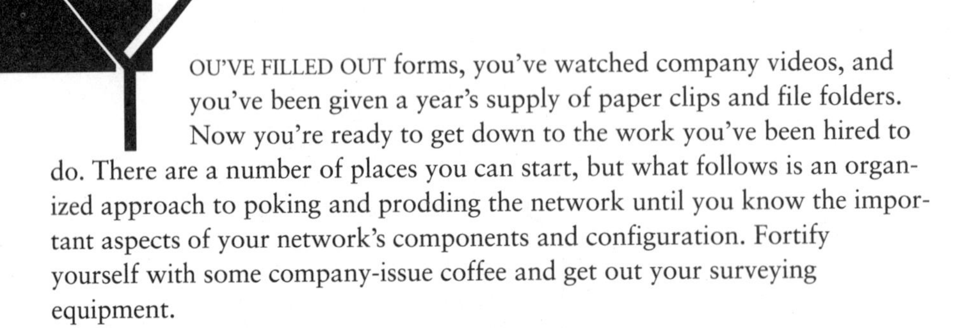

YOU'VE FILLED OUT forms, you've watched company videos, and you've been given a year's supply of paper clips and file folders. Now you're ready to get down to the work you've been hired to do. There are a number of places you can start, but what follows is an organized approach to poking and prodding the network until you know the important aspects of your network's components and configuration. Fortify yourself with some company-issue coffee and get out your surveying equipment.

Bring a pad of paper, a sharp pencil, and copies of the File Server Worksheet found in the NetWare Installation manual. You don't need elaborate tools at this point!

Turn to the Highlights section for a brief preview of the most important information and to the Checklist section for a more thorough list of items to investigate. Use your triage skills to determine the depth of information you can gather immediately; if you must move on immediately to other issues, save the detail items for later.

The Vital Information

THE FOLLOWING LISTS are tailored to two levels of physical layout investigation. If you're swamped by meetings and problems await you, you'll want to collect the information discussed in the Highlights section. These issues are the fundamental bits of information that identify the physical layout of your network and allow you to talk intelligently about its design and configuration. The Checklist items are a comprehensive compilation of network information that will be useful to you. There's no garbage in either section; you'll want to know every bit of this information. Unfortunately, you may not have the time or opportunity to immediately investigate these items thoroughly.

Highlights

At this stage of investigation, you need to identify several portions of the network you manage. First, locate the NetWare servers and record the following information:

- Names
- Locations
- IPX internal network numbers
- Speed ratings
- NetWare-reported memory
- Reported hard disks
- Reported volumes
- Loaded name spaces

Next, determine which non-NetWare machines are likely to be connected to the NetWare networks. Then, identify the following network components:

- Cabling type
- Physical topology
- Communications protocols employed
- Network interconnection equipment
- NetWare server–connected internetworks

For each NetWare server, identify:

- Number of user licenses
- Number of currently active users
- File server utilization rate

Consult the Checklist for potential sources of information and for an expanded list of tasks.

Checklist

The Checklist provides the bits of information you'll want to uncover, and even better, it shows the tools you can use to bring the important networking information to light. These tasks and tools are explained in more detail throughout this section.

	TASK	SERVER STATUS	TOOL
❑	Locate server name	Up	CONFIG console command
❑	Locate server internal network number	Up	CONFIG console command
❑	Determine processor rating	Up	SPEED console command
❑	Find RAM reported by NetWare	Up	MEMORY console command
❑	Determine number of hard disks	Up	INSTALL console utility
❑	Locate networks connected to	Up	CONFIG, DISPLAY NETWORKS console commands

	TASK	SERVER STATUS	TOOL
❑	Identify the network driver versions	Up	CONFIG console command
❑	View the NetWare-reported hard disks	Up	INSTALL console utility
❑	Determine microprocessor model/speed	Down	Inspection
❑	Identify bus architecture	Down	Inspection
❑	Determine memory installed	Down	Inspection
❑	Identify network interface cards	Down	Inspection
❑	Locate disk controllers	Down	Inspection
❑	Determine number of hard disks installed	Down	Inspection

Inspecting the File Servers

THE NETWARE FILE servers, Microsoft Windows NT servers, UNIX hosts, and LAN-connected minicomputers and mainframe computers are the first components you'll want to investigate. If you want to know about a network, you have to know the servers. Your understanding of what the servers do will expand with time, and network connection and load issues will be addressed, but first you should investigate the machines themselves. This section discusses the servers; the next section, Inspecting the Host Systems, discusses the host systems.

NetWare file servers primarily exist to distribute files and share network resources such as printers and modems. Because NetWare functions as a multiprotocol router, the file server can also handle communications between clients on dissimilar networks if the proper hardware and software is installed. For the moment, concern yourself with some of the basic server information outlined in this chapter. Collect more detail as you go along or when you have a chance for more leisurely exploration.

Network View of Server Configuration

At this point, you should introduce yourself to the NetWare file servers. As it turns out, servers don't much care who you are. However, the prudent administrator will learn several basic things about the servers immediately. These bits of information can be found using the CONFIG command from the console prompt.

The NetWare server console prompt is a colon.

Try to avoid learning anything twice. Most network administrators inheriting anything but the smallest, most underutilized networks do not have the luxury of uncovering the same information repeatedly. To maximize the return on your investment of time, try to record the most important information as you go along:

- Write down what you learn about each server.
- Label each server with its name and internal network number.
- Label each hub, concentrator, or multistation access unit (MSAU) with its network number.
- Tag each cable coming from a server into a hub.

Chanting the MAU, MSAU Mantra

You're likely to encounter several kinds of network connection devices. The most common terms for these devices are concentrators, hubs, MAUs, and MSAUs.

Concentrators connect several communications circuits to a smaller number of circuits.

Hubs are devices that allow multiple workstations to attach to a network. *Active hubs* amplify the network transmissions they receive and can increase the distance between nodes on the network. *Passive hubs* only split the signal and pass it on to multiple stations.

Media access units (MAUs) once referred to hubs and concentrators used for ARCNet and Ethernet implementations.

Multistation access units (MSAUs or MAUs) referred to the similar devices used to connect Token Ring nodes.

These days, the terms *MAU* and *MSAU* are used loosely and interchangeably. Either term is probably referring to a multistation access unit.

Masking tape and a marker work acceptably for tagging network components; anal retentives and those administrators with high-profile networks or large amounts of free time will want to invest in a labeling machine and cable-labeling equipment.

The Console Prompt

The prompt for a NetWare file server is a colon. Many users are used to seeing DOS prompts, which show a drive letter and often a path. Others are familiar with the OS/2 prompt, which encloses the drive letter and path with square brackets.

SYSTEM	PROMPT
DOS	C:\DATA\NOTES>
OS/2	[C:\DATA\NOTES]
NetWare client	F:\DATA\NOTES>
NetWare console	:

Using the CONFIG Console Command

The CONFIG command is entered at the NetWare console prompt on a file server.

```
:CONFIG
```

CONFIG displays information about the server:

File server name

IPX internal network number

It also displays information about each of the server's network adapters:

LAN driver and version number loaded for the board

Slot number, I/O port, and interrupt assigned to the board

The node address for the board

The frame type used by the board

The name used by the board

The LAN protocol bound to the board

The network number of the cabling connected to the board

The server configuration information is displayed on the screen as shown in Figure 1.1.

Servers with many network adapters and multiple LAN transport or communications protocols scroll one screen of information at a time.

Finding the Server Name

Each NetWare server must have a name. These names are often descriptive and indicate the function or department supported by the file server (for example, SALES, SYSTEMS). Other names use literary or historical themes (for example, NAPOLEON, PROKOFIEV). Whimsy, fantasy, and sci-fi are also popular (for example, THORIN, BURBLE). If a theme is discernible, its

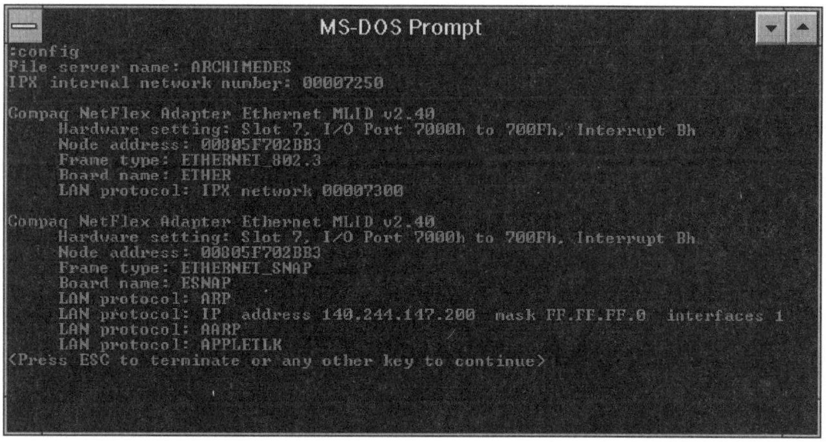

FIGURE 1.1 The information displayed by the CONFIG command on a file server console.

MS-DOS Prompt

```
:config
File server name: ARCHIMEDES
IPX internal network number: 00007250

Compaq NetFlex Adapter Ethernet MLID v2.40
     Hardware setting: Slot 7, I/O Port 7000h to 700Fh, Interrupt Bh
     Node address: 00805F702BB3
     Frame type: ETHERNET_802.3
     Board name: ETHER
     LAN protocol: IPX network 00007300

Compaq NetFlex Adapter Ethernet MLID v2.40
     Hardware setting: Slot 7, I/O Port 7000h to 700Fh, Interrupt Bh
     Node address: 00805F702BB3
     Frame type: ETHERNET_SNAP
     Board name: ESNAP
     LAN protocol: ARP
     LAN protocol: IP  address 140.244.147.200  mask FF.FF.FF.0  interfaces 1
     LAN protocol: AARP
     LAN protocol: APPLETLK
<Press ESC to terminate or any other key to continue>
```

value may simply be in differentiating machines while maintaining a relatively accessible pool of possibilities. A naming scheme can also provide information—and misinformation—about how the network is used or structured. As shown in Figure 1.2, the servers' names are SNYDER, KAPP, and THEDER.

Determining the Internal Network Number

The server's IPX internal network number is a unique identifying number for the server's internal router. This definition is succinct, but it may not be completely clear. The distinction between a network number and an internal network number is noteworthy.

Each server has at least one network adapter, also called a network interface card or NIC. These adapters physically connect the server to the cabling that makes up the network. You can think of the cabling systems that make up the networks as city streets. In NetWare's terms, the street names are hexadecimal (base 16) numbers in the range of 1 to FFFFFFFE. The layout of these streets is called the *topology*.

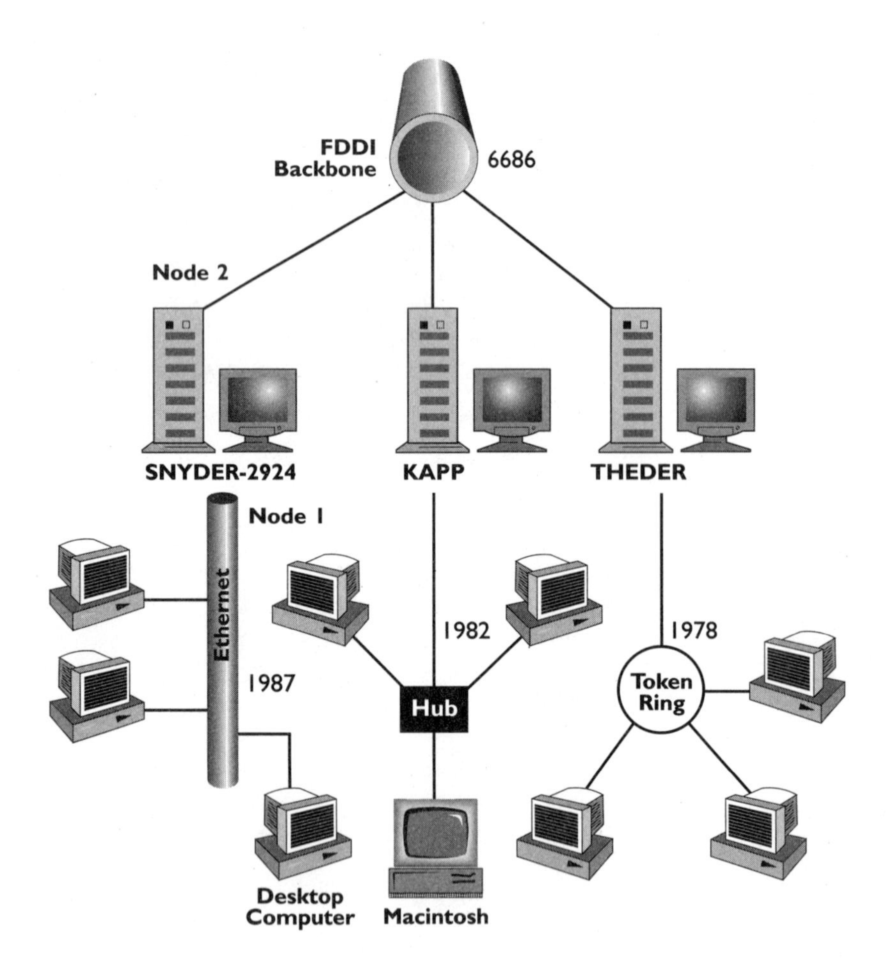

FIGURE 1.2 This internetwork has three servers, SNYDER, KAPP, and THEDER, each supporting workstations on different topologies and access methods.

Servers and clients on any given cabling system have address numbers as well. These addresses are the network node numbers. The combination of a node number and network number give the equivalent of a full street address.

A network server with multiple NICs has multiple network addresses. It has only one internal network number, however. In Figure 1.2, SNYDER is Node 01 on Network 1987 and Node 02 on Network 6686. SNYDER still has only one internal network number, however: 2924.

If the node and network numbers are equivalent to street addresses, an apt analogy for the internal network number is the zip code. The internal net is how network data is routed to a specific server for distribution along the network cabling systems it serves.

Identifying Server Hardware

You know the names and addresses of the servers. Now it is time to delve further and find out more about the server machines themselves. You'll have to "look under the hood" for several of the following configuration items. This generally requires that you down the server and remove the case or cover to expose the components inside.

You can bring a server down by issuing the DOWN console command at the file server console prompt. The server issues a warning if users have files open. Try to get all files closed before taking the server down to prevent corruption of data.

If your predecessors have left documentation from the manufacturer, packing slips, or inventory records, you'll be in position to defer this major step. If you've been left adrift, however, you'll want to schedule some downtime to explore the servers.

Taking a server down is never a trivial issue, even when the users have gone home and nobody is around to interrupt or disturb you with frustrated cursing. Disk drives in marginal condition often spin indefinitely but may not spin up and mount when you reboot the machine. Intermittent problems caused by interrupt conflicts, cabling degradation, and improper termination can often turn nasty (or appear only) when the server is restarted. Downing the server isn't a bad thing, but as my father says, there's risk inherent in changing states in a system.

Even if you have access to documentation or lists of equipment, it's a good idea to open the servers anyway. You may find that the most recent information you can unearth is out of date. You may also find that an unscrupulous predecessor has absconded with memory or add-in boards. It's a good idea to become familiar with the internal layout of your systems so that if disaster strikes, your learning curve won't be as steep.

Remember that a file server is simply another computer; its components and design may be more sophisticated in some ways, but it is not fundamentally any different from the PCs you and your clients use.

Uncovering Processor Information

NetWare lacks a method of directly identifying the microprocessor used in a file server, but you can use the SPEED console command to determine the relative performance level indicated by NetWare. From the console prompt, issue the command:

```
:SPEED
```

NetWare returns a number indicating the relative speed of the processor. If the speed is lower than you expect based on the processor model you find, check to see whether a high-speed setting can be issued for the server; some machines default to non-turbo mode and run at a much slower clock speed than the maximum.

NETWARE RATING	RELATED PROCESSOR
95	80386SX
120	80386DX (16 MHz)
1830	80486DX (66 MHz)
3660	Pentium (66 MHz)

A microprocessor is a chip or a set of chips that execute the calculations and comparisons done by software. The microprocessor's time is split between the various hardware components via interrupts. Most microprocessors are capable of multitasking—servicing multiple programs and processes simultaneously.

Intel dominates the NetWare server market, but the list of Intel-compatible processors that can be found in server-class machines—some from very reputable vendors—is growing. The increased competition is mostly at the middle and low ends of the microprocessor market, partially because Intel's massive development operation now has an incentive to push the high-end technology past what its competitors can provide.

INTEL 80386 AND COMPATIBLES Intel's 80386 microprocessor family is the lowest-powered processor that runs the versions of NetWare that are currently sold. Older versions of NetWare (version 2.x and earlier) were quite different in many ways from NetWare 3.x and 4.x. If you've inherited a network with older versions of NetWare running on the servers, upgrade to a currently

supported version of the product. See Chapter 12 for a discussion of immediate upgrades.

See the NetWare section in Chapter 2 for a discussion of the differences between the various versions of NetWare.

Although the 386 is the minimum processor required, it is still a highly advanced, complex chip. The 80386 can run at clock speeds from 16 MHz on early models to 40 MHz on some compatible chips from vendors other than Intel. This means that 16 to 40 processor cycles are executed each second. The 80386 has a 32-bit architecture internally and externally, although Intel's 80386SX uses 16-bit communications externally. This stifled external data bus was developed because at the time the 386 was designed, few IBM-compatible computers used data bus designs greater than 16 bits. The design practice of making a microprocessor faster internally than externally is common because most bus, add-in board, and peripheral designs lag behind leading-edge chip design. (After all, it would be foolish to develop a 256K-bit adapter board before 256K-bit buses and processors were available.)

The Intel 80386DX chip and most of the compatible microprocessors from other vendors use the full 32-bit bus externally. The 386 can address large amounts of physical memory and virtual memory—enough that many operating systems running on the processor cannot address the full 4GB of physical memory the 386 can use. NetWare 3.x can use the full 4GB of RAM, but you're not likely to see an installation with anywhere near that amount. For the most part, the limitation has been how much RAM can physically be located on the motherboard or memory bus. Of course, few installations would require this much RAM on a NetWare file server, and most administrators would find the price tag for the full complement of RAM prohibitive. The full 4GB of RAM for $150,000 would be a steal.

The 386 does not have an internal math coprocessor; math functions can be more efficiently processed if the 80386DX or 80386SX chip is coupled with an 80387DX or 80387SX math coprocessor. These chips are separate items that plug into a 386 system's motherboard and handle floating-point math procedures.

INTEL 80486 AND COMPATIBLES These microprocessors run at faster clock speeds, from 25 MHz to 100 MHz in the 80486DX4. They also combine a microprocessor, a math coprocessor, and a 4KB RAM cache onto a single chip. A RAM cache is memory that instructions are stored in to improve system speed. The 4KB cache is not large enough to be sufficient by itself, so most 486 systems include an external RAM cache, usually ranging in size from 64KB to 512KB.

The improved speeds found in the 32-bit 486 processors are partially provided by another design that allows the chip to perform faster when executing commands internally than when communicating with the rest of the system. Clock doubling and tripling is commonly used to allow a chip that runs at 25 MHz or 33 MHz externally to process internal commands twice as fast—50 million or 66 million instructions per second for clock-doubled chips, and 75 million or 100 million instructions per second for clock-tripled versions.

PENTIUM The Pentium chip, the next in Intel's line, is a faster, more advanced microprocessor. It contains 3.1 million transistors, almost three times as many as the 80486. It is available in clock speeds ranging from 60 MHz to over 100 MHz.

Intel named the Pentium to diverge from the 80x86 naming scheme the chip manufacturer started with but could not trademark. The name isn't bad, but it led to speculation that the next generation processor might be called the Sexium, a less appealing moniker. The Pentium's successor is currently being referred to as P6.

Some early Pentium systems were not designed to cool the microprocessor adequately, and the stocky chip was known to overheat; newer designs and a variety of third-party cooling devices keep the heat generated by the processor from being an ongoing problem. The Pentium has a beefed-up floating-point unit (FPU) built in, although this enhancement is of less interest to file and database servers than it is to process servers and math- or graphics-intensive workstations.

P6 The P6, which Intel began developing concurrently with the Pentium, is Intel's next-generation microprocessor. It combines a reduced instruction set (RISC) design with the inherited complex instruction set (CISC) aspects of the 80x86 family. The P6 includes a synchronous 256KB Level 2 cache on a 64-bit processor bus, which may standardize performance somewhat between machines designed by different vendors. Although Intel is also including a 16KB Level 1 cache, it is serious enough about the need for an integrated Level 2 cache that it is manufacturing super-fast (10-nanosecond or less) SRAM to enhance performance further.

The Pentium Bug

The Pentium processor was produced in large quantities with a flaw that caused large-scale calculations to return erroneous results. Although the problem appears only when extremely large numbers are manipulated, users were outraged when the news was leaked.

The result of the calculation (48.999999÷41.9999999)×41.9999999 should be 48.999999, but my flawed Pentium-based system returns 48.99987692969. Another example is 4195835–((4195835÷3145727)×3,145,727), which should return 0 but comes up with 256 on a buggy Pentium.

Intel initially indicated that it would not recall the chips, but it later set up a program to replace the defective processors with newer chips.

Frustrated users spread jokes like this one: How many Pentium programmers does it take to screw in a light bulb? Three. One to stand on a chair holding the bulb and one to spin the chair around.

Intel's P6 chip was previewed early in 1995 and is expected to be available in small quantities in late 1995. Several computer manufacturers anticipate having P6-based systems available in time for the 1995 Fall Comdex trade show.

The P6 also includes a new system bus that allows up to four processors to work in harmony. With PowerPC processors threatening to invade the desktop and designs from AMD, Cyrix, and others promising more bang for the buck in Intel-compatible systems, Intel has more reason than ever to ratchet up performance in its processor line.

Looking at the Server Bus

A computer's bus is the path that system components and add-in boards use to communicate with the microprocessor. Since NetWare servers act primarily as *file* servers rather than *applications* servers, they are mainly concerned with opening files as clients request access to them.

Applications servers are simply user-accessible network machines that run programs. While NetWare is an excellent file server system, it is not as well suited to running applications, in part because its protection of memory is not as strong as its other features. Although Novell is encouraging development of NetWare-based applications, most notably database NetWare Loadable Modules (NLMs) such as Oracle and Lotus Notes, NetWare faces competition from UNIX products and Windows NT, which run applications rapidly and safely.

The biggest burden on the server is usually on the memory and drives. Since the bus ties these frequently accessed components to the microprocessor, the ability of the bus to handle large amounts of information simultaneously is vital to acceptable network performance. Thus, it is important to know the bus *bandwidth*—the amount of data that can flow along the bus. Some bus designs also provide certain other advantages and disadvantages.

Boards and Resources

The boards installed in a server or workstation communicate with the computer's microprocessor via *interrupts*. Each board is assigned an *interrupt request* (IRQ) number; the microprocessor monitors the IRQs and responds to the corresponding device when a request for attention is seen.

Two more kinds of resources used by add-in boards relate to the way the boards access the computer's memory and microprocessor. The *I/O port* setting indicates the address of the board's interface to the microprocessor, while the *memory address* or base I/O number indicates the starting address of the computer's memory available to the device.

Proper resource configuration prevents multiple devices from attempting to use the same IRQ or I/O port and keeps a device with large memory requirements from overwriting memory assigned to another device.

ISA The Industry Standard Architecture (ISA) bus was used in the IBM PC AT systems and persists in most workstation designs today. It is a 16-bit bus (though you can find many 8-bit adapters that do not use the full bandwidth because of low input/output requirements or as a cost-reducing measure). The ISA bus connector is illustrated in Figure 1.3. The prevalence of the ISA bus was one reason Intel produced the 80386SX, the microprocessor with the 16-bit external design.

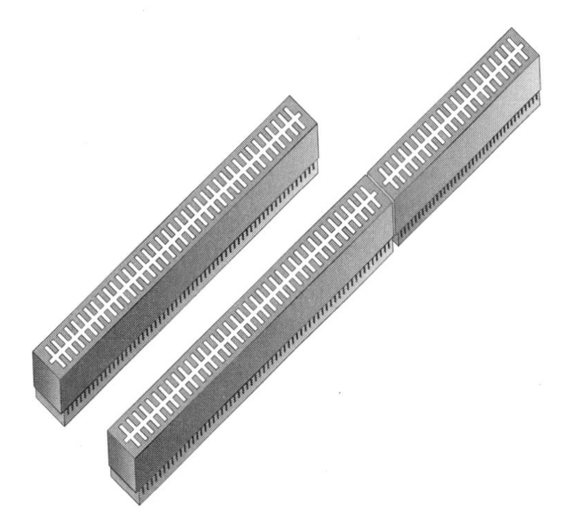

FIGURE 1.3
ISA bus connectors with one slot accept 8-bit boards, those with two slots accept 8-bit or 16-bit boards.

Sixteen-bit boards have two sets of connectors that plug into the expansion bus, which is usually on the computer's motherboard. A 16-bit ISA board is shown in Figure 1.4. The length of the boards varies by manufacturer, board function, the year it was produced, etc. *Full-length* boards theoretically should snuggle into the expansion bus connectors while the non-exposed end slides through a board support. Because of variations in board length and computer system layout, this fit does not always work as well as it should.

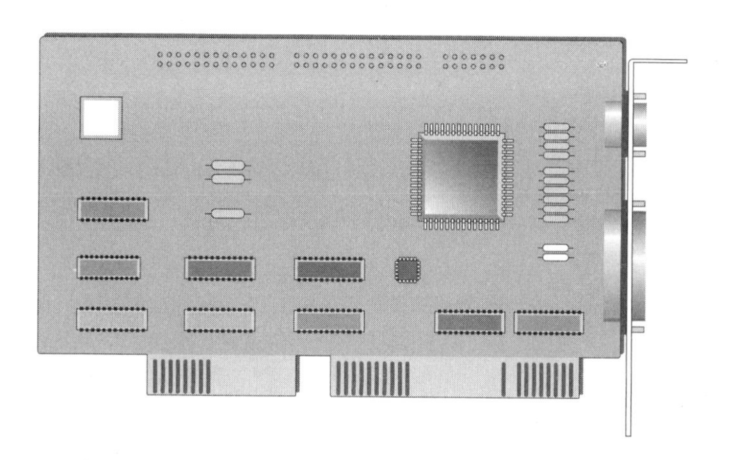

FIGURE 1.4
Sixteen-bit ISA boards have two sets of contacts that slide into the connectors on the motherboard.

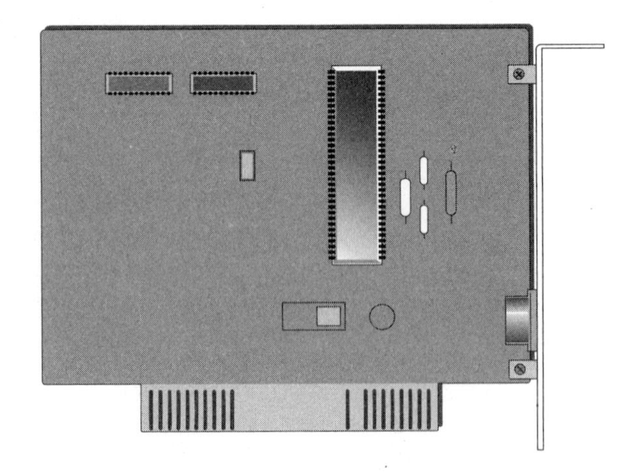

FIGURE 1.5
Eight-bit ISA boards have a single set of contacts that mates with the ISA connector. The second connector on a 16-bit slot is unused.

Eight-bit boards use only one of the connector sets and are often very short. An 8-bit ISA board is pictured in Figure 1.5. Avoid using 8-bit boards, especially in servers that handle lots of traffic, because their limited bandwidth is a liability. A serial/parallel I/O card on a file server may never be used and doesn't need to be upgraded, but an 8-bit network card would hamstring the operation of the network.

MICRO CHANNEL The Micro Channel Architecture bus, or MCA bus, is a 32-bit bus used by IBM in its original PS/2 line of personal computers. Figure 1.6 illustrates a Micro Channel bus connector. Later PS/2 machines do not necessarily use the Micro Channel bus, which never became tremendously popular.

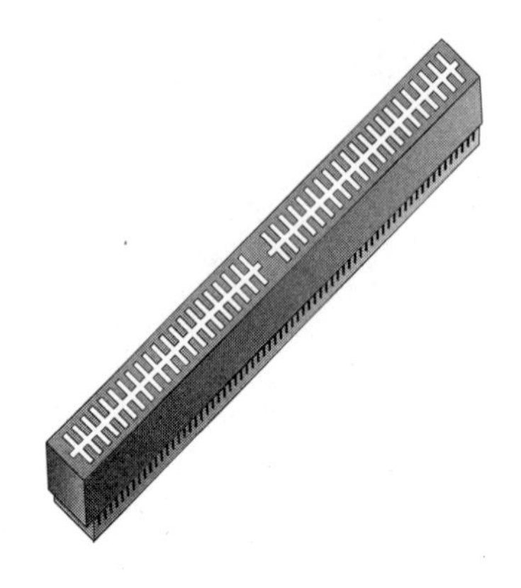

FIGURE 1.6
Micro Channel bus connectors provide 32-bit communications and bus-mastering but are not compatible with ISA boards.

IBM's design had some advantages, but it had two dramatic flaws. One was lack of compatibility with ISA boards. Ah, lack of backward compatibility strikes again. The second flaw only exacerbated the first flaw: pricing on the boards was so high that users were not inclined to discard their perfectly useful ISA-based machines to use Micro Channel systems.

The Micro Channel Architecture was once referred to as the MCA bus, but when the Music Corporation of America (MCA) got wind of this IBM abbreviation, they filed a flurry of lawsuits. Now we diligently use the non-infringing Micro Channel name.

One of the advantages of the Micro Channel architecture is its inventorying process. The system does a self-check on start-up and checks the boards that are in place to make sure no changes have been made to the configuration. Even better, Micro Channel boards have a *bus-mastering* capability that allows them to communicate directly across the bus rather than requiring the microprocessor to be involved in each transfer of data. Bus-mastering frees the computer's microprocessor to work on other operations. A Micro Channel add-in board is shown in Figure 1.7.

Micro Channel boards are usually distinguished by a blue plastic strip at the end of the board opposite the external connectors. This strip often lengthens the board and slips into the retaining clip in the computer's chassis.

FIGURE 1.7
Micro Channel add-in boards often have a blue plastic strip extending the length of the board so it can snap into a support in the case.

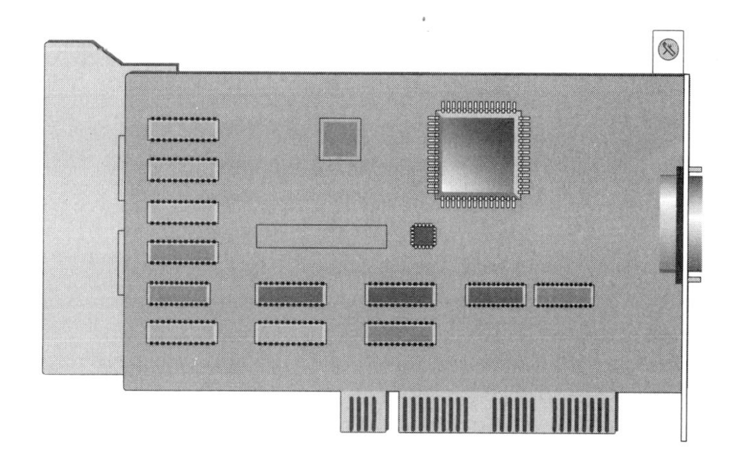

EISA The Extended Industry Standard Architecture bus is a 32-bit bus design that is backward-compatible with ISA add-in boards. The EISA design is frequently used in file servers because it is mature and stable, employs bus-mastering, has good configuration functionality, and is not outrageously expensive. Figure 1.8 displays an EISA connector.

FIGURE 1.8
The EISA bus provides 32-bit communications and bus-mastering. Its connector can also accept ISA boards.

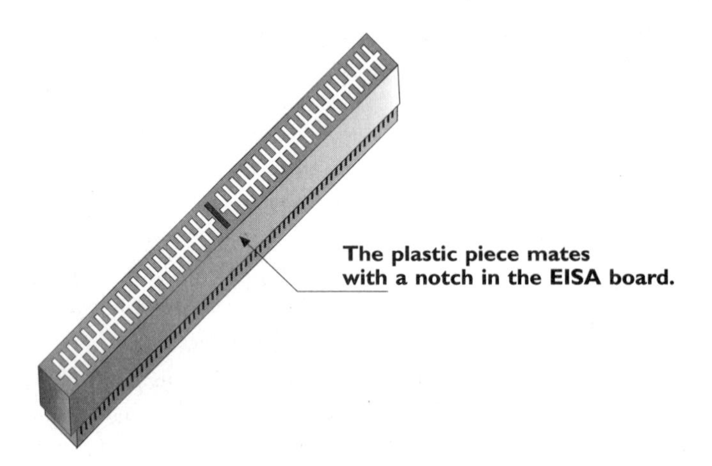
The plastic piece mates
with a notch in the EISA board.

EISA systems, like Micro Channel systems, are aware of the boards installed and check them when the system is started. EISA systems are generally aware of additions and subtractions of memory, the presence of boards that are expected or new, and the disposition of system resources, such as interrupts and memory locations. This awareness allows the administrator to configure the machine without stepping on toes by accidentally using an interrupt already claimed by another board.

Unfortunately, although ISA boards work perfectly well in EISA systems, they do not provide the information necessary for the configuration software to recognize how they use system resources. If your machines contain ISA boards, be sure you know how they are configured—the memory locations, interrupt requests (IRQs), and direct memory access (DMA) channels they claim—and check to see that they don't conflict with the EISA boards. Intermittent problems can be caused by conflicts that slip through the cracks.

EISA boards have two sets of connectors placed close together. An EISA board is illustrated in Figure 1.9. Although its data path is wider than ISA designs (32 bits instead of 16), the EISA bus is not as fast as more recent board designs that also use a faster data path.

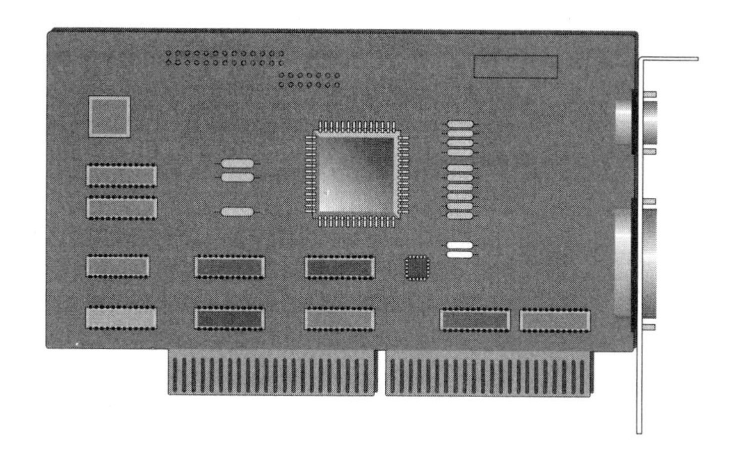

FIGURE 1.9 EISA add-in boards feature two sets of contacts with a notch in the set closest to the external connectors.

VESA LOCAL BUS The VESA local bus (VL-bus) standard was created by the Video Electronics Standards Association and is based on the standard local bus design found in ordinary Intel-compatible computers. The *local bus* is used—even in older computers—to tie the microprocessor to memory and to a math coprocessor, if present. The local bus is essentially a direct connection to the microprocessor and uses microprocessor speeds. Unfortunately, microprocessors do not have enough power to extend the standard local bus to additional devices, and even if output is increased, decoding logic is required to link external devices to the processor. A VL-bus connector is shown in Figure 1.10.

The VESA standard expands on the 80486 processor bus. Controller logic identifies the information intended for local-bus boards and peripherals and separates it from information addressed to standard ISA bus destinations. Communications between the VL-bus boards and the microprocessor are handled directly. This allows data to move between the board and the microprocessor many times faster than the ISA standard and several times faster than even the 32-bit EISA and Micro Channel architectures. Figure 1.11 illustrates a VL-bus board.

FIGURE 1.10
VL-bus connections can run at clock speeds up to 66 MHz, providing much faster performance than previous bus designs.

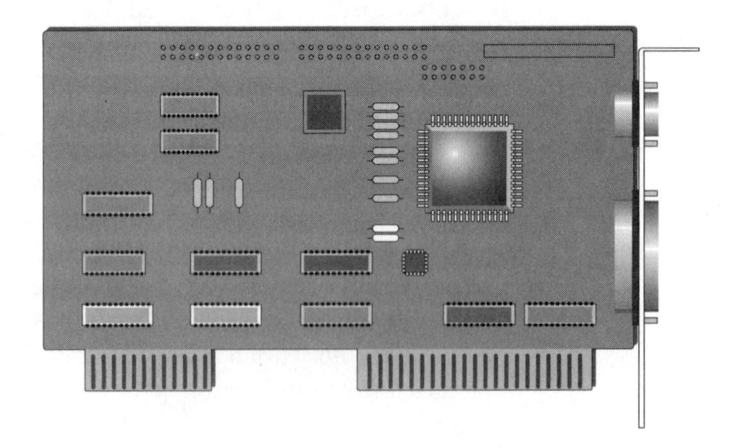

FIGURE 1.11
VL-bus add-in boards use 32-bit paths to communicate with each other and the microprocessor.

PCI The Peripheral Component Interconnect was developed by Intel using a *mezzanine* bus design in which the PCI logic isolates the boards on the PCI bus from the microprocessor and other components on the system's local bus. A PCI bus connector is shown in Figure 1.12.

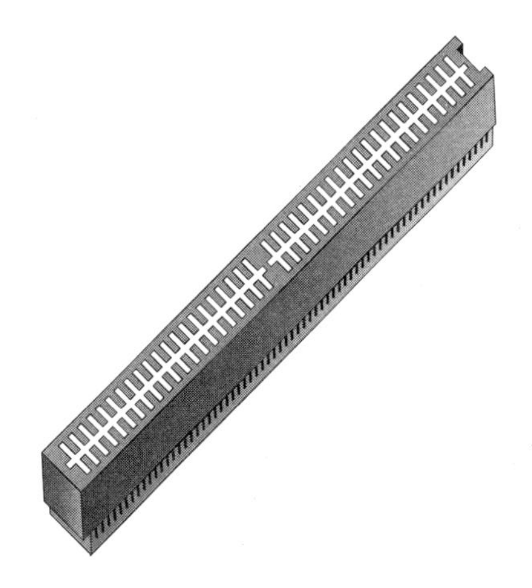

FIGURE 1.12
PCI bus connectors support 32-bit communications, providing bus-mastering and processor-speed independence.

Some advantages of this isolation are that PCI boards work independently of the processor's speed and can perform effective bus-mastering. Another advantage is the promise of "plug and play" operation of PCI boards, which can be configured automatically by the isolating PCI logic. One disadvantage of this architecture is the separation imposed by the PCI logic, which means that the boards cannot communicate as quickly with memory or the microprocessor. A PCI add-in board is shown in Figure 1.13.

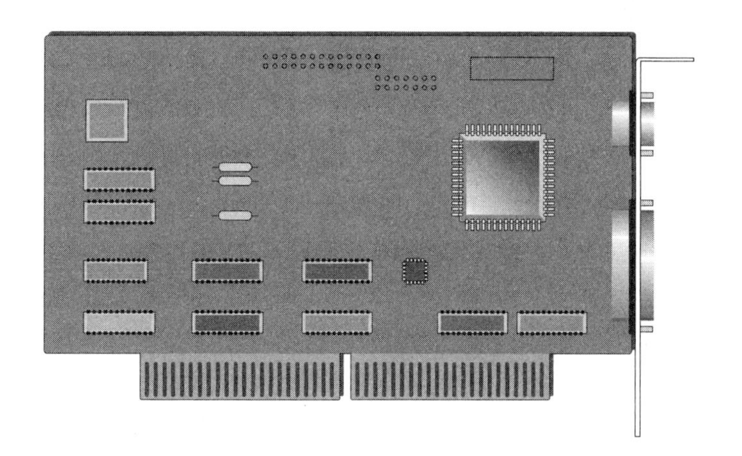

FIGURE 1.13
PCI add-in boards offer the promise of "plug and play" operation in the future as well as high performance right now.

RAM

The amount of random access memory, or RAM, accessible to NetWare can be determined by executing the MEMORY console command. From the console prompt, issue the command:

```
:MEMORY
```

The more memory, the better. ISA and Micro Channel systems may report only 16MB of RAM. If you believe more memory is installed than is being reported, you can use the REGISTER MEMORY console command on these systems to allow NetWare to address more than 16MB. EISA systems can automatically register memory beyond 16MB; the command can be added to the STARTUP.NCF file to implement this registration.

```
Auto Register Memory Above 16 Megabytes = ON
```

DMA can cause problems with memory registration, but current hardware and drivers should not cause trouble.

RAM is where most of the work is performed in both file servers and client systems. If you come from the UNIX workstation world, you may be surprised at how little main memory is generally contained in a NetWare server, let alone in a client microcomputer. Some servers that were high-end systems a short time ago can physically accommodate only 128MB of RAM. By comparison, I know of a project in which fast access requires that microprocessor layouts be stored in 1.5GB of RAM on a UNIX workstation.

DRAM Dynamic random access memory (DRAM) is generally used as main memory on file servers and workstations. Dynamic RAM needs to have its contents refreshed periodically, which slows down performance by adding refresh overhead. File servers and workstations typically use 30-pin or 72-pin SIMMs (single inline memory modules), which are small circuit cards containing one or more DRAM chips. Both SIMM types are illustrated in Figure 1.14.

The older 30-pin models are usually found in 4MB, 1MB, and 256KB configurations and usually need to be matched in pairs or sets of four. The newer 72-pin versions can be obtained in configurations up to 64MB and can often be mixed and matched like candy from the supermarket bins. Thus, you may have one 32MB SIMM, one 16MB SIMM, and two 8MB SIMMs, plus 8MB soldered to the motherboard of your server, for a total of 72MB of memory on the server.

FIGURE 1.14
SIMMs are typically found in older 30-pin or newer 72-pin models. The 72-pin versions have a notch in the connector edge.

It is important to know which chip configurations your servers use so that you can determine what sizes and speeds to keep as spares. Some computers cannot use SIMMs larger than a certain size. (For example, some systems work fine with 1MB, 4MB, and 8MB SIMMs but cannot read 16MB SIMMs and return error messages on start-up.)

The speed of a DRAM chip typically ranges from 60 ns (nanosecond), which is very fast, to 90 ns, which is significantly slower. It's no surprise: faster DRAM costs more.

An emerging type of DRAM is becoming more common on Pentium-based systems, which require faster delivery than normal DRAM chips provide. Extended Data Out (EDO) DRAM yields about a 10 percent improvement in system performance by reducing the number of wait states required to synchronize the fast processors with main memory.

SRAM Static random access memory (SRAM) retains its contents without being refreshed. As a result, it runs between four and five times faster than DRAM. Unfortunately, SRAM is quite expensive, and although some vendors

NetWare Memory Requirements

NetWare 4.1 comes with a relatively complex formula for determining the necessary amount of server RAM. The simplified version follows:

AMOUNT OF RAM	NEEDED FOR
8MB	Baseline requirement
2MB	Remote installation
2MB	Add-in NetWare products; PSERVER, MONITOR, INSTALL, SERVMAN
Disk Space x 0.008	File Allocation Tables, Directory Entry Tables
1MB–4MB	Additional cache buffer RAM

have produced machines that used SRAM for main memory, it is very unusual to find such systems. Instead, SRAM is used as cache memory, storing frequently or recently accessed information to avoid having to do a slower lookup from main memory for commonly performed operations.

SRAM is produced in smaller chip densities than DRAM, and for 12 ns memory, the fastest SRAM generally available, you can expect to pay about $20 for 32KB. Slower, 25 ns SRAM can be obtained for less than $10 in the same size.

VRAM Video random access memory is dual-ported DRAM intended specifically for use in graphics adapters. VRAM is also more expensive than DRAM, but because it is used to provide faster video performance and because file servers tend to have minimal graphics equipment (a brand new server typically has VGA or SVGA built into the motherboard and doesn't need anything more when running NetWare), VRAM is not likely to be found in any of your NetWare servers.

VRAM's dual porting means that it has two data paths, allowing faster access to the contents of the memory chips. The dual porting also has an impact on prices. Expect to pay twice as much for VRAM as for DRAM of the same size and speed.

Disk

Hard disk information can be viewed via the INSTALL console utility.

1. From the console prompt, enter the following:

```
:LOAD INSTALL
```

2. Select the **Disk Options** entry.

3. Look at the **Partition Tables** entry. A list of disk drives that can be seen by NetWare is produced. By selecting each of the disk drive entries, you can see how the drives are partitioned. Be sure to check the results you find here with the results of your visual inspection of the server's drive bays or disk subsystem.

Since NetWare's primary function is serving files, hard disk space, configuration, redundancy, and performance will likely occupy a fair portion of your time. The good news is that hard disk prices have fallen dramatically, and at the same time, the amount of disk storage available in a single device has been increasing. You will also need a floppy drive, and a CD-ROM drive is extremely useful for loading software.

Operating systems and applications software have become particularly large compared to the capacities of floppy disks. NetWare and Windows NT use more than 20 diskettes each. Many network utilities take more than 5 diskettes each, and large applications you may run on your network often take more than 12 diskettes. A CD-ROM can save you the time you would have to spend switching diskettes, and it also spares you the surprisingly common phenomenon of mislabeled installation diskettes.

DISK CONTROLLERS As you might expect, disk controllers are add-in boards that control the flow of data to and from disk drives. Two main kinds of disk controllers are in use today: Integrated Drive Electronics (IDE) and Small Computer Systems Interface (SCSI). Both interface standards have been enhanced with more advanced specifications, and both are often found in client microcomputers and file servers. NetWare also provides support for other device interfaces, such as the Enhanced Small Device Interface (ESDI) and the Seagate ST-506 interface, but these older designs are not well suited to the size required by and stress put upon network disk drives.

The IDE design provides on-disk intelligence to enhance performance and simplify connections to the drive. An Enhanced IDE (EIDE) standard breaks the 528MB limitation imposed by the original IDE standard. IDE controllers typically can work with two hard disks and two floppy drives at a time. This makes them quite sufficient for workstation needs, but only lightweight NetWare servers will be adequately served by this capacity. Furthermore, the IDE interface typically does not control the high-capacity, high-speed tape drives desired by most network administrators.

Enhanced IDE CD-ROM drives are available on many new systems at reasonable prices, but they are not a good choice for NetWare servers. Although NetWare can be installed from a non-SCSI CD-ROM drive and can mount a non-SCSI CD-ROM drive, many users have experienced problems when installing or attempting to mount these drives. If you want to install NetWare from a CD-ROM, or if you wish to attach CD-ROM drives to a NetWare server for access by your users, SCSI is the way to go. If you already have an IDE or EIDE CD-ROM drive, check with the manufacturer for NetWare-compatible drivers.

SCSI (pronounced "scuzzy") drives have three advantages over other designs: high capacity, high throughput, and daisy-chaining compatibility. Nine gigabyte SCSI drives are commonly available, and since a single SCSI interface board, or *host adapter*, can control up to seven devices, the large amounts of disk space NetWare has theoretically been able to handle are now more reasonably accessible. A SCSI chain is shown in Figure 1.15.

IDE devices can be faster in certain cases, but the flexibility of the SCSI design makes it a natural for use in file servers. SCSI chains can be finicky, however, and proper chain *termination*—the attachment of resistor packs to each end of the SCSI chain—is imperative.

Although it may seem like an advantage to use the SCSI-chaining ability to connect your hard disks, tape drives, and CD-ROMs to a single host adapter, it's not. The SCSI bus communicates with each component on the chain at the same speed, so when the system starts up, the host adapter negotiates the slowest speed on the chain and uses that speed for every device connected to it. Separate your hard disks onto their own adapters, and consider how your other peripherals are used to determine whether they need their own adapters.

FIGURE 1.15
The CD-ROM drives in this SCSI chain use SCSI IDs 1 and 2, while the tape drive uses ID 4. Four more devices could be added to this chain.

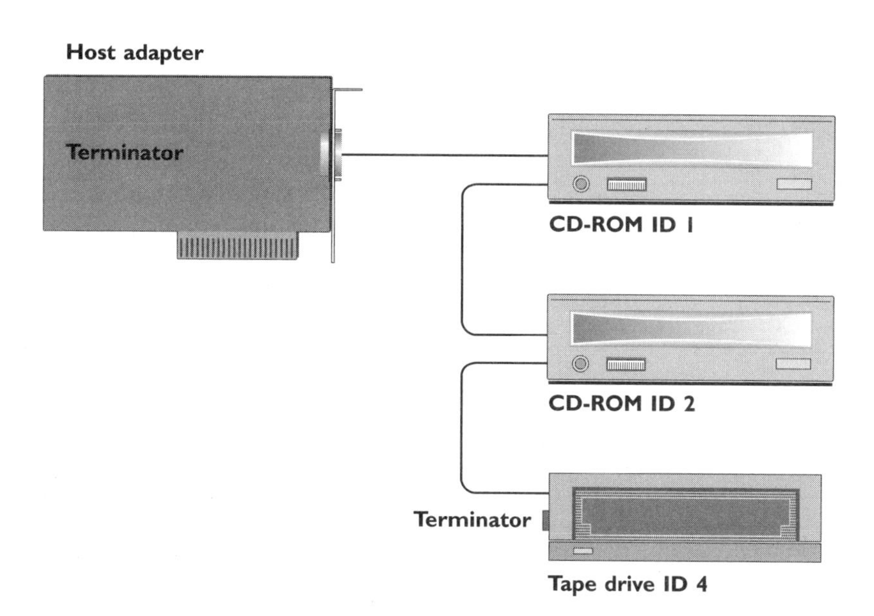

HARD DISK DRIVES Hard disk drives store large quantities of data and are much faster than floppy disks, tapes, and CD-ROMs. Although you can get portable models, most are not intended to be moved. The best characteristics you can hope for in hard disks are reliability, capacity, and speed. Reliability is measured in two ways as far as most network administrators are concerned: first, how much work do *you* need to do to configure the hard disks and keep them running; and second, how far will the *manufacturer* stand behind them with a warranty? Five-year warranties on hard disks are often provided by certain manufacturers at little noticeable markup; spending extra money to purchase a drive with a longer manufacturer warranty is always a good investment.

Access time is also important in hard disks, although most high-capacity drives have access times lower than 12 milliseconds (ms). Older drives will generally be lower capacity and will be slower. Four-gigabyte drives are currently available in a half-height, 5¼" form factor, and larger-capacity drives are usually found in full-height, 5¼" units.

Access time is the measure of how long the drive takes to access and send data after the request is issued by the system.

The hard disk itself consists of multiple magnetic material–coated platters and a head that reads and writes to the platters, which are sealed to prevent the influx of moisture and dust. Each drive is configured into a number of tracks, sectors, and cylinders. Tracks are sections of the platters divided into concentric bands. Sectors are pie-slice sections of the platters, and cylinders are parallel tracks on multiple platters in one drive.

One of the performance numbers you'll want to pay attention to is *average access time*, which should be lower than 10 ms for the multigigabyte drives typically found on modern networks. Make sure you compare apples and apples: look at access times that include *latency*, the period during which the platter spins into position after the head is in place.

Another significant performance number is the *average data transfer* rate. Although a maximum throughput number can be interesting, the sustained average is the most useful number you'll find. It gives you an idea of the transfer speed to expect from the drive during normal use. Look for sustained average transfer rates approaching .5 MB per second.

Finding Volumes of Information

Network disk drives, like client disk drives, are partitioned into logical segments that may take up all available space on a drive or a smaller portion of the physical space available. These partitions are further subdivided into the disk spaces that can be seen by users: volumes. Volumes may consist of an entire partition or a portion of a partition, or they may span multiple partitions. All NetWare servers have a volume named SYS; it may be the only partition, or there may be others.

Mounted NetWare volumes can be identified using the VOLUMES console command. From the console prompt, enter:

```
:VOLUMES
```

NetWare responds with a list of the volumes that have been activated (mounted), along with the *name spaces* that have been loaded for each volume. The example network shown in Figure 1.1 includes a server with Macintosh clients; running VOLUMES from KAPP would generate a response like this:

```
The following volumes are mounted:
SYS        DOS
APPS       DOS
UDATA      DOS, MAC
```

The INSTALL utility can be used to identify volumes that NetWare is aware of but that are not currently accessible to users. All volumes on partitions NetWare can see are reported by the **Volume Options** entry. Volumes can be mounted by executing the MOUNT command from the file server console. The server attempts to mount all the volumes on the server when the MOUNT ALL console command is issued.

```
:MOUNT volume_name

:MOUNT ALL
```

Inspecting the Host Systems

I USE THE TERM *host systems* to refer to any number of systems that are very different but have one similarity: they are all big enough blips on the network radar to require description. Thus, these machines may not perform the same kinds of tasks as NetWare servers, but they are important enough to the network to merit some notice. A nondescript UNIX box performing nothing but Domain Name Service (DNS) on your Internet-connected network would certainly be a host by this description. Your IBM VM systems, with bundles of mission-critical data, or your HP or DEC systems, with accounting applications and data, would likely be important enough to fall into this category. A Windows NT server tied to the NetWare network via TCP/IP or IPX/SPX would absolutely fall into this category.

There is such a mishmash of equipment and software that can be connected to a NetWare network (and can perform useful functions when connected!) that a detailed rundown of the equipment you're likely to find in each case could fill more than a book in itself. However, the methods of connecting those systems to NetWare networks are much more accessible. They're also the most important part for a network administrator to understand and control. So you need to know what kinds of machines are connected to the network, but you need to know more about the connections than you do about the machines themselves.

Identifying Host Hardware

The beauty of large computer systems is that they are...large. You won't have any problems identifying a VAX and its attendant equipment. You also won't have any trouble finding an associated IS department, or at least some computer operators who can tell you what systems they know about, what they do, and where they're located. You'll find these machines in chilly computer rooms, with libraries of tapes and banks of terminals.

A bigger problem comes from less-centralized systems like UNIX workstations that form powerful subnetworks attached to your main NetWare system. Heavily equipped boxes may lurk in closed offices with no physical (or word-of-mouth) evidence of their existence.

This is one reason to draw a mental line as quickly as you can around the physical equipment that you are responsible for. If you can't find it, then leave it off that iteration of your understanding of your empire. As meticulous as you need to be in understanding what you have and what is happening on the NetWare side, you must be able to punt when you find yourself lost in a foreign area. Concentrate instead on understanding where systems *can* tie into your network. If everything was running smoothly before you came aboard, and if everything continues to run smoothly, you may never uncover some of the quirks of the whole network. Pray for this circumstance, but do not expect your prayers to be rewarded. Instead, expect angry users to approach you at some point, wanting to know why you trashed their systems. You can then introduce yourself and make a good impression by knowing your half of the equation.

Verifying Host Connection

The fact that a minicomputer, Windows NT box, or UNIX box exists in the same company, department, or room of a company does not in any way imply that the host in question is physically connected to the network cabling or communicates with the NetWare network. Organizations have been known to have multiple independent computer systems and users with dumb terminals and network workstations vying for attention on the desktop. This is generally true of companies with changing needs and technologies, especially when a "legacy system" is being phased out over a period of time. If the new data and the old data are logically independent, there's little use in integrating

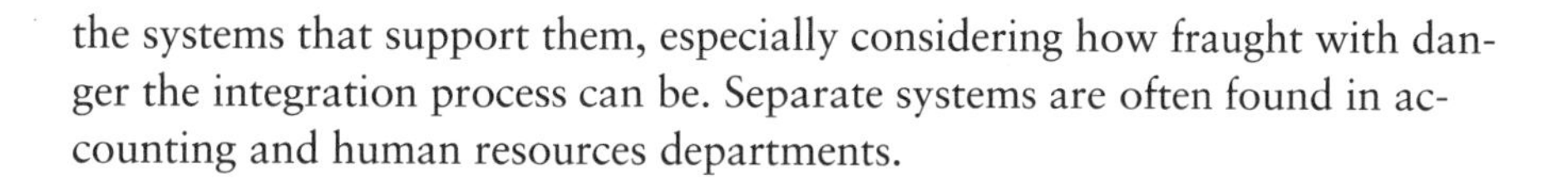

the systems that support them, especially considering how fraught with danger the integration process can be. Separate systems are often found in accounting and human resources departments.

See the section titled Understanding Network Protocols in Chapter 2 for a detailed discussion of protocols used to connect diverse systems.

However, you should check the host systems you're aware of to see whether they are connected. The most common connection methods are via TCP/IP, which is a very common protocol found outside NetWare networks and is handled relatively well by NetWare's internal routing, and IPX/SPX, the NetWare native transport protocols. Gateway products allow network users to send information to and receive data from minicomputer or mainframe systems, encapsulating the data into IPX/SPX packets to be routed by NetWare servers on the LAN. These gateways are particularly useful for IBM's Systems Network Architecture (SNA) products and other proprietary systems. Although a variety of software solutions allow non-NetWare operating systems to use the IPX/SPX protocols, these packages generally slow the hosts significantly. Running TCP/IP on the NetWare server to link to other systems is usually a better bet.

TCP/IP links are useful because so many systems can use the protocol—including NetWare. The Transmission Control Protocol/Internet Protocol (TCP/IP) transport in NetWare routes IP traffic between networks and uses the unfortunately acronymed Routing Information Protocol (RIP) to communicate network configuration information, allowing routers to configure IP forwarding automatically. NetWare also allows IPX networks to *tunnel* IPX information across internetworks that do not normally support IPX routing.

NetWare's Network File System (NFS) provides file and printer sharing functionality between NetWare resources and NFS users and also allows X Windows users to access NetWare server consoles. The FleX/IP product also provides access to resources on NetWare networks for UNIX users.

Identifying Existing Network Topologies

NOW THAT YOU know the major players in your network's social scene, it's time to see how they meet and interact. The previous section identified the individual servers and uncovered evidence of physical connections. This section discusses the physical cabling systems underlying the network structure.

Understanding Bus, Star, and Ring Topologies

The three cabling topologies you are likely to encounter are bus, star, and ring topologies. *Wireless* and *point-to-point* topologies are also used, but these are significantly less common.

Wireless topologies typically use radio frequency (RF) signals to link client machines to interconnected hubs. The major advantage of this topology, naturally, is that the client machines can move—for example, you can roam through the office with your laptop, maintaining your network connection wherever you go. This technology is still maturing, however, and security is still a concern for RF communications links. Security can be a major concern for businesses with sensitive data, and let's face it, very few organizations don't believe their data is both confidential and vital. Wireless network connections are also expensive, but once the technology becomes more widely accepted, the cost is likely to decline.

One common use for wireless networks is the immediate creation of a temporary network. Situations that require intensive work at remote sites can use wireless technology to good advantage. If disasters destroy your cabling system, a wireless network can provide a workaround until the physical connections can be established again.

Point-to-point networks, on the other hand, are not likely to become any more common; these rock-solid networks contain links between each node and every other node on the network. PC hardware is not particularly well suited to this kind of layout (you can't have very many network boards in a system before you run out of IRQs, for example), which is probably overkill for systems in the NetWare world. Point-to-point connections might be reasonable on file servers in a high-traffic, mission-critical network, but client connections should probably use a more common design.

Looking at Star Topologies

The systems connected to KAPP in Figure 1.16 are connected using a physical star topology. Each client has a connection to the hub, so if a single "leg" fails, the only machine affected is the one on that particular cable. The central connection point allows somewhat easier management and troubleshooting, and a variety of cable types can be used, including the very popular unshielded twisted pair (UTP).

In a star topology network, expect to see a hub with a number of patch cables connecting in from client machines or a punch-down panel. These

FIGURE 1.16
The physical star topology connects each node—client systems, servers, or network-connected peripherals—to a central hub.

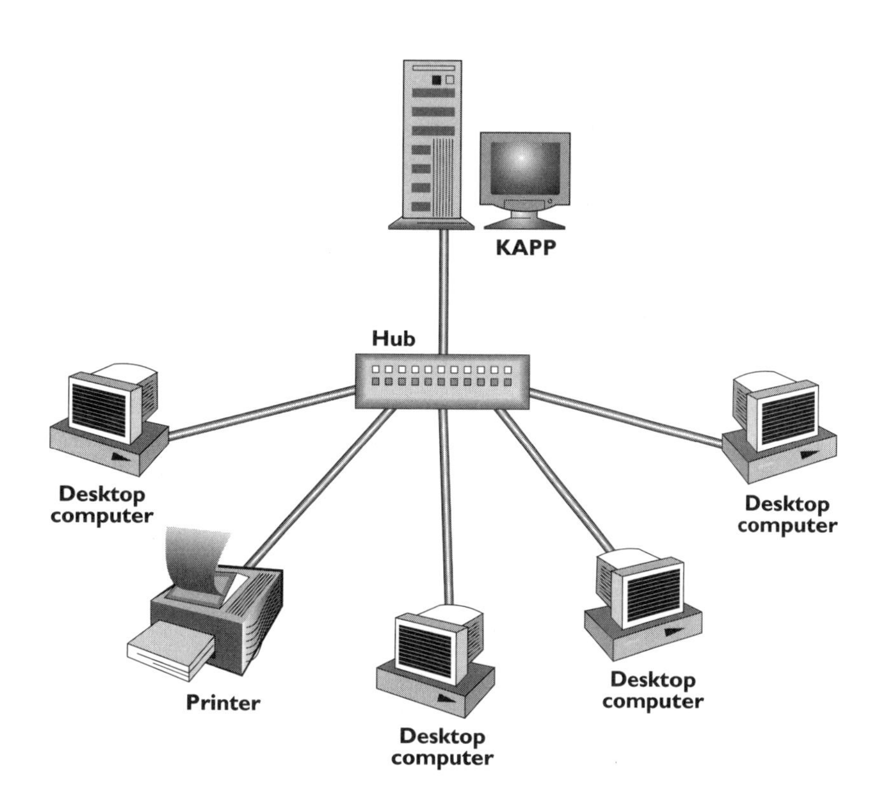

hubs may be centrally located, but they may also be hidden in wiring closets and other out-of-the-way places and then tied together with fiber lines or other cabling systems.

A punch-down panel or block is a solderless connector used to connect telephone wires. The wires are pushed—punched—down into teeth that penetrate the insulation. Although punchdowns were formerly used for telecommunications, they are now frequently found in data communications situations where twisted pair cables carry network traffic.

Looking at Bus Topologies

The systems connected to SNYDER, shown in Figure 1.17, are tied together with a bus topology. All the machines are tied to a single cable running through the area. Each end of the trunk cable is terminated with a *terminator*, a resistor that identifies the end of the cabling. Network traffic flows from each node on the network to the trunk and is broadcast in both directions along the trunk until it is claimed by another node or reaches the end of

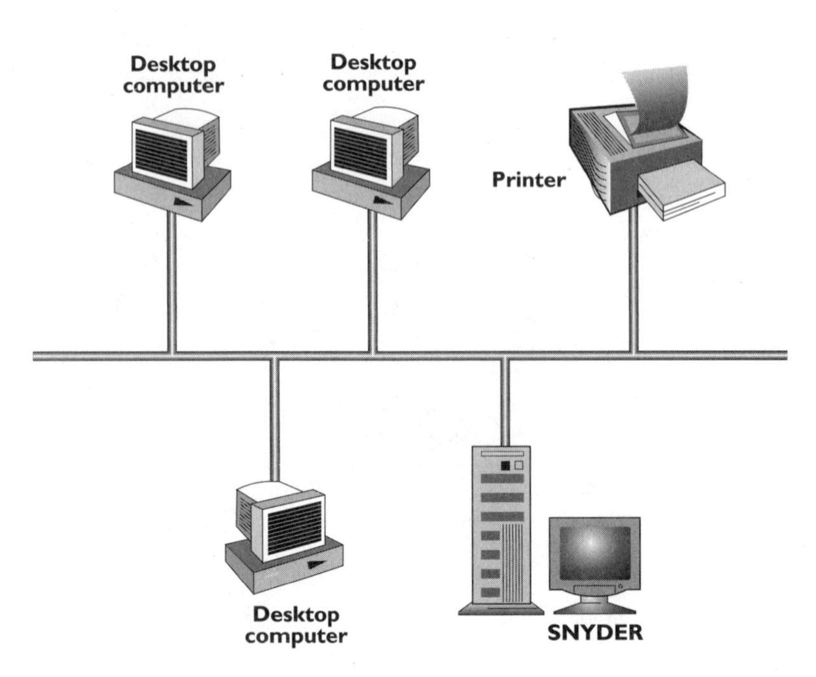

FIGURE 1.17 The bus topology links each network-connected node to a single cable with a terminator at each end.

the trunk run. One advantage of this topology is that a hub is not required (this reduces expense but requires that you have appropriate terminators on hand). However, bus topologies are less fault tolerant because heavy traffic and cable failures are not handled gracefully.

Expect to see thick or thin Ethernet (we'll take a look at these in a moment) on a bus network, with thin Ethernet coaxial cable connected to T-connectors at each node and thick Ethernet trunks tapped into by vampire taps that connect to ports on the nodes' NICs.

Vampire taps, sometimes called vampire clamps, earned their name because they feature two fanglike taps that pierce the coax cable and make contact with the two conductive portions of the coaxial line. The fangs are uneven in length so that one reaches the inner conductor and the other reaches only the outer conductor.

Looking at Ring Topologies

The network connected to THEDER shown in Figure 1.18 employs a ring topology. The nodes on the network are connected in a ring around which data flows until one of the nodes claims it.

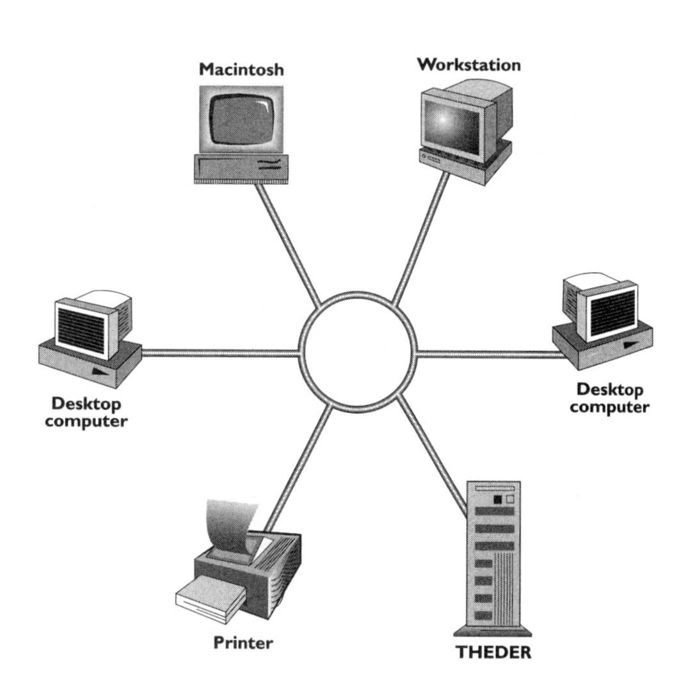

FIGURE 1.18 The ring topology uses a single cable connected at each end. Each node connects to the ring and claims its data.

Dual-counter-rotating rings, like the *backbone* network linking the three servers shown in Figure 1.19, provide a greater degree of fault tolerance because a failure of a single ring does not completely bring down the network.

FIGURE 1.19
Dual-loop-counter-rotating rings use two physical connections flowing data in different directions so that a single cable failure does not bring the network down.

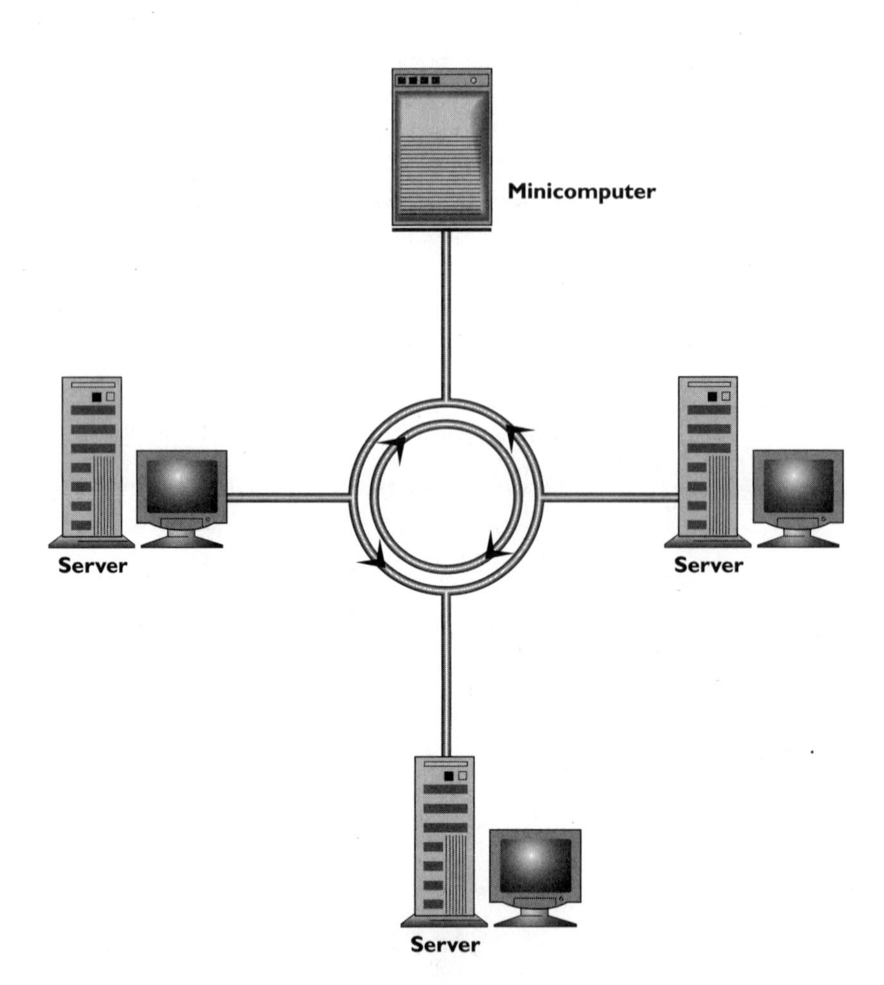

Although ring topologies are available on other networks, the most common use is in Token Ring, which is a little complicated because it appears to have a star topology. Nodes are physically connected to a multistation access unit (MAU) in star fashion, but the electronic signal running through the MAU actually runs in a logical ring shown in Figure 1.20.

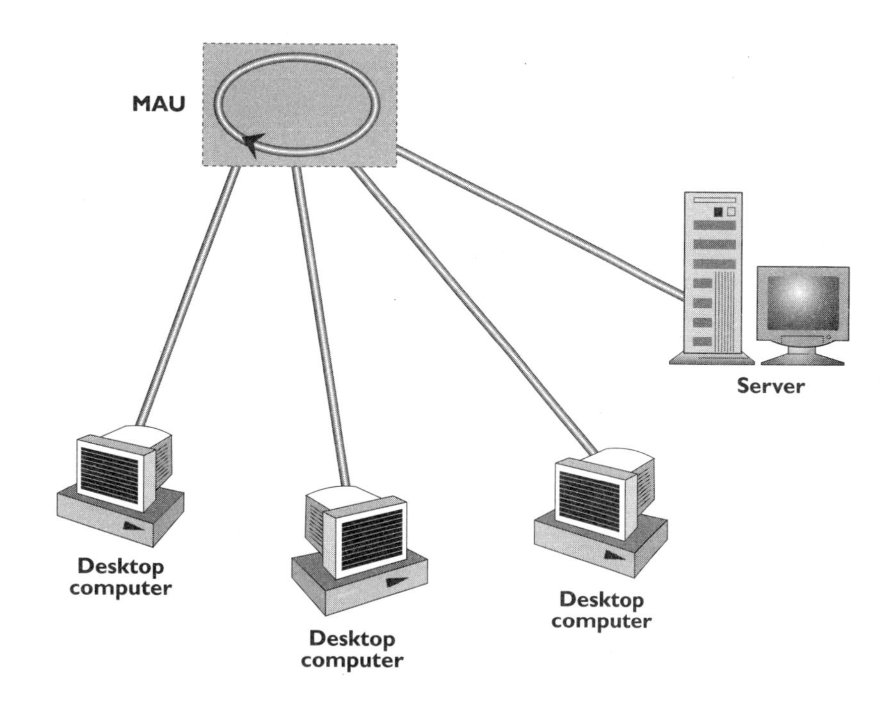

FIGURE 1.20 The Token Ring configuration appears to have a physical star layout, but the data in the multistation access unit (MAU) flows in a ring.

Identifying Ethernet Access Method Implementations

Ethernet is the most common network access method in use today; it is a mature standard that supports a wide range of transport protocols and several different cabling types. Ethernet is *nondeterministic*; that is, data going out onto the Ethernet bus doesn't know where it's going. Instead, it heads along the wire until it is accepted by a node or eliminated by a terminator or by a collision with another packet. All active nodes hear the data broadcast by other nodes. The data is accepted by the node to which the data is addressed. The nodes on an Ethernet bus attempt to determine that the bus is clear before they send data, and when a node receives data, it sends an acknowledgment. When collisions occur because nodes send data at the same time, the nodes that sent the data resend the information after a randomly determined delay.

The best way to identify the Ethernet access method and frame type running on your network is to check the server consoles to see which LAN protocols are reported by the CONFIG console command. Ethernet running on NetWare 3.11 servers is likely to report the Ethernet 802.3 frame type. Ethernet running on NetWare 3.12 and 4.x servers is likely to be using the Ethernet 802.2 frame type—although "evolved" networks may use both frame types. Macintosh clients and TCP/IP may add Ethernet_SNAP and Ethernet_II frame types.

This configuration obviously has some inherent problems. The more traffic on the network, the more likely that collisions will occur. Because collisions require that data be sent again, more collisions mean slower response times. Although Ethernet is theoretically capable of 10 megabits per second (Mbps) speeds in its primary flavors, this performance can be dramatically degraded by large numbers of nodes active on the same network because all the users are sharing the 10Mb bandwidth. Your mileage will vary depending upon the load your users are putting on the network. If the collision lights on your Ethernet hubs are blinking wildly, you may want to consider redistributing users when you are more familiar with the network's layout.

Working with Thick Ethernet

Thick Ethernet, or 10Base5 Ethernet, uses heavy-gauge coaxial cable, which consists of a conductive center wire wrapped in an insulating material, which, in turn, is wrapped in another conductor and then covered in a protective material—often Teflon. This cable is safer and easier to pull, but it is more expensive than other types of cable. Coaxial cable is illustrated in Figure 1.21.

This heavy cable makes up the bus, while nodes are generally connected by a cable with *DIX* (15-pin Digital/Intel/Xerox) connectors to a transceiver unit that connects with a vampire tap (with two "teeth" of unequal length that pierce the coax cable and make contact with the two conductive layers) at the bus.

Thick Ethernet is fairly expensive but allows long cable runs and provides reasonable handling of heavy traffic loads.

FIGURE 1.21
Thick and Thin Ethernet use different gauges of coaxial cable, which is composed of a conductive center, insulating material, another conductive layer, and protective coating.

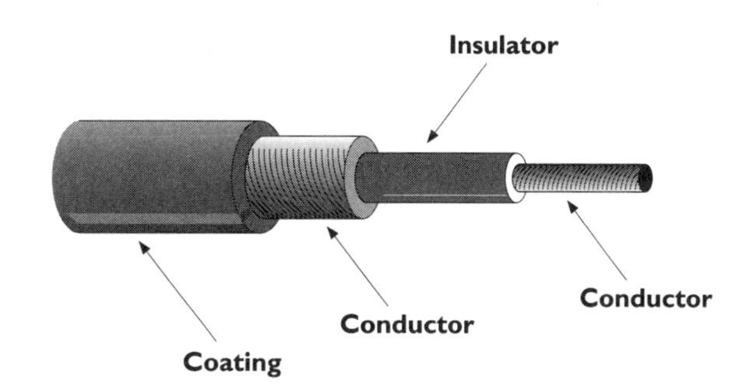

Working with Thin Ethernet

Thin Ethernet is also known as 10Base2 Ethernet or "Cheapernet." Thin Ethernet uses a smaller diameter RG-58 coaxial cable than Thick Ethernet and, instead of transceivers and vampire taps, uses T-connectors on the nodes to connect to the Ethernet bus. The cabling uses BNC connectors, which have a male portion (a barrel) with pins that rotate into a secure position in the female portion. A Thin Ethernet line connecting two systems via T-connectors is shown in Figure 1.22. Fifty-ohm terminators end the bus.

Thin Ethernet has lower overall cost, but its overall length is more limited than that possible with Thick Ethernet, and like Thick Ethernet, it is not tolerant of cabling problems because of its bus topology. It is convenient for small

FIGURE 1.22
A Thin Ethernet bus connects to nodes via T-connectors with BNC connectors.

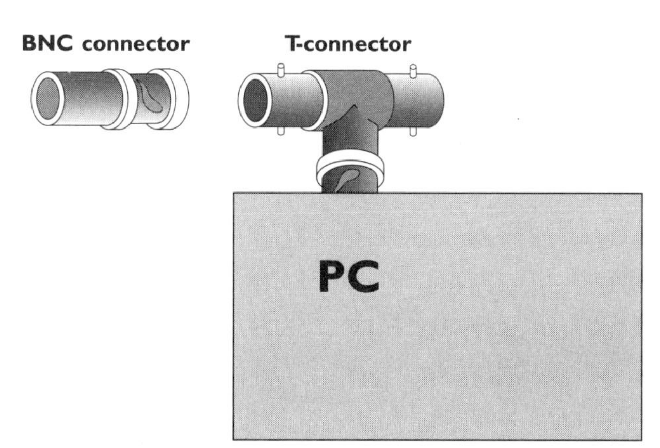

networks, however, especially because it does not require the additional expense of transceivers (used with Thick Ethernet) or hubs (used with 10BaseT).

Working with 10BaseT

10BaseT Ethernet uses unshielded twisted pair (UTP) cabling in a star topology. Each of the nodes uses an RJ-45 connector, which looks like an ordinary phone jack on steroids, and a length of UTP cable to reach the center of the star, which is a device known as a hub or concentrator. RJ-45 and RJ-11 connectors are shown in Figure 1.23.

10BaseT Ethernet was devised to take advantage of wiring that already exists in many buildings, but most of the wiring in use is voice-grade and not highly suitable to network communications. Using Category 3, 4, or 5 cabling is a better idea than hoping to make use of older cable. Because UTP is familiar to most telecom workers and cable installers, getting the wiring done for a 10BaseT job should not be any problem.

FIGURE 1.23
RJ-45 connectors look like larger versions of the familiar RJ-11 phone jacks and hold four pairs of wires.

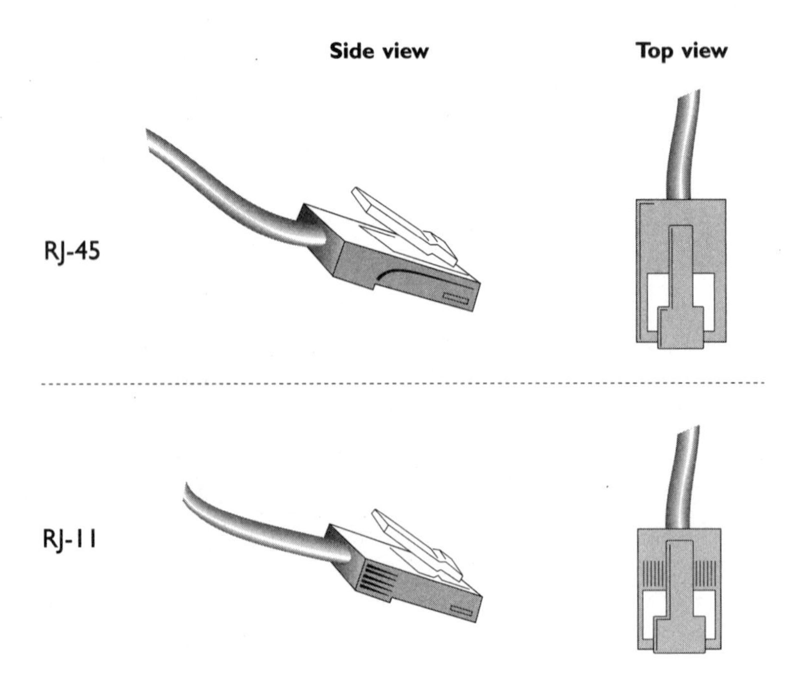

Make certain that each office is wired with at least two network UTP runs. Doing so avoids problems with UTP cabling, which can be relatively delicate. Also, be sure that your punch-down panels, patch panels, and cables use RJ-45 connectors rather than RJ-11 (telephone) connectors. A cable tester is a wise investment for network administrators who have 10BaseT networks.

The best thing about 10BaseT Ethernet is the use of the star topology, which is more resilient than bus topology because a single network cable failure won't normally take down the entire network. Naturally, if the cable that fails is the line from the hub to the server, the distinction is not likely to be appreciated by the users who can no longer reach their files and applications. An additional benefit is that heavy traffic loads are handled more gracefully than on Thick or Thin Ethernet because of improved routing. On the downside, interference from sources of electromagnetic force (called electromagnetic interference, or EMI) can be problematic, and overall cable lengths are somewhat limited.

Pondering Emerging Ethernets

The standard shared 10BaseT Ethernet that is so common in business settings has two big problems. The first is that adding users to the network adds collisions—which means network bandwidth is used by data that will have to be retransmitted. The second problem is that the 10 Mbps theoretical maximum is not great enough for the kind of large-scale data transfer many companies are interested in. Moving large images across an Ethernet connection, especially if the network is busy, can be a problem.

The answers to these questions are still emerging, but solutions are already available. The bandwidth problem is addressed by *switched Ethernet*, which employs intelligence in the hubs to provide the full 10 Mbps bandwidth to each of the connected nodes, rapidly switching between them.

The throughput problem is being addressed via emerging 100 Mbps Ethernet solutions. 100BaseT and the 100VG AnyLAN implementations offer the speed required for high-load applications such as videoconferencing.

Identifying Token Ring Implementations

Token Ring was developed by IBM and continues to develop primarily with IBM's input. The Token Ring standard yields high-performance, high-reliability networks that are physically connected in star topologies but logically work as ring topologies. The Token Ring architecture uses MAU units, which are somewhat similar to Ethernet concentrators, to connect nodes. The MAUs themselves are connected via ring-in (RI) and ring-out (RO) connectors, which create a loop of MAUs. Figure 1.24 illustrates a Token Ring MAU. If the network contains only one MAU, its RI and RO connectors are joined to each other. Token Ring is capable of running at 4 Mbps or 16 Mbps; most currently available NICs work at either speed.

Unlike Ethernet, which is nondeterministic, Token Ring relies upon the passing of a token around its logical ring to determine which node can talk at any moment. This *deterministic* architecture does not involve the packet collisions and the resulting network overhead found in Ethernet networks. As a result, many users find that their 4 Mbps Token Ring networks perform about the same as Ethernet networks.

FIGURE 1.24 The Token Ring MAU connects the network nodes and creates a central ring using special ring-in and ring-out connectors.

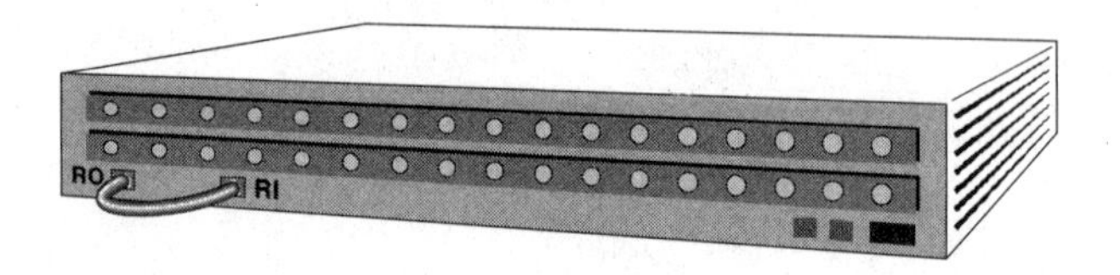

Token Ring cabling used to be IBM Type 1 shielded twisted pair (STP) only. IBM's STP cable design handles traffic well and is not easily affected by EMI. However, the widespread availability of UTP cabling can also be leveraged in a Token Ring network, which can handle the same kind of UTP wiring as used in 10BaseT networks. Although this cable is not ideal for many reasons, it is especially convenient in mixed environments using both Ethernet and Token Ring, because the existing cabling system can be used with whichever NICs and hubs are appropriate.

Switched Token Ring implementations are currently available, though there are fewer options than in the Ethernet world. In fact, as IBM provides more support for Ethernet networking, and as other vendors drop out of Token Ring markets, the user base for Token Ring may continue to shrink. Cost per node and the development and proliferation of Ethernet nodes are the major factors in this decline; the Token Ring architecture itself is sound and effective.

Identifying FDDI Implementations

Fiber Distributed Data Interface (FDDI) transmits data at the speed of light, providing 100 Mbps speed and excellent reliability—for a price. Although fiber-optic cable installation and maintenance prices are falling, they are still prohibitive for most networks. Fiber will be used in future high-speed networks, although it will likely share roles with the promising-but-not-yet-solidified Asynchronous Transfer Mode (ATM) and 100 Mbps implementations of Ethernet. FDDI uses a ring topology with two rings running in opposite directions, as shown in Figure 1.25.

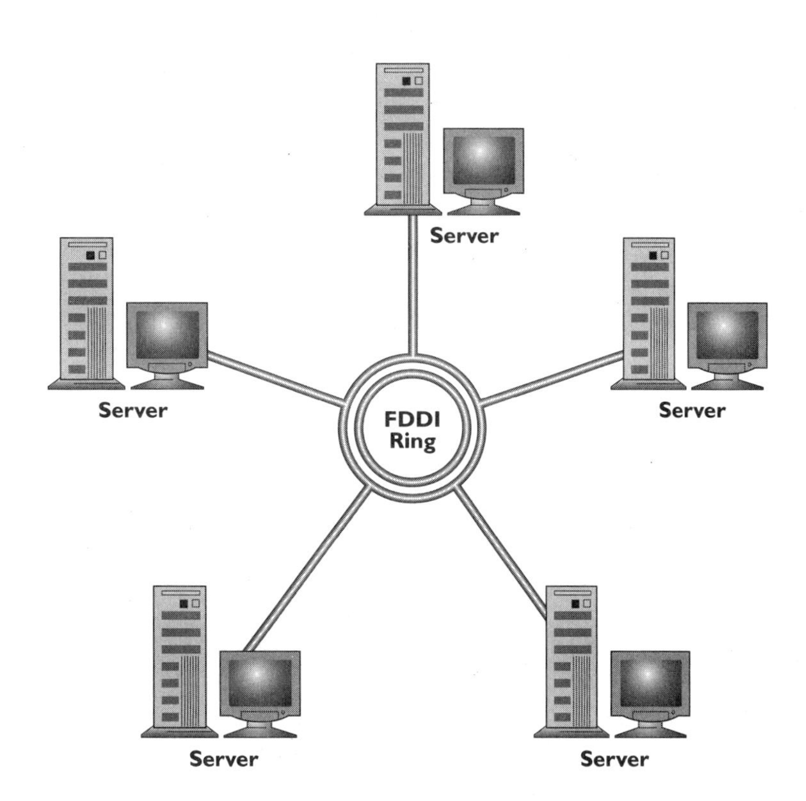

FIGURE 1.25 An FDDI network uses fiber-optic cabling in a dual-ring topology to provide reliable, high-speed communications.

Not all fiber in use is FDDI. Transceivers are available to connect network devices such as hubs and routers; the fiber used in these configurations provides high-speed connections but does not actually make up an FDDI network. Fiber implementations in Ethernet, Token Ring, and ARCNet transmit data at the speed of light but don't improve overall throughput past the limits of the access method in use. You can't slow down the light beams in the fiber, but you can't speed up the transceivers spitting data onto the other cabling systems, either.

Fiber can be fairly sturdy, but it is often quite delicate. Avoid bending fiber to a sharp angle, which can cause transmission problems or breakage. Also avoid exposing your eyes to the light emitted from a broken cable or cable end.

Identifying ARCNet Implementations

ARCNet is a relatively old technology that uses a token-passing scheme similar to Token Ring's across a star or bus topology. ARCNet isn't typically found in newer networks in part because it is relatively slow, providing 2.5 Mbps throughput. It also has relatively tight length limitations, and its token-passing scheme is not inherently efficient because tokens are passed on the basis of each NIC's ARCNet number. However, its deterministic architecture and low packet overhead make good use of available bandwidth. ARCNet networks use active and passive hubs to connect multiple nodes. Active hubs amplify the network signal before passing it along, allowing greater distances between nodes than passive hubs, which merely split the signal between multiple output lines. RG-62 coax cable is used most frequently, though UTP is also used, and fiber is found occasionally. An ARCNet network is displayed in Figure 1.26.

ARCNet uses manager-assigned node addresses on the NICs, unlike Ethernet cards, which are preprogrammed with unique addresses, and unlike Token Ring cards, which are preprogrammed with unique addresses but often allow a change of address through configuration. Because the ARCNet tokens are passed by address rather than by sequence on a ring (as Token Ring tokens are), the addresses should be set to improve performance. Another unique aspect of ARCNet is its timeout setting, which indicates how quickly a NIC expects another node to respond. Changing the timeout setting from the 31 microsecond default is one way to improve the standard distance limits, but the longer wait in turn reduces performance—not something you wish

FIGURE 1.26
ARCNet often uses a physical star topology from an active hub, which regenerates the network signal before passing it along.

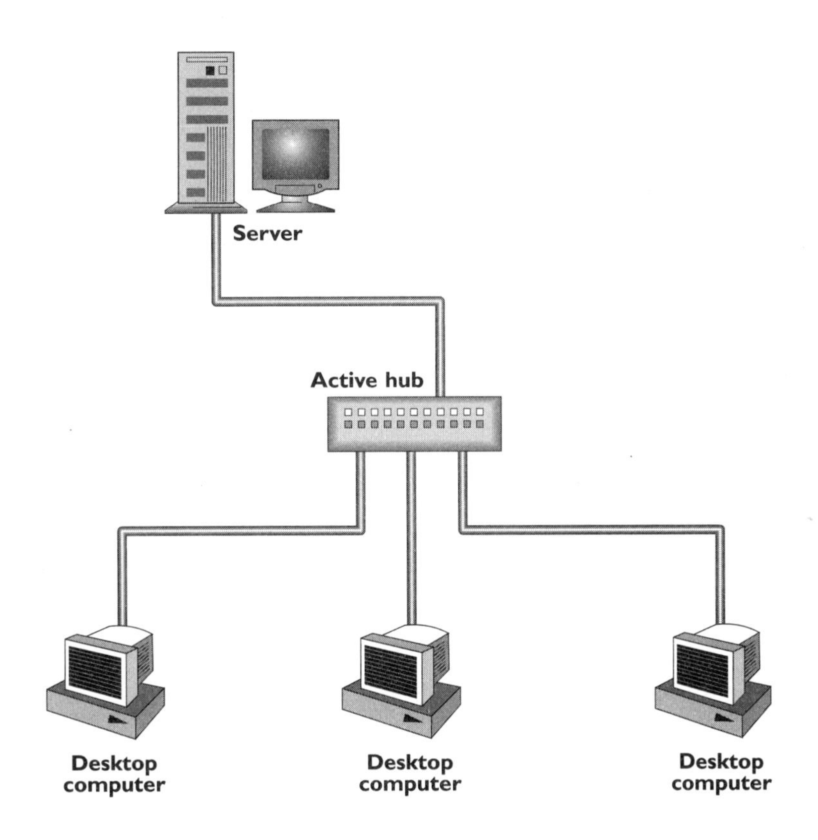

for in a topology that starts off so slowly. Check your ARCNet NIC documentation to see if timeout settings can be altered.

Locating Network Interconnections

THERE ARE SEVERAL common kinds of connections between networks. Since networks are simply cabling systems, we can see that in the example network shown in Figure 1.2, the networks 1987, 1982, and 1978 are connected into an internetwork. These interconnections are provided via network 6686, an FDDI network acting as a *backbone* for the network. The backbone is a network that links servers on an internetwork so that information can quickly be routed from one network to another. As shown in Figure 1.2, the backbone FDDI hub has connections to SNYDER, KAPP, and THEDER.

Although the interconnection was provided through an external device in Figure 1.2, the routing functions built into NetWare can make a server a network interconnection. This situation is shown in Figure 1.27.

FIGURE 1.27 Data on this network is routed internally through the server SMITH and also through a dedicated router.

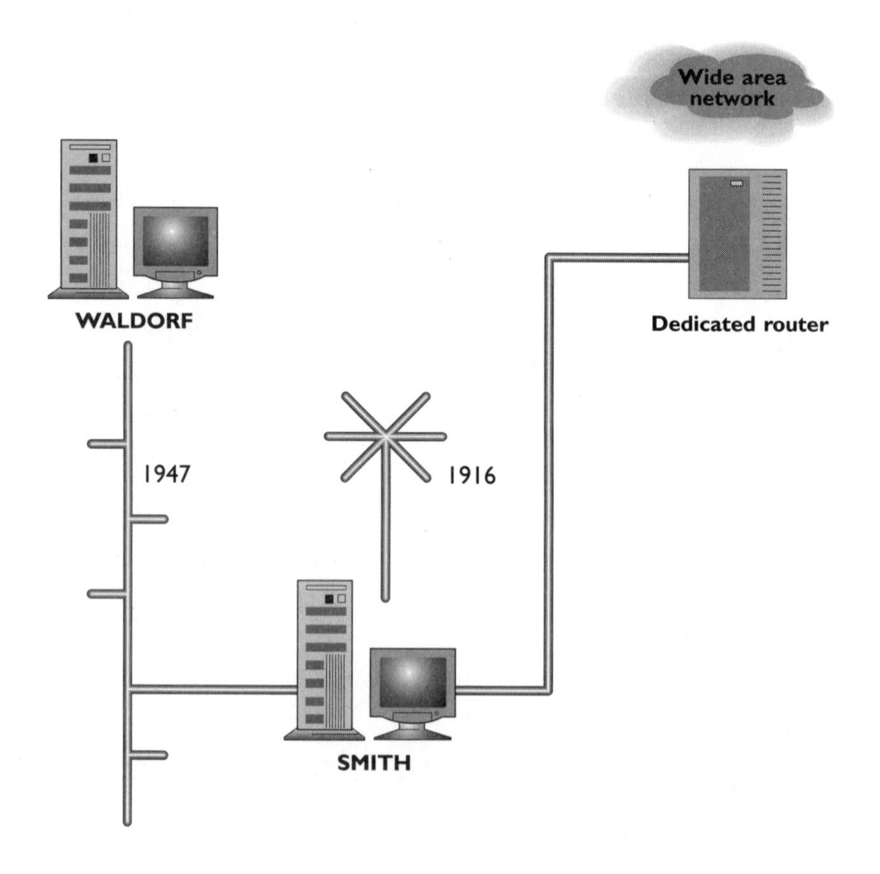

In this case, WALDORF is a server on 1947, a bus topology network. SMITH connects to 1916, a star topology network. But notice that SMITH also connects to the 1947 network and to the router. SMITH is a network interconnection because it connects multiple networks using NetWare's internal routing.

Labeling the equipment and the cabling in the network is important, but it isn't really sufficient. Draw a network diagram showing the servers and networks. You don't need to indicate client machines; just make certain you know the server names and internal network numbers, and show the links between those servers and the networks they serve. The number and location of client systems will be important when you're troubleshooting your bus network or if you have users on daisy chained hubs. Hand-drawn maps are adequate, but if your siblings inherited all the artistic skills in the family, you may be more comfortable using a network diagramming package or even a simple drawing package. Visio works quite nicely and comes with network stencils featuring standard topologies and machine types. Well-drawn maps are useful to you, but they can also be effective when you're explaining something to management...especially if you're asking for money to improve a poor network design!

Locating Network Connections at the Server

The CONFIG console command is a good way to identify server-based network connections. Since each active NIC indicates which network it is connected to, you'll be able to determine which interconnections occur at each server.

Active NICs are those that have drivers loaded. Be sure to do an inventory when you have a chance to make sure that NICs or other pieces of equipment aren't tucked uselessly away inside your server.

You'll also know which protocols are running across that network. If TCP/IP is loaded on a NIC, the IP number for that network interface is indicated.

Make a note of the version of the driver that is being used for each NIC. Later, you can check with the vendor (via a BBS, an online service, or the Internet) to see whether an update is available. Much of the network administrator's time can be spent ensuring that the most current drivers and modules are being loaded. The components that provide much of the functionality in NetWare are called NetWare Loadable Modules (NLMs). There may be dozens of these modules on each server.

Another way of identifying the network layout structure is by using the DISPLAY NETWORKS console command from one server:

```
:DISPLAY NETWORKS
```

As shown in Figure 1.28, this command generates a list on the console that shows the network numbers on your internetwork, along with the distance from the server in number of hops (the number of networks away) and the time NetWare expects a packet to take getting from the current network. This time is reported in ticks, which are 1⁄18 of a second. Any of the network numbers displaying a 0 for the number of hops are connected to the server where the command was run.

FIGURE 1.28 The DISPLAY NETWORKS console command displays the connected network numbers with their distances in "hops" and the time in "ticks" to reach each network.

```
MS-DOS Prompt
:display networks
   00000001  5/6     00000004  5/6     00000013  2/2     00000019  4/5
   0000001A  4/9     00000020  4/5     00000021  4/5     00000023  4/5
   00000024  4/5     00000025  4/5     00000026  4/5     00000027  4/5
   00000029  4/5     00000030  4/5     00000040  4/5     00000041  4/5
   00000042  4/5     00000043  4/5     00000044  4/5     00000046  4/5
   00000047  4/5     00000049  4/5     00000060  4/5     00000062  4/5
   00000063  4/5     00000064  4/5     00000065  4/5     00000066  4/5
   00000067  4/5     00000068  4/5     00000070  4/5     00000073  4/5
   00000074  4/5     00000075  4/5     00000076  4/5     00000079  4/5
   00000081  4/5     00000083  4/5     00000084  4/5     00000086  4/5
   00000089  4/5     00000090  4/5     00000091  4/5     00000092  4/5
   00000093  4/5     00000094  4/5     00000095  4/5     00000096  4/5
   00000097  4/5     00000098  4/5     00000099  4/5     000000E1  3/4
   00000100  4/5     00000101  4/5     00000300  5/6     00000301  5/6
   00000304  5/6     00000306  5/6     00000311  4/4     00000330  5/6
   00000335  4/4     00000400  5/6     00000410  4/4     00000430  5/6
   00000435  4/4     00000500  4/5     00000501  4/5     00000502  4/5
   00000503  4/5     00000504  4/5     00000505  4/5     00000506  3/4
   00000507  5/6     00000508  4/5     00000509  5/6     0000050A  4/5
   0000050B  3/4     0000050C  5/6     0000050D  5/6     0000050F  4/5
   00000510  4/5     00000609  4/5     00000611  4/5     00000614  4/5
   00000640  4/5     00000642  4/5     00000645  4/5     00000649  4/5
   00000691  5/6     00000749  4/5     00000811  4/5     00000951  3/3
<Press ESC to terminate or any other key to continue>
```

Locating Network Connection Equipment

Network connection equipment can take many forms, from modems providing asynchronous access to the network to more complex data service units, routers, and bridges. Smaller networks may not have any of these connections, while larger networks are likely to have many. Unfortunately, NetWare's built-in tools are relatively inefficient ways of checking on these network connections. However, these devices are likely to leave "spoor" that you can use to hunt them down.

Physical Presence Look for boxes that say "Cisco" or "Bay Networks."

Mystery Networks If you've got more networks reported from your servers than you expect, scour the wiring closets and phone rooms.

Existing Network Maps Network interconnection devices are usually expensive and are likely to have made it onto any maps your predecessors may have generated. Look especially for any black boxes connected to "network clouds."

Network Management Tools These software packages can be the equivalent of bloodhounds when you're hot on the trail of interconnection equipment. See Chapter 14 for more details.

Working with Network-Connected Modems

Modem connections are slow. Let me repeat that: *Modem connections are slow*. They are not fast, they are not responsive, they are not particularly reliable. However, since they're inexpensive and convenient, they're likely to be a part of any network you find yourself managing. Modem connections generally work as network-connected nodes, either single units or in modem pools connected to communications servers, or as remote-control connections, in which a remote machine takes control of a locally connected network machine via modem and special software.

MODEM-CONNECTED CLIENTS Remote nodes connected via modems on standard telephone lines are slow. They're *really* slow. With all the network activity that is usually running on 10 Mbps network lines attempting to run over a phone connection with perhaps a tenth of the throughput, it's no wonder everything takes so long through a serial connection. The biggest advantage of a remote-client connection is that the connection is transparent; there's no remote-control software to worry about. The best way to avoid problems with remote-connected clients is to run executable files from the client and only use the phone line connection to access data on the network. This minimizes the impact of the limited phone line bandwidth. Don't expect to be able to dial into the network and run programs at anything resembling network (read that as "acceptable") speeds.

One remote node software package available is Novell's NetWare Connect, which also allows dial-out capabilities for network users and remote-control client operation. Funk Software's Proxy and Telepartner International's RemoteVision are two additional remote connection software packages. AirSoft's AirAccess is designed for remote node connections via packet radio connections. Cisco, Attachmate, Rockwell Network Systems, and Shiva all offer hardware and software designed to support remote nodes.

REMOTE-CONTROL CLIENTS Clients who use remote-control software to dial in to the networks need to have a machine ready to accept the call and make a network connection. The remote machine runs the remote-control software, while the computer on the other end of the phone line runs remote-control software and the usual network client software. This arrangement can be somewhat faster than remote connections, although GUIs like Microsoft Windows add graphical overhead that can reduce performance. Another problem is that the network-connected machine is generally beyond the control of the remote user, so power outages, energy-conscious coworkers, or dropped network connections can be problematic. Some of these problems can be resolved by power-management hardware on the local machine that can be instructed to perform a reboot in case of a crash.

Remote-access software is available from several manufacturers. Some highly rated packages include Microcom's Carbon Copy, Norton-Lambert's Close-Up, Stac Electronics' ReachOut, Symantec's pcANYWHERE, and Triton Technologies' CoSession.

Working with CSU/DSU Connections

Channel Service Units (CSUs) and Digital (or Data) Service Units (DSUs) are devices used to connect digital T1 lines, which are standard copper twisted-pair phone lines carrying digital signals that are regenerated at close intervals. T1 lines and fractional T1 lines are commonly used to connect wide area networks and enterprisewide networks. CSU/DSUs connect to the ends of T1 lines and provide signal termination, checking services, and broadcasting services. Most systems that include T1 connections should have redundant connections; if connectivity over long distances is important enough to merit the expense of a T1 leased line, it makes sense to provide backup. The CSU and DSU functions can often be found in a multiplexer (mux), which is a device that allows multiple signals to travel along the same physical wiring to maximize the use of communications circuits.

Working with Network Hubs

Network hubs include 10BaseT Ethernet concentrators, ARCNet active and passive hubs, and Token Ring MAUs. Each of these units works differently in its network topology, but each acts as a central connection point—and as a central point of failure. Many vendors currently offer "stackable" hubs, which provide a chassis or a chaining mechanism and allow the addition of additional ports and management modules. Some MAUs allow use of STP and UTP connections from the same physical box (as separate logical rings), and some hubs allow Token Ring and Ethernet ports to coexist in the same chassis. (Management of both networks is another story indeed.)

It is important to locate the hubs in your network; adding users and networked peripherals is much easier when you know where to connect them, and hubs can sometimes hang or become crippled by high collision rates. The connection LEDs on hubs make it easy to see how many viable connections are in place at any point in time.

Working with Bridges

Bridges are network connection devices that direct the flow of network data between network segments. Bridges can act primarily to segment network traffic, preventing data from crossing unless it is intended for an address on the other side. Bridges can also be coupled to provide long-distance communications, although this can degrade performance. Bridges read the destination address on the data they encounter and allow through only the data with legitimate business on the other side. Because the bridge needs to be able to read the address, it is protocol specific; since it reads only the address, it is relatively fast. Different types of cabling and NICs can happily be connected by a bridge as long as the communications protocol is the same.

A bridge can connect networks with different kinds of cabling if both networks use the same communications protocol, so a 10BaseT network running IPX/SPX could be connected by a bridge to a 10Base5 network running IPX/SPX.

Bridging information can be based on an address table you manage or on a table the bridge creates dynamically by polling nodes on the network periodically.

Working with Routers

Routers are more complex than bridges and work with higher-level information and addressing. Unlike bridges, which combine physically separate networks into one logical network (thereby becoming effectively transparent to the network), routers connect separate networks and allow data to pass only if it belongs to a destination on a connected network. The degree to which a router uses intelligent path selection to pick the best route for the data affects the speed penalty imposed by the routing.

NetWare itself acts as a multiprotocol router, but although it is the cheapest router you'll find (since you already own it), it isn't necessarily the most efficient. Router costs can be very high, but most large networks use dedicated routers to provide better network data flow. Because routers typically use subnetwork addressing, they discard some addressing information before sending data to its destination. This allows more efficient links, which is particularly important over expensive, low-bandwidth wide area connections.

Working with Gateways

Some of the highest-level network interconnections are gateways. These devices connect disparate communications systems and perform translations between addressing, packet composition, operating software, and data formats. Gateways are complex and expensive and are generally useful for connecting systems that share data like electronic mail.

Determining User Load and Location

WHEW! THAT'S A lot of different hardware to be looking at. Now that you've kicked the tires a bit and checked out the paint job on your "previously owned" network, it's time to have a look at how the network is running right now.

The most important aspect of the network load is user distribution. The number of users you have on each network and server will have more to do with network performance (not to mention mundane issues like user licensing and disk space) than anything else. Ultimately, you'll want to know what the users are doing and why, but since we've got to walk before we run, let's first figure out how many users are on the network and where they are.

Looking at the Load on a File Server

Before checking on the distribution of users, have a quick look at how the server is running. The MONITOR console utility is a good way to look at any NetWare server's vital statistics. More detailed information can be generated by network analysis software, but for "getting to know you" purposes, enough information can be gleaned from the MONITOR screens to give you an idea of the load being placed on each server.

To use the MONITOR console utility, load the NLM from the console.

```
:LOAD MONITOR
```

After the command is executed, the MONITOR Main screen, similar to the one shown in Figure 1.29, appears at the server.

FIGURE 1.29
The main screen of the MONITOR console utility provides a variety of server information, including the NetWare version, number of user licenses, number of connected users, current processor utilization, and server up time.

```
MS-DOS Prompt
NIRVANA:modules
MONITOR.NLM
  NetWare 386 Console Monitor
  Version 1.75    October 26, 1992
  Copyright 1992 Novell, Inc.  All rights reserved.
STANDARD.NLM
  ARCserve Standard Tape Support  Version 5.01d
  Version 5.01d   March 8, 1994
  (C) Copyright 1990-1994 Cheyenne Software, Inc.  All rights reserved.
TAPESVR.NLM
  ARCserve SCSI Tape Driver
  Version 5.01d   March 15, 1994
  (C) Copyright 1990-1994 Cheyenne Software, Inc.  All rights reserved.
ASPI50.NLM
  ARCserve SCSI Board Driver
  Version 5.01d   February 17, 1994
  (C) Copyright 1990-1994 Cheyenne Software, Inc.  All rights reserved.
ARCSERVE.NLM
  ARCserve Scheduler
  Version 5.01d   March 17, 1994
  (C) Copyright 1990-1994 Cheyenne Software, Inc. All Rights Reserved.
<Press ESC to terminate or any other key to continue>
```

File Server Up Time

This number indicates the time that the file server has been running since it last came up. If you're looking at this number on your first day in a new network administration position, you'd like it to be high—ideally more than a month. This would indicate a certain amount of stability that you can assume (initially, at least) will continue while you learn the ropes. If the server has been up less than a week, you'll want to find out why, and you should try to find out who was the last person to restart the server.

Utilization

Server utilization is a percentage indicating how busy the server is keeping its processor. If the percentage is high—over 50 percent on a continual basis, or spiking up past 70 percent—you'll want to investigate to see what is occupying the processor. If a server is providing file access to network users, even many users and many requests, processor utilization would not be very high; expect something around or below 10 percent on average. If utilization is higher, it is likely that a process is running that is burdening the system. A network backup module may be working hard, or the disk drives may be remirroring after falling out of synchronization—or some other process is bogging down the system. High utilization is generally be noticed by the users, who will experience lower performance than usual.

If you do see very high utilization at this point, select the **Processor Utilization** entry from the **Available Options** menu. If there is no **Processor Utilization** entry, press the Escape key to exit MONITOR, and answer Yes when it checks to make sure you want to unload the NLM. From the console prompt (cycle through the active screens by pressing Alt-Escape until you see the colon prompt), type:

```
:MONITOR /P
```

This loads the MONITOR utility with the processor utilization option enabled. This option indicates the relative load placed on the microprocessor by each of the active processes. Often a LAN driver or host adapter (identifiable by their IRQ numbers) is taking up an inordinate share of the processor's time.

Connections in Use

Finally, check the number of connections in use. Compare it to the number of user licenses indicated at the top of the screen (next to the version of NetWare on the left side of the title bar). Select the **Connection Information** entry from the **Available Options** menu and quickly scroll through the user list. Does it list mostly unique user logins or are there many multiples of certain login names? This **Connection Information** identifies only the login names used for various sessions, which doesn't really tell you how many actual users are connected, but it does give you an idea of what to expect to see.

Looking at User Locations and Connections

When you have checked the relative usage on the various servers, compare the results. Are certain servers running NetWare licensed for more users than others? How close to license capacity are the servers? Do some appear to be more heavily burdened?

Now compare the user load results by server to the network connections you've identified. Are some physical networks more heavily laden than others? Does the distribution of network interconnection equipment make sense given your understanding of which servers have the most usage? The answers to these questions should not be set in stone; your understanding of the network is still evolving at this point. However, if there are discrepancies between what seems reasonable and what appears to be in place, these are avenues for further exploration.

Hey, that's quite a bit of stuff you've looked at. You have looked at the servers and the host systems in your predominantly NetWare network and identified the most important hardware components installed in them. You have identified the physical topologies connecting the servers and their clients and have located the important connection and routing points along the network. You have used a number of basic NetWare utilities to find information about how the network is connected. In Chapter 2, Into the Pit: Investigating Network Operating Systems, you'll look at the networking software installed on your systems.

Into the Pit: Investigating Network Operating Systems

HAVING GOTTEN A handle on the equipment installed in your new situation, you're ready to have a closer look at the network operating systems in use. Take a quick trip to the water cooler, tidy up the papers on your desk, and dig a little into the structure and strengths of the products you'll be managing. Although many different products are available, the network operating systems most frequently encountered are various flavors of UNIX, Microsoft's Windows NT Server, Banyan's VINES, and naturally, Novell's NetWare. These products provide varying levels of connectability, and in some cases, different versions of these products can provide somewhat different functionality, reliability, and connectivity. The preferred protocol-level interactions between these network operating systems are also of interest, in part because most of the products run most efficiently when they use particular protocols.

The Vital Information

WHILE THE LAST chapter focused on exploration, investigation, and note taking, this chapter includes background information on some of the most popular network operating systems. If you'd rather not take the time to look at the comparative information for each of the operating systems covered here, you can gather the data germane to your inherited network and move on.

If you want to move on, first identify the UNIX (or UNIX variant) systems, Windows NT servers, and VINES servers installed on the network. Identify the NetWare versions in use on the file servers. Locate any peer-to-peer networks in your domain using Windows for Workgroups, LANtastic, or Personal NetWare. Find the communications protocols in use on the network, and determine the software interfaces used to connect dissimilar systems.

Chapter 1 focused on gathering information about the NetWare servers on the network; you'll want to have your list of NetWare servers ready to add information to, and you should also keep the list of host systems ready.

Identifying NOS Products in Use

ALTHOUGH THIS BOOK assumes you administer a NetWare-centric network, multiple network operating systems are found in many organizations. Strengths and weaknesses of the products, multiple development paths or decision-makers, personal bias, and sometimes plain confusion conspire to scatter multiple products throughout a company's internetwork. This can be a learning experience for administrators coming from a single-product background. Because the evolution of enterprise networking is likely to continue to involve multiple products and protocols being patched together in mission-critical situations, a more cynical view is that administrators will want to check as many boxes as possible to pique the interest of future employers. In any event, playing with unfamiliar computer toys can be both fun and profitable. Since UNIX, Windows NT, VINES, and NetWare are the heavy hitters in the networking arena, we will take a look at each of them.

Several popular peer networking products are available; Microsoft's Windows for Workgroups is quite popular, and Artisoft's LANtastic and Novell's Personal NetWare offer a number of benefits to users tired of using the *sneakernet* to physically move data from one microcomputer to another. However, while these products provide paths for data flow, they are not designed to handle the kind of ambitious network flow typically found in NetWare environments. Still, many users work on peer network operating systems, and while you are not likely to be asked to integrate the peer systems into your client/server network, a little knowledge can't hurt. Besides, it's fun to pronounce the acronym for Peer Network Operating System (PNOS).

UNIX

UNIX is a mature, 32-bit operating system that is available from a large number of vendors on a wide range of machines. Its multitasking features are outstanding, and its primary networking protocols are the ones used on the Internet. UNIX is suitable for very large-scale organizations and is generally packaged with a tantalizing assortment of utilities, compilers, and other goodies. So why aren't there more UNIX users in mainstream businesses?

Look around…there are many UNIX users in mainstream businesses. However, there has long been a mutual dislike between UNIX users and users in the DOS world, and since NetWare's primary strength started off with its similarity to DOS, it's not surprising that the UNIX crowd would disdain the NOS. Some aspects of NetWare are understandably distasteful to those who aren't used to such limitations: Novell's operating system is nonpreemptive, which leaves some of the "we run this ship on a tight schedule" gang shaking their heads; furthermore, NetWare's NLMs have more control over their own destinies than UNIX aficionados care for, in part because NLMs sometimes end up overwriting parts of each other in memory. This is admittedly untidy, and we who are used to it simply eliminate the offending modules, cursing enthusiastically.

On the other hand, users coming from the DOS world are a bit put off by the many variations of UNIX, the slower response time typical of UNIX systems, and the unfriendly command set. UNIX vendors are doing their best to resolve these problems, and their products have many strengths, not the least of which is their natural application as Internet-connected machines acting as World Wide Web (WWW) servers. It's likely that we will see more integration between NetWare and UNIX systems as time goes by.

A UNIX History Lesson

UNIX traces its roots to 1969, when it was created by AT&T's Ken Thompson and Dennis Ritchie. After the initial implementation, the software was written and developed in the newly created C programming language. UNIX was designed as a multi-user, multiprocessing operating system.

A Familiar Name

UNIX co-creator Dennis M. Ritchie's name is probably familiar to hackers, who may know him as co-author of the C programmer's bible, *The C Programming Language*. Ritchie initially designed C for the implementation of UNIX on DEC's PDP-11 minicomputer. (Ken Thompson created a predecessor named—you guessed it—B, for UNIX running on the PDP-7.) Like UNIX, one of the greatest strengths of C is its relative platform independence. C code can readily be moved from one system to another by being recompiled to run on different platforms. C compilers themselves can be relatively easily created and easily moved from one platform to another. This pervasive portability is convenient for software developers, hardware vendors, and users alike.

In 1974, users at the University of California at Berkeley acquired a DEC PDP-11 16-bit minicomputer and a copy of UNIX. By 1979, the gung ho Golden Bears had produced three iterations of the UNIX software with additional utilities and enhancements. Two of the Berkeley Software Distribution (BSD) versions of the operating system were based on the initially obtained version of UNIX, while the third—known as 3BSD—was based on the 32-bit Bell Labs 32V software. The Defense Advanced Research Projects Agency (DARPA) spurred further development of 4.1BSD with several more enhancements.

Cal's Computer Systems Research Group (CSRG) then produced two versions of UNIX in which the AT&T code had been rewritten. While the BSD software had required a software license from AT&T, these CSRG products, NET/1 and NET/2, were distributed without requiring purchasers to obtain source code licenses from either AT&T or Berkeley. AT&T's UNIX Systems Labs (USL) responded to NET/2 with a suit alleging that AT&T licenses were still required.

In the end, the University of California got out of the UNIX distribution business, USL was sold to Novell in December 1992, and everyone decided to play nice. In the big picture, UNIX gained quite a bit by being enhanced by the Berkeley group, especially because AT&T was doing little to spur the aggressive development and distribution of the software. The networking enhancements and utilities added in the BSD releases are now part of the versions of UNIX available from many different vendors on many different platforms. Roll on, you Bears!

Understanding the Nature of the Beast

Most of the current implementations of UNIX are based on one version or another of AT&T's System V kernel (a noticeable exception is NeXTStep, which uses the Mach kernel). UNIX is a multi-user, multitasking system that can support large numbers of users on a single processor (even on Intel hardware, on which a 80386-based machine can handle over a hundred users simultaneously). However, performance appears to be slower than on DOS and Windows systems, in part because a UNIX system handles more tasks than DOS-based systems even dream of handling. UNIX runs much more happily on systems with plenty of RAM—count on 32MB for a smallish system; one site I know of uses 1.5GB. Since many current implementations take advantage of the instruction sets available on the most powerful processors, powerful hardware pays off. Performance tuning generally pays significant dividends on UNIX systems.

Since UNIX uses central processing rather than the distributed model employed by NetWare systems, data does not have to travel from the point on the network where it is stored to another point on the net where it is processed; these tasks can occur on the machine that initiated them. This reduces the amount of network activity required. Thanks to the Berkeley extensions, UNIX speaks TCP/IP fluently, making it a natural for Internet connection and Web server activities. UNIX tools are more complex and more powerful than what is available in the single-tasking DOS arena.

While UNIX is available on a wide range of platforms and is theoretically portable to any hardware powerful enough to support it, it has some limitations on the Intel platform. Although most versions include graphical interfaces, generally based on X Windows, support for Microsoft Windows is somewhat limited. DOS-based applications (including Windows apps) are run using the *virtual machine* capabilities of the Intel 80x86 architecture. Since the virtual machine emulates an 8086 or 80286, full-fledged DOS applications that try any sort of funky control over memory may not run properly. Furthermore, the virtual machine emulations limit Windows to running in standard mode, which is not particularly desirable.

Windows Standard Mode offers only task switching; enhanced mode is required for the cooperative multitasking offered by Windows. This is the major disadvantage of standard mode. Since standard mode does not recognize the VxD virtual device drivers, it may not work with all the software you'd like it to.

Who Is in Control of UNIX?

UNIX development and standardization issues became more significant as a result of two occurrences. BSD stopped releasing new software, no longer providing direction and functionality enhancements. Then USL was sold to Novell, a company often criticized for being too focused on its meat-and-potato client/server NOS and mispositioning its UNIX products. The herd of vendors attempting to differentiate and sell their UNIX products are aware that users want "open" architectures. Since the desire to differentiate and the desire to standardize are somewhat contradictory goals, you can understand part of the problem faced by users and vendors alike. The vendors responded to the users' need for open architectures by turning to the age-old solution of forming committees. Quite a few industry organizations, some of which are nonprofit, are working to promulgate standards for UNIX, UNIX-like operating systems, and UNIX components.

The Common Open Software Environment (COSE) initiative was trumpeted by several of the biggest players in the UNIX world and was supposed to push standardization of graphical user interfaces. Unfortunately, the differences among the implementations of graphical desktops in the member companies' products has slowed progress. The X/Open organization is intended to standardize application programming interfaces (APIs) to ease applications development across multiple platforms. The Open Software Foundation (OSF), another industry-sponsored group, supports the OSF/1 version of UNIX and the Motif graphical user interface. Other OSF initiatives include the Distributed Computing Environment (DCE) and Distributed Management Environment (DME) for applications development and systems management, respectively. Meanwhile, the IEEE standards body has defined the 1003 family of POSIX standard. POSIX defines a UNIX-like operating system that theoretically provides portability but does not seem particularly relevant to real-world situations and problems.

The UNIX Flavor Taste Test

Everybody and their brother (except for my brother, so far) has a version of UNIX. IBM has AIX, which seemed to fall out of IBM's grand systems architecture for a time but reappeared with a vengeance on the RS/6000 platform. HP/UX, A/UX, Ultrix, and others contend for attention but appeal primarily to users of Hewlett-Packard, Apple, and DEC systems, respectively. Some of the more interesting versions are worth brief descriptions.

UNIXWARE UnixWare is the result of a union between USL and Novell (Novell effectively gained full custody when it bought USL from AT&T at the end of 1992), who jointly founded Univel. Novell has indicated a plan to integrate UnixWare and NetWare in future implementations, but at the moment, UnixWare is being marketed as a UNIX client operating system for NetWare environments and as an operating system for network application servers.

UnixWare includes powerful and easy-to-use tools for network administration, although support for NetWare Directory Services (NDS) under NetWare 4.x is not available in UnixWare 2.0. It handles both TCP/IP and NetWare's native protocols, and it includes a strong GUI. The NetWare UNIX Client File System (NUCFS) allows UnixWare users to access NetWare volumes. Novell has been criticized for hiding the light of the System V Release 4.2 (SVR4.2) under its NetWare-centric bushel, but it isn't surprising that Novell, knowing that its bread is buttered with its PC-platform NOS, seems satisfied targeting UnixWare as part of its enterprisewide NetWare solution.

SOLARIS SunSoft's Solaris traces its lineage back to SunOS, which was the UNIX implementation found on Sun Microsystems' popular workstations for some time. The widely available Network File System (NFS) and Network Information Service (NIS) features, which centralize the administration of files and users, originated in SunOS. Solaris has an enterprisewide focus and provides IPX/SPX support and strong ties to the Intel platform. It was one of the first products to support symmetric multiprocessing (SMP), combining multiple processors in a single system to increase power and performance.

Although symmetric multiprocessing systems can provide increased performance, they can also be configured to allow system redundancy and therefore fault tolerance. In this mode, the SMP system can switch control to a secondary processor if the primary processor fails. Most SMP systems do not simultaneously provide fault tolerance and increased performance, however.

SCO UNIX The Santa Cruz Operation's SCO UNIX has long been *the* UNIX solution for users on Intel hardware, holding more than 30 percent of the multi-user UNIX market. SCO is working to improve connectivity between Microsoft Windows clients and its UNIX servers to expand into a broader market rather than the less sexy transaction-processing segment it dominates.

Some of SCO's Windows-related products allow clients to gracefully access UNIX system resources such as printers and SQL databases.

LINUX Linux is a variant of UNIX that has one major advantage: price. Can you say "public domain"? I knew that you could, and many other users are entering the UNIX waters by wading in at the shallow end. For under a hundred dollars, you can get a distribution copy of Linux with utilities and electronic documentation. You can run the software on an 80386-class machine with 8MB of RAM, though you won't be setting any world speed records by doing so. The availability of Linux means that network administrators, hackers, and homemakers everywhere can experiment with UNIX systems and Web links with a discarded machine and a minimal investment. The beauty of this situation is that hobbyists and spare-time coders are already generating a wealth of information and add-ins for Linux. Your value-added reseller probably won't be much help if you run into problems, but for exploration or purposes that are not mission-critical, Linux is hard to beat.

NEXTSTEP One of these UNIXs is not like the others…one of these UNIXs doesn't belong….Unlike most versions of UNIX, which are based on different versions of the SVR4 kernel, the NeXTStep operating system, developed by former Apple visionary Steve Jobs, uses the Mach kernel. This NeXT-generation offering features an object-oriented design that pervades its structure. Its Workspace Manager GUI is very well designed, and multimedia features have built-in support: this is not your father's UNIX. Graphics, video, and audio integrated into the operating system package make this a very sexy product, but NeXTStep is even more snooty about hardware than most strains of UNIX. Give it all the RAM you can handle, take advantage of the decline in disk prices to give it plenty of elbow room, get a nice turbocharged processor, and enjoy an unusual level of applications support.

If you're running NeXTStep, you will want at least a 100 MHz 486-class microprocessor with 24MB of RAM to run in color. Don't bother with a hard disk smaller than 500MB; 1GB would be a better idea. These numbers aren't completely out of line with machines running Windows and DOS, but the additional pep you provide a NeXTStep machine pays greater dividends.

Windows NT

Can we talk? When I first installed Microsoft's Windows NT, version 3.1, I wasn't particularly impressed. I didn't like its NetBEUI transport, and I didn't care for the interface, which looks like Windows for Workgroups. I figured it was a bad joke that logging into the network involved the "three finger salute" (Ctrl-Alt-Delete). I really disliked the performance I got when I accessed SQL Server data on an NT server from an NT client.

But I have changed my mind about NT. Version 3.5 is faster than its predecessor (although NetWare is still faster for file and print services). It offers SMP support and uses the additional processors efficiently. Its support for IPX and TCP/IP is welcome in most networking environments. Microsoft also offers support for IBM's Systems Network Architecture (SNA) networks. Security and network management features are acceptable, and installation is easy if the hardware is sufficiently compatible. I still loathe Microsoft Mail, which comes bundled with NT, but other options are available, including Lotus Notes, the integrated database and messaging software.

NT is a 32-bit operating system that is competitively priced and has the full influence of the software industry's heavyweight behind it. Whether Microsoft's business practices seem fair to users, competitors, or courts, the company's marketing and clout are likely to continue to push NT into more organizations. As long as the software continues to develop as it has between versions 3.1 and 3.5, the system will certainly be appealing from the system administrator's perspective. Microsoft is hoping to build the kind of support infrastructure around NT that Novell has created for NetWare; one strategy Redmond has copied is a training and certification program. One of the Microsoft Certified Systems Engineer exams is waived for NetWare- and Banyan-certified applicants.

VINES

Banyan Systems traditionally held sway over the large enterprisewide network market with its Virtual Networking Software (VINES) NOS. VINES is a UNIX-based, multiprocessing-capable system that features the StreetTalk global naming service. StreetTalk identifies network users and resources and replicates changes to the network Access Rights List (ARL) between servers. Novell's global naming service, NDS, appeared with NetWare 4.x. VINES also provides database access for Oracle and SQL databases based on StreetTalk entries, allowing centralized network management of database resources.

Although VINES is UNIX-based, it doesn't use TCP/IP as a native protocol, but it can emulate TCP/IP. VINES has a loyal following, and although its overall NOS market share is less than 10 percent, it is used in roughly half of the enterprisewide networks connecting more than fifty users per server. The availability of NetWare 4.x with NDS has convinced some VINES users to switch to Novell's product, but Banyan's purchase and integration of BeyondMail and long-awaited enhancements like fail-safe login (allowing users to access the network even if their local StreetTalk server is down) will likely ameliorate the situation.

Banyan's Enterprise Network Services (ENS) product provides access to network resources across heterogeneous networking systems. ENS is available for UNIX, Windows NT, VINES, and even NetWare networks. The product is seen not only as a solution to the common problem of internetwork incompatibility, but also as an alternative to vendor solutions such as Novell's NetWare Directory Services. Banyan sees ENS as its future in the networking industry.

NetWare

Wir sind hier wegen dem Bier. Or in this case, we're here because of NetWare. Various versions of Novell's flagship NOS make up a whopping 70 percent of the installed networks. The product's success is not coincidental; NetWare is a fast, reliable operating system that looks enough like DOS to have become popular and offers enough support for assorted network protocols and diverse client operating systems to have survived despite changes in the landscapes of businesses. NetWare's compatibility and modular design have put Novell at the front of the networking class. Other network operating systems offer some intriguing advantages, but Novell seems to be willing to push development in the areas that are most compelling to the majority of users.

Look at that Power!

NetWare in each of its modern incarnations has used several features to boost its performance to consistently outstanding levels when providing access to files stored on the server. NetWare's fundamental design as a file server means that it specializes in retrieving files for clients; this design enhances performance by off-loading the execution of applications to the client machines. This *distributed processing* philosophy is a very different approach than that taken by UNIX (or Windows NT, for that matter). Directory and file caching, directory hashing, and elevator seeking are all used by NetWare to improve its file access performance.

One area in which NetWare 2.x and 3.x needs some improvement is in its handling of users and groups of users. These "objects" are stored in a system database referred to as the bindery. Binderies are created and maintained independently on all the servers in an internetwork, making management of a large, distributed network difficult. This flaw is addressed in NetWare 4.x.

Directory caching places the Directory Entry Table (DET) and File Allocation Table (FAT) into server memory. The DET lists directories, file names, and file and directory properties and links the file name entries to the File Allocation Table, which stores the file names and locations. NetWare quickly accesses files and directories because these "file address books" can be consulted in RAM rather from disk. Directory hashing is the process of creating an indexed DET in memory; the indexing improves performance by reducing the amount of time required to find the correct entry in the DET.

File caching is the process of storing frequently used files in main memory so that access is faster. If you store your company's electronic mail files on a NetWare server, the 15 users logging into the network at 9:35 a.m. after pouring their coffee and shooting the bull for half an hour will be able to access the mail executable and the central address book file much more quickly than they will be able to access their individual mail files. But don't expect them to notice or thank you. Of course, if 150 people log in at 9:35 a.m., the point of diminishing returns will probably be reached and the server will be so busy handling the sudden user load that the added performance provided by file caching will be outweighed. Still, Novell says file access can be improved a hundred times if a file is cached.

Elevator seeking maximizes the efficiency of disk drive accesses. This process determines the physical locations of the files being accessed and selects a sequence that allows the disk heads to follow a smooth path over the drive platters. This maximizes the efficiency of the head motion, reducing wear on the disk hardware and enhancing file retrieval performance. Elevator seeking is similar to an efficient method of grocery shopping: instead of following the order of the list you created before you went to the supermarket, moving randomly from one aisle to another, you start on one side of the store and select items off the list as you pass them.

NetWare 2.x

Although you probably won't be able to buy NetWare 2.x anywhere but at a garage sale (my advice is to get the oscilloscope instead), vestigial traces of it may be tucked away somewhere. Run—do not walk—to your nearest authorized reseller and get yourself a modern version of NetWare. While you're at it, make sure you get hardware that runs a modern version of NetWare. NetWare 2.x varies dramatically from subsequent versions in hardware support and in design.

SYSTEM SPECIFICATIONS NetWare 2.x used a different core structure than subsequent versions. Version 2.x predates Intel's 80386 microprocessor and lacks much of the power afforded by the 386 architecture. It supported the ISA and MCA bus designs, could handle up to a hundred users on a single server, and allowed DOS, OS/2, and Macintosh clients to use network resources. Those resources aren't very impressive by today's standards; a NetWare 2.x server could address only 12MB of RAM and only 2GB of disk space carved into volumes no larger than 255MB.

ARCHITECTURE The single biggest difference between the architecture of the 2.x products and that found in later versions is the lack of modularity in 2.x. These products contained standard core operating system code, but network and disk drivers had to be selected before a specific installation of NetWare would operate. Once the drivers were selected, the operating system could be generated and run. If you wanted to change drivers, however, you were forced to recreate the operating system from the core and the new driver components. The server would accept add-in applications called Value-Added Processes. VAPs were run on the server but were loaded separately. Hard disks on NetWare 2.x servers had no DOS partition; they were completely under NetWare's control.

NetWare 3.x

NetWare 3.x (originally called NetWare 386 because it took advantage of the more powerful architecture built into Intel's 80386 microprocessor) supports millions of users worldwide. Its modularity allows additional functionality to be integrated into NetWare servers, and its performance has made it the premier network operating system.

SYSTEM SPECIFICATIONS NetWare 3.x can access the full 4GB of RAM addressable by the 80386 processor; its 32TB maximum disk storage space could all be allocated to a single 32TB SYS volume if you wished (good luck). Up to a thousand users can be logged into a single server from DOS, OS/2, and Macintosh clients. File exchange with UNIX systems is supported via NFS. File servers can be duplexed—set up to run identically and redundantly—for highly fault-tolerant systems using SFT III in NetWare 3.1x and later versions.

ARCHITECTURE Version 3.x separates the drivers and services that were centralized in the 2.x operating system. The result is an NOS that is highly configurable on the fly. Applications, drivers, and utilities that run on the server are run as NetWare Loadable Modules (NLMs) that can be loaded and unloaded while the server continues to run. This makes it much easier to update drivers and alter network configurations.

STRENGTHS AND WEAKNESSES NetWare 3.x is in widespread use in networks of all sizes and architectures. From small, relatively loosely organized groups like not-for-profit organizations to global businesses, NetWare 3.x is used to share files and resources and to connect to other networking systems. It features extensive support for the most popular access methods and for the universe of physical topologies.

Its ability to support the most popular client platforms and interconnect with the most popular host systems using the most popular protocols and standards has made it a dominant product. Its speed, security, and modular architecture have also contributed to its success. However, it lacks unified management tools, using instead a variety of utilities to perform different administrative tasks. It also lacks the kind of global access to internetwork resources that has been the strength of VINES for years. NetWare servers are highly connectable, but they must be managed one server at a time and do not cleanly share resources. Because NetWare leaves processing to the client machines and focuses instead on providing fast access to file and print services, it isn't intended for use on applications servers.

NetWare 4.x

NetWare 4.x builds on the performance strengths of its predecessors and goes a long way toward integrating network administration and resources. Version 4.1 resolves several of the inelegant aspects of the early releases of Version 4.0.

Most of the less-impressive aspects of NetWare 4.x have been corrected in version 4.1. One problem was that earlier versions of the NetWare Directory Services (NDS) were not able to merge two NDS trees. This defeated the purpose of the NDS somewhat, since a single point of management at the top of the tree is a major goal of NDS. Another problem involved deleting and re-adding users, who then could not be managed using the standard utilities. Memory faults, login problems, and replica errors were also eliminated in the 4.1 release.

Since the majority of the code used in NetWare 4.x was used in NetWare 3.12, version 4.x literally uses the previous version as its basis. This continuity can provide at least a small measure of certainty to administrators concerned about the stability of the new system. One other noteworthy feature is the addition of data compression on network volumes.

INSTALLATION ISSUES NetWare 4.x can be installed relatively automatically using the "simple" installation procedure. This installation creates a single-level NDS structure that can be modified if necessary. The custom installation procedure allows the administrator more latitude in the creation of the NDS design. NetWare 4.x can be installed over DOS or OS/2, and upgraders can use "across-the-wire" upgrades to add new servers or update existing servers to the new version. Installation across the wire uses existing servers and network connections to provide a high-speed installation process run across the network. Installation can also be performed via CD-ROM.

NETWARE DIRECTORY SERVICES (NDS) The Directory Services structure is a centrally managed but distributed database containing the names of an organization's users, disk volumes, servers, printers, and other resources. NDS replaces the binderies of individual servers used in NetWare 2.x and 3.x and allows users to access the resources they need by logging in only once.

Attaching to multiple servers is a major headache in NetWare 3.1x networks. As your network resources expand and your users become more sophisticated, your users will begin to need global access to data. Executives may want to look at

employee data stored on the accounting and human resources servers. The production staff may want to look at the scheduling databases maintained on the product management servers. Although this data sharing is a good thing, it is also a hassle because you'll have to manage separate NetWare 3.1x accounts on each of the servers for each of the users involved. Your login scripts will become filled with groups performing automatic attach-and-map functions to drive letters you will have to keep straight. Not a pleasant scenario.

The NETSYNC utility merges NetWare 3.1x binderies into NDS as appropriate and allows management of an internetwork containing 3.x and 4.x servers. NDS also lightens the load of network administrators, who can manipulate network objects and access to those objects without moving from server to server. Graphical administration utilities for Windows and OS/2 are finally included with the client software—though these same utilities also accompany NetWare 3.12.

Windows for Workgroups

Windows for Workgroups has many strengths, including its price and its ubiquitousness. Many computer systems come with WFW already installed over DOS. It has a graphical interface and is also a peer networking product, although many users have WFW installed on their standalone machines. WFW works admirably and quickly as a client to Windows NT, and it can also connect to NetWare servers whether or not it's also used for peer networking.

WFW recognizes a variety of NICs and can completely configure many of them. Although NetBEUI is the standard communications protocol, other protocols (including IPX and TCP/IP) can be used singly or combined with NetBEUI. These protocols sit on top of the Network Driver Interface Specification (NDIS) layer, which allows protocol sharing on the client. NDIS 3.0 runs in protected mode, requiring less than 5KB of conventional memory and running faster than previous NDIS implementations.

WFW is an acceptable peer network with good file and printer sharing, simple configuration (if all goes well), and wide compatibility. Microsoft Mail is bundled free, but in this case, you definitely get what you pay for. WFW is most interesting as a network client because its support for a variety of networks and its familiar interface makes it a reasonable option for many business networks.

Microsoft Mail is an adequate product with a clean interface and a great price. It is reasonably easy to set up and configure, but customizing its client software can be a chore. Its performance on a WFW network is poor, and it has been plagued with some management inelegancies—my least favorite is the problem with shrinking mail file sizes. The administrator couldn't compress the files; the users had to compact their own databases. This problem has been resolved in an update to the program. Some of the features I take for granted in other packages, such as blind carbon copies and mail routing, are not standard features, though a routing form can be obtained from Microsoft. The package includes no file viewers and has no rules-based message handling features. It's fine, but if you want a sophisticated mail package, look elsewhere.

See the Windows 95 section in Chapter 5 for a look at the improved networking functionality built into Microsoft's long-awaited client software.

LANtastic

Artisoft's LANtastic is a mature, stable, and highly expandable peer networking solution. Its support for NetWare and Windows for Workgroups (using Open Datalink Interface or Network Driver Interface Specification drivers) is more complicated than its standard connection using proprietary 2 Mbps or Ethernet peer connections. TCP/IP and Macintosh support is available, and LANtastic has long allowed CD-ROM sharing. Version 6.0 of Artisoft's peer networking software is available for DOS, OS/2, and Windows.

Artisoft offers the LANtastic Dedicated Server (formerly CorStream), a NetWare 4.x-based network operating system supporting up to a hundred users. Artisoft makes use of the power of NetWare 4.x (including certain NLMs) but provides shortcuts and automatic configuration routines that provide some insulation from the complexity and inelegance of some of NetWare's tools. The LANtastic Dedicated Server allows devoted LANtastic users to take advantage of the benefits of a true file server.

Personal NetWare

Novell's entry into the peer networking market should really be considered only by those who want to take advantage of its ties to its big brothers, the full NetWare 3.x and 4.x products. If you have a NetWare server-based network but want to provide peer access, Personal NetWare is probably the product for you. Personal NetWare's strongest feature is Single-Network View, which is a database of network objects replicated across the entire peer network. Since users are allowed to access network resources without worrying about where they are connected, the single login feature found in NetWare 4.x is also available in Personal NetWare. Other NetWare 4.x features are available, including network auto-reconnect, which reestablishes network connections when a server goes down and comes back up, and the Virtual Loadable Module (VLM) client drivers.

Understanding Network Protocols

IPX AND TCP/IP HAVE already been mentioned repeatedly; they are commonly used communications protocols. NetBIOS is also frequently encountered, and although it is not really a network protocol, it acts rather like one. A good basis for comparison of the protocols and near-protocols is the OSI model.

To find the protocols being routed on your NetWare server, look at the results of the CONFIG command. You'll find IPX bound to the NICs, but you may also find TCP/IP and AppleTalk. Since NetBIOS is not a routable protocol, you'll find it being emulated on the client machines. Look for the NETBIOS.EXE file being run when a client system starts or logs into the network.

The OSI Model

The Open Systems Interconnection (OSI) model of network activity is useful as a conceptual tool for distinguishing the various tasks that are handled between the hardware being fed bits of data and the user being notified that various network resources are ready for use. The seven-layer model has been embellished by a large number of protocols and implementations by the International Organization for Standardization (ISO) and networking product vendors; these implementations are generally expensive and lack the maturity and stability afforded by other protocols that are more widely used. Perhaps one moral of the story is that standards organizations are not the best forums for development; another might be to avoid organizations and standards whose abbreviations are palindromes. Regardless, the OSI model can provide a useful framework for understanding what functions are performed by any particular process or protocol. Most protocols do not use all the layers in the OSI model.

Working from the top end (the portion of the model closest to the user) down, the OSI layers are Application, Presentation, Session, Transport, Network, Data Link, and Physical, as shown in Figure 2.1. Each layer communicates only with the layers next to it.

FIGURE 2.1 The OSI communications model divides communications between computer systems into seven layers.

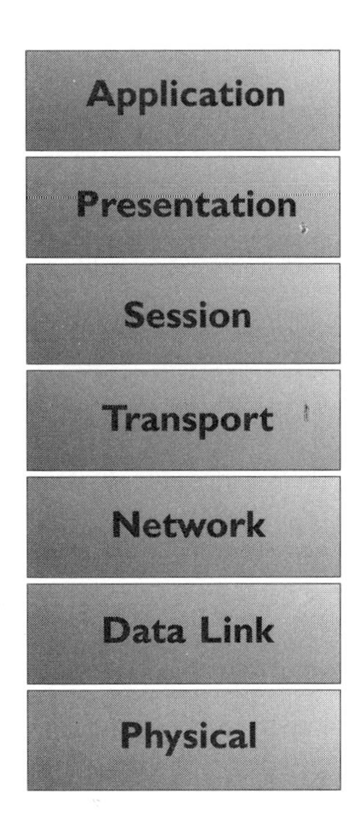

Application Layer

The Application Layer communicates the existence and availability of network services (including file manipulation, print services, electronic mail support, and database services). The existence of these network resources can be broadcast periodically, as implemented in NetWare's Service Advertising

Protocol (SAP), which announces the presence and availability of NetWare servers on the network each minute. This obviously has the disadvantage of filling the network with traffic that various nodes may not care about. The inclusion of NDS in NetWare 4.x allows the clients to decide when they want to know what resources are available, reducing network traffic. The Application Layer also manages interaction with the local operating system, allowing the client to make use of network services, either by redirecting requests made at the client station to the appropriate network resources or by connecting via terminal emulation to the network resources.

Presentation Layer

The Presentation Layer tidies up data being shared between systems using different conventions for interpreting data, such as ASCII and EBCDIC. Differences ranging from disparities in character sets to dissimilar file and data storage methods are resolved at this layer to prevent systems that use different hardware and software from stumbling over their differences. It's a bit like the Star Trek Universal Translator, ensuring that all parties understand what's being said by translating it to their native tongues.

Another analogy for the Presentation Layer is the Babel Fish, a peculiar creature described in Douglas Adams' The Hitchhiker's Guide to the Galaxy. By placing the leech-like creature in your ear, you could immediately understand words said to you in any language. Note that the problem with this analogy is that the Babel Fish is a mystical creature that always works, while the Presentation Layer and the Star Trek Universal Translator must understand what the two systems are saying.

Session Layer

The translation of data from one system to another is made possible by the Session Layer, which establishes and relinquishes connections between systems to facilitate data transfer. The Session Layer "opens hailing frequencies" between systems and arranges the terms of information transfer, including what should happen if portions of the transmission are lost and which direction(s) data will flow. The Session Layer is also responsible for ensuring that the data flow is complete and then hanging up the phone—terminating the connection it initiated.

Transport Layer

The Transport Layer addresses the content of the data flow, ensuring that data is in the proper sequence and that its component pieces are intact. While the Session Layer is concerned with the channels across which the data flows, the Transport Layer's focus is on the data itself. The Transport Layer makes sure that data intended for a bad connection is stored or rerouted so it will eventually reach its destination.

Network Layer

The Network Layer handles communications from one network to another, selecting different network routes based on the intended destination of the information being sent. The Network Layer software can be found in network devices that route data between interconnected networks. Routing paths can be stored in static tables or can be updated depending on prevailing network conditions. The Network Layer works with logical (network) addresses; physical addressing is determined at the Data Link Layer.

Data Link Layer

At the Data Link Layer, information is packaged for transmission on the network. The data is given a destination address and a return (source) address and is inserted into containers appropriate to the local network's arrangement. The *media access protocol* indicates how traffic is handled on the network; that is, is network communication controlled by a token-passing system such as Token Ring? Or is a contention-based Ethernet approach appropriate?

Physical Layer

The Physical Layer is rooted in reality. It comprises the media (usually cabling) that make up the network, the devices that interconnect the cabling, and the physical characteristics of the signals being broadcast over the media in place. These signals need not be transmitted over cabling, of course. Cellular packets, microwave, and radio frequency communications work equally well and still involve physical equipment sending and receiving information.

Applying the OSI Model

If you're at all like many of the network administrators I know, you may have learned the OSI model's structure in a class and relearned it for a certification exam. Quite a big deal is made of the model, especially given that few viable systems directly follow it and not any successful, widely implemented products adhere to the standard.

However, understanding the OSI model is an indication that you understand what kind of activities are going on in a network environment. Okay, that may not give you a warm, fuzzy feeling, but maybe this will:

Follow the OSI model from the lowest level when you are cold-troubleshooting your network. If you know a likely cause for the problem, go ahead and resolve it. But if you are experiencing an unfamiliar problem in an unfamiliar system, working up the model is a good approach. You almost always catch the really stupid problems more quickly, and it helps you rule out other possibilities. Ask basic questions: Is the machine physically connected to the network? Is the client running the correct frame type for the network it's on?

Common Protocol-Like Things

Now that we have a common basis for comparison, let's look at the specific products and standards found in many networking environments.

IPX/SPX

Novell's Internetwork Packet Exchange and Sequenced Packet Exchange protocols are the native transport methods found in NetWare. The IPX network communications protocol handles communications between nodes and happily chats with the NetWare client shell or emulation programs. SPX builds upon and complements IPX, offering features such as guaranteed delivery of data.

Novell's NetWare Link Services Protocol (NLSP) is another IPX enhancement that improves routing functions at the Network Layer, eliminates Routing Information Protocol (RIP) and SAP broadcasts, and makes more efficient use of network bandwidth. By default, NLSP transmits routing information only when services or routes are changed or every two hours.

SPX2 is a transport protocol that Novell recently developed in conjunction with AT&T. While standard SPX guarantees packet transmission, it requires the receipt of a reply for a packet before it transmits the next packet. SPX2 allows multiple packets to be queued and transmitted before acknowledgment of receipt is received. SPX is also limited to 576-byte packets, while SPX2 can negotiate the largest possible packet size agreeable to the systems involved.

TCP/IP

The Transmission Control Protocol/Internet Protocol, collectively referred to as TCP/IP, is everywhere. TCP/IP is not the official protocol of the 1996 Olympics, but it is the official protocol for the Internet. That alone makes it a powerful presence in the networking world, but its development in the public domain has made it a strong and widely accepted protocol. Department of Defense (DOD) funding, including money that went to the University of California at Berkeley to add and enhance network support in UNIX, fueled early implementations. The protocols are documented in close to two thousand Requests for Comments (RFC) files available from several electronic sources. IP runs at the OSI Network Layer, which corresponds to the Internet Layer in the DOD model (see Figure 2.2). TCP is the corresponding transport protocol (Host-to-Host Layer in the DOD model, as shown in Figure 2.2).

The RFC files can be obtained via File Transfer Protocol (FTP) from the InterNIC Directory and Database Services site and other sources on the Internet and can be purchased on CD-ROM from InfoMagic.

Some common TCP/IP application-level protocols using TCP include Telnet, a common terminal emulation protocol, FTP (File Transfer Protocol), which not surprisingly allows file transfer as well as file and directory access and transfer, and SMTP (Simple Mail Transfer Protocol), which routes electronic mail on the Internet (much like the Message Handling System, or MHS, routes e-mail on NetWare systems).

FIGURE 2.2
Using a layer structure similar to the OSI model, the Department of Defense communications model illustrates relationships between computer systems.

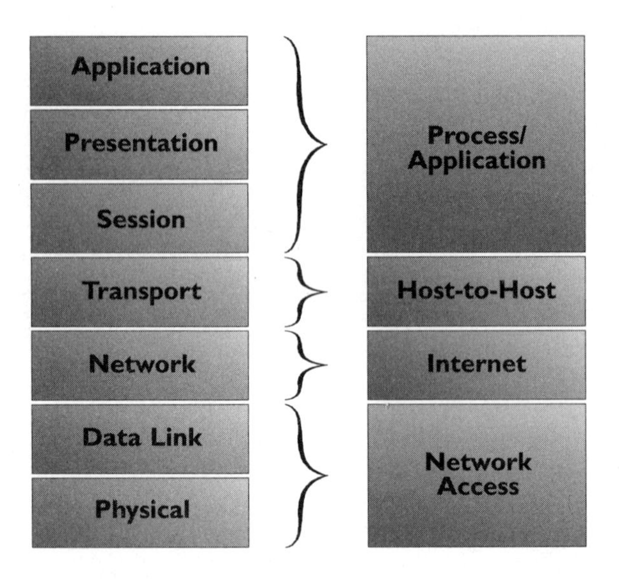

Telnet is the most basic terminal emulation protocol. It allows a system to connect to a TCP/IP host as a terminal to make use of the services available from that host. You can dial up your UNIX network from a Telnet-equipped PC and check your e-mail, for example. The FTP protocol is somewhat more complex; instead of having the remote host do all the work, FTP allows you to look at the files on the remote host and copy them to your machine. You can also FTP files from your machine to the remote host. This is particularly useful for documentation and device drivers, which are inevitably available somewhere on the Internet. You need know only the address and how to invoke your FTP software to get what you need. Many sites allow anonymous FTP—access by any user who logs into the system as "anonymous".

INTERNET ROUTING The IP protocol handles the routing of information around the Internet. When an application in the upper model layers has data to communicate, TCP adds a header identifying the source process, the data sequence, and acknowledgment information. IP then adds another header, creatively named the IP header, to the message to specify that it came from TCP and to indicate the source and destination network addresses. IP passes the data on to be tagged with hardware addresses, placed in an appropriate frame, and passed on to its destination. An example of header-equipped data is shown in Figure 2.3.

FIGURE 2.3
Data is tagged with the TCP and IP headers and the hardware addresses and is placed in the correct frame before being routed via IP.

INTERNET ADDRESSING Internet addresses can be wonderfully succinct, especially considering how many users can be addressed. The Network Information Center (InterNIC) manages the distribution of Internet network numbers. (It is also the "keeper of the cheese" for the current TCP/IP protocol specifications). The numeric Internet address consists of four hexadecimal bytes and includes enough information to identify both the network and the node on the network. The first byte determines the *class* of the numeric Internet address.

Class A networks have a first byte in the range from 0 to 127. These networks use the first byte to indicate networks and the last three bytes to indicate the node. This means Class A organizations cannot have many servers (since there are only 128 of them), but they can have 16,777,216 nodes each. Even if you've inherited a multimillion-user network with one server, you won't be able to get a Class A network address because they have all been assigned.

Class B networks have a first byte in the range from 128 to 191. These networks use two bytes to identify the network and the other two bytes identify the unique hosts.

Class C networks have a first byte in the range from 192 to 255. These networks are defined by the first three bytes and use the final byte to indicate the nodes. The three network classes are illustrated in Figure 2.4.

These networks can use masks to break up the network into subnetworks to segment traffic. The default mask for a network eliminates the network's portion of the Internet address, effectively setting those bytes to 0. The mask sequence is decimal 255 (hex FF), so a Class B default mask would be 255.255.0.0.

Since numeric addresses can be difficult for humans to remember, Internet addressing also includes alphanumeric host and domain names. A specific

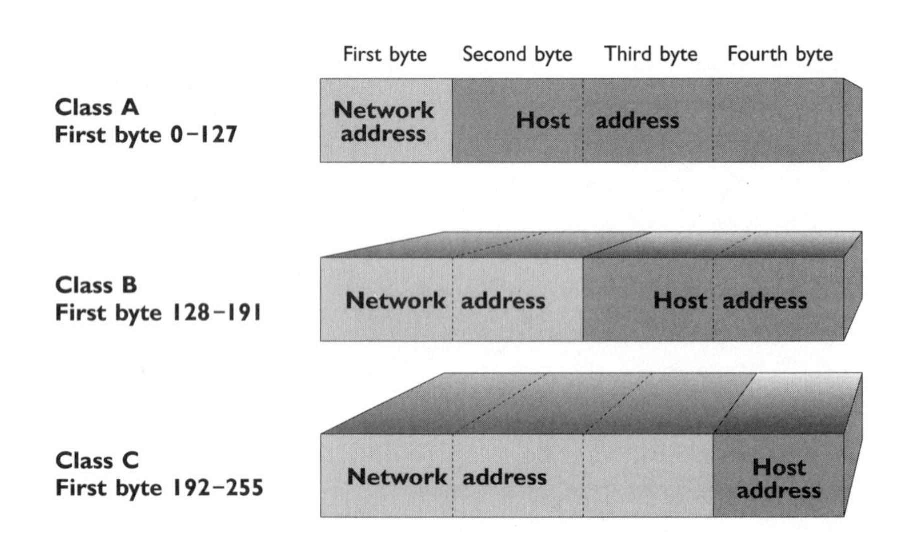

FIGURE 2.4 Internet addressing is divided into three classes of networks, which use different bytes for addressing based on the contents of the first address byte.

host's name is attached to names identifying its networks. The broadest separation of these networks are the standard Internet domains (in the United States—international addresses usually have a domain indicating the country):

DOMAIN	USED BY
ARPA	Internet management
COM	Corporations
EDU	Universities
GOV	Government agencies
MIL	Department of Defense
NET	Network
ORG	Not-for-profit organization

With enough subdomains in an address, things can get relatively squirrely, but alphanumeric addresses are still easier for most people to remember and associate with something meaningful than sets of four numbers. For example, I find ftp.microsoft.com much easier to remember than 198.105.232.1, which is the corresponding numeric Internet address.

The relationships between the Internet names and numeric addresses are maintained in host files on NetWare servers and on Domain Name Service (DNS) servers, which can dynamically associate names and aliases with addresses and can share information with other DNS servers.

DNS servers can run a number of different operating systems. The most important function they perform is associating names with numbers. This name service allows you to enter the name or alias for a machine rather than its numeric address. Reverse name service allows other systems to find an entry in a DNS that links your numeric address to the Internet name you claim is yours. Your name needs to be in a DNS for this to work. NetWare servers maintain a list of hosts they know about in the HOSTS file, which is found on the SYS volume in the \ETC directory.

NetBIOS

NetBIOS is not actually a network protocol in the same sense as IPX/SPX and TCP/IP are. It is an application programming interface (API) used mostly by IBM. Its 16-byte addressing takes a "first come, first served" approach to associating addresses to users. Since it isn't routable, it is often found packaged in TCP/IP on large networks, which isn't particularly efficient. NetWare and some other systems provide support by emulating NetBIOS. Unfortunately, NetWare's NetBIOS software takes up about 30KB on the client machine and cannot safely be loaded into high memory.

Lotus Notes used to rely on NetBIOS connections, which was particularly unfortunate because the groupware package is targeted at large organizations with enterprisewide information-sharing needs. Notes now supports both IP and SPX connections as well.

NetBEUI

NetBEUI (NetBIOS Extended User Interface) is a NetBIOS-derived protocol championed by Microsoft and used in Windows NT and Windows for Workgroups. Support for NetBEUI is incorporated into Microsoft's Win32 API, which makes it convenient to call from applications. That does not make it a good protocol, unfortunately. Like NetBIOS, it is not routable. Since Windows NT supports both IPX/SPX and TCP/IP, either of those protocols is a better choice for most NetWare-based networks.

AppleTalk

AppleTalk is an OSI-based protocol suite that includes LocalTalk, the built-in connectivity solution found on Macintoshes for years, and EtherTalk and TokenTalk, which support standard topologies running at reasonable speeds. Like the NetBIOS-style protocols, AppleTalk allows first come, first served assignment of node addresses. AppleTalk zones, the standard groupings of resources, cannot be centrally registered. AppleTalk's advertisement of these resources is inefficient and produces relatively large amounts of network traffic. Since Macintosh systems can run TCP/IP protocols, one solution for administrators with Macintosh clients on a NetWare network is to use the EtherTalk or TokenTalk protocols running TCP/IP.

Centralization Makes Sense

You probably aren't familiar yet with how your organization views and treats its network administrator. Reactions usually range from mindless hatred to disdain to indifference...and sometimes they approach appreciation. One way you can improve your stock with users is to implement changes that improve performance without upsetting the ways they do things. This is not always easy, but in some cases, changes are long overdue.

I know of an organization of engineers who work mostly on Macintosh systems. The organization itself is distributed across the globe, but its employees work on a contract basis and there is no real in-house IS staff. The organization was able to create a network that connects its offices on multiple continents, but since no one was ever concerned about improving the connection, users on the West Coast of the United States had a full view of and access to Macintosh zones on the East Coast.

Transmission between sites ran at abysmal speeds that were easily improved upon by removing the chatty AppleTalk, which was sucking up bandwidth and money advertising services to users thousands of miles away. Printers in the affected offices had to be networked on an Ethernet network, but the inherently higher speeds of the full Ethernet connections also improved performance in each of the offices.

Exploring Software Interfaces

IF YOU HAVE gotten the impression that I think IPX/SPX and TCP/IP are the protocols of choice for NetWare-based multiplatform networks, you're absolutely right. Both are widely used, mature technologies that boast high speeds despite high reliability rates ensured by receipt confirmation. Building a network of any size that incorporates nonroutable protocols is asking for trouble. Additional options may develop in time, but at the moment IPX/SPX and TCP/IP are the best choices.

If your network includes dissimilar platforms running IPX/SPX and TCP/IP, you have simple ways of finding out who and what is connected to the network.

IPX/SPX Protocols in Common

If your clients are running IPX/SPX, you're in great stead. You can use the standard NetWare tools to identify active users and the networks they connect to without any problem. NetWare doesn't care whether the client runs a full installation of Windows NT or uses OS/2 Warp or is the squarest of NetWare Tested and Approved systems running the latest VLMs. Each of these systems may have unique installation, configuration, and attachment problems, but once they're up and running, they're just three NetWare users.

TCP/IP in Common

As pretty a picture as the all-IPX/SPX concept is, it's not very realistic. Many popular systems don't include IPX/SPX support, and many of those that do use inefficient software solutions that yield poor network performance and also slow other tasks on the host to a crawl. Go ahead, enjoy the thought of such a clean network for a few more minutes, but then disabuse yourself of the notion that you can attain (or keep, depending upon your inheritance) that NetWare nirvana.

Running TCP/IP on a diverse network isn't bad. Many products are available that support a wide range of TCP/IP functions and utilities for NetWare clients, and plenty of products allow TCP/IP users to access the riches of the NetWare network.

Accessing UNIX Hosts

NetWare users can access UNIX hosts through your network by using one of two main options. Users can load a TCP/IP stack at the PC and on the NetWare server so that the TCP/IP information can move from the UNIX host through to the client. If the server runs TCP/IP, IP is bound to one or more NICs.

A protocol stack is a bit of memory-resident software that handles the protocol-related information on the system. A common DOS stack is the TCPIP.EXE software used by Novell's LAN Workplace for DOS. A common Windows stack is Trumpet, a dynamic link library (DLL) that runs in Windows and handles TCP/IP communications.

The other solution is to employ a gateway to translate the information contained in the host's TCP/IP communications into something that the IPX/SPX-speaking client can handle. See the Working with Gateways section in Chapter 1 for more information about this approach.

TCP/IP EMULATION The first of these two approaches is taken by LAN Workplace for DOS, a Novell package that loads a TCP/IP stack on the client. The TCP/IP module uses about 20KB of RAM and is fed configuration information in the NET.CFG file (see the NET.CFG section in Chapter 5 for more detail).

The LAN Workplace product includes tools for DOS and Windows; the simplest of these is the ever-useful PING. To check the connection from a client machine, use the command:

```
C:\>PING host_address
```

The function should return a notification that the host is alive. Figure 2.5 shows a successful PING from DOS.

If it doesn't, move through the OSI model from the bottom to the top to find the problem. The physical connection must be viable all the way from the client to the host system; TCP/IP needs to be carried that entire distance. The results of an unsuccessful PING attempt from a Windows utility in the LAN Workplace package are displayed in Figure 2.6.

FIGURE 2.5 The PING command indicates that another TCP/IP-connected machine is running and is connected to the network.

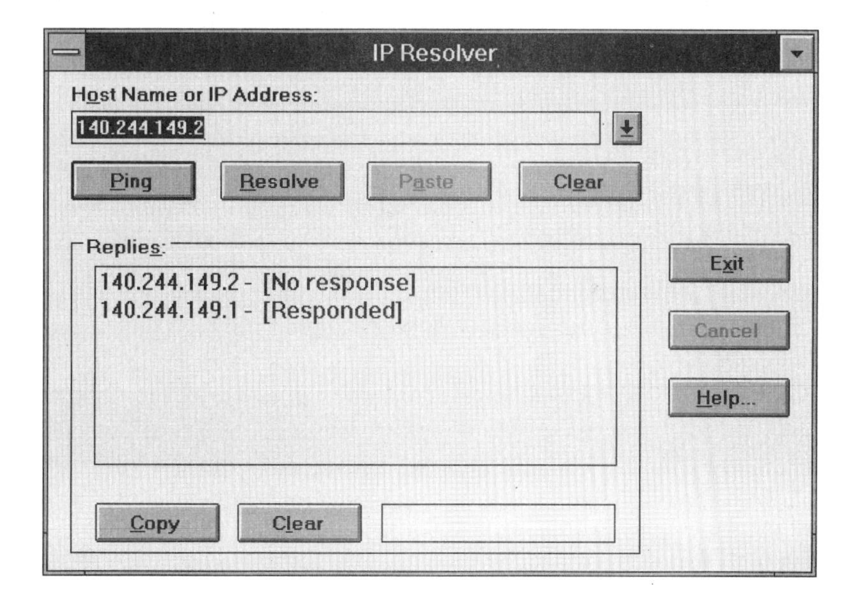

FIGURE 2.6 An unsuccessful PING attempt gains no response. The failure may be due to a machine or network being down or to improper configuration.

Other LAN Workplace utilities include FTP for file transfer between DOS and UNIX and a corresponding Windows utility, Rapid Filer. Other utilities in the package allow remote access of files on the client machine, terminal emulation, printing, chatting with remote users, and resolution of IP names.

Server-based solutions that allow network stations to use TCP/IP include Novell's LAN WorkGroup and Firefox's NOV*IX.

GATEWAYS A TCP/IP gateway on a NetWare network allows communication from the client to use IPX/SPX only. Multiple protocols do not need to run over the client NICs; instead, translation between the two systems takes place at the gateway. This solution allows for less configuration on the user end; users do not need their own IP addresses because the UNIX host believes access is coming from the gateway.

Accessing NetWare Systems

Novell provides support for UNIX clients wishing to access NetWare resources, including files and printers, through several different packages. FLeX/IP provides basic file transfer and print features, while NFS Server and NFS Gateway provide the full power of the Sun-originated NFS file system.

FLEX/IP FLeX/IP manages access to files on NetWare servers via FTP and also makes print queues available to users on UNIX hosts. Access to files can be limited to certain users with specified passwords, but security is not the strongest feature of this file access method, which can leave files on *attached* NetWare servers available to FTP clients. Access to printers is handled by mapping UNIX usernames to one or more login names on the NetWare server.

NETWARE NFS NetWare can run NFS on the server, making it appear identical to other NFS machines as far as UNIX clients can tell. NFS performance is good on NetWare machines, which are optimized for file-serving tasks like these. The NFS Server product also provides printer access to UNIX clients. NFS can also be implemented using the NFS Gateway product, which allows nearly seamless cross-access by users of both systems.

Once again, we have covered quite a bit of ground in this chapter. We have looked at the development and functionality of some of the major networking software products, investigated the structure and implementation of some of the most significant network protocols, and explored some of the software connections that allow different network systems to communicate with one another. In Chapter 3, we'll return to the nitty-gritty by investigating the division of work and resources around the network.

W³: Identifying What's Where and Why

IN CHAPTER 1, you took a tour of your "previously owned" network, looking for vital information about what kinds of servers and connections exist. In Chapter 2, you took a closer look at the network operating systems that are typically found in a NetWare network and briefly studied methods of communication between systems. Now you get to take the first steps toward relating the hardware and software to the actual work that's done in your new environment.

One policy to file away for reference is that the most successful network administrators understand not only the systems they manage, but also the work those systems need to facilitate. It is vital that you understand the workings of your network, but it is also important for you to absorb the overall work flow in the organization. This combination of technical and organizational expertise allows you to optimize your network's performance on the level that counts: getting more work done rapidly and reliably.

Okay, I'll get off the soapbox; it's time to look at the data on the network for the first time. You can gain some understanding about what happens on the network by looking at how data is distributed among servers and among disks and volumes on those disks. The applications stored and the processes running on the network can provide another level of appreciation for the network design, and the location of peripherals on the network gives another glimpse into the sensibility of the existing network structure.

The Vital Information

WHAT YOU WANT to take from this chapter is an understanding of what work is done on each server, and furthermore, which users attach to each server. Division of work happens logically on network machines and in business groups alike; your eventual goal will be to segment usage of the network logically to reduce network traffic and enhance network reliability and speed. Use the following checklist to mark your progress during your network investigation.

COMPLETED	TASK
❑	Create network map showing server names and network interconnections.
❑	Create volume map for each server showing volume structure, volume size, and major files.
❑	Check previous network documentation for clues about network use.
❑	Interview technical staff, management, and users for information about network use.
❑	Look at access rights to see who can access data.
❑	Look at login scripts to see who regularly maps to data.
❑	Check free space on volumes.
❑	Identify the network modules and processes in use.
❑	Identify networked printers and other networked peripherals.

Dividing Work by Server

THE DIVISION OF data among servers is the most basic level of separation provided. In NetWare 2.x and 3.x environments, user access to resources on servers the users don't log into is relatively difficult to design, create, and manage. The global access to network services in NetWare 4.x is an improvement, but the physical location of data still dictates network traffic patterns. The kind of work done on each server also determines what degree of reliability is required. We'll use some of the information gleaned during this exploration to determine the disaster response in Chapter 4.

Logical and Physical Networks

The NDS (NetWare Directory Services) feature in NetWare 4.x creates a *virtual network* by making the resources more transparently accessible than they are in NetWare 3.x and NetWare 2.x environments. Although the centralization of resources and management makes network peripherals and data more accessible, it does not make the underlying physical network any more efficient. Since data is still routed between servers on the physical network, network design should attempt to place users in the same area as the peripherals and servers they access most.

Investigation at this level can be relatively quick; in smaller networks, look at the servers first and approach coworkers once you have a basis for discussion. Particularly large networks, especially those distributed over a large corporate campus, can be more problematic. Maximize the use of your time by consulting with existing IS or technical staff before you go exploring.

Identifying What Goes On

If the network is small enough to be approachable, have a look around before you talk with users about the network. Smaller organizations may contain fewer people who have a good idea of the network landscape, and you may be able to find enough information by looking at a few servers without asking basic questions of somebody whose knowledge level you can't yet assess. Now is the time to make some sense for yourself and see what you can determine.

Learning from Server Names

Server names are loaded with potential. Sure, they may sound frivolous, stupid, mundane, or meaningless, but they can indicate functions, histories, and even interrelationships. Even if they have no intrinsic value, the information you have already collected about the servers' hardware, operating systems, network connections, and protocols can be extremely useful in putting together a mental picture of what's going on.

Look at the server names you collected in Chapter 1 for meaning. Do the names describe functions? In my network, some of the servers are named for the departments that use them. Of course, CUSTOMER01 and SERVICE01 both seem like they could describe the Customer Service department, but they actually describe two different groups, the Customer Support group (CUSTOMER01) and the Customer Service group. They're not very interesting names, but they're functional.

The first server I managed was named ARCHIMEDES, which is a fine name, but it's a little long and people sometimes had trouble spelling it. Despite these problems, it was always fun to refer to the server going down as the Archimedes Screw. The name itself doesn't have any meaning in the network context, but it did fit into a scheme that called for Greek philosophers in our area of the WAN at that time.

These kinds of associations—groups of servers sharing location, common function, or age of installation—are useful when you're distinguishing one new machine from another. Take advantage of these associations if you see them. Don't fret if you don't. The sample network names shown in Figure 3.1 weren't chosen randomly, but their origin and connection is rather obscure.

Create a map of the servers and associate them with the networks they connect to (see Figure 3.1). Place the servers along one axis and the physical network on another. Look at how the servers connect to each other and think about how they physically and logically relate to each other. There may be little correspondence between how the network is distributed, how the users access it, and how data flows. But better designs optimize traffic flow over the heavily used routes and reduce the number of hops that data needs to travel. If the network isn't optimized yet, you can make design modifications a priority.

I encourage you to manually create maps, in part because the mapping process requires you to understand some of the network layout, and in part because you can be sure of the maps you create. A number of software packages are available to perform the mapping for you. If you use them, remember that they can make mistakes and cannot convey information about connections that should exist but don't. Quyen Systems' NetViz, Microsystems Engineering's SysDraw, and HavenTree's

FIGURE 3.1
The server names KAPP, THEDER, and SNYDER are not complicated, but the names themselves don't convey much information to most users.

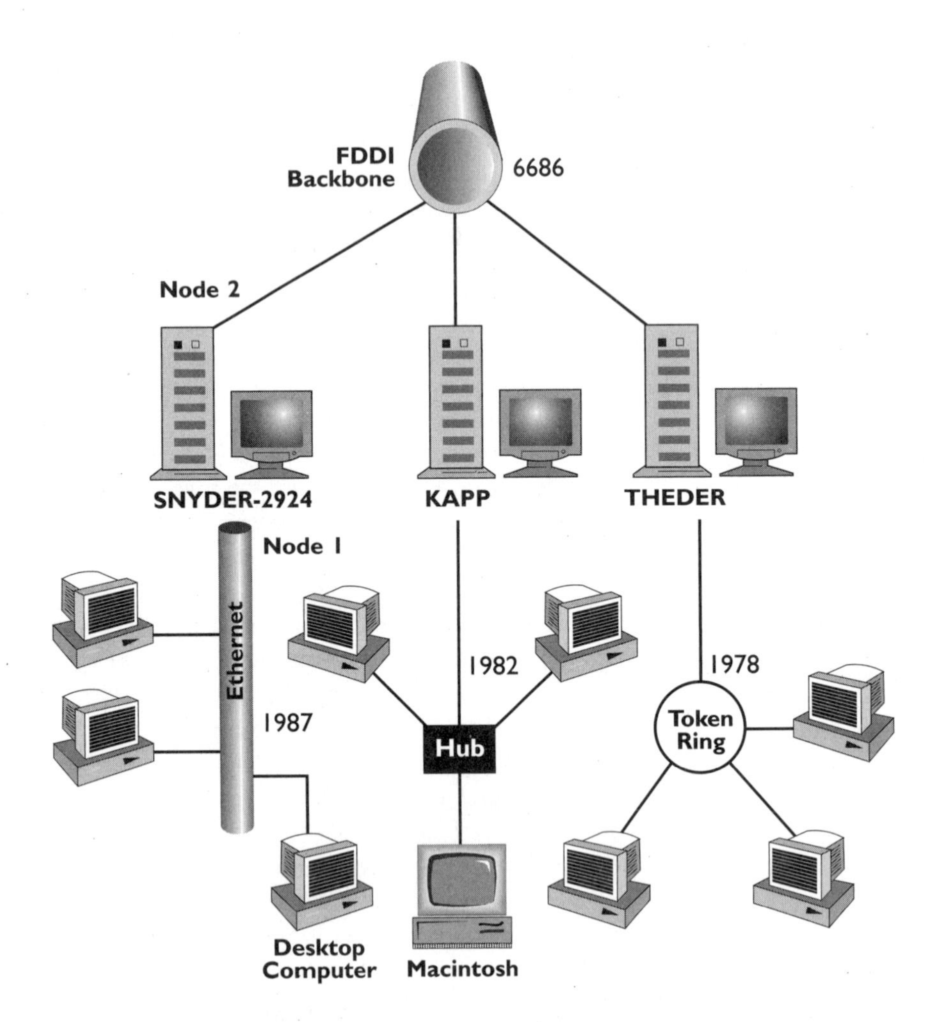

NodeMap are three products that provide varying degrees of drawing detail, layout accuracy, and component database support. You will probably want a package like one of these, which lists for approximately $299 to $995.

If you don't have a sense for how data and resources are distributed across the network, don't worry. You're laying the groundwork that will make the details more meaningful…once you extract them.

Learning from Volume Names

Volume names are another hit-and-miss proposition in an inherited network. You know you'll have a SYS volume; sometimes that is the only volume installed, which makes it easier to avoid running out of space on the SYS volume but complicates restrictions on user space. Large volumes spanning multiple drives have more possible points of failure; drives in RAID (redundant array of inexpensive disks) systems are seen as one device and can accommodate only eight volumes total. Figure 3.2 shows two volume structures.

Instead of storing data on the same drive segments each time a particular volume is written to, a RAID system stripes data across multiple drives. This provides faster access times because multiple drives can be collecting or writing parts of the data at once. It can also provide fault tolerance when an additional parity drive is included. A parity drive stores error-checking information that allows data to be restored if one of the drives fails. RAID is described in more detail in the Redundant Array of Inexpensive Disks section in Chapter 4.

These restrictions at both ends of the spectrum encourage volume design to fit into the middle ground whether it is carefully composed or thrown together helter-skelter. If you're faced with names like VOL1 and VOL2, or with USER and APPS, the association of the volumes with the servers is an important one.

A network map showing the server's volume structure can be very useful. As shown in Figure 3.3, you can expand down from the volume level as you explore further, or you can simply indicate the kinds of applications and data that can be found in each volume.

Asking About What Goes On

If your network is too imposing to quickly investigate in any reasonable way, talk to your coworkers to find out where to start. If you have had a chance to look at the names of the servers and volumes in your new empire, you can inquire about the network components with a rudimentary understanding of how things are arranged.

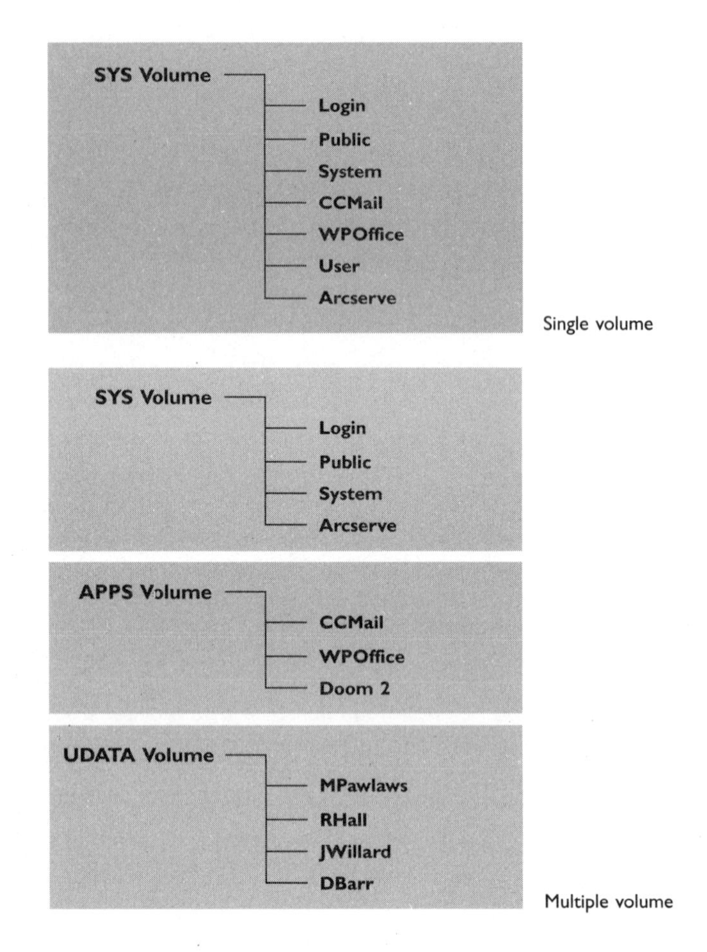

FIGURE 3.2 Two approaches to volume structure: an easily created, single-volume, multiple-directory structure and an easily managed, multiple-volume structure.

The Reference Material

Reference material fits into the section on talking to people because the reference files represent the understanding of their creators. If the network is exhaustively documented, you know only that a large quantity of data is available; you don't know how reliable it is. One way of testing the veracity of any records you find is to see whether they jibe with the information

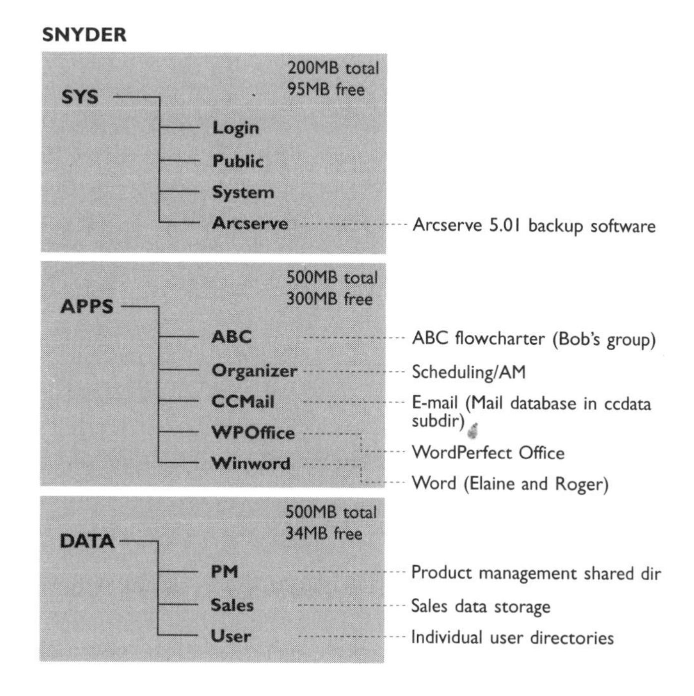

FIGURE 3.3 A map of SNYDER's volume structure indicates where the most important applications and data are stored and where the most free space is located.

you've already collected. Are the servers on the same networks in your new lists and maps as they are in your predecessor's? Are machines missing from the existing server lists? If so, the documentation is a story that isn't necessarily credible. Keep it as a historical reference, and take a grain of salt whenever you need to consult it.

Documentation to Look For

Although any kind of information can come in handy, the pieces you really want to get your hands on are the ones that help you determine the network's history. You can collect your own data about its current status, and its future is in your hands, but purchase orders, network maps, hardware and software documentation, error logs, systems requests, and proposals are all potential sources of information that can help you understand what the network has done in the past and how it has evolved to its current state.

If the documentation appears to be in order, say a quick prayer of thanks, and donate a little extra to your charity of choice. You're lucky, and the rest of us envy you. Current, reliable documentation is a wonderful resource when you're getting to know a new system. Remember to retain a small degree of skepticism, however. Never take what you see on paper to be the gospel truth, and never fall into the worse pit: disputing what you see with your eyes because of what you see on paper. If CONFIG says a particular NIC's IP address is 1.1.1.1, that's what the server thinks it is, even if your documentation says otherwise. Fix the server, then update the documentation.

Having current docs can be burdensome in one way: if you inherit spotless information, you'd better keep it that way. Having a snapshot view of the hardware and software installed on the network, a history of the errors encountered and solutions employed, and the map of interconnections is essential for communicating with your managers, employees, vendors, and value-added resellers.

The Reference People

You're not ready to go from office to office soliciting opinions about network functions and performance. You want to build on what you already know, and because what you already know at this point is purely technical in nature, the next step is to talk to the technical people who have been around longer than you. You can then proceed to identify managers whose input can give you a better idea of the daily needs of the network's users.

TECHNICAL STAFF When I say *propellerheads*, I mean it in absolutely the nicest way possible. If you're part of an Information Systems organization, you probably won't be able to swing a cat without hitting somebody who can tell you which servers and data are considered most vital. Computer operators and help desk staff are often excellent resources, but you must keep their perspectives in mind.

Computer operators are generally process-oriented. They know which of the tasks they perform get the most attention (usually the most yelling when something goes wrong), but they are often insulated from the business and production aspects of the company. Take time to introduce yourself, and get an idea of what the operators spend their time doing.

Help desk staff is a great resource for a variety of reasons. It'll be able to tell you which users have the most problems and which will tax your network resources the most. However, help desk staff is often separated from the strategic information involved in managing a network of any size. Find out what its major problems are and who the biggest attention-getters are, but rely on more senior IS staff for a better view of the big picture.

The relative competence or incompetence of a manager is hard to know immediately. Someone who appears ignorant or timid may turn out to be shrewd, while someone who seems decisive and confident may actually make decisions too quickly. Don't judge anybody yet. If you must, grumble to your cat about your coworkers' stupidity when you get home, but when you're at work, you are employed in a service position and your customer is everybody, including your coworkers and managers. Resist the temptation to assume that a manager who last was involved in a hands-on technical role 15 years ago lacks the ability to understand and resolve problems.

Rather than getting off to a bad start with IS managers, make use of them. Try to bolster your understanding of the users and processes described by the operators and support staff with more strategic issues, such as departmental missions and goals, intermediate- and long-range plans, and organizational structure. If you can get your hands on an organizational chart showing divisional and departmental heads, become familiar with it. Use your interaction with IS management as a bridge to the rest of the company.

In the event that you *are* the IS staff, don't be downhearted. You get to play all the roles at once, and you will certainly learn about the network's use in practice.

DEPARTMENTAL MANAGERS The departmental managers are a good source of information one level less technical. Armed with the layers of information you've gathered from other sources, you're equipped to have a chance of understanding their production needs. Try to avoid allowing your conversations with the managers at large to digress to laundry lists of complaints. At this point, you are gathering information only about what needs to be done; your fresh perspective is an asset in this situation because you have a chance of approaching the network's function from directions that have not previously been explored.

Avoid having a meeting with multiple managers if you can. Group mentality tends to cause harmonic resonance in people: if somebody brings up a subject, others often agree verbally whether or not they have anything fresh to add. Your approach can be somewhat less formal; obtain a rundown on what the network is most important for in each group.

A sales department may need to have its contact and order databases open all day to be productive; in this case, quick response getting servers up and running is tantamount, but after the sales staff goes home at 5:00 p.m., the servers aren't utilized at all. An editorial production staff may have deadlines around which the network's reliability and availability are critical, but at other times access may be less critical. A database programming staff may need access to a wide range of servers for testing and may run processes at night that keep the database files open during the scheduled backups.

In each case, you need to know *what* the group is doing and *how* they do it. Detail at this point is less vital than getting as many pieces of the big picture as possible. For the finest point of granularity, you'll go right to the horse's mouth, so to speak.

The End Users

These are the card-punching workers whose efforts make the product or provide the service that keeps your salary coming. Unless you find yourself in a very small organization indeed, you won't be going from workstation to workstation pursuing suggestions and opinions. Instead, integrate your inquiries into your exploration of the physical network.

As you walk around the office, introduce yourself to some of the people you see. If you have the opportunity on a NetWare 3.x network, use the USERLIST command to identify the network that various workers are tied to. The /a option identifies the network segment they connect to:

```
c:\>userlist /a
```

Figure 3.4 shows the system response to the USERLIST command.

You can also use the WHOAMI command from client stations to see which users are logged into multiple servers. You don't need to look at all the users; just try to get an idea of why those who map to multiple servers do so. Look at the login times to see whether the attachments happen simultaneously, possibly through login scripts or with batch files that connect them to multiple servers at login. Figure 3.5 shows the system response to the WHOAMI command.

```
c:\>whoami
```

FIGURE 3.4
The USERLIST command can be used to determine the IPX number of the networks users connect to.

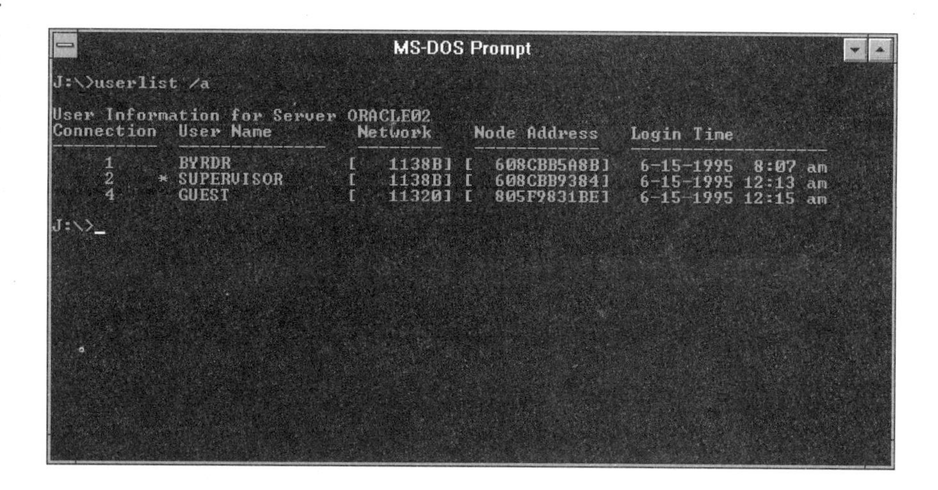

FIGURE 3.5
The WHOAMI command indicates which servers a user is connected to and provides details about each server and connection.

```
MS-DOS Prompt
C:\>whoami
You are user SUPERVISOR attached to server TEST01, connection 30.
Server TEST01 is running NetWare v3.11 (100 user).
Login time: Thursday  June  15, 1995  8:12 am

You are user MMILLER attached to server ARCHIMEDES, connection 32.
Server ARCHIMEDES is running NetWare v3.11 (100 user).
Login time: Thursday  June  15, 1995  8:15 am

You are user SUPERVISOR attached to server ORACLE02, connection 2.
Server ORACLE02 is running NetWare v3.12 (10 user).
Login time: Thursday  June  15, 1995  12:13 am

You are user SUPERVISOR attached to server ORACLE01, connection 7.
Server ORACLE01 is running NetWare v3.11 (20 user).
Login time: Thursday  June  15, 1995  12:23 am

C:\>
```

Look at menu systems, hot keys, batch files, or Windows icon properties to see what applications the users are running and whether they're invoked from a local drive or a network drive. Ask the users about their daily routines. Get a feeling for what's happening; don't concern yourself with inventorying software or mapping users at this stage. You're simply preparing for the next level of analysis: what is on the server's hard disks?

Segmenting Work by Disk and Volume

SINCE MOST FILE servers have multiple disks and multiple volumes, administrators and users have to decide where the applications and data will reside. Sometimes the locations are determined logically; in other networks, those who have sufficient rights spread the data across disks and servers and let the bits fall where they may. You can check the distribution of the data by looking at how the disks and volumes are used.

Disk Use

Disk use is of interest because you need to know the size and status of the physical disks being accessed. You want to know where to find the most stress on the system, and a single drive may have multiple active partitions that all contain important, frequently accessed data. Reading from and writing to a disk drive causes wear on the disk, and although drives can be expected to last several years, there is no sense in considering them expendable. You can also enhance performance a little by balancing load across physical disks.

Knowing the disk characteristics is also useful. This information can be gathered using the MONITOR console utility.

1. Type `LOAD MONITOR` from the console prompt.
2. On the **Available Options** menu, select **Disk Information**, which lists the physical disks that can be seen by the disk controller.
3. Select each of the drives to view information about it. The **Drive Status** window is shown in Figure 3.6 and includes the following information:
   - Disk driver
   - Disk size
   - Number of partitions
   - Mirror status
   - Hot fix status

- Partition blocks
- Data blocks
- Redirection blocks
- Redirected blocks
- Reserved blocks

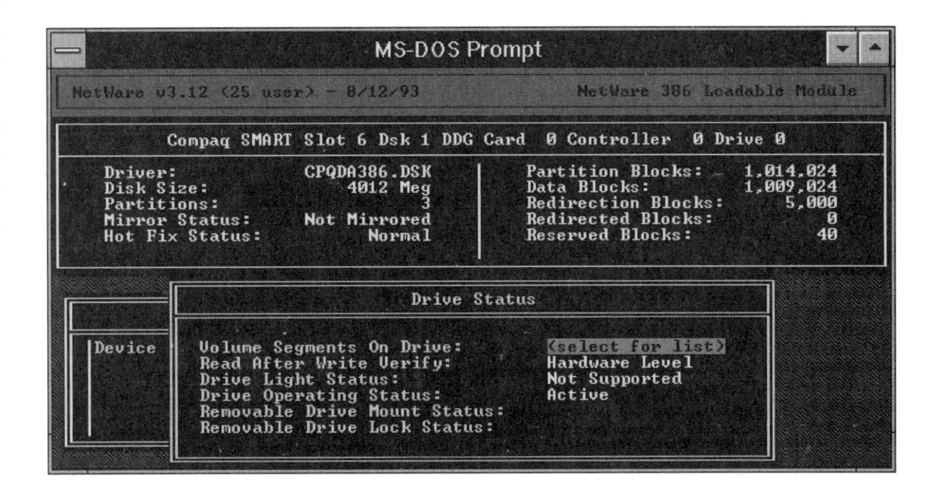

FIGURE 3.6 The Drive Status window in the MONITOR console utility contains useful information about the configuration and status of each of the server's hard disks.

The information provided by **Driver, Disk Size,** and **Partitions** indicates the disk driver loaded on the server to control the hard disk, the total size of the hard disk, and the number of partitions the drive is formatted into, respectively.

Mirror Status indicates whether data is written to multiple hard disks. This is a fault tolerance feature that is described further in Chapter 4. The possible settings are **Mirrored, Not Mirrored,** and **Remirroring:**

Mirrored	Multiple disks write information placed on the drive. The mirrored drives are matched bit by bit.
Not Mirrored	Mirroring is not currently installed or active.

Remirroring	The system is in the process of updating the drives to match the data on the secondary drive to the data on the primary drive. This process generally slows the server noticeably.

Hot Fix Status indicates whether the hard disk redirection function is operating properly. This setting should read **Normal**; if it indicates **Not-Hot-Fixed,** the drive needs to be replaced.

Hot Fix redirection allows NetWare to mark bad blocks on the disk when it has trouble reading from or writing to the disk. Two percent of each hard disk's space is allocated to Hot Fix redirection by default; the percentage can be increased using the INSTALL console utility, but changing the setting will destroy data on the disk.

The number of **Partition Blocks** indicates the total number of blocks on the partition. Blocks are 4KB by default, but the setting can be set for each volume. The block size can be read from the **Volume Information** screen in the INSTALL console utility. The partition blocks are divided into **Data Blocks** and **Redirection Blocks.** Data blocks are available to NetWare for storing data; redirection blocks are dedicated to Hot Fix.

Redirection blocks are further divided into two categories: **Redirected Blocks** and **Reserved Blocks.** The redirected blocks have already been used for Hot Disk, while the reserved blocks are held in reserve, waiting to store redirection tables for the Hot Disk system.

Follow these steps to access the Volume Segments window, which is illustrated in Figure 3.7. The Volume Segments window indicates how the volumes are spread across the disks.

1. Type `LOAD MONITOR` from the console prompt.
2. Select **Disk Information.**
3. Pick a disk from the ones listed in the **System Disk Drives** window.
4. Select **Volume Segments On Drive** to see the list of volumes.

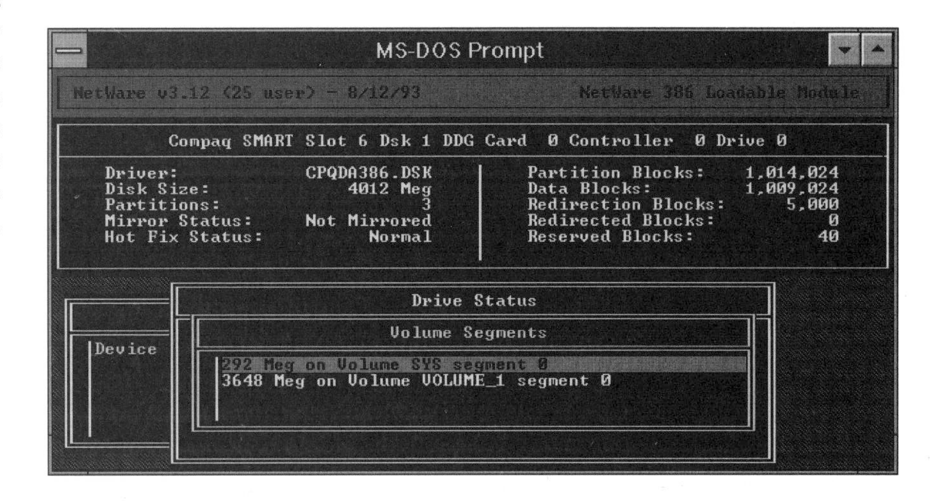

FIGURE 3.7
The Volume Segments window in the MONITOR utility shows all the volume segments located on a single device or array.

Volume Use

The information you have been pursuing in this chapter is simply *how the system is used*. The suggested approach has been one of building on the evidence you collect from the system by interviewing the users. This provides a framework for interpreting the most valuable clues: how the network resources are configured for use by your organization. The fundamental division of data from a user and process perspective is at the volume level. Whether or not your server supports global access to resources, those resources are allocated on the volume level.

There are three places to look for information about how the volumes are used: user access rights, login scripts, and space in use.

- User access rights indicate who *can* access the data.
- Login scripts indicate *how easily* users can access the data.
- The space in use on the volume indicates how rich (or how bloated) the resource is.

User Access

User access rights can be viewed in the directory structure of any volume. This information is useful for providing context for the rights settings. The FILER utility runs from a NetWare client workstation and can display file and directory information, including which users and groups have been granted *trustee rights* to a directory. Trustees are users or groups who are explicitly assigned a particular level of access to a file or directory. The rights used in NetWare 3.x and 4.x networks are File Scan, Read, Create, Write, Erase, Modify, Access Control, and Supervisor. Each of the rights is represented in NetWare utilities by its first letter.

Trustees are users or groups who are explicitly assigned a particular level of access to a file or directory.

Follow these steps to look at the contents of a volume and its directories:

1. Start the FILER utility by typing the utility name at a network drive prompt on a client workstation.

   ```
   Z:\>FILER
   ```

2. Select the path to the desired volume from the **Select Current Directory** entry.
3. Choose the **Directory Contents** entry to see the subdirectories and files at this level.

By selecting one of the listed directories or files, you can copy or move files and directories; change the server, volume, and directory you're pointing to; or view information.

The Inherited Rights Mask (IRM) for each file and directory controls the inheritance of rights from parent directories. The mask allows only specified rights to filter down from a directory to subdirectories or files. This allows greater control over security by requiring rights to be assigned directly to the file or directory being protected.

The **View/Set File Information** and **View/Set Directory Information** options display screens showing information about files and directories; notice the **Inherited Rights Mask** entries and open the list of **Trustees.** The letters in the IRM section are the rights that can be inherited from parent directories. Figure 3.8 shows the **Set File Information**.

If you find that FILER won't run because the client machine doesn't have enough memory to load all the file and directory information, you can use command-line utilities instead. Type `TLIST` *at the appropriate network drive prompt to see the trustee list for a given directory. TLIST is also faster than FILER for retrieving trustee right information.*

FILE SCAN This right allows users to see files and directories. If it is set at the file level, it allows the file name to be viewed even if the directory is not tagged as viewable. In other words, File Scan rights at the file level imply File Scan rights to the directory level containing the file.

READ This right allows users to open and run files. Set at the directory level, it allows Read access to all files in the directory. Ordinarily, users with Read access are also granted File Scan access. However, there may be circumstances when certain files are retrieved by a process the user is running, and you do not want to provide File Scan access to the user.

CREATE This right allows the creation of files and directories. Users require this right to save a file or copy a file to a directory.

WRITE This right allows users to modify files. It provides for opening an existing file and saving it once changes have been made. You need not have Create rights to save a file you have changed.

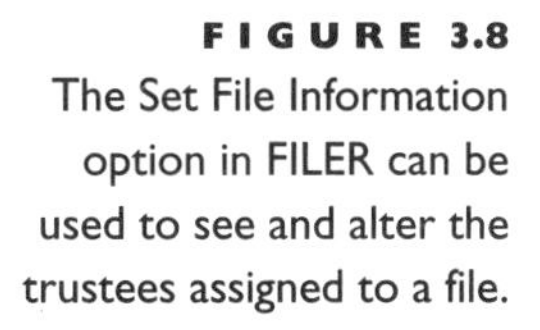

FIGURE 3.8 The Set File Information option in FILER can be used to see and alter the trustees assigned to a file.

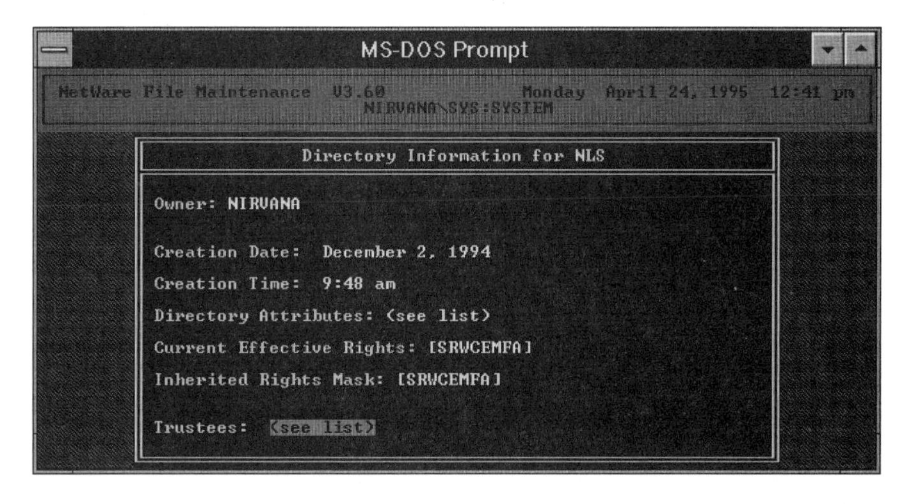

ERASE This right allows users to delete files and directories.

MODIFY This right allows users to change file and directory attributes and rename files and directories. It does not allow users to modify file content.

Attributes are properties of files and directories that affect access and operation. Attributes override rights settings. Attributes (and the letters used to represent them in NetWare utilities) are Archive Needed (A), Delete Inhibit (D), Execute Only (X), and Shareable (S). Attributes are discussed in more detail in Chapter 8.

ACCESS CONTROL This right allows users to grant F, R, C, W, E, M, and A trustee rights for themselves or other users. It also allows modifications to the IRM.

SUPERVISOR This right provides all of the access allowed by the preceding seven options and cannot be blocked out by the IRM. The Supervisor right allows the user to grant Supervisor access to others and to alter the IRM. The S right is therefore powerful and difficult to control.

Supervisor access isn't something you want to give away freely. Since the Supervisor right is so powerful, reserve it for users who can be trusted to use it safely. Being a supervisor in an organization in no way justifies Supervisor rights. And you can tell them I said so.

Percentage Full

Another way to gauge the volume usage on a NetWare file server is to see how much space is available. This issue is important to be aware of because a volume that is almost full is one that needs cleaning or expanding.

Since most users are not terribly concerned with weeding files out of the volumes they use, you'll have to help them with the gardening. Weed whackers not being available yet for network systems, you'll have to investigate file usage to free up space on the existing drives, or you'll have to install more hard disks. See Chapter 9 for information on restricting use of volume space, and see Chapter 14 for a discussion of tools that allow you to keep track of free volume space to avoid problems.

USING CHKVOL TO VIEW AVAILABLE DISK SPACE CHKVOL is a NetWare command that reports the amount of disk space on a volume. It displays the total space on the disk that can be used to store data, the amount of disk space taken by files and deleted files, and the amount of space remaining. It also reports the amount of that free space accessible to the user issuing the command. CHKVOL runs from a client station and provides a "moment-in-time" snapshot of the volume space available. Command-line options allow access to multiple volumes and even multiple servers.

```
Z:\>CHKVOL

Statistics for fixed volume KAPP/SYS:

Total volume space:                    300,000 K Bytes
Space used by files:                    76,260 K Bytes
Space in use by deleted files:          45,360 K Bytes
Space available from deleted files:45,360 K Bytes
Space remaining on volume:             223,740 K Bytes
Space available to TTAYLOR:            223,740 K Bytes
```

USING VOLINFO TO VIEW AVAILABLE DISK SPACE The VOLINFO utility, which can be run from a NetWare client station, displays the names of the server volumes, the total space on each volume, and the amount of space available on each (see Figure 3.9). It also indicates the number of directory entries that have already been allocated on the volume, the number of directories NetWare has allocated to the volume, and the number of available directory entries. DOS files, subdirectories, and trustee lists each use one directory entry.

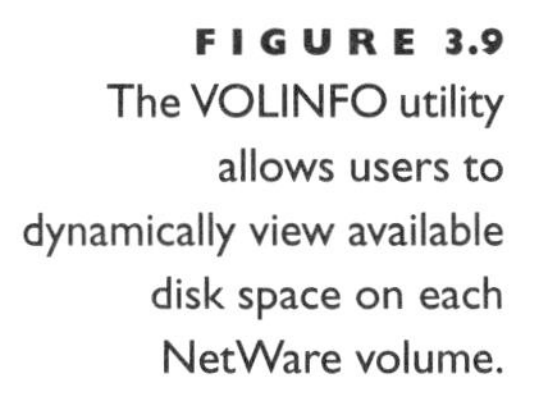

FIGURE 3.9
The VOLINFO utility allows users to dynamically view available disk space on each NetWare volume.

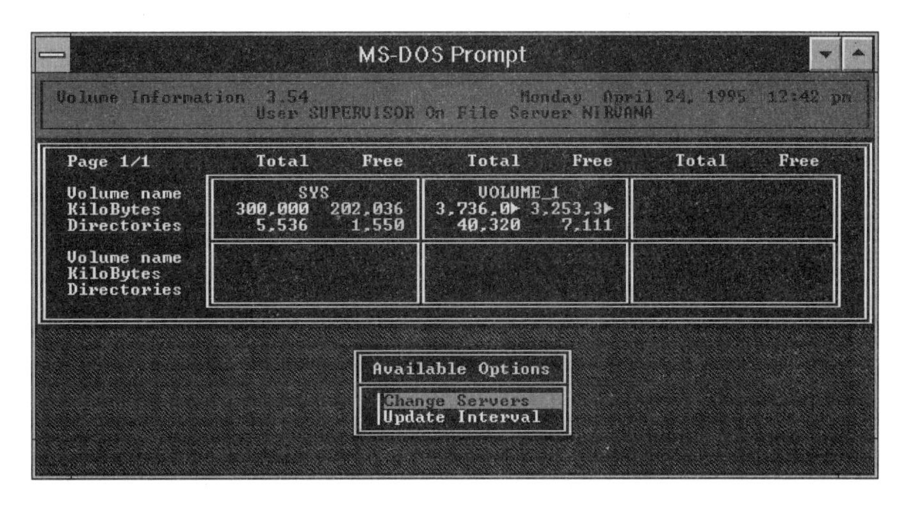

On volumes with the Macintosh name space loaded, Macintosh files use two directory entries each.

The advantage of using VOLINFO is that it has a user-configurable polling rate and updates you on how the free disk space is changing. Check the space next to the numbers listed in the Free column. An arrowhead pointing up indicates that more free space is becoming available, and an arrowhead pointing down indicates that more space is being used.

THE DYNAMIC VOLUMES CHKVOL and VOLINFO do not provide a very complete idea of the long-term dynamic of disk usage; VOLINFO's dynamic information compares only the current information with the information from a previous update. For more effective use, use a scheduling utility to execute a CHKVOL command each day; record the information, and keep a log of the space available. You don't need to study it daily, but you should have additional data points to see how much space has been taken up historically.

One other way to look at disk space is by using the directory command from a network client machine. Use some of the options and comparisons to look for large files, then files by user, files that have not been accessed in a year, and files created in the past day.

The following command looks for files larger than 1MB in the Z drive's root and in all its subdirectories. The /si option specifies a filter by size, the gr option indicates that the file size needs to be greater than the specified number, and the /sub option broadens the search to include subdirectories:

```
Z:\>NDIR /si gr 1000000 /sub
```

The following command looks for files created by the username RHALL. The /ow option specifies a filter by owner, and the eq option indicates that the search includes files created by a particular user. The not eq option would exclude files owned by the specified user.

```
Z:\>NDIR /ow eq "RHALL" /sub
```

The following NDIR command looks for files that have not been accessed after January 1, 1995. This is particularly useful for finding old and unused files. The /ac option indicates a filter by access date, and the bef option requests a list of files accessed before the specified date.

```
Z:\>NDIR /ac bef 1-1-95 /sub
```

To look for recent files, substitute the aft option. The following command looks for files that were created after October 1, 1995. The /cr option indicates the command uses the creation date as a filter.

```
Z:\>NDIR /cr aft 10-01-95 /sub
```

Identifying Network Processes

NETWORK PROCESSES INCLUDE a variety of add-in software that takes advantage of NetWare's modular architecture. These NetWare Loadable Modules (NLMs) include the necessary but unexciting disk and LAN drivers, but quite a few optional modules provide extended operating system functionality. Some network applications run an NLM component that acts as an agent on the server.

Identify the name and version number of each of the NLMs on your system and record the information. It can be useful when troubleshooting and to ensure that your servers all use the same and most recent modules.

Using MODULES to Identify Network Processes

The MODULES console command lists each of the server tasks that is not a component of the central operating system. Since relatively few core components are in NetWare 3.x and NetWare 4.x, you can expect more than 20 modules on even lightly loaded servers. Figure 3.10 shows a sample MODULES screen.

```
:MODULES
```

Using MONITOR to Inspect Network Process Load

The MONITOR console utility shows its usefulness again by displaying another take on the server process picture. Not only does MONITOR display the modules loaded on the server, it is even more useful because it displays the system resources used by each module.

FIGURE 3.10
The MODULES console command displays all the modules running on a NetWare server.

```
MS-DOS Prompt
:modules
STANDARD.NLM
  ARCserve Standard Tape Support
  Version 5.01e   August 1, 1994
  (C) Copyright 1990-1994 Cheyenne Software, Inc.  All rights reserved.
STANDARD.NLM
  ARCserve Standard Tape Support
  Version 5.01e   August 1, 1994
  (C) Copyright 1990-1994 Cheyenne Software, Inc.  All rights reserved.
TAPESVR.NLM
  ARCserve SCSI Tape Driver
  Version 5.01e   August 21, 1994
  (C) Copyright 1990-1994 Cheyenne Software, Inc.  All rights reserved.
ASPI50.NLM
  ARCserve SCSI Board Driver
  Version 5.01d   February 17, 1994
  (C) Copyright 1990-1994 Cheyenne Software, Inc.  All rights reserved.
ARCSERVE.NLM
  ARCserve Scheduler
  Version 5.01e   May 20, 1994
  (C) Copyright 1990-1994 Cheyenne Software, Inc. All Rights Reserved.
<Press ESC to terminate or any other key to continue>_
```

Follow this procedure to see the systems resources used by each module:

1. Start MONITOR by typing `LOAD MONITOR` at the console prompt.
2. From the **Available Options** menu, select **System Module Information** to see the list of modules on the **System Modules** window, which is shown in Figure 3.11. By selecting the module name, you can see the size of the module, the name of the file used to load it, and several resource tags.

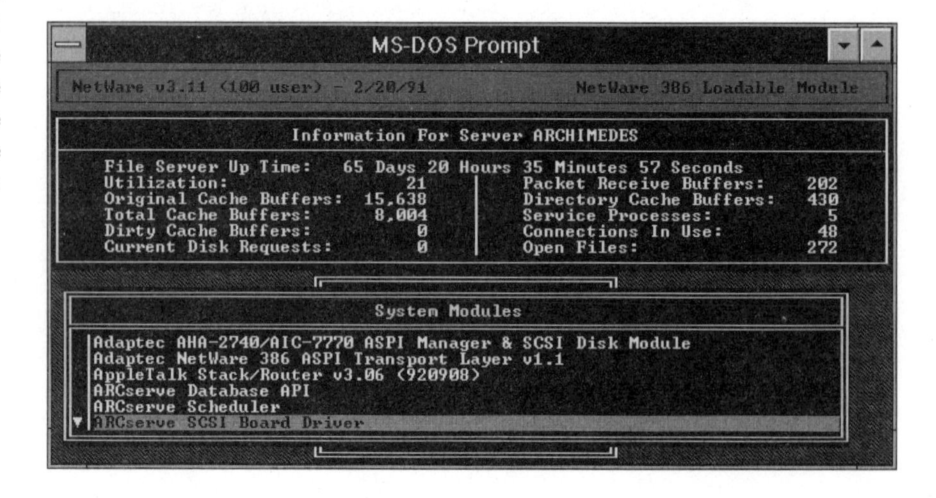

FIGURE 3.11
System modules can be viewed by selecting the System Module Information option in the MONITOR console utility.

3. By selecting the **Resource Tag** option of choice, you display the tag name, the module name, the resource type being used by the module, and the amount of that resource type in use by the module.

Finding Networked Peripherals

THE FINAL STEP in this trail of investigation is to identify the networked peripherals installed: printers, CD-ROM drives, modems, and so on. One way to identify connected peripherals is to look for related modules running on the server. Another way is to look for physical connections and work backward. Networked printers can be handled and identified in several different ways, but they are usually easy to find.

Printers are the most common network-connected peripheral devices, but you'll frequently find several others in NetWare networks. CD-ROM drives are becoming common because software to address them (CDROM.NLM) is now included in NetWare 3.12 and 4.x. Since CD-ROMs are also the preferred method of software distribution at the moment, it is beneficial to know where you have drives available. Tape drives are often found in use as backup devices, and modems are still used for dial-in, dial-out access and asynchronous communications.

Peripheral-Related Server Modules

If you're tracking the wily networked peripheral, server modules are good spoor. Adapter boards and tape drive device modules are often found in network MODULES listings. CD-ROM drives are often connected to servers as volumes using special VLMs. The RS232 NLM is usually running on servers with modems connected for remote management. Dial-in products sometimes use NLMs to identify and manage calls on the dial-in devices.

Look at the MODULES listing for these kinds of entries. If you find a module and cannot find any corresponding hardware in use, the module may be a vestigial remain of a previous configuration. Avoid unloading modules from the server during normal processing hours, however. NetWare does not ensure memory integrity, and module loading and unloading can sometimes cause abends (abnormal ends to server processing—server crashes).

Working Backward from a Networked Peripheral

In some instances, the peripheral itself is visible and may even be in regular use. You may not be able to ascertain which server it connects to because of distance or convoluted cabling systems. In these instances, attempt to identify the network connection. If you can trace the peripheral back to its connection to the network, you can reduce the number of possible network connections. You may also be able to connect a test machine at the same point and execute a USERLIST /A to see which network connection is being made.

If the network connection is non-unique (that is, if the physical network has connections to multiple servers), you have to look elsewhere for information. One place to search for clues is the MONITOR utility's **Active Connections** window, where you may find names that look like device names (strings of numbers or peripheral-sounding names). Figure 3.12 shows an **Active Connections** window with a list of peripherals. Remember to use what you know of the network naming conventions to gather clues.

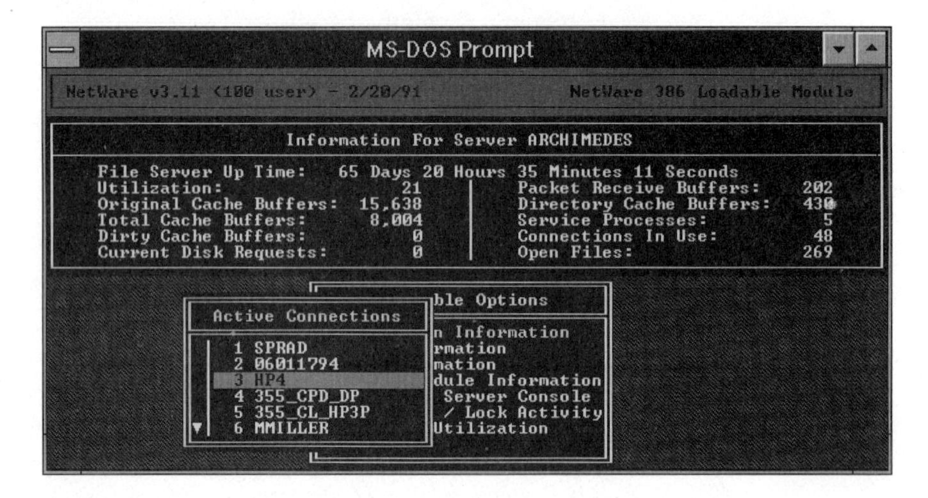

FIGURE 3.12 Some network devices can be discovered by checking the names on the MONITOR utility's Active Connections window.

Identifying Network-Connected Printers

Networked printers are managed in a separate utility called PCONSOLE. This utility runs on a client machine and allows the configuration of *print queues*, which are where print jobs are stored, and *print servers*, which are the processes that actually manage and perform the printing.

PRINT SERVERS Print servers can run on dedicated workstations, on file servers (handled by an NLM), and on hardware connected to the printers. You'll want to know several things about each print server, as shown in Figure 3.13.

For each print server, you can see the file servers allowed to connect, the list of users notified when the printer has a broadcast message (when it wants to complain about being offline, for example), the configuration of supported printers, and the list of queues whose jobs go to each of the supported printers.

FIGURE 3.13 The PCONSOLE utility's Print Servers and Print Server Information windows allow you to view and configure print servers.

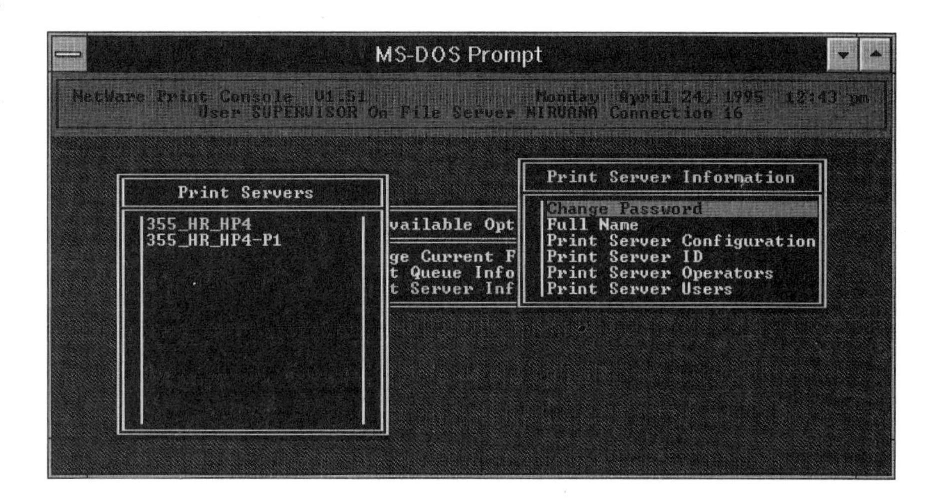

In addition to the standard print server utilities provided with NetWare, some third-party print server manufacturers include their own software. Two common examples are HP's JetAdmin, which comes with its JetDirect print server boards, and Intel's NPAdmin, which comes with its NetPort print servers. These programs generally perform competently, although NPAdmin's older versions had a nasty habit of crashing servers when configuring complex print server arrangements.

PRINT QUEUES The **Print Queue Information** option in PCONSOLE shows the list of jobs lined up in the print queue; queue operators and job owners are allowed to modify the print jobs in the queue.

The **Current Queue Status** window, shown in Figure 3.14, shows the number of entries waiting in the queue for service by the print server. It also shows the number of servers currently attached to the queue. Operators can enable or disable user, print server, and file server access to the queue from this screen.

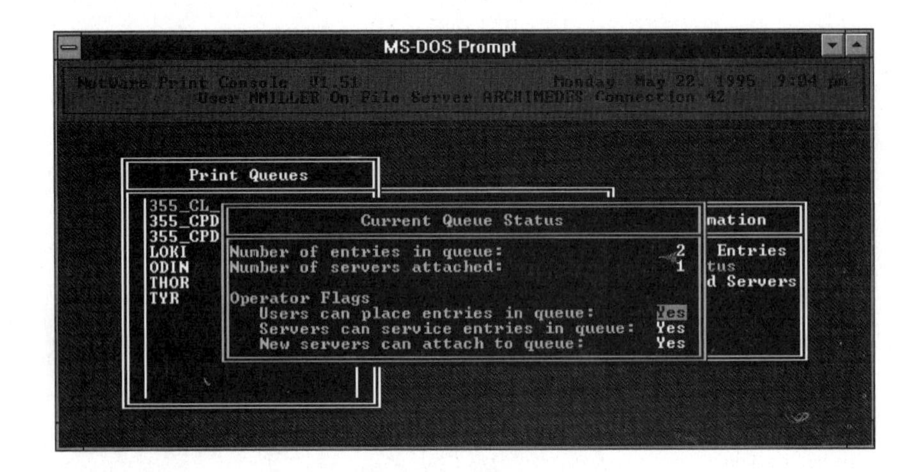

FIGURE 3.14 The status of a printer queue can be viewed in the PCONSOLE utility, which runs from a NetWare client workstation.

Currently Attached Servers shows the names of servers currently connected to the print queue, and the **Print Queue ID** screen displays the name of the queue's bindery object on the server.

The remaining entries provide lists of *queue operators*, who are users with authority to modify and remove print jobs and queue definitions, *queue servers*, which are the print servers that can service the queue, and *queue users*, who are users with access to put print jobs in the queues.

This chapter has begun the association of the network's uses with its layout and operation. You should continue to expand your understanding of how the network is meeting business needs and where it can be improved, but your understanding of the division of data among servers, the kinds of NetWare modules employed on the servers, and the configuration of network peripherals provides a fundamental basis for your understanding of how the network is used.

Lightning Strikes: Preparing for Disaster

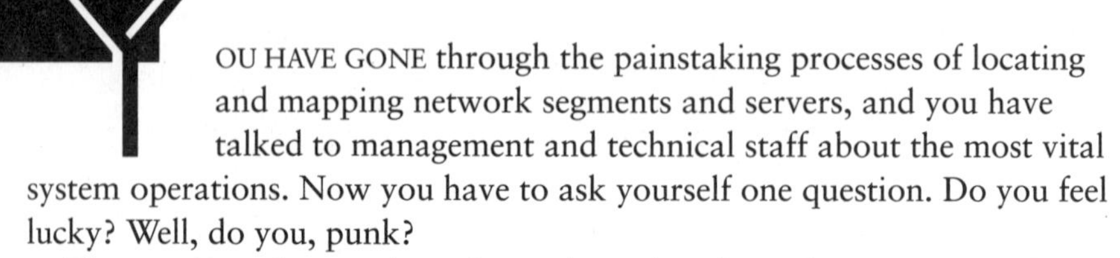

YOU HAVE GONE through the painstaking processes of locating and mapping network segments and servers, and you have talked to management and technical staff about the most vital system operations. Now you have to ask yourself one question. Do you feel lucky? Well, do you, punk?

The previous chapters have focused on identifying the structure and components of an inherited NetWare network. Having gained this fundamental understanding of the new systems, you are ready for your first course of action: preparing for disaster. It may seem a mite early to be acting on the information you've gathered, but the bottom line is that you already have enough data to decide on a disaster-preparedness plan and to ensure that your network will survive a disaster. As you develop a greater understanding of what the network needs to do, you can modify the plans you make here, but the last thing you need to deal with in a new network environment is the nightmare of recovering from a disaster for which you were not at all prepared.

The Vital Information

THIS IS AN important, heavy-duty chapter. You're being asked to ensure that the power supply is steady and backed up, the temperature and humidity of the server environment are correct, that appropriate system redundancy steps are employed, that the system for making backups is reliable, that spares of vital components are available, and that a disaster recovery plan is developed.

COMPLETED	TASK
❑	Determine which users must be able to work and which processes must continue running at all times.
❑	Ensure continuous power to the equipment needed to keep the essential processes running.
❑	Provide sufficient backup power to gracefully shut down file servers.
❑	Devise a procedure for server shutdown.
❑	Measure temperature of server environment.
❑	Move, enclose, or ventilate servers to ensure appropriate temperature, humidity, and dust levels.
❑	Identify current system redundancy levels—disk mirroring or duplexing, RAID, or SFT III.
❑	Add system redundancy as required by vital data.
❑	Select appropriate backup equipment and software.
❑	Develop backup and verification schedule, and arrange off-site storage of backups.
❑	Create an inventory of the vital spares for critical network parts.
❑	Develop an overall disaster plan to deal with total destruction of the network assets.

Ensuring Power Supply

THE QUALITY AND state of the power you feed to your network servers and communications equipment can have tangible effects on their reliability and performance. Your network's fuel source is its electrical power, and your network is what it eats. If the network loses power, even for a short period of time, the network will have problems; if the power is too weak or too strong, the network will have problems.

Preventing Sudden Power Loss

Power loss can be a major problem for a network storing mission-critical data. If your users have data files open on the servers when a loss in power occurs, the data can be lost. If the power fails late in the day, your users could lose an entire day's work. And if your backup process is intermittent, unreliable, or—heaven help you—nonexistent, you may lose additional days of work. If vital data disappears or cannot be accessed, you'll be answering to a company of angry users who feel that the data loss is your fault.

The best way to head this prospect off at the pass is to make sure that you have backup power that can kick in when the utility company's power fails. This supply must be sufficient to power the systems you need to keep up and running. The backup power supply must also be able to notify a person or process that the power has failed and that powering down is necessary.

Network Uninterruptible Power Supplies

The components that make up your network need different levels of protection from power failure. You must decide which network elements need to continue running at all times, which ones should stay running just long enough to be powered down gracefully, and which ones can lose power completely at a moment's notice and without supervision. Then you need to select equipment that will provide the levels of protection you target for each network element.

DECIDING WHAT NEEDS PROTECTING The components that need the most protection are the ones that are most critical to your organization's needs. If communications links are the lifeline of your company's sales, the mail gateway and telecom lines need the highest levels of protection so that they run at all times. If you provide database services to dial-in customers, your database server must continue to run throughout a power outage. On the other hand, the server you are using to test the latest release of some applications needs to remain running only long enough to be taken down in an orderly fashion. In any event, the information you received from your organization's managers in the earlier chapters should be sufficient to identify the most critical company undertakings.

Remember to relate the portions of your network; if the client machines do not have any independent power supplies, you will not need to keep their printers running, and their file servers need not remain up throughout the power failure for the users' sake. By the same token, if you expect your users to be able to access mission-critical equipment, they need power supplies for their client systems and throughout the route their data travels. If users connect to one server and route through a second server to reach the third, all three servers and their corresponding connection equipment must have power, as shown in Figure 4.1.

FIGURE 4.1
If certain users must be able to work during power outages, be sure to allocate power supplies so that they can connect to the mission-critical equipment.

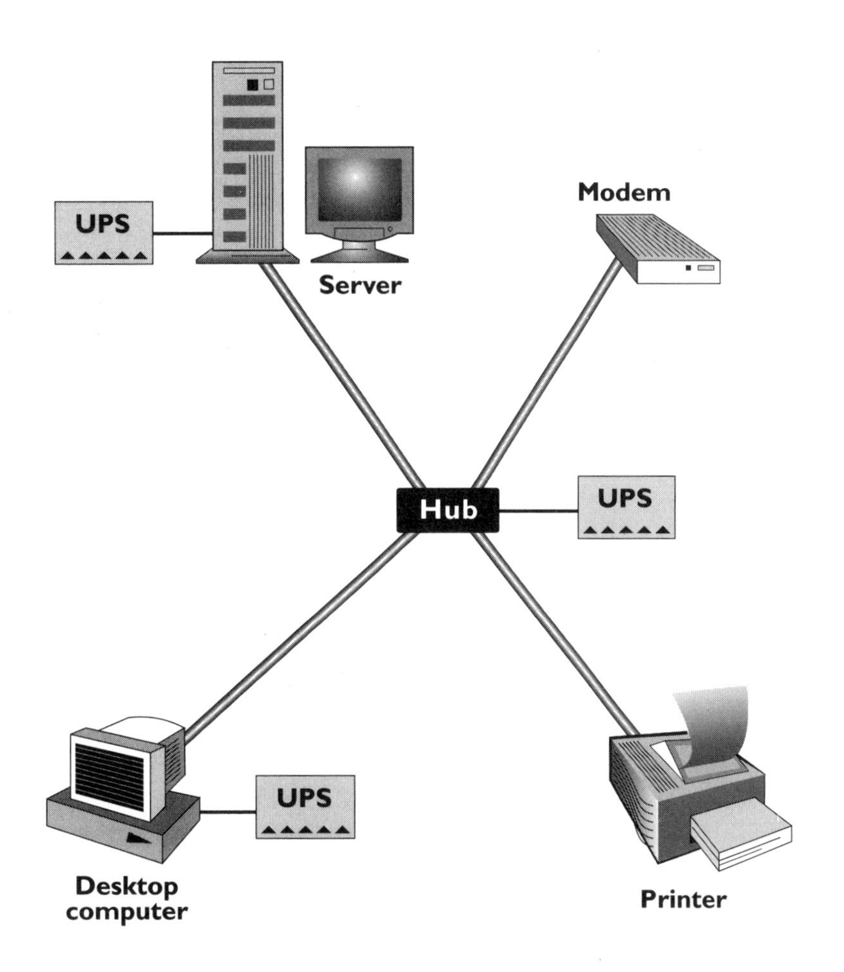

Those units that do not merit full-time power may require varying amounts of up time; most user workstations can be shut down much more quickly than most file servers. Simply dismounting drives on the file servers can take a long time in many cases, and some processes may need time to be stopped and unloaded. From what you learned about the volume sizes and the processes running on the servers, estimate the time it will take to bring the file servers down.

Taking the server down can require a fairly long time depending on the number of users connected, the number of processes running, and the size of the disks attached. Expect 10 minutes for a server of any size, with more time required if the server has enormous volumes mounted, databases that must be manually closed, or many user connections you wish to kill to make sure their files are shut properly.

If servers need to transfer data somewhere before going down, add the transfer process time to your estimate. Make sure that the existing equipment can handle the load of the devices connected to it for the period of time you've calculated it needs to perform. Be conservative in your estimate so that you have time to deal with other emergencies that may come up during an outage.

CHOOSING AN UNINTERRUPTIBLE POWER SUPPLY You can purchase a 400-watt uninterruptible power supply for less than two hundred dollars, but in most applications, you'll want more power for your servers, which may need to power a number of hard disk drives and other peripherals.

Power supplies in the 1,200-watt to 2,000-watt range can typically handle individual servers with plenty of time to shut down in an orderly fashion. List prices range from $700 to $2,400 for these products, depending on the frills and features you select.

The three common types of UPS systems available are offline, online, and line-interactive.

Offline UPS systems are the simplest. They contain a battery, a DC-to-AC converter, and circuitry that detects a loss of power and switches on the battery. The battery then provides the power output to the connected systems until the power returns or the battery's charge is drained. When the power comes back on, the battery recharges itself. The amount of time an offline UPS needs to detect power loss varies; 4 milliseconds or less is the desirable response time.

Power Conversions

The power coming from the wall outlets uses *alternating current* (AC), which switches its polarity from positive to negative. Utilities in the United States provide AC at 110 volts switching 60 times per millisecond (60 MHz). European power suppliers use 220 volts at 50 MHz.

Computer systems use *direct current* (DC), which provides constant polarity. Batteries supply DC power, but because UPS devices plug into the AC input of the computer system's power supply, the batteries in a UPS generate DC power that is converted to AC power, passed over the power cord to the computer, and converted to DC again for use by the system components.

Online UPS systems provide the system with power at all times. These UPSs are constantly charging their batteries so they can provide a continuous flow of clean power.

Line-interactive units are essentially offline systems with voltage regulation built in. These UPSs respond more reliably to low-power situations but reserve battery power for real emergencies.

Look for the following features in your UPS systems:

FEATURE	DESCRIPTION
SNMP management	Proprietary management software is often quite good, but Simple Network Management Protocol (SNMP)–compliant UPS systems are best for administrators who make use of general management software, such as ManageWise or the NetWare Management System.
Monitoring functions	The UPS should connect to a file server's serial or mouse port or should include an add-in board that allows the UPS to notify the file server (via an NLM) that the power is out. Monitored systems can automatically perform shutdown routines.

FEATURE	DESCRIPTION
Correct connections	Make sure that you match connectors; you want your electrical line and your UPS to use the same kind of connector. Also check that the power available on the circuit can fully power the UPS.
Level monitoring	Many UPS systems have a built-in display that indicates how much load is being placed on the unit. This is a good way of checking capacity and battery condition. Some UPS products also support remote monitoring via modem links.

OTHER POWER CONDITIONING EQUIPMENT Loss of juice isn't the only power-related threat your systems face. Variations in voltage are quite common; the aging power infrastructure in the United States does not provide flawless delivery, especially in remote areas. Heavy loads can cause brownouts, and "noise" on poorly situated power lines can affect the quality of AC power. Quality UPS systems protect against these conditions, but some products are available for equipment that doesn't need to run during power outages.

Surge suppressors should be placed on client machines and other equipment that does not have to stay running during a power outage. These devices prevent too much energy from reaching the sensitive electronic devices you want to protect. Look for quick activation times, preferably less than a nanosecond, and a large energy dissipation level, ideally over 400 joules. Look for devices that protect from much higher power levels with a fuse. Most vendors of quality suppressors insure equipment protected by the devices. Try to obtain surge suppressors indicating that a proper ground is established and that the suppressors are still running correctly; suppressors can burn out just like other equipment can.

Isolation transformers, which reduce noise on a circuit, and line regulators, which control voltage on power and telecommunications lines, can also be useful in network environments.

Check for Signs of a Struggle

Fluctuations in power levels can cause catastrophic failure of network devices and components, but more often than not, power disturbances result in intermittent problems. If there are many phantom occurrences and problems with a particular device or computer, check to see what kind of power conditioning and protection is in place, and check the status of the protection being used.

The kinds of strange behavior to watch for include systems suddenly restarting, keyboards or printers locking up, display fluctuations or failures, power supplies burning out, network connections being dropped, telecommunications links losing connections, and opened files being trashed or filled with garbage.

Remember to start at the hardware level when you're troubleshooting a problem and have no leads. Work from the ground up; you can't get much closer to the ground than the power supply.

Maintaining the Server Environment

YOU WANT TO keep your hardware happy in as many ways as possible. You've made sure it is eating right, and now you want to make sure it is dressed properly. Well, you want to ensure that it runs at the proper temperature.

If your servers and networking equipment reside in a central computer room, you have probably inherited an environment-controlled system. Organizations that have downsized from large computer systems generally have appropriate temperature, dust, and humidity controls in place because the older equipment was even more finicky than the current LAN systems. Very new buildings often include an IS center with elaborate controls. If you are somewhere in the middle ground, you'll have to make other arrangements.

Temperature

The first issue to take up is the temperature of the computer room. If all the systems are located in one area, this will be much easier to arrange than if you work in a distributed environment. Arrange to put thermometers in each of the areas containing network hardware. Since thermostat readings on the building temperature control devices may not be reliable, use an indoor thermometer.

Computer systems dissipate heat through cooling fans providing ventilation through the chassis. They also dissipate heat through the chassis itself. This means that the systems should have free air intake and outflow openings and that the ambient air temperature should not be very high. Although the chilly computer room is not the most delightful place to work on a cold day, a low temperature can keep computer and network equipment running at temperatures that reduce wear on circuitry. Too much heat can literally cook components, and even less catastrophic temperature levels can cause device failures.

If your temperature levels are inappropriate, you'll need to find a way to change them. If the equipment you're concerned about is all located in a single room, it is easier to provide climate control. If the building is not equipped to reduce the temperature in a single room, air conditioning systems can refrigerate the air and maintain a proper operating temperature.

These systems can also control humidity, and some filter out dust particles. If you have ever taken the cover off a computer and have seen the colonies of dust bunnies frolicking in the power supply intake and under the motherboard, you know how much dust is in the air.

Temperature ranges vary from product to product; my Compaq equipment specifies an operating range of 50° to 95° Fahrenheit, (10° to 35° Celsius), which is pretty reasonable. Unfortunately, when the environmental controls go on the fritz in a remote server room, you can exceed that level without knowing it. PCubid Computer Technology produces a microprocessor heat sink with a built-in fan and a temperature probe port for a digital thermometer. Berkshire Products offers the PC Watchdog, which trips an alarm when the system temperature rises too high.

Other Environmental Factors

You can't get away with just regulating the temperature of the system—keeping dust and other contaminants out of the environment is also important. Make sure that your air conditioning filtration system is clean and operational. Dust buildup is most harmful to mechanical devices such as disk drives, but it can also interfere with air flow within server or peripheral cases, reducing the effectiveness of the fans and causing internal temperatures to increase significantly.

Humidity can also be harmful. Check the tolerances of the media in use to see what levels of humidity are acceptable. High humidity can cause tape to stick to itself and may even cause rusting in severe cases. Low humidity can cause some media to become brittle.

Tests on hard disks and other devices indicate that major temperature and humidity fluctuations are more damaging than longer exposure to slightly higher or lower levels. My Compaq equipment indicates a very broad range of relative humidity levels, 8 to 90 percent. I keep tabs on the humidity levels to try to avoid major changes.

Employing System Redundancy

SYSTEM REDUNDANCY INVOLVES running multiple systems to ensure continued operation of the network in case of a device failure. The most common forms of system redundancy involve hard disks. This approach makes sense because NetWare has traditionally been primarily a file server technology (as opposed to an applications server technology, in which disk contents are not as vital). Data is usually the most important element on a NetWare network, and because disk drives are among the most heavily used devices and are prone to failure, disk redundancy is an appropriate fault tolerance feature.

The three forms of disk subsystem redundancy you're likely to encounter are disk mirroring, disk duplexing, and redundant array of inexpensive disks (RAID). *Mirroring* writes all data to two hard disks so that if a single disk fails, the other can continue to run, keeping users up and data safe. *Duplexing* uses two disk controllers to address two devices; this provides the safety of mirroring but eliminates the disk controller as a single point of failure. *RAID* generally involves *striping* data across multiple drives, usually with parity information saved so that data can be rebuilt when a single device fails.

The most extreme and most secure version of system redundancy supported in the NetWare world is SFT III, a system fault tolerance scheme in which two servers are duplexed, generally over high-speed connections. If a single component or even an entire system fails, an SFT III system can continue to run using the remaining server. NetWare 3.11, 3.12, and 4.x support SFT III, but the version in 4.x is an improved version.

Disk Mirroring

Disk mirroring provides a basic level of system redundancy, addressing the primary point of failure on most NetWare networks. As shown in Figure 4.2, mirroring writes data to two different devices each time NetWare writes to

Mirroring and the DOS Partition

The DOS partition on a NetWare server's disk drive is a small partition formatted with DOS. Although the volumes viewable by NetWare users are located on NetWare-formatted partitions, the server boots from the DOS partition and can access files on that partition. Some administrators keep copies of the system start-up files, STARTUP.NCF and AUTOEXEC.NCF, on this DOS partition to ensure that they are accessed only by the console (or remote console).

The DOS partition is not mirrored or duplexed by NetWare's fault tolerance features. Only NetWare partitions are duplicated. This means that if the disk drive containing the DOS partition fails, you lose the SERVER.EXE file stored there as well as any other information you need. Don't be lulled into a sense of security by your duplexed or mirrored systems; make copies of the DOS partition periodically—certainly every time you make configuration changes. Some systems include EISA configuration information on a system partition rather than on diskettes; if your system uses a system partition, use the EISA configuration utilities to duplicate the contents of system partitions periodically.

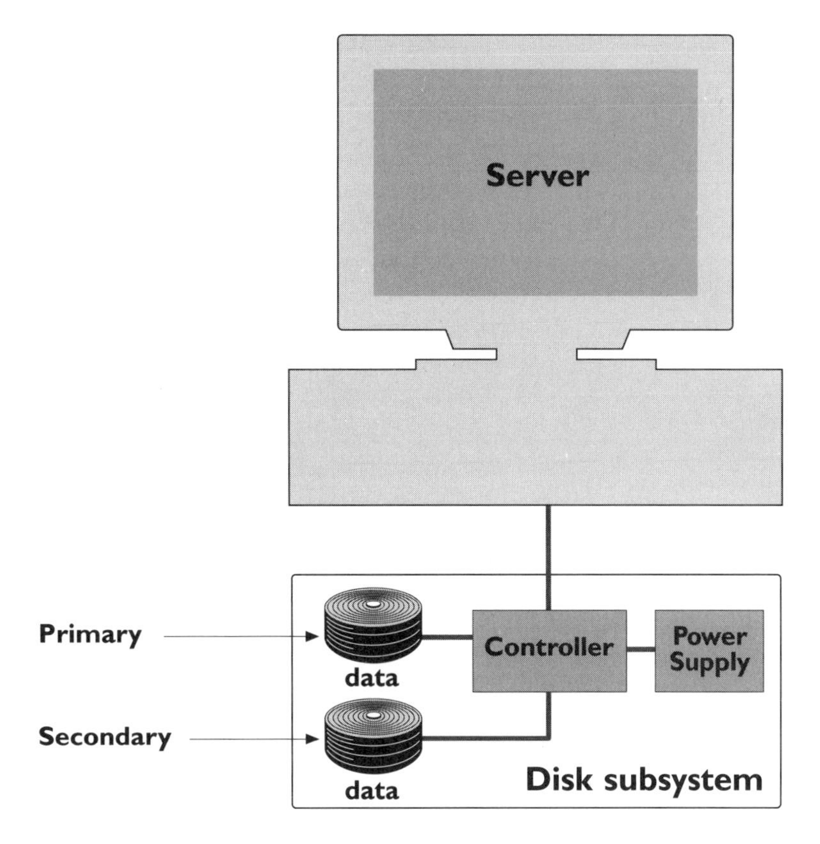

FIGURE 4.2 Mirrored disk subsystems write data simultaneously to two disks. The system checks to ensure that the two sets of drives are synchronized.

the hard disk. One of the drives is marked as the primary disk (or master disk), and when discrepancies occur between it and the mirrored (secondary or slave) disk, the data is copied from the primary disk.

If a single drive should fail, a mirrored system continues operating, using the remaining drive. After the secondary drive has been repaired, the mirrored disks can be synchronized. If the master disk fails, the system still operates, but be careful when repairing and reinstalling the failed master disk. Change the secondary disk to the primary disk before you remirror the system; this way, the most current data is tagged as the master data.

You can set and check mirroring by using the INSTALL console utility.

1. Enter `LOAD INSTALL` from the console prompt.

2. Select the **Disk Options** entry from the **Installation Options** menu.

3. From the **Available Disk Options** menu, select **Mirroring.** You can inspect mirrored partitions or set mirroring from the **Disk Partition Mirroring Status** menu. Here are descriptions of the available partitions:

STATUS	DESCRIPTION
Mirrored	The partition is currently mirrored. Select a logical partition from the **Partition Mirroring Status** list to see which devices are mirrored.
Not Mirrored	The partition is not currently mirrored.
Out of Sync	The partition is marked for mirroring, but the physical disks do not currently contain identical data. When a partition is being remirrored, the master disk indicates **Mirrored,** and the secondary disk indicates **Out of Sync.**

Remirroring begins as soon as NetWare can write to mirrored drives marked Out of Sync. If a drive fails but is still active (for example, if the Hot Fix area is completely filled so that data can no longer be redirected from problem areas), the server may commence a process in which it attempts to resynchronize the drives. The process continues until the server encounters a problem on the failed drive. At that point, the server abandons synchronization for the moment but attempts it again repeatedly. Since remirroring can take hours to finish and utilizes the processor somewhat, user performance may be noticeably worse during remirroring.

One of the problems with disk mirroring is that a disk controller failure defeats the redundancy of the system because there is no controller redundancy. Because controllers are relatively stable and hardy, this is not usually a major problem. However, it does leave a single point of failure.

Disk Duplexing

Disk duplexing overcomes that single point of failure problem by providing separate disk channels for the redundant disks. In most cases, this means that two chains of disk drives connect off two separate disk controllers. Duplexed systems should include separate power supplies for each disk subsystem. Like disk mirroring, this provides high reliability because a single component failure can be tolerated; unlike disk mirroring, failure of a disk controller or disk subsystem power supply can be tolerated. Disk duplexing is even more expensive than disk mirroring, requiring 50 percent overhead for power supplies and hard disk controllers as well as the standard 50 percent disk drive overhead imposed by mirroring.

Disk mirroring and disk duplexing share a performance-enhancing benefit called *split seek*. When NetWare has a request to read from disk, the system selects the disk that responds faster. Duplexed disks can further improve performance by reading from separate disks when multiple read requests are received simultaneously. Duplexed systems can write more quickly than mirrored systems because different controllers are handling the data being written to the drives.

Although most systems use pairs of disks to provide fault tolerance, it is possible to link up to eight physical partitions to create one duplicated logical partition. Even with disk drive prices dropping dramatically, adding multiple additional mirrored or duplexed drives is not cost effective and may be indicative of paranoia. Unless your system has incredibly bad disk drives, immeasurably vital data, and unbelievably large capital budgets, consider eliminating additional mirrorings and making use of the other partitions as additional disk space.

To make a mirrored partition available as a new volume segment, use the INSTALL console utility.

1. Enter `LOAD INSTALL` from the console prompt.
2. Choose **Disk Options** from the **Installation Options** menu.
3. Select **Mirroring** from the **Available Disk Options** menu.
4. Select the desired partition from the **Partition Mirroring Status** list.
5. Select the hard disk desired for unmirroring.
6. Press Delete.
7. When the disk is listed as being Out of Sync, you can select it and press F3.

If both drives in a mirrored pair fail, data is lost. Duplexing does not solve this problem, and although it is more secure than mirroring, multiple component failures can still be a problem in a duplexed system. Verified data backup should be performed as frequently as necessary to ensure recovery from a catastrophic failure.

Redundant Array of Inexpensive Disks

RAID comes in a variety of flavors based on the same concept: data can be *striped* across multiple disks for faster performance and improved fault tolerance. While disk duplexing and mirroring create duplicate partitions with identical data, RAID's fault-tolerant permutations write data only once but split it between drives. Additional information used to restore data if one of the disks fails is stored on a *parity* disk or is also striped across the system's drives.

RAID's different implementations are referred to as *levels*. Although RAID Level 0 through Level 5, which were developed by University of California at Berkeley researchers, are established, there are some variations on the concepts that are being touted as RAID Level 6, RAID Level 7, and RAID Level 10. Although there is general consensus about what the first six RAID levels entail, RAID definitions are still developing. The RAID Advisory Board is an industry organization of over 50 vendors who oversee the RAID definitions. It is less important to be certain of the RAID level implemented on a disk subsystem than to know what specific performance and fault tolerance features it employs. The most common RAID implementations are described in Table 4.1.

TABLE 4.1 Defining Features of the Most Common RAID Implementations

RAID Level	Description	Performance	Fault Tolerance	Application
Level 0	Disk striping only	Very fast reads and writes	No fault tolerance	Heavy I/O applications
Level 1	Drive mirroring/duplexing	Fast reads, slow writes	Completely redundant drives—high fault tolerance	Critical data applications
Level 2	Disk striping across mirrored disks with bit- and parity-checking	Good throughput by reading from multiple disks	Effective fault tolerance plus error isolation	Large systems such as minicomputers

TABLE 4.1 Defining Features of the Most Common RAID Implementations (continued)

RAID Level	Description	Performance	Fault Tolerance	Application
Level 3	Byte striping across data disks; dedicated parity disk	No parallel reads and writes; parity disk causes write bottleneck	Tolerates a drive failure	Video and other applications with large, sequentially accessed files
Level 4	Block striping across data disks; dedicated parity disk	Good read performance, especially with large files. Write operations bottlenecked by parity disk access	Survives loss of a disk	Read-only applications
Level 5	Block striping of data and parity information across all disks	Parallel reads and writes improve speed; some versions must read parity data before all writes, reducing write performance	Handles failure of one drive	Database storage and retrieval

RAID Level 0 is not really fault tolerant, but it is used in some systems to enhance performance. Level 1 is merely the mirroring and duplexing discussed previously. Level 2 is usually found in the minicomputer world because it is more robust than other methods but offers little advantage in the NetWare environment. Level 3 stripes data bit by bit between drives and maintains an additional drive with parity information. Level 4 also uses a separate drive for parity information but stripes data in blocks. Level 5 is the most frequently used level in NetWare systems; it stripes data and parity across all the drives in the subsystem.

What Is Parity?

Parity can sound a little bit magical; the notion of a five-disk system in which an entire disk can be removed without a loss of data is somewhat mind boggling. The way that RAID Level 5 systems provide hot swapability requires spreading the parity data among the drives in the system rather than storing it on dedicated drives.

When a RAID Level 5 system writes to disk, it stores the first block on one drive, the second block on another drive, and so on, until the data is all written. The system calculates an error-correcting code based on *odd parity*.

Although NetWare defaults to a 4,096KB block, let's assume a 1-byte block for convenience. If a NetWare operation writes 2 bytes to disk, 10010001 and 00011000, the RAID system stripes the first byte to the first disk, the second byte to the second disk, and a parity byte, 10001001, to the third disk, as shown in the illustration.

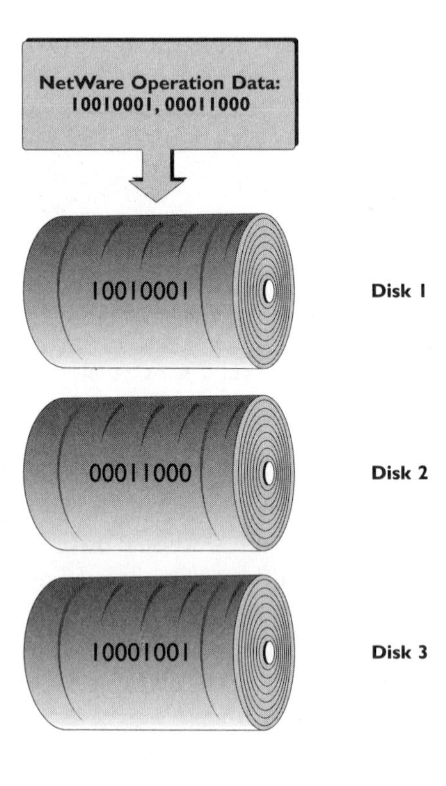

(continued)

Where did the parity byte come from? The byte is created by performing an XOR (exclusive OR) on the other bytes. An XOR sets each bit to 0 unless exactly one of the corresponding bits is 1. Thus 0 XOR 1 = 1, 0 XOR 0 = 0, and 1 XOR 1 = 0.

How is the parity information useful? Here's how. If the vice president of marketing, mesmerized by the flashing lights and intrigued by the handy plastic handles on the RAID drives, pulls out the second drive, the system can figure out what data was stored on it by looking at the byte of information on the first disk and the parity byte. As shown in the second illustration, any bits that are set to 1 on the first disk and also in the parity byte must have been 0 on the missing disk (because only 1 XOR *0* = 1). Any bits that are set to 0 on the first disk and 1 in the parity byte must have been 1 on the missing disk (because only 0 XOR *1* = 1). Any bits that are set to 0 on the first disk and 0 in the parity byte must have been 0 on the missing disk (0 XOR *0* = 0). And any bits that are set to 1 on the first disk and 0 in the parity byte must have been 1 on the missing disk (1 XOR *1* = 0). Make sense?

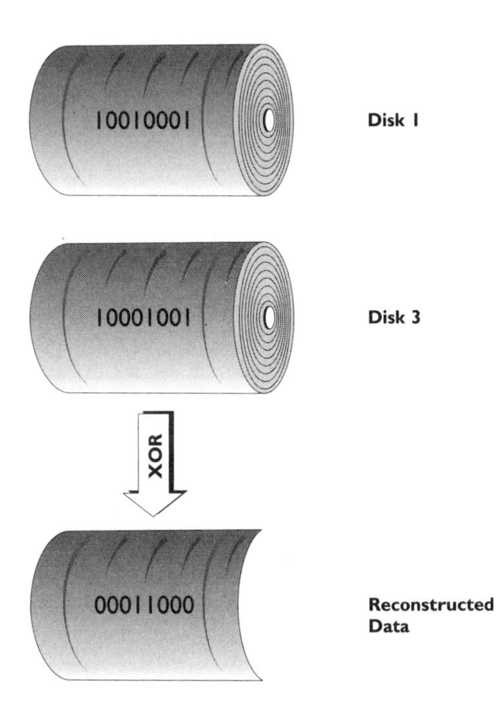

RAID Level 0

RAID Level 0 provides no fault tolerance. Its primary purpose is improving performance; since data spans multiple physical drives, multiple reads and writes can be performed simultaneously. This is great for systems with heavy I/O demands. Unfortunately, Level 0 is crippled when failures occur. Since no parity information is stored on Level 0 subsystems, the failure of a single drive results in the failure of the whole volume. Furthermore, data cannot be recovered if a single drive fails.

Because of this weakness, be aware of Level 0 systems on your network. Consider duplexing these systems, which won't degrade performance because the redundant writing occurs simultaneously. It can be expensive, however, because it requires an additional RAID subsystem. A seldom-referred-to RAID system is Level 1, which is simply mirroring.

Some vendors refer to systems with the combined Level 1 and Level 0 (mirrored and striped data) as RAID Level 10, but this level and description are not part of the original RAID definitions that have been widely accepted and implemented.

RAID Levels 3 and 4

RAID Level 3 and RAID Level 4 combine data striping across drives with an additional drive that stores parity information. The parity information consists of data that allows the system to recreate data when a disk fails. Level 3 stripes data at the byte level, while Level 4 stripes data at the block level. RAID 3 is suited to situations where the goal is fast sequential reading of a large file. Because the striping level in RAID 3 is so small, however, all drives are typically involved in each transaction, so only one read or write can be performed at once.

Since RAID 4 allows multiple simultaneous reads, its read performance is better suited to addressing multiple smaller files. Both systems are slowed during write operations because they must write to the parity disk during each write operation. Access to the parity disk becomes a bottleneck in these configurations.

RAID 3 is suited best to situations in which a single file is accessed most of the time—for example, a huge centralized database. RAID 4 is more appropriate for situations in which several small files are accessed simultaneously—for example, a program that consults several on-disk configuration files.

RAID Level 5

RAID Level 5 does not distinguish between data and parity disks. Each device in the Level 5 array contains both data and parity information. The data is striped at the block level. Multiple read and write operations can be performed simultaneously; because multiple drives are used for most read and write operations, RAID 5 performance is better than that of single-drive systems. The more disks in the array, the more efficiently the reads and writes can be performed, so Level 5 performance actually improves as more disks are added to the subsystem.

RAID Level 5 is not as fast as RAID Level 0 because of the parity information that is stored, but the ability to *hot swap* drives makes the performance difference worthwhile for most NetWare networks. Hot swapping allows a faulty drive to be removed from the array and replaced with a functional drive. The system continues to operate and the data can be rebuilt on the new drive after it is installed.

Although RAID Level 5 can be implemented at the software level, these versions are usually 30 percent slower than RAID Level 5 systems running at the hardware level. Despite the relative youth of the RAID concept, a variety of solutions are available, including integrated RAID controllers and drive subsystems in Compaq's ProLiant line of file servers.

SFT III

The trend toward downsizing and migrating data from centralized systems to NetWare client/server configurations has contributed several features to NetWare networks themselves. One feature that is developing and becoming more popular is SFT III, server mirroring. This is the highest level of NetWare's System Fault Tolerance. In an SFT III system, a critical server is connected to a nearly identical system. If one of the systems experiences a failure, the other can continue processing and serving users. This degree of fault tolerance is attractive for mission-critical applications, where loss of access to data or applications for any period of time could severely affect business.

SFT III comprises three processes running on the two mirrored servers. Each server runs the Mirrored Server engine (MSEngine), which enables the server mirroring itself. These identical processes are fed by IOEngines, which are I/O processes running on each server, communicating with the server hardware and routing information to the MSEngine.

The SFT III server connections are established using the Mirrored Server Link (MSL), which is a high-speed connection between the servers. The MSL connection speed is important because it dictates the overall speed of the mirrored servers. The MSL maximum distance is important because physical separation can be vital to system redundancy. MSL adapters installed in each server maintain the "twin" connection; a list of currently approved MSL boards is available via Novell's Faxback system at 1-800-414-5227.

Although some SFT III sites may need to have a server available at all times when users at the same location can access it, other sites need around-the-clock access and reliability. Long-distance connection stability is important in these networks because a relatively local disaster such as a flood, earthquake, or accidental sprinkler discharge should not take both mirrored servers out of action.

Using Backup Equipment

ALTHOUGH FAULT TOLERANCE is a desirable feature, most networks periodically encounter problems that require recovery. Whether your mirrored pair of disks fails together or one of your users accidentally deletes a file, you'll want to keep periodic backups of your data.

Since most of the data that is vital to an organization is also dynamic, backups usually need to occur frequently. Most sites perform daily backups of varying degrees of completeness. Daily backups are fine, but they have three main problems. One problem is that the volume of data being backed up requires an inexpensive medium. Another problem is that daily backups may be adequate generally, but if the data is changing during the course of a workday, turnaround time on a restoration of the stored backup may be too great. Finally, files are often open during a daily backup, preventing access and ruining the integrity of the backup.

For the moment, we will concern ourselves with the question of how to effectively store large quantities of important data without going broke. After we look at the equipment most likely to meet our backup needs, we can progress to finding ways of scheduling backups to maximize efficiency.

The three devices that are generally most effective for performing backups are tape drives, writable optical disk drives, and hard disks. Diskettes do not hold enough data to be a viable option even for workstation backups. Certain tasks, however, are still appropriate for diskettes, particularly EISA configuration file storage and DOS partition backup. Network backup of a single 1GB volume to 1.44MB diskette would practically be a life's work.

Understanding NetWare's Backup Structure

Novell's Storage Management Services (SMS) backup engine comprises several modules that run on the backup host system (the destination server) and the target systems (the source servers and workstations). The SMS structure includes the host portions and target components shown in Figure 4.3 and 4.4.

At the top level of the SMS structure lies the Storage Management Data Requester (SMDR). This process runs on the host server (look for a server module name in the form SMDR*xxx*.NLM) and manages communications between the backup software and the processes running on the source machines, the *target service agents* (TSAs). See Figure 4.4.

The backup software itself accepts input from the SMDR and communicates it to the Storage Device Interface (SDI). Although NetWare includes the SBACKUP.NLM backup software, it isn't particularly sophisticated. Cheyenne's ARCserve, which features a Microsoft Windows interface and maintains a database of archived files, or Palindrome's Backup Director, which has excellent tape management features and a tight DOS interface, yield better performance and are much more robust. They're worth the expense.

The SDI process manages communications between the backup software and the hardware-specific device drivers found at the root of the SMS structure. The hardware device drivers are specific to the interfaces and devices used by the backup host system.

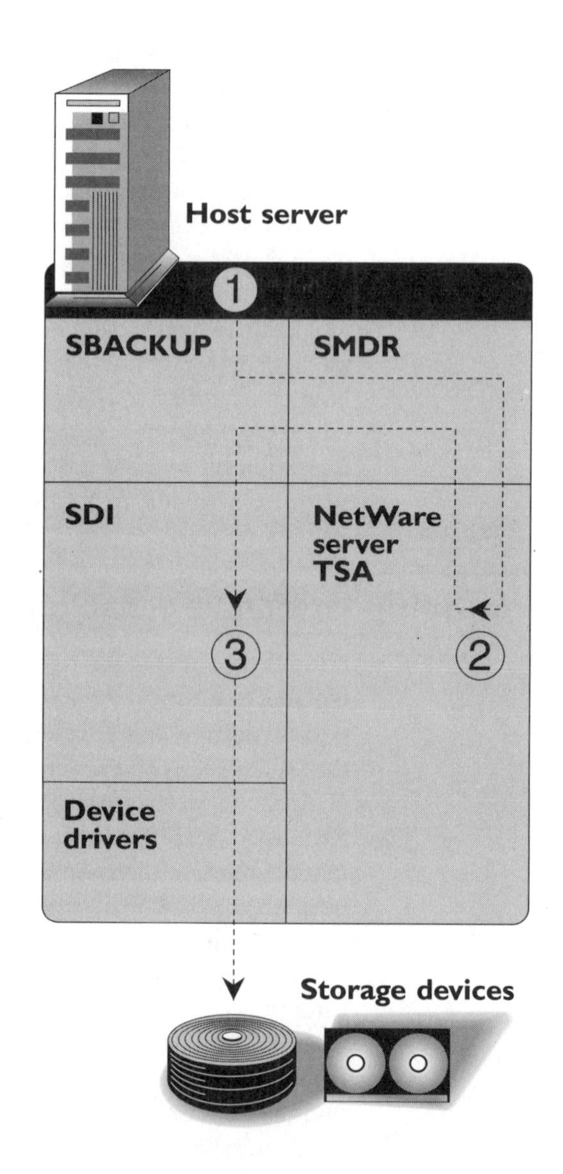

FIGURE 4.3 Storage Management Services host modules move data from the host system to the backup hardware.

The target service agent runs on the system that needs backing up. The SMS design supports several different kinds of agents, including server TSAs, database TSAs, and workstation TSAs.

FIGURE 4.4 Storage Management Services target service agents link the source systems to the host system.

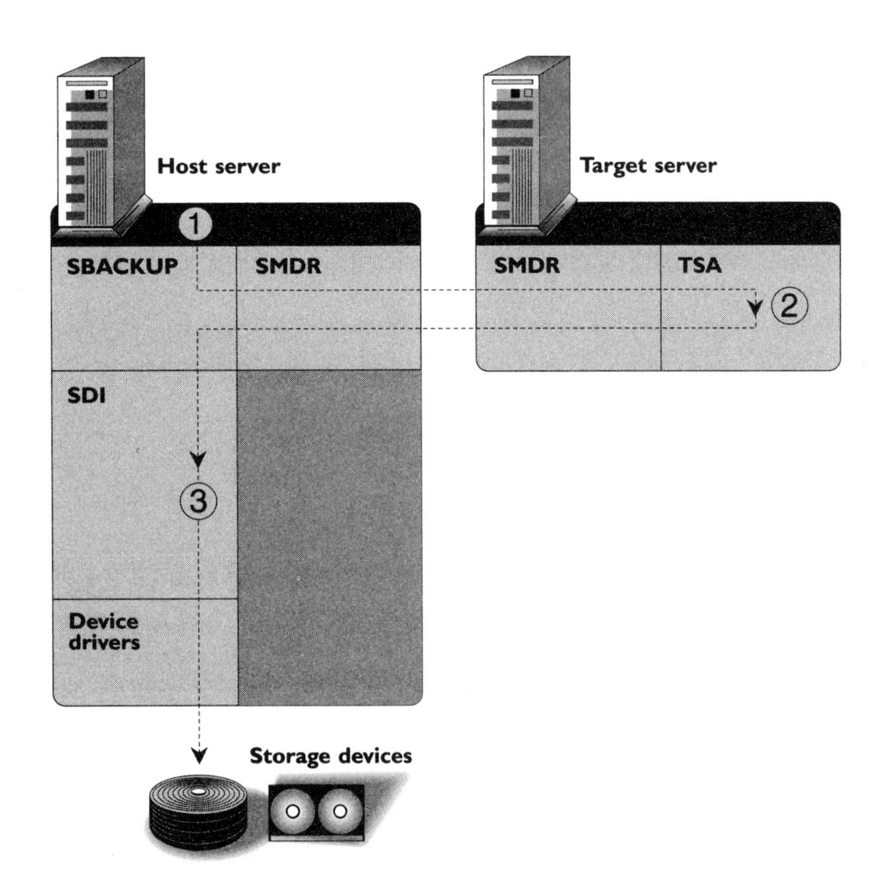

The server to be backed up needs to run the server TSA (look for a server module name in the form TSA*xxx*.NLM). Even if the source server is also the destination (host) server, the TSA must be loaded. The database TSAs also reside on file servers and work on several different kinds of databases, including the directory service database in NetWare 4.x networks.

The workstation TSAs include a process running on the host server and a memory-resident agent on the DOS or OS/2 workstation needing backup. Centralized workstation backup can be very useful, but the large size of current local hard disks makes this a time-consuming and hard-to-manage process.

Tape Drive Backups

Tape drives are slow when compared to other storage technologies, but they offer one compelling advantage. Their cost per megabyte makes them by far the most suitable media for data backup. They also offer the benefit of being highly portable. Unfortunately, their speed and vulnerability to damage demand that you pay more attention to them than you will want to. Later in this chapter, we'll discuss structuring the backups to provide maximum data coverage with minimal hassle, but for the moment, let's look at the technology available and at the limitations of tape.

Tape backup for digital audio tape (DAT) drives costs roughly a nickel per MB for the tapes themselves. Recordable CD-ROM stores 650MB per disk and costs slightly more per megabyte than DAT tape. New 3.5" magneto-optical disks storing 230MB cost a quarter per MB.

Make Sure It's Doing Something

When you're looking at the current backup systems, make sure that physical connections and processes are running for each backup device. A colleague told me that when he was looking over the backup equipment of his inherited NetWare network, he saw the Operations staff label and insert a tape into one particular drive each night, then remove and log it the next morning. Since he wasn't sure what the drive was backing up, he asked the operator, who didn't know either. The source name on the label didn't mean anything to my colleague, who looked to see which server the drive connected to. It didn't. A power cable was connected to the drive, but there was no SCSI cable. The drive turned out to be a vestige of a server that had been phased out. Make sure all the equipment in *your* inherited network is being used.

Tape Backup Technology

Although QIC-40 (quarter-inch cartridge) and QIC-80 tapes are suitable for use with standalone PCs, their capacity is relatively limited, and they require a separate pass over the tape to verify a backup. These drawbacks make them undesirable—and uncommon—in NetWare backup systems.

Easily the most common backup medium in NetWare networks is digital audio tape (DAT). DAT uses two write heads contained in a rotating drum. The heads pass over the tapes at an angle, resulting in a write pattern that looks like a helix, as shown in Figure 4.5. Two read heads also contained in the drum compare the data written to the tape to ensure that it is backed up properly; mistakes are immediately identified and rewritten.

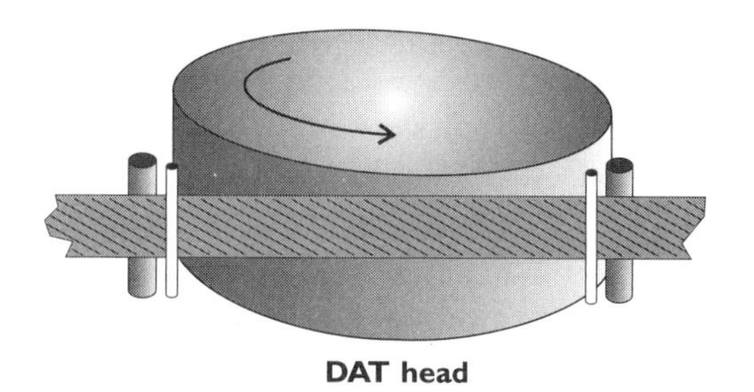

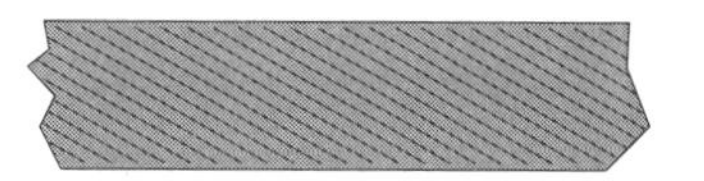

FIGURE 4.5 Digital Audio Tape (DAT) heads write in a helical pattern on the tape. The read and write heads are contained in a drum rotating at an angle to the tape.

Tape Backup Performance

Although there are several variations on the DAT format, they are similar in performance and capacity. With data compression on the fly, theoretical throughput reaches 60MB per minute. Real-life data is highly unlikely to be transferred at these rates because actual throughput is heavily dependent on the compressibility of the data being written. Complications such as alternate name spaces and precompressed files can slow throughput to under 10MB per minute, even with a fast backup package running on a dedicated SCSI host adapter attached directly to the server in question.

Backups running over network connections are further slowed by the capacity of the network; even if there are no users occupying bandwidth on your Ethernet network when the backup runs at 1:00 a.m., the 10MB per second network connections can be a performance bottleneck. Hanging tape drives off a network backbone running FDDI or 100 Mbps Ethernet would be a more effective solution.

Tape Backup Capacity

Compression ratios have a large impact on the capacities of backup tapes. The multigigabyte capacities advertised by many drive manufacturers can be achieved only if compression is incredibly efficient. File-tracking information that can be preserved by many backup packages can speed access during the restore process, but it can add significant amounts of data to the tape, especially if a backup includes many small files. In most cases, expect significantly less real-life data to fit on a single 90- or 120-meter DAT tape. If you are backing up three 2GB volumes that are mostly full, don't be surprised if you need two tapes in your drive that touted 8GB storage capacity.

Unfortunately, having to swap tapes during backups is irritating at best. As drive capacities and the expectations for NetWare storage capacities have increased, tape storage has not kept pace. One ameliorating factor is the advent of affordable DAT autochangers. These devices contain multiple tapes in a single box. A combination of hardware and software controls allow the backup to proceed on the number of tapes it requires. Autochangers with larger capacities can also be configured to manage the backup process without administrator supervision. These devices are a tremendous boon to managers with large amounts of data and small operating staffs.

Optical Disk Backups

Some organizations use writable optical disks for their backups because optical disks are less sensitive to environmental conditions than tapes are. Because optical disks typically can store less than 1GB of data each, this option is not cost effective for frequent backups. It can be useful for long-term archival storage, however. Write-once, read-many (WORM) optical disk jukeboxes are not supported by all backup software, but they provide a stable medium with life expectancies in the decades.

Hard Disk Backups

Many organizations have multiple shifts, processes that run around the clock, or workaholic users who are in the office at all hours. In each of these cases, keeping files closed all night for backup is not a reasonable course of action. In many situations, certain volumes are in high demand all day; in these cases, moving files to another volume on the same server can provide partial backup. Although it is safer to back up these files to removable media, moving the files to a backup volume provides first-line backup. It also allows the backup process to run at slower tape speeds—on the backup volume. Of course, this approach doesn't handle backups of the NetWare bindery or NDS, which are open while users are connected.

How to Make Use of Hard Disk Backups

Another way in which hard disk backups can be useful is to provide periodic backup during the day. One organization I worked for keeps its workflow-tracking data in a custom FoxPro database residing on the network. Users update the information during the day from walkup stations and personal workstations, so the files are open all the time. When some new NLMs started causing server abends, these database files were trashed. Recovering data from the previous night's backup took several hours using the backup software available. The work input on the day of the crash was lost; getting the previous day's file took half a day, and having the users manually update the database with the lost day of work took half a day.

To fix this problem, we added a workstation on the network that closed the database files and copied them to its hard disk every 30 minutes. It retained two copies of the database files at all times. The new worst case was that an hour of data would be lost, and the restoration process was automated and fast. Since the workstation itself was a low-powered machine destined for the bone yard, the cost of coding the backup procedure and installing a NIC saved days of lost data and lost opportunity costs.

Developing Backup Procedures

KNOWING WHAT KIND of backup equipment is in place or is appropriate to your network is only the first step. A viable disaster-recovery plan requires a backup procedure that provides adequate coverage for yourneeds and works with your technological tools and limitations. The foremost rule to keep in mind is that the less sophisticated you make the backup process, the more easily somebody else will be able to perform it properly.

The less sophisticated you make the backup process, the more easily somebody else will be able to perform it properly in your stead.

With that ease-of-use caveat in mind, you should consider three issues when devising a backup procedure. The first is to determine how backups will be preserved and identified in case disaster strikes and the backups need to be used. The second issue is the frequency and content of the backup. The third concern is that of implementation: who will perform the backup, and how will the reliability of the backup process be monitored?

Keeping Tabs on the Backup

Storing the data is only part of the backup process. Getting to the data is just as important and requires more ongoing work. Managers should ensure that recent data is quickly accessible so that files deleted by mistake can be restored even when the SALVAGE utility cannot help.

SALVAGE is a utility run from a network drive prompt on a DOS client workstation. Files that have been deleted but not yet overwritten can be resuscitated by SALVAGE, but if the deleted files reside on a volume that is low on space or has high file turnover, files become inaccessible to SALVAGE relatively quickly.

Easily accessed recent backups are also useful for rapid restore operations in case disaster strikes. Easy access must be balanced with security, however.

It makes sense to think that if your mirrored or RAID Level 5 disks fail to the point that you need to do a complete restore, something catastrophic may have happened. If your network equipment is trashed when your building burns to the ground during a riot, your easily accessible backups are going to be ruined, too.

Don't forget to turn virus scanning on in your backup software to make sure your nicely stored and labeled tapes aren't infected.

To ensure that your network backups are useful, catalog and label each tape with vital information, and periodically store your backups offsite.

CATALOGING AND LABELING WITH CONFIDENCE Your backup routines are producing a "product" you'll want to be able to quickly and accurately find in the future. Some backup software packages store inventories of tapes by date and name, which saves you the trouble of keeping your own database of contents. If your software doesn't perform this function, it is a good idea to keep a record of the dates and tapes used for the backup. The record can be an electronic database or even a spiral-bound notebook. You'll want to keep tabs on the following information, as shown in Figure 4.6:

- Tape name(s) or number(s)
- Backup date
- Extent of backup
- Retention date
- Backup content
- Errors reported

The tape name or number is identifying information that will always be associated with that particular tape, regardless of what data it currently contains. The tape should be labeled with this information so that it can be identified uniquely. Common approaches are code numbers (L00045) or names (SNYDER F WEEK 2). Use the existing approach if it suits you or phase in a new system as you make changes to the backup procedures.

The backup date should be straightforward. One possible source of confusion is backups that begin after midnight. "Thursday night's backup" may

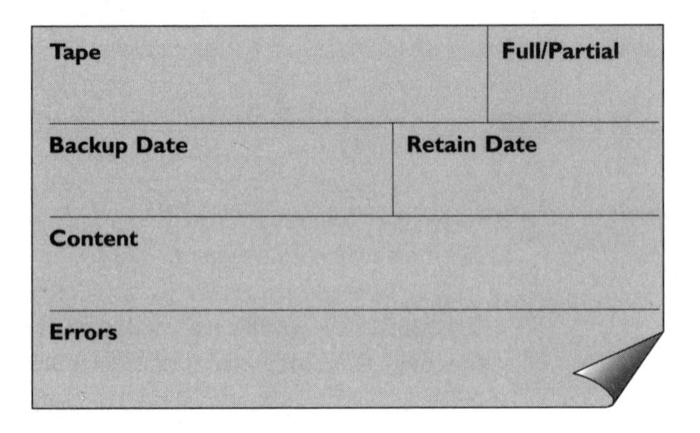

FIGURE 4.6
A tape label containing the vital information allows quick identification and retrieval of the appropriate tapes.

have Friday's date if it runs after midnight. Just pick a description (call it the Thursday backup or the Friday backup), and refer to it consistently. Put the corresponding date on the tape and in your log.

The extent of backup entry indicates whether the tape contains a full backup or a partial backup. If every backup you do is a full backup, this information will not be important. If you use the *differential* or *incremental* techniques described later in the What Do We Want to Keep? section, indicate which one has been performed.

Grandfathers in the Tower: Tape Use Patterns

The most common rotation patterns are the *grandfather-father-son* (GFS) and *Tower of Hanoi* strategies. These methods are similar in concept: a pattern of use is employed to make tape use and retention predictable and sensible.

GFS uses a "grandfather" tape once per month (usually the last full backup), a "father" tape once per week, and "son" tapes daily. The grandfather and father tapes are full backups, while the son tapes can be partial backups. The son tapes are used most frequently but contain fewer files. This approach is sometimes modified to provide long-term archiving; grandfather tapes are often archived for years.

The Tower of Hanoi approach adds a parallel "family" of tapes. Instead of using the same father and sons each week, a second father tape is added with corresponding son tapes. These two groups of tapes are kept together, alternating every two weeks. Variations on this approach typically add more families and include long-term archiving.

The retain date indicates how long a backup should be kept before the tape can be used again. Since using a fresh tape for each backup is almost never cost effective, tapes are usually recycled and saved in a regular pattern. The retain date indicates how long the tape should be saved.

Backup content refers to the files, directories, volumes, or servers being saved. This content is not likely to be dynamic; if you can fit your entire server's contents on one tape, this entry can simply indicate the server name. If you restore a few volumes to each of two tapes, indicate which volumes are backed up on which tapes. This will make finding the correct tapes much easier when you need to restore particular data.

Errors reported are important because they may indicate that a backup won't be useful for its ultimate purpose—restoration of network data. Don't get caught up in backup as a process and lose sight of the goal, which is to have the network data available if something goes wrong. Errors reported by the backup software may include users with open files preventing access, problems with the backup job description, or even hardware problems. Most network backups are done on SCSI tape drives, which makes them susceptible to the chronic SCSI problems with cabling and termination. If your SCSI chain has problems, your backup device may disappear from the network... better look to see.

The tape label itself does not need to include every detail about the backup set. A sample label is shown in Figure 4.7. The important parts are the host name, the tape number if multiple tapes are used, the backup date, and the tape name or number. The tape's identifying name and number should be on a separate label that is not removed; the other information can be placed on a label that is updated or removed and replaced each time the tape is reused.

Always remove one label before adding another to a backup tape. Multiple labels may interfere with the proper operation of the backup device and can even cause the tape transport to stick. And that's bad.

WHAT DO WE WANT TO KEEP? The fundamental question you want to ask when you decide how to approach the backup method is "what do we want to keep?" The second question you want to ask is "what is the best way to keep it?" The answers to these questions depend on your situation." A full backup, your initial answers should be "everything" and "whichever way is restored provides these answers, but a full nightly backup can require quite a

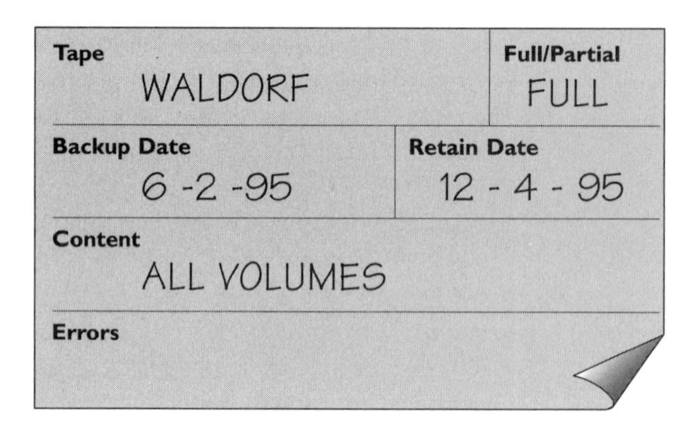

Tape
WALDORF
Full/Partial
FULL
Backup Date
6 -2 -95
Retain Date
12 - 4 - 95
Content
ALL VOLUMES
Errors

FIGURE 4.7
Backup tape labels should include the vital information needed to recover data.

few tapes and take a very long time on large networks. Many network administrators perform a full backup once per week and then perform partial backups during the workweek. Two popular forms of partial backups are *incremental* and *differential* backups.

Full backup stores everything, including pesky bindery or NDS databases. These backups are the basis for any disaster recovery plan because they are the primary link to how the network data looked on a given day.

Incremental backups are performed in conjunction with periodic full backups. Incrementals store all files that are new or have been altered since the last full backup. The big advantage of an incremental backup is that only a fraction of the data on the network is likely to change on any given day. Storing only the changes requires less tape space and allows much faster backups. Restoring the network to its former glory involves restoring the last full backup and then the incremental backups that followed it. In an incremental system, if your full backup was performed on Sunday and your disaster took place on Friday, you'd have to restore the full Sunday backup plus the Monday through Thursday incremental backups. This process can take a long time, and the backup integrity relies on five different tapes.

Differential backup addresses the inefficiency of restoring a network from an incremental backup. Instead of saving the changes made each day, the differential backup stores the changes made since the last full backup, which means that the network can be restored with a full backup and a single differential backup tape, saving time and eliminating some possible points of failure.

Reserving Spares and Repairs

NO DISASTER RECOVERY plan is complete without providing for spare parts in case network components should fail. The wisdom of the "spares and repairs" philosophy comes with balancing the expense of stocking additional parts with the likelihood of failure and the potential downtime involved.

Evaluating the Likelihood of Failure

If you have ever worked for the government or for government contractors, you may have some experience with determining statistics for failure probabilities and MTBF (mean time between failures). The kind of elaborate calculations required for failure analysis used in government contracts is of no use to you. Cast it aside immediately unless you are still in the employ of a government agency or contractor.

Your best guide to evaluating the chances of failure for your network components is common sense. The most complex equipment and the most frequently used equipment are the most likely to fail. Unfortunately, the most complex equipment is usually the most expensive. On the other hand, the most frequently used devices are typically quite affordable.

Server Equipment

The disk drives are the most likely devices to fail in a NetWare server, which is one reason so much attention is paid to the backup and fault tolerance features of a network. Other components that are relatively likely to fail are SIMMs, SCSI host adapters, and NICs. A good policy is to keep a spare drive of each drive type found on the network and to keep one spare each of memory, disk controllers, and network adapters. Random device failure is not likely to strike multiple devices at once, and if your power is adequately monitored, you are not likely to have components failing en masse unless a major disaster occurs. Monitors and keyboards can generally be found among the spares available for end users; check to see whether the servers use the same connectors as your client systems do.

To minimize downtime from hardware failures, keep a spare drive of each drive type found on the network and one spare each of memory, disk controllers, and network adapters.

Keeping spares of other server components, including motherboards and built-in power supplies, may be more difficult to justify. If your budget allows it, purchase a spare server of the same class as the existing machine (or upgrade an existing server and use the old system as a spare). When you purchase servers, make sure on-site support is provided for a reasonable period of time. Standard warranties range from one to five years depending on the vendor and how much extra money you are willing to spend. Value-added resellers (VARs) may also be able to provide you with emergency equipment. Expect at least a one-day turnaround time for service from vendors and VARs, even when they promise turnaround in hours. Two-day response time is usually considered quick in the real world.

Before you determine how long a warranty or support contract you want to obtain, you need to decide how long the server will be viable and what in-house resources you have to repair it. If your business requires leading-edge technology, don't worry about extending a server warranty past two or three years. The server will be outdated by then. If you have extensive spares and personnel capable of troubleshooting problems, purchasing support from a VAR is probably unnecessary.

Peripheral Equipment

The peripherals most prone to failure are printers. Because printing is a mechanical process that involves dirt (in the form of paper residue and toner or ink) running through the device, it is an inherently risky undertaking. A printer is too much like a copy machine to be a completely dependable piece of office equipment. Although devices from HP, IBM, and other vendors are quite reliable, they are still a likely point of failure.

Large organizations should be able to keep spare printers on hand, but if your organization spends money more conservatively, redeploying other network-connected printers can be a solution. Procure a full-capacity printer for your own use, and deploy it if another device fails. Service contracts can be helpful, but since production reports and executive memos are not likely to wait while your service technician is dispatched, have another option in mind.

Other network peripherals, such as network modems and CD-ROM drives, are usually less expensive. If you have many of them, or if they are used for mission-critical data access, keep a spare or two. Time will tell whether the devices themselves are prone to failure, but if you forego keeping a spare part, record the reasons for that decision so that you can defend yourself when problems arise.

Network Equipment

The biggest failure points for network connectivity are the connections themselves. Cables can be damaged by careless handling, accidental breakage, or even roving bands of rats. Keep plenty of spare cables (with connectors) on hand, including extra long cables that can route around trouble spots on the network in case of problems. Cable terminators used on bus topologies should also be stored to handle an emergency cabling addition or modification.

Network communications devices are another story. Hubs and MSAUs are relatively expensive and are generally hearty enough that they aren't problematic. On the other hand, the center of a star topology is a single point of failure that can affect many users. If you can afford to keep extras, do so. If you can't, have a plan in hand to minimize the damage if a hub should fail.

Spare bridges, routers, and other sophisticated network equipment are hard to sell to management in all but the largest organizations. A $75,000 router is a critical part of your network that isn't likely to be easily bypassed, either. For these pieces of equipment, a service contract is a necessity. Spending $10,000 to get half-day response time for a single device may not seem like much bang for the buck, but unless you can create a contingency plan to handle the failure of a router, accept the expense as an operational necessity.

Gauging Losses Due to Downtime

Although losses due to downtime should be considered for any network disaster preparedness plan, it seems that most purse strings are relatively open to fault tolerance and backup schemes but snap shut when spare equipment is on the table. Perhaps this is because management can see the backup and fault tolerance equipment being used and therefore considers it working for its money. Management should also consider the losses due to lost data, employee downtime, and corporate loss of face.

If you take a look at some of the horror stories covered in networking and business journals, you should be able to find a suitably terrifying description of losses due to downtime. More ammunition in the battle to justify disaster preparedness comes in the form of figures from Infonetics Research, which reports that average revenue lost from a one-hour LAN segment outage was $78,000; the highest outage costs ran up to $500,000 in business losses.

Estimating the Value of Lost Data

If a system failure results in the loss of data that cannot be recovered, you can perform a rough calculation of the cost of that lost data.

1. Determine the number of employees using the system for important data.
2. Find the annual revenue generated per employee by dividing the gross annual revenue of the department or organization by the number of its employees.
3. Calculate the daily revenue generated by each employee by dividing the result from Step 2 by 250 workdays per year.
4. Determine the revenue generated by the network users by multiplying the result from Step 1 by the result from Step 3.
5. Identify the percentage of the day's data that cannot be recovered.
6. Calculate the lost data's value by multiplying the result from Step 4 by the result from Step 5.

Estimating the Cost of Wasted Employee Time

The time that employees spend twiddling their thumbs while the problem is fixed can also be determined in rough figures. The time you and your staff spend repairing the problem should be included (include yourselves as employees using the system).

1. Determine the number of employees using the system for important data.
2. Estimate the time required to solve the problem.

3. Approximate average user pay per hour.

4. Calculate the value of wasted time by multiplying the answers from Step 1, Step 2, and Step 3.

Estimating the Cost of Corporate Loss of Face

Determining this value is a more difficult process, and it can vary from organization to organization. The way to come up with a procedure is to evaluate the sources of revenue and determine how failures can impact the bottom line. If loss of data means that your bids cannot be made by deadline and your organization loses contracts, a fairly straightforward correspondence exists between downtime and revenue. If repeated loss of data prevents products or services from reaching customers in a timely fashion, those customers may find other sources, and you may lose revenue due to customer attrition. Even if you cannot devise a reasonable formula, an explanation of this concept should accompany your requests for disaster recovery expenditures.

Designing Disaster Recovery Procedures

A VARIETY OF POTENTIAL disasters may beset you and your network, and creating a single plan to encompass them all is unrealistic. It's also a waste of time. Creating an integrated disaster-support document is not something you should be spending your time on yet, if ever. Instead, focus on the disasters that are most likely to happen and address the worst-case scenario. As your understanding of the network develops, you may want to alter the plans you create now. The changes you make to the network and its management may also change the approaches you describe. For the moment, do some brainstorming to identify possible problems and resolve them. Get your staff involved; they may be able to think of disasters that have happened or could happen.

Addressing the Worst Case: Total Destruction

If a natural disaster or some other cataclysmic event destroys your computer center or your entire building, are you in any situation to recover? Probably not, and it may not seem like there is much to be done in such a case. That kind of pessimistic thinking will never get you decorated for business valor. Do what you can to preserve data, information about the current network layout, and information about which service providers and VARs can help you reconnect and rebuild.

Data Preservation

Your well-designed data preservation plan includes off-site storage, and a good thing, too. The frequency with which you supply the off-site facility with backup tapes will dictate the amount of data you lose to a large-scale disaster. Weekly transfer of tapes containing full backups is probably a good baseline. Even if your circumstance does not allow storage with an off-site storage service, you should be making copies of your backup tapes to take home. Put them somewhere where they'll be safe from extreme temperatures, humidity, and curious cats. If the data is too sensitive or proprietary to leave the site in your hands, it is too valuable to be stored anywhere but a reliable off-site service.

Network Layout Documentation

The maps and lists of equipment you compiled during your investigations in the previous chapters were not made simply for your health. This information allows you to approach a reconstruction effort. You'll know what equipment has to be replaced, what the critical data is and where it was stored, and how the whole system was tied together. This information should be stored with your off-site vendor or in another safe location (keep it with your copies of the backup tapes if worse comes to worse).

Contact Information

The first call to be made in a total disaster is not likely to be one you make. The insurance company will need to be notified of the extent of the loss. Include the insurance contact's name and number in your disaster plan so that accessing this information will not be a bottleneck in an emergency. Telecommunications providers will need to be contacted to resume communications services if your LANs are connected over any distance, so include the appropriate numbers in your plan. If your company has worked with particular vendors or VARs in the past, your records should indicate the organizations and your contact names and numbers for each. Naturally, the off-site vendor's name and number should be recorded with your account number.

Addressing Other Circumstances

Other circumstances will have to be addressed individually. Some possibilities are more likely than others, and some plans will be easier to verify or test than others. Spend some quality time identifying possible equipment failures or other minor disasters and evaluating your response options. Come up with a response plan for each reasonable situation you can imagine. Some possible disasters include:

- Theft of equipment. In more than one incident, organized bands of thieves have broken into a business and torn open the file servers to steal the SIMMs. At roughly $50 per MB, server memory can be a very valuable asset, especially if you're using 32MB SIMMs. Leading-edge microprocessors are also popular targets for theft. Of course, collateral damage is often caused when the server cases are forced open and the chips are removed.
- Failure of a disk drive. This *will* happen. Know what you will do.
- Failure of a server add-in board. Host adapters, NICs, and even graphics boards are known to give up the ghost. Have a recovery plan devised.
- Server hardware failure due to unknown factors. The server goes down, and you cannot bring it back up. What do you do now?

- Lost telecom connection. If mud slides take out your T1 lines, your WAN goes down. How do you keep mission-critical e-mail flowing?
- Virus strike. A virus infects your system and eats data. How do you go about getting clean data and moving on? See Chapter 8 for further discussion of security issues like this one.

Notification Procedures

Make sure that the computer operations staff and facilities department know to notify you in case of a network or site emergency. Leave your home phone number or pager number with the computer room staff and make sure that the facilities manager includes your numbers in the emergency plan.

This chapter has focused on the kinds of steps that should be taken to ensure that your network can withstand common disasters, such as temporary power outages and component failure. It has also outlined the steps involved in creating and implementing backup procedures and a disaster recovery plan; these measures will help you recover rapidly from emergencies that damage the network. An understanding of the vital data that resides on the network and of the important business activities that require network support is vital to the successful design and implementation of disaster preparedness plans. In the next chapter, we move away from the servers and their centralized data to investigate the network client systems.

Scoping the User: Examining Client Systems

I N THE PRECEDING chapters, our focus has been on the important network equipment and its use. Now it is time to investigate the user configurations in your inherited network. There are many different ways to connect client stations to a NetWare network, and many different local operating systems can be used with NetWare. We will look at the most common client platforms and connection information.

You don't need to look at every client on your network at this point. Please don't. Instead, use what you know from the login scripts and what you learned in Chapter 3 from your interviews with technical staff, managers, and users to determine which groups of users have standard job descriptions or work activities. Take a cursory look at their hardware, and then have a look at the different *kinds* of systems in use.

The Vital Information

BEFORE YOU LOOK at the client software configurations, determine which client hardware is in place. Then identify the client operating systems and the network client software involved for each group of users. The following checklist can help you keep track of the information you find.

COMPLETED	TASK
❑	Find PC hardware in use.
❑	Locate Macintosh hardware in use.

COMPLETED	TASK
☐	Identify DOS-based PCs and check NetWare client software configuration.
☐	Check Windows-equipped PCs for NetWare support and Windows update files.
☐	Locate PCs using Windows for Workgroups and check network client configuration.
☐	Identify PCs using Windows 95 and check network client configuration.
☐	Check client software configuration on Macintosh systems in use.
☐	Look over OS/2 systems for proper connection and network configuration.

Identifying Client Hardware

THE PRECEDING CHAPTERS focused on the network servers, hosts, and communications equipment. For most users, however, the network is transparent at that level. They may not know the names of the servers they attach to, let alone the volume names they map to. They are much more concerned with the machines that sit on their desks and on which they do their work. If they cannot connect to the network—whether they've forgotten their passwords, moved their machines and lost physical connections, or are logging into a server that is down—they're likely to tell you that the "network is down."

If you are the entire IS staff, you will clearly need to be supporting these users, ensuring that they can continue to be productive. Even if you have a staff of technicians who set up PCs and deal with the client needs, there is often a gray area where a client technician cannot find the connection problem on the user's machine. So you'll want to know what your users are using and doing not only because your network's design and development depend on your understanding of these issues, but also because you may be called on to answer questions about problems encountered by users.

Although IBM-compatible hardware is most frequently found in NetWare networks, Apple's Macintosh computers occupy business niches that are often connected via NetWare. NetWare 4.x includes the Macintosh support software and will accept as many Macintosh clients as the NetWare license allows (version 3.12 comes with a five-user license for its NetWare for Macintosh software). Most other hardware you'll encounter comes from manufacturers of UNIX-based systems; because these typically use TCP/IP for communications, they are not likely to use the standard NetWare client software.

IBM PC Compatibles

IBM-compatible microcomputers are the most widely used business computers, and they are also found in many homes. The components found in the IBM-compatible world are very similar to those that can be found in file servers. Processors, buses, memory, and disks can be identical, although there are differences in what is "standard" in the server and client hardware categories.

Manufacturers who make IBM-compatible PCs that are found in business settings include big names such as Compaq and IBM, but quite a few mail-order vendors, including Gateway 2000, Dell, Austin, and Zeos, are also frequently found in business settings. Manufacturers such as Packard-Bell, Canon, and AST Research are common sights in small computer retail stores, computer superstores, and even department stores—and you'll find them in businesses, too.

The bottom line in the PC world is supposed to be that the vendor provides a package of components and competes on the basis of price, availability, and support policies. This is mostly true, but some manufacturers work harder to ensure compatibility and interoperability. Some components are better supported and use drivers that are more frequently updated than others. Although the NIC in a client machine is the only hardware that is introduced by networking, NIC drivers can sometimes conflict with other software, especially when the user machines are attempting to optimize memory settings in the resource-starved DOS environment.

Configuring memory in a system with NIC drivers and the NetWare client software can be an adventure. Some drivers hang the system if you attempt to load them high (the NETBIOS.EXE emulator provided with NetWare is an unfortunate example). The default NIC settings can also be a problem; for example, 3Com's excellent 3C509 NICs default to IRQ10, which is also the interrupt used by Compaq's Business Audio driver. A quick reconfiguration via the 3Com setup software straightens out the situation, but it may take you some time to identify such problems.

The model of microprocessor used in an IBM PC–compatible client machine has little to do with its network interoperability. Any fully Intel-compatible 80386, 80486, or Pentium-class processor should have the performance and capacity to run the client software adequately.

Bus design is not often a limiting factor for network connectivity either. Although the ISA bus is the *de facto* standard in desktop PCs, MCA, EISA, VL-bus, and PCI NICs are available, and portable computer users even have the option of using PC cards (the official but infrequently used name for PCMCIA—Personal Computer Memory Card International Association—add-in cards) to connect to Ethernet or Token Ring networks.

Apple Macintosh

The Apple Macintosh has long supported peer networking via built-in network ports. These LocalTalk connections are exceedingly slow—at 230 Kbps, it's faster than a modem and slower than the kinds of network access methods discussed previously—and are not very useful in most modern network environments. Older machines with expansion slots support the addition of add-in NICs, and newer Macintoshes have integrated Ethernet or Token-Ring connections.

Older Macintosh models typically use the NuBus expansion bus. Various vendors manufactured Ethernet, ARCNet and Token-Ring cards for these systems. If these older Macintosh systems, such as Macintosh IIsi, IIci, and IIfx models, exist in your organization, it is generally a better idea to upgrade to more recent models than to invest in connecting machines that are presently quite limited in power. I don't think the new Macintosh machines are terribly well suited for general business use, but these older machines highlight the Macintosh's limitations.

Newer Motorola 680x0-based Quadra and PowerPC models typically include a proprietary connector that allows connection to an Ethernet or Token

Ring network via an external transceiver. Be sure that any transceivers you order have the appropriate connectors for your cable topology.

Configuring Client Network Software

NETWARE'S CLIENT FOCUS has long been the DOS platform. Because NetWare was developed as an extension of the DOS world—it looks and acts like DOS as far as its users are concerned—NetWare's client focus made quite a bit of sense. The dominance of DOS in the business world made this an even better approach. As GUIs were bolted on top of DOS and as OS/2 and Macintosh clients needed network connections, their support has evolved. Support for each platform varies in sex appeal, but all the major PC and Macintosh operating systems are supported enough to allow file and print sharing to an acceptable degree.

DOS

NetWare's support for DOS is important for DOS-only and DOS/Windows systems. The current client software architecture combines Open Datalink Interface (ODI) support for multiple protocols running on NICs with Virtual Loadable Modules (VLMs) acting together as the NetWare DOS Requester. The ODI/VLM design is modular and highly configurable, and it is the path of future development for Novell. If your network uses the older IPX/NETX client software, updating the clients should be one of the update tasks on your list.

You can identify the version of DOS installed on a PC by typing `VER` *at the DOS prompt. The system returns the version number installed. The latest version of Microsoft MS-DOS is 6.22. IBM PC-DOS version 7.0 is available, while Novell's DOS 7 is no longer being developed.*

IPX/NETX versus ODI/VLM

The IPX/NETX approach used in earlier versions of NetWare worked just fine, so why was it abandoned? The ODI/VLM approach is better for several reasons, but flexibility and modularity are the keywords in this comparison.

IPX.COM managed the flow of data between the NIC and the NetWare shell. IPX.COM was generated for each different NIC by running the WSGEN utility. WSGEN combined and configured the IPX.COM elements by using a NIC driver provided by Novell or the NIC manufacturer (designated by a .LAN extension) and the IPX.OBJ file. The latter was a generic object file that contained the data management information for the workstation software.

NETX.EXE is a series of NetWare shell files that identify commands intended for NetWare handling and spirit them away from DOS, through IPX.COM, and onto the network. Early versions of the shell were specific to the DOS version in use and were named NET3.COM, NET4.COM, and NET5.COM. Subsequent versions were simply named NETX.COM and later, NETX.EXE. The EMSNETX.EXE and XMSNETX.EXE files make use of expanded and extended memory, respectively.

The ODI/VLM approach uses the Link Support Layer (LSL) file, LSL.COM, which manages data flow between the NIC's MLID (Multiple Link Interface Driver, the network adapter driver) and the protocol stack. The protocol stack itself runs as IPXODI.COM on IPX/SPX networks or TCPIP.EXE on TCP/IP networks. The DOS Requester is loaded next. The Requester is composed of multiple .VLM files, each of which performs a specific function. This modular design facilitates expandability, customization, and more efficient use of memory.

The best reason to use the ODI/VLM architecture is because Novell has ceased development in the IPX/NETX arena. The proliferation of new and exciting acronyms comes in as a close second.

DOS Client Building Blocks

The files you can expect to see on client machines depend on how old the network is and how recently the clients have been updated. Don't be surprised if you do not see any .VLM files on the client machines; VLMs are relatively new and are not universally in place. If you don't see VLMs in use, you'll probably see NETX used with ODI drivers.

ODI AND NETX This approach loads the Link Support Layer (LSL) software, the NIC driver (called a Multiple Link Interface Driver or MLID), the protocol stack, and then the NETX.EXE shell. These utilities are usually loaded in the AUTOEXEC.BAT file or in another batch file called from AUTOEXEC.BAT, or they're manually invoked by the user. STARTNET.BAT is automatically created and placed at the beginning of the AUTOEXEC.BAT file by the latest client installation software. NET.BAT is another common file name used by network administrators. The STARTNET.BAT or NET.BAT file may look something like this:

```
rem LOAD NETWORK DRIVERS
lh LSL.COM
lh 3C509.COM
lh IPXODI.COM
lh NETX.EXE
```

Although this approach is not leading edge, it is acceptable, and it does not necessarily require updating immediately. Check to see that the dates on the driver files are the most recent ones available; if they're not, make updating these files a priority.

ODI AND VLM This approach is the most current, encouraged wholeheartedly by Novell. The visible difference is that NETX.EXE is not loaded; instead, VLM.EXE is loaded.

```
rem LOAD NETWORK DRIVERS
lh LSL.COM
lh 3C509.COM
lh IPXODI.COM
VLM.EXE
```

The VLM file attempts to wedge as much of itself into extended memory (XMS) as possible as a first choice or if instructed to do so with the /MX option. Since a full complement of .VLM files can fill the VLM memory-resident portion to about 100KB, you should push as much of that overhead into high memory as is possible. The /ME option loads VLM contents into expanded memory (EMS), and the /MC option forces VLM files to be loaded into conventional DOS memory.

The VLM Files

A dynamic set of VLMs is available. One reason that the architecture encourages modularity is so that Novell and third party vendors can develop VLMs with additional functionality. The VLMs are loaded based on the instructions placed in the NET.CFG file. Required .VLM files perform a variety of functions.

BIND.VLM This VLM file handles bindery compatibility and services. It looks at the Preferred Server setting in the NET.CFG file to identify the file server the client will attempt to connect to first.

CONN.VLM This VLM file manages connection information, providing information to other client software and establishing connections as requested. It sets the maximum number of connections to eight unless another setting is specified by a Connections setting in the NET.CFG file.

FIO.VLM This VLM file manages access to files residing on the network. The PB Buffers setting in the NET.CFG file can configure this file for using packet-burst communications, which improve communications performance by accelerating the transfer of multiple packets heading for the same destination.

GENERAL.VLM This aptly named VLM file handles general VLM business. This file references the NET.CFG entry specifying First Network Drive.

In older versions of the client software, the DOS LASTDRIVE command was set to the last drive letter accessible by DOS (usually E, leaving F as the first NetWare drive letter). The VLM implementation sets the LASTDRIVE entry to Z and uses the First Network Drive line of the NET.CFG file to identify the first drive letter usable by NetWare.

IPXNCP.VLM This VLM file creates NCP (NetWare Core Protocol) headers, builds packets, and sends the "signed" packets to the ODI driver. NCP packet signatures are used to prevent unauthorized network access. The Signature Level setting in the NET.CFG file should be appropriate to the level set at the file server console. The default Signature Level on the client is 1, which signs packets only if requested by the server. The default Packet Signature Option on the server is 2, which signs packets if the client is capable of signing.

NETX.VLM This VLM file handles calls to API functions of the older NetWare shell. It provides backward compatibility for applications that expect the shell software to be loaded.

NWP.VLM This VLM file manages interactions with servers, including logging in and out, accepting broadcast messages, and dealing with the bindery or NDS.

REDIR.VLM This VLM file acts the most like the NETX.EXE file does, handling DOS redirection. REDIR identifies network calls and routes them to the appropriate NetWare process and allows DOS to handle its own calls. This feature gives the user the ability to use DOS and NetWare functions from the same prompt.

SECURITY.VLM This VLM file signs NCP packets and performs other packet security functions.

OTHER VLMS PRINT.VLM redirects printing from the workstation, allowing capture to network printers. AUTO.VLM allows automatic reconnection for NetWare 4.x clients that lose a network connection. NDS.VLM is used by NetWare 4.x for interfacing with the NDS global services. RSA.VLM is another 4.x-specific security module.

NET.CFG

The NET.CFG file, usually found in the \NWCLIENT directory on a local network drive, contains a variety of configuration options that are consulted when the network software is loading on the client machine. The most important of these options indicate the NIC driver in use and specify the appropriate frame type. VLM modules can be configured based on entries in this file, and optional VLM modules can be loaded. General network client configuration information can also be specified.

NETWORK CLIENT CONFIGURATION INFORMATION These settings are inherited from an earlier version of the NET.CFG file called SHELL.CFG. NET.CFG supersedes SHELL.CFG, but since all the SHELL.CFG configuration settings work in the new configuration file, you can copy the SHELL.CFG file to a new file called NET.CFG and add any additional options that are necessary. See Table 5.1 for selected generatl configuration options.

TABLE 5.I Selected General Configuration Options

OPTION	DEFAULT	DESCRIPTION
IPX Packet Size Limit	4,160 bytes	Reduces memory use by specifying smaller maximum packet size. Range from 576 to 6,500 bytes.
IPX Retry Count	20 retries	Increasing retries allows connectivity when networks drop many packets.
IPX Sockets	20 sockets	Some applications require more than the default number of sockets
SPX Abort Timeout	540 ticks	Increasing this setting from the default may keep long-distance connections from terminating prematurely.
SPX Connections	15	Specifies the number of SPX connections the client can use simultaneously. Mostly of interest for print server PCs, which need a setting of 60.
Cache Buffers	5 cache blocks	These 512-byte buffers cache files locally; adding additional buffers may improve I/O processing.
File Handles	40 open files	This setting controls the number of network files the client can have open simultaneously. Many database applications require more open files.
Local Printers	no default	This setting is most useful when there are no local printers (Local Printers = 0). Adding this line prevents Print Screen operations from being directed to DOS, which can hang the workstation.
Max Tasks	31 tasks	Controls the maximum number of tasks that can be simultaneously active. Windows and other multitasking environments can conceivably require more tasks, though I would be impressed to see this happen. The setting range is 20 to 128 tasks.

TABLE 5.1 Selected General Configuration Options (continued)

OPTION	DEFAULT	DESCRIPTION
Preferred Server	no default	This setting indicates the name of the server the client will attempt to connect to. Without this line, the client will attempt to connect the closest server.
Read Only Compatibility	Off	This is a rarely used option that allows read only files to be opened by a call that implies write access. Even with this setting on, attempts to write to the file generate error messages.
Set Station Time	On	This line allows the client to accept or decline the synchronization of the workstation's clock with the time set on the file server.
Show Dots	Off	DOS and Windows normally display the single dot (.) and double dot (..) directory entries, but NetWare does not normally display them on network volumes. Navigation in the Windows File Manager is easier if Show Dots is enabled.

NOTE: Additional settings can configure the NetBIOS emulation file when it is loaded. These options can be found in the installation documentation provided with NetWare.

ODI CONFIGURATION INFORMATION These options indicate the MLID driver in use and can specify hardware configuration, including the interrupt and I/O port address used by the NIC, the NIC's memory address, and the frame type used to communicate with the server. The LSL configuration can also be modified for use with the TCP/IP protocol stack. The ODI configuration is set using the following parameters:

```
LINK DRIVER drivername
     INT NIC_IRQ_setting
     PORT NIC_I/O_port_address
     MEM NIC_memory_address
     FRAME frame_type
LINK SUPPORT protocol_stack_and_frame_type
     BUFFERS number_of_LSL_buffers
     MEMPOOL LSL_buffer_size
```

Make sure your client frame type is correct for your network. If Ethernet 802.3 is the frame type running on the network, new client installations will sometimes be unable to locate a file server. This is because most installations now default to Ethernet 802.2. A server has to be using the same frame type as the workstation attempting to find it.

VLM CONFIGURATION INFORMATION These settings allow customization of the VLM settings when the VLM files are loaded. The following is an example of the VLM configuration portion of the NET.CFG file:

```
NetWare DOS Requester
     Auto Reconnect = ON
     Connections = 16
     First Network Drive = J
     Signature Level = 2
     Load Conn Table Low = ON
     Large Internet Packets = ON
```

Microsoft Windows

Microsoft's graphical user interface has grown up since its early implementation as a clumsy runtime GUI. Version 3.1, at this writing the most widely used iteration, is relatively stable, relatively easy to use, and extremely popular. Microsoft has leveraged its popularity into quite a marketing tool for its applications and future operating systems. Windows for Workgroups is a peer networking version of the software that also works quite well as a Windows NT client and interfaces relatively comfortably with NetWare networks. Windows 95 is a much-ballyhooed and long-awaited version of the GUI that nearly eliminates DOS as an underlying structure.

Microsoft Windows 3.1

Windows 3.1 is currently the most-used interface in the world of microcomputing. Most computer manufacturers and resellers bundle DOS and Windows with each system they sell, giving the GUI a major leg up compared to products like OS/2. Windows 3.1 is everywhere, and accordingly, most applications run by business users are Windows applications.

IBM is now bundling OS/2 Warp with its computer systems, a move that may increase exposure to Warp somewhat. IBM previously bundled only Windows and its version of DOS with its systems.

The biggest problem with Windows is that it is bolted on top of the DOS operating system. It is therefore limited by the memory constraints imposed by DOS. It adds some of its own limitations, however. Windows uses several different kinds of resource pools. As applications run, they use workstation memory, but they also use Windows resources. Even a system with 32MB of RAM can run out of DOS memory or Windows resources, and running out of either one will at the least prevent applications from running. At worst, you can experience a system crash and data loss.

From a networking perspective, very little network support is built into Windows. Limited printing and network connection management utilities are included; the core network connectivity is provided at the DOS level. The Windows Print Manager allows connection to network queues as shown in Figure 5.1.

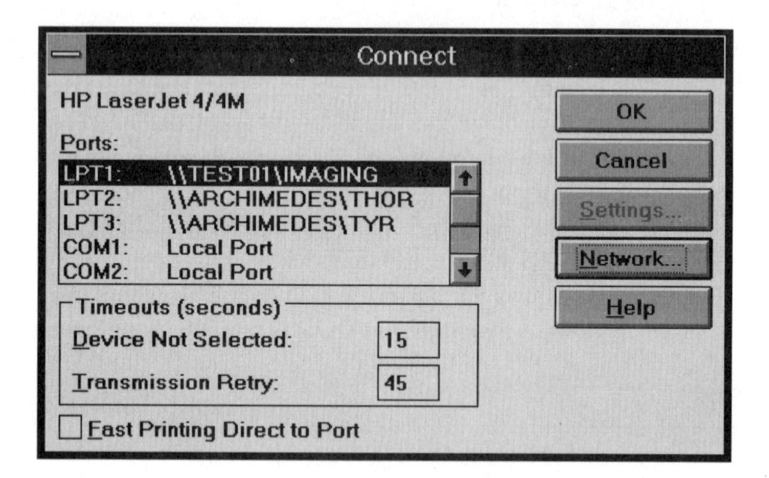

FIGURE 5.1 The Print Manager in Microsoft Windows provides some network support by allowing users to print to network queues.

The File Manager utility in Windows allows connections to NetWare file servers and allows network mapping as illustrated in Figure 5.2.

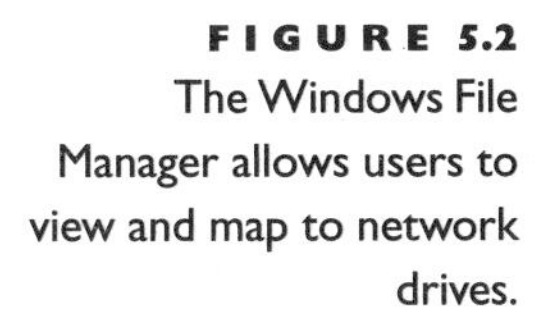

FIGURE 5.2 The Windows File Manager allows users to view and map to network drives.

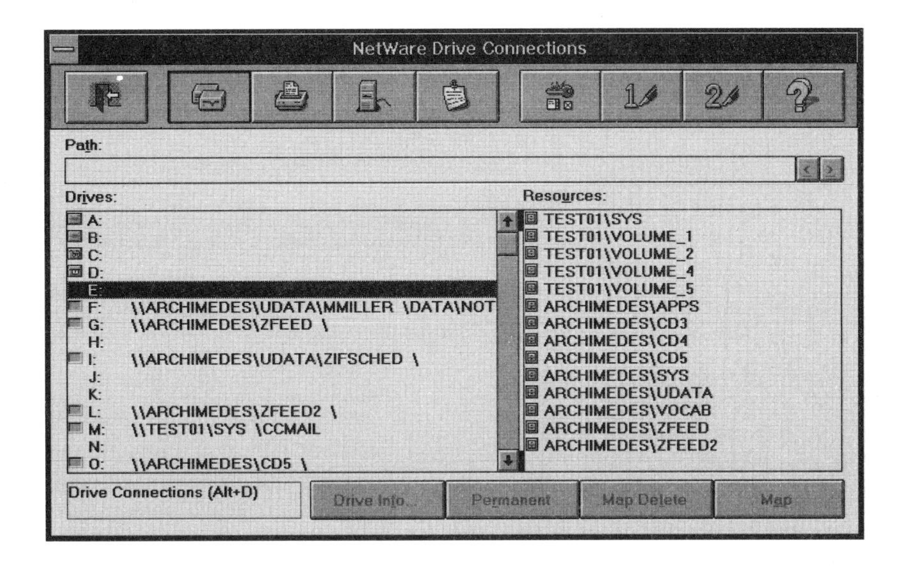

Network administrators looking at Windows client setups should be concerned with three issues. Windows needs to be aware of the network connection, the latest Windows and DOS client files need to have been installed, and the NetWare client utility should be running.

WINDOWS SUPPORT FOR NETWARE NETWORKS Check to see that the client machine has NetWare support installed in Windows by running the Windows Setup program from Windows or by executing the SETUP.EXE program found in the Windows directory. The Windows version of the setup program is shown in Figure 5.3.

FIGURE 5.3 The Windows Setup program indicates whether NetWare support has been installed.

Windows Setup

Options Help

Display:	QVISION 2000 16-bit 32K colors
Keyboard:	Enhanced 101 or 102 key US and Non US
Mouse:	Compaq Mouse/Trackball
Network:	Novell NetWare (shell versions 3.26 and above)

If the network support option indicates None Installed, install the appropriate NetWare version as shown in Figure 5.4. The options for the Windows shell version correspond to the shell or redirecter version in place at the DOS level.

FIGURE 5.4
The Change Systems Settings options offered in the Windows Setup program allow you to select the correct NetWare shell.

Change System Settings

Display: QVISION 2000 16-bit 32K colors

Keyboard: Enhanced 101 or 102 key US and Non US keyboards

Mouse: Compaq Mouse/Trackball

Network: Novell NetWare (shell versions 3.26 and above)

OK | Cancel | Help

UPDATING NETWARE AND WINDOWS FILES NetWare and Windows have a history of contention, especially when DOS applications or windows are open on the desktop. The worst manifestation of the process-level bickering between the two programs is referred to as the *Black Screen of Death*. The Black Screen generally appears when a DOS application is running on a NetWare-connected Windows system. Windows abruptly disappears from the screen, leaving a blinking cursor in the upper left hand corner of the screen. A cold reboot (pressing the reset button or turning the power off and on again) is required to restart the system, and any unsaved data is lost.

The Black Screen was widespread and was the subject of much Novell and Microsoft finger pointing. Fortunately, updates to Windows and NetWare software are available to eliminate this problem. Originally called DOSUP*n* and WINUP*n* (where *n* was an indication of the version of the patch files), these updates solve several problems and are now split into multiple files that can be selected based on the client configuration. Find the most recent update files, and create batch files to upgrade your user configurations. Doing so greatly reduces the support headaches you experience as a NetWare manager with Windows clients.

See Assembling Parts of the Puzzle, later in this chapter, for information on Novell's NetWire services, which are electronic sources of update files.

NETWARE USER UTILITY FOR WINDOWS The standard utility for Windows users is included with the latest client software and updates. It is better than the previous version and does a reasonable job of making servers, volumes, and printers available for Windows users. To connect to a NetWare server using the utility, click on the Servers button, highlight the server to attach to, and click on the Attach button. Figure 5.5 shows the Windows user utility.

FIGURE 5.5
Attaching to a NetWare server using the Windows user utility, NWUSER.

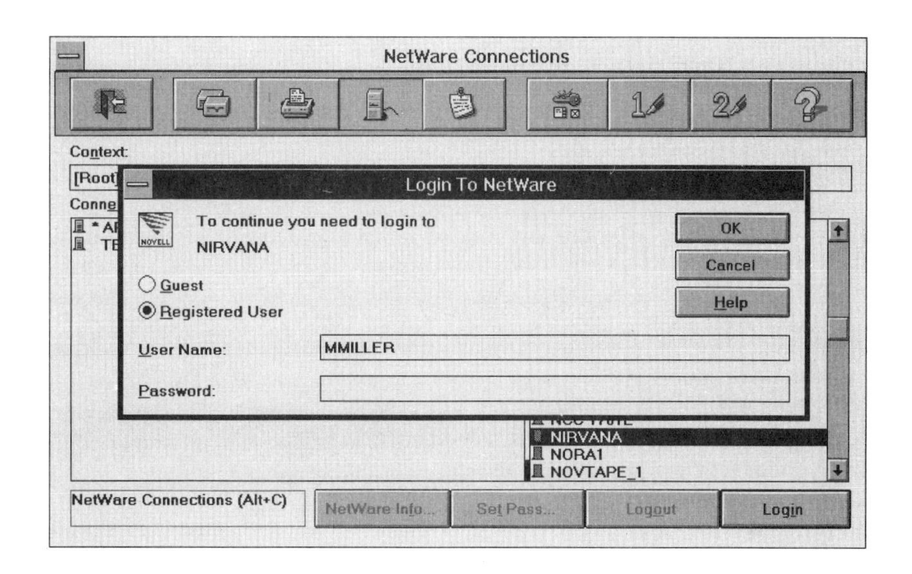

Printer capturing and capture configuration can also be performed in the utility, as can mapping to NetWare volumes and directories.

The connection between DOS shells from Windows and Windows itself is not foolproof from a networking standpoint. If your users running Windows shell out to a DOS prompt and then forget that they're running Windows, they can run into trouble if they log out of the network. Returning to Windows will cause a system crash.

Windows for Workgroups

Windows for Workgroups (WFW) is Windows with peer networking support and some minor interface enhancements. It is still DOS-based and relies on the NetWare software loaded in DOS. WFW 3.1 does not support the NetWare ODI drivers, though WFW 3.11 does.

After making sure that the network client software has been loaded in DOS, follow these steps to check NetWare support on a WFW system:

1. Start Windows for Workgroups.
2. Open the **Windows Setup**.
3. From the **Options** menu, select **Change Network Settings**.
4. Click on the **Networks** icon to display the installed networks.

Novell NetWare should be one of the installed networks, as shown in Figure 5.6.

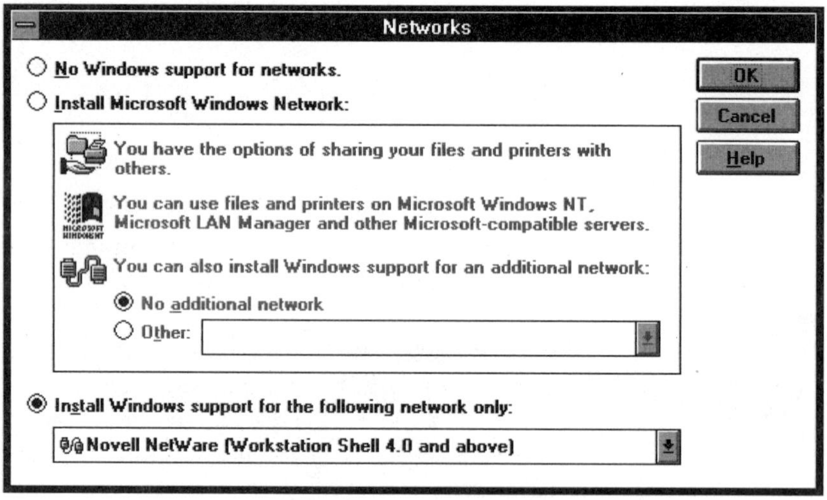

FIGURE 5.6
Network support can be selected in the Networks dialog box in Windows for Workgroups.

Windows for Workgroups modifies the CONFIG.SYS and AUTOEXEC.BAT files to provide NetWare support. The CONFIG.SYS file loads a driver to support simultaneous use of Microsoft's NetBEUI protocol and IPX. It also contains a LASTDRIVE setting that reserves certain drive letters for DOS and WFW.

```
DEVICE=C:\WINDOWS\MSIPX.SYS
LASTDRIVE=P
```

The AUTOEXEC.BAT file runs versions of IPX and NETX that replace the NetWare-generated files.

```
C:\WINDOWS\MSIPX
C:\WINDOWS\NETX
```

Follow these steps to perform further customization of NetWare's interaction with WFW:

1. Open the **Control Panel**.

2. Double-click on the **Network** icon.

This should display the **NetWare Settings** dialog box, as shown in Figure 5.7.

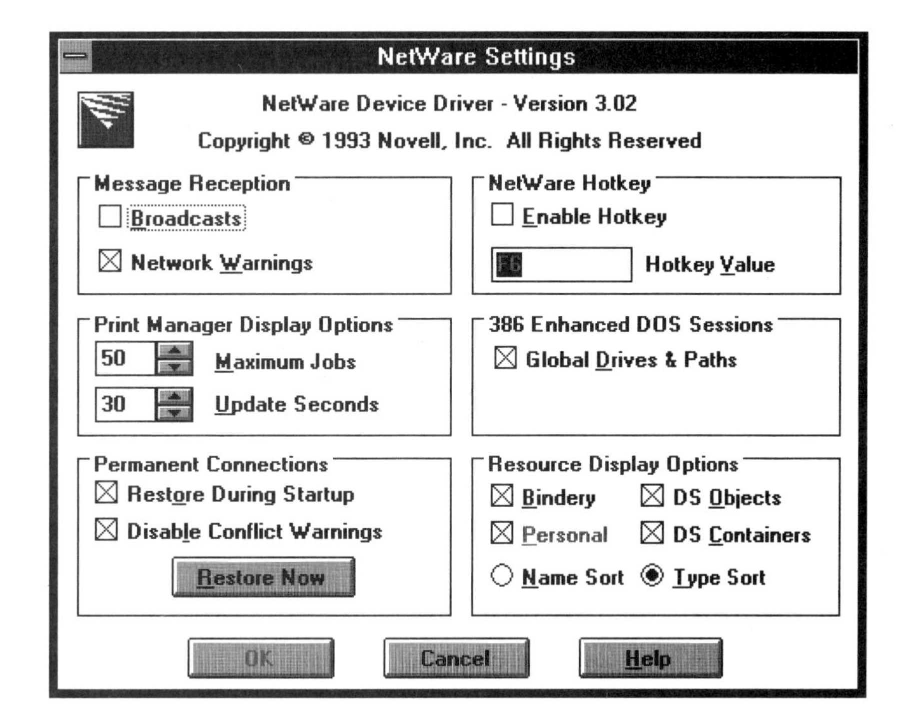

FIGURE 5.7
NetWare settings can be specified from the Network icon in the Control Panel.

Windows for Workgroups is not the fastest NetWare client system you'll find. Its performance is much better as a client to Windows NT.

Windows 95

Windows 95 is the next-generation version of Windows that eliminates all but the most obscure traces of DOS from the GUI design. Windows 95 is ready to run on client machines for NetWare networks, and it supports the NetBEUI, IPX/SPX, and TCP/IP protocol stacks. Support is also planned for VINES and other operating systems. Windows 95 also provides peer-to-peer networking services similar to those in WFW. Additional utilities planned for Windows 95 include tools to allow network client performance analysis and an SNMP agent to allow network management of client systems.

The Windows 95 network driver configuration screen is shown in Figure 5.8.

Macintosh

Apple's system software is a mature operating system with an outstanding GUI. It's prone to crashing, but that's hardly a unique criticism in today's operating system market. The Macintosh has built-in networking functionality and therefore doesn't require traditional shell or redirecter programs. The Macintosh Chooser utility can be used to access network resources once the file server has been made Macintosh-ready. Novell's NetWare Tools utility adds additional functionality.

Native Network Support

The Macintosh Chooser lists the available AppleTalk zones. As you select each zone, you can see the file servers associated with that zone. Double-click on the server you want to start the login process. The Macintosh doesn't require additional software on the client end; it runs just fine as is.

AppleTalk runs over several different topologies, including LocalTalk, EtherTalk Phase 1, EtherTalk Phase 2, or TokenTalk. Make sure the appropriate topology is selected and installed in the Extensions folder.

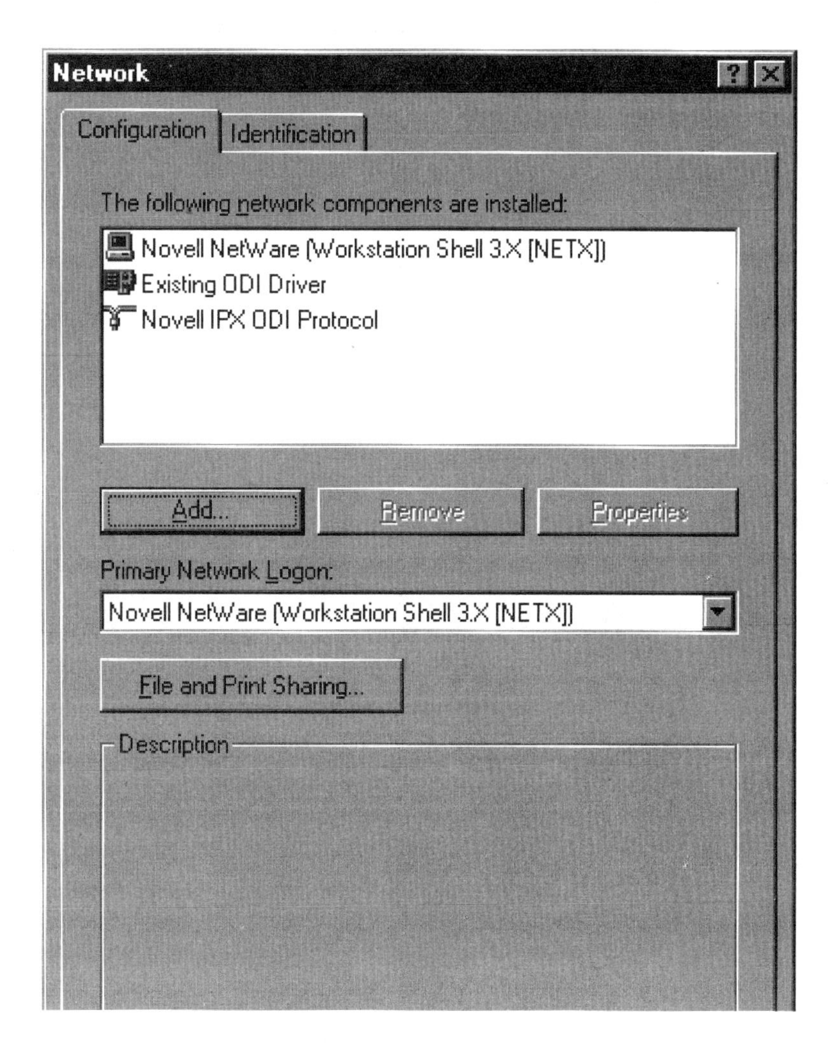

FIGURE 5.8 The Windows 95 network driver configuration screen allows easy configuration of client workstations.

Server volumes can be selected to be opened, and volumes can be tagged to automatically be added to the Macintosh desktop on startup. Network volumes are represented by an icon that looks like a file cabinet with the top drawer open. The icons can be dragged to the trash can icon to remove them from the desktop; removing all network volumes from the desktop causes a logout from the server.

Installing the Macintosh Software on a Server

The NetWare for Macintosh product is included with standard NetWare packages with a 5-user license, and a 200-user license package is also available. This package allows the AppleTalk transport to run on the NetWare server as an additional protocol.

AppleTalk Phase 2 requires the Ethernet SNAP frame type, while the older Phase I transport requires Ethernet II. The appropriate frame type should be loaded after the standard 802.2 Ethernet frame type running IPX in the AUTOEXEC.NCF file:

```
LOAD NE3200 PORT=300 INT=2 FRAME=ETHERNET_802.2
NAME=SLOT1IPX
LOAD NE3200 PORT=300 INT=2 FRAME=ETHERNET_II
NAME=SLOT1ETALK
```

The next step for establishing Macintosh support is to load the AppleTalk NLM on the file server. Each AppleTalk network needs a unique internal network number or range of numbers in decimal format. Each internal network number can have an associate zone name used to advertise network resources. The server is advertised in the first zone listed.

```
LOAD APPLETLK net=1492-1493 zone={"SYSTEMS","SALES"}
```

After the AppleTalk module is loaded, the protocol should be bound to a NIC. The zones should be included in the BIND statement unless a ATZONES.CFG file is maintained to relate internal network numbers with zone names.

```
BIND APPLETLK to SLOT1ETALK net=1492-1493 zone={"SYS-
TEMS","SALES"}
```

The AFP.NLM module provides file service for Macintosh users accessing volumes with the Macintosh name space installed. AFP autoloads when those volumes are mounted. ATPS.NLM is the AppleTalk Print Services process, which enables AppleTalk access to network printers.

Apple's System 6 software can only see volumes up to 1GB in size. System 7 doubles this limit to 2GB volumes. This has not traditionally been a problem for peer-networked or standalone Macs, but on NetWare networks with large amounts of disk storage, this can be an important limitation. Make sure the network volumes with the Macintosh name space loaded are not too large to be accessed by your clients.

NetWare Utilities for Macintosh

Novell's add-in client software provides additional access, security, and information beyond what the Macintosh System software includes. The main components are the NetWare Tools desk accessory and the User Authentication Method (UAM) security utility.

NETWARE TOOLS This utility is stored in the System folder and provides messaging similar to the NetWare SEND and BROADCAST utilities, information about file and directory rights, and user and group information. The NetWare Tools desk accessory is shown in Figure 5.9.

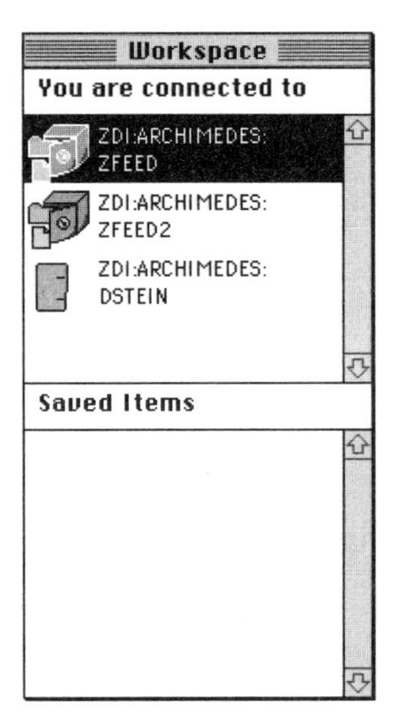

FIGURE 5.9
The NetWare Tools desk accessory allows access to file and user information.

The desk accessory can be used to list users, create users, and delete users, as shown in Figure 5.10.

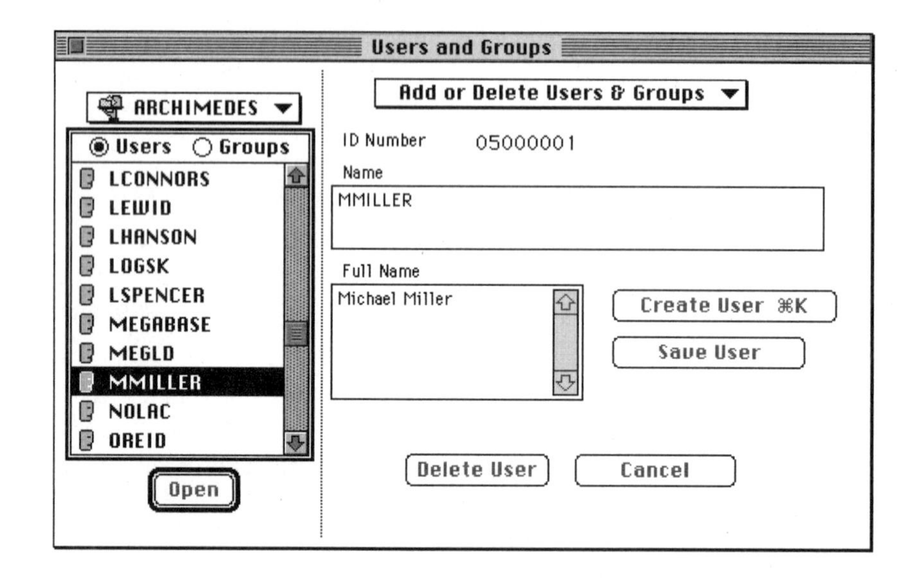

FIGURE 5.10
The NetWare Tools desk accessory can be used to view, add, and delete network users.

It can also be used to view and change group information, as shown in Figure 5.11. Although its appearance is dissimilar, this desk accessory is very much like the SYSCON utility in DOS.

If you look at the network volume information rather than the user information portion of the Tools, you find functions that list effective rights for volumes, directories, and files, as shown in Figure 5.12.

You can also use the Tools to assign individual rights to users or groups. An interesting feature of this utility is its use of rights "packages." These packages are sets of rights that are commonly combined for a particular function. Descriptions of the particular rights assigned by each package are displayed on the fly, as illustrated in Figure 5.13.

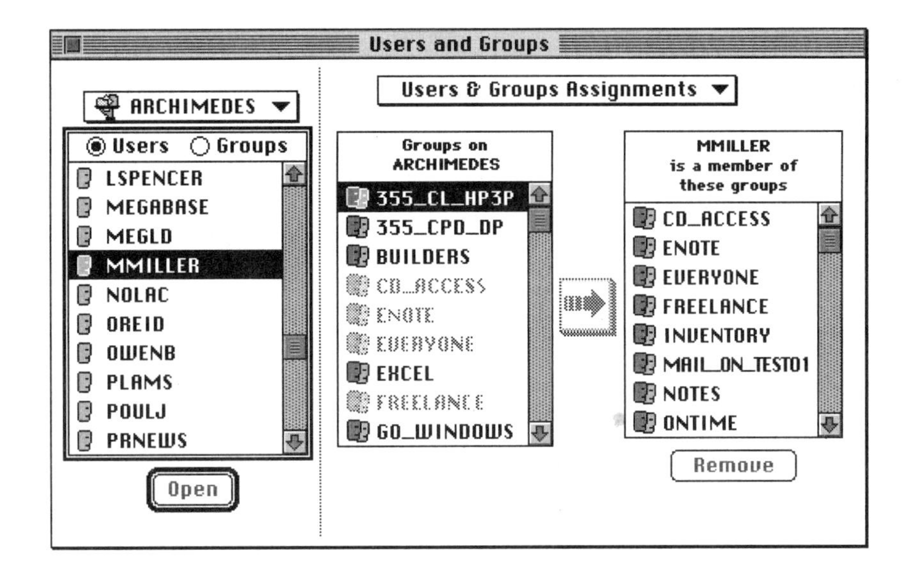

FIGURE 5.11 NetWare Tools can be used to view the groups a user currently belongs to and allows group additions and subtractions.

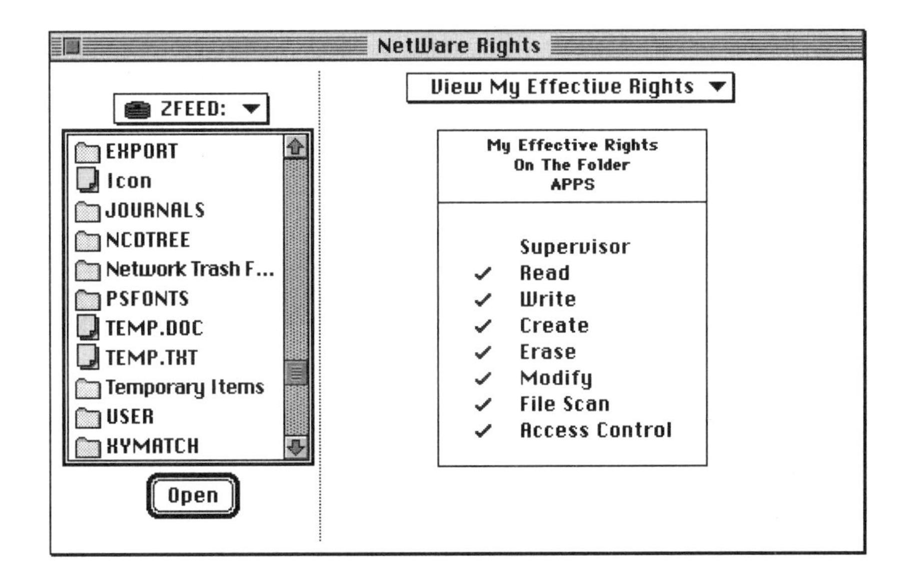

FIGURE 5.12 The NetWare Tools accessory allows you to view effective rights on a NetWare volume.

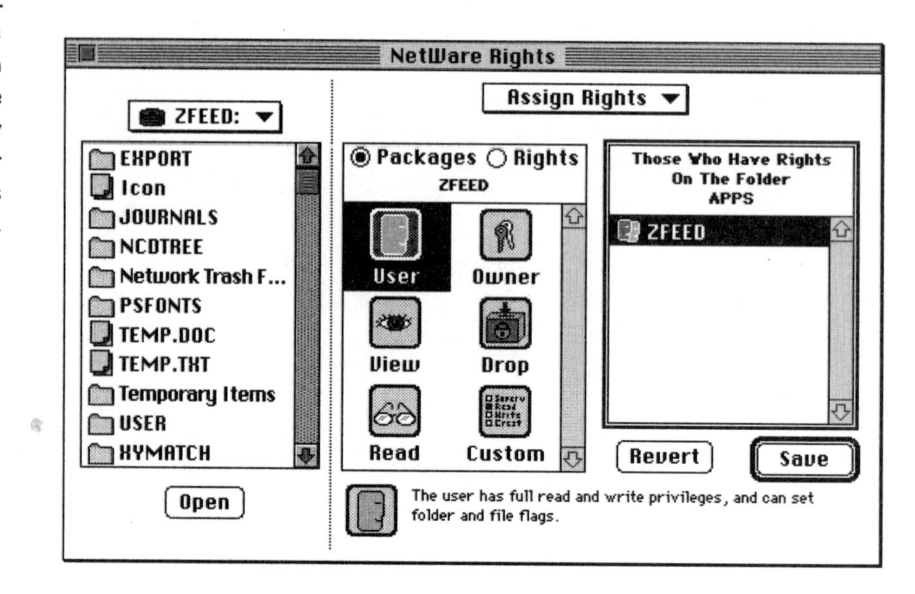

FIGURE 5.13 NetWare rights can easily be set in the NetWare Tools utility by associating users or groups with rights packages.

USER AUTHENTICATION METHOD The User Authentication Method (UAM) software resides in the System folder and provides enhanced password security. The UAM software includes the following features:

- Allows passwords up to 63 characters rather than the eight characters allowed by AppleShare.
- Uses NetWare's encryption on passwords before they head out onto the wire. AppleShare offers only plain or scrambled text.

OS/2

IBM's latest, greatest desktop operating system is OS/2 version 3.0, known as Warp. It is a robust multitasking, multithreaded OS that comes with useful applets and options for DOS and Windows support. Its NetWare support is very much like that in previous versions, which were also based on NetWare's OS/2 Requester. Although this implies a certain degree of stability in the underlying technology and although it does not require additional server configuration like Apple's system software does, awkward interactions are still to be found in the interaction between OS/2 and NetWare. The NetWare client utility for OS/2 is illustrated in Figure 5.14.

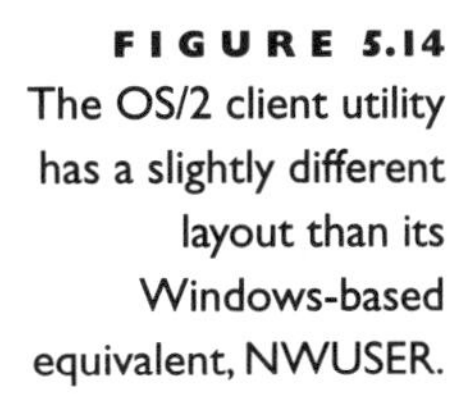

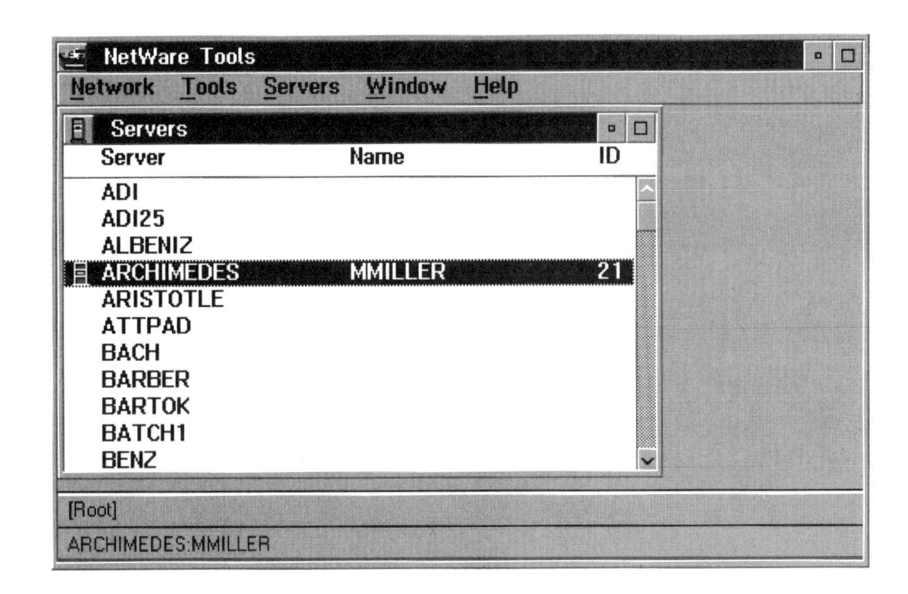

FIGURE 5.14
The OS/2 client utility has a slightly different layout than its Windows-based equivalent, NWUSER.

IBM's OS/2 Warp Connect attempts to make connecting to TCP/IP, IPX/SPX, and NetBIOS/NetBEUI networks easier and more efficient. It's a step in the right direction, but it lacks the ease of installation and use of an integrated network client. This is one area in which Windows 95 has an advantage over OS/2.

Assembling Parts of the Puzzle

Connecting an OS/2 system to a NetWare network requires several pieces available from different sources. The client software, ODI drivers, and other device drivers required to get the system running can require some searching and some troubleshooting. Furthermore, client system configuration can be a complicated and imposing task.

Novell's most recent version of the OS/2 client software is included on the NetWare 4.1 CD-ROM, but some slightly updated files are available from online sources such as NetWire, Novell's series of forums on CompuServe. An even better place to get Novell files is the Novell World Wide Web site. Those who are Internet connected but lack a Web browser can use the File Transfer

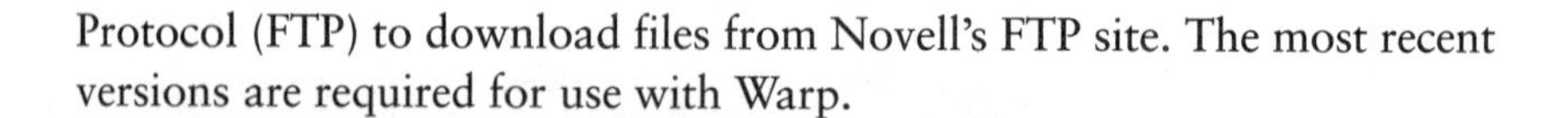

Protocol (FTP) to download files from Novell's FTP site. The most recent versions are required for use with Warp.

On CompuServe, enter `GO NETWIRE` *to get to Novell's forums. You can access the site ftp.novell.com via anonymous FTP. The Novell WWW home page is at www.novell.com.*

The ODI drivers provided by IBM and Novell are mostly for older, extremely common NICs. To get the client running properly, look on the bulletin boards, FTP sites, or CompuServe forums supported by your NIC vendor.

3Com drivers can be obtained from ftp.3com.com, which can also be reached via WWW at www.3com.com. Compaq drivers can be obtained from ftp.compaq.com, which can be reached via WWW at www.compaq.com. Intel drivers can be found at ftp.intel.com, which is pointed to by the Web page at www.intel.com. You get the idea.

The NET.CFG file used by an OS/2 system is nearly identical to the one used by a DOS system. A few more details may be of interest, such as Named Pipes support for the unroutable NetBIOS protocol IBM prefers, but most of the entries will be familiar. Although Novell includes OS/2 help files explaining the possible entries and listing syntax, building the files manually is more complicated than it should be.

Finally, a successful OS/2 connection requires that the rest of the system be stable. Despite OS/2's generally effective crash protection, the operating system can be finicky about differences in hardware, so as the administrator of a network with OS/2 users, be sure you get the most recent device drivers and configuration information available from your component vendors. Yet another reason to standardize workstation equipment as much as possible.

Using a Connected OS/2 System

After the system is configured and running, OS/2 works well. The standard NetWare utility allows users to attach to servers and map to drives, and network connections and mappings can be saved and automated using OS/2 .CMD files. The application is very similar to the Windows user utility.

One thing to be careful about is the difference between the OS/2 commands and utilities included on the NetWare server and the standard DOS commands and utilities. Although OS/2 can support DOS, native OS/2 versions of the NetWare programs are required for workstations attached through OS/2. These programs are found in the SYS:PUBLIC\OS2 and SYS:PUBLIC\LOGIN\OS2 directories on the file servers.

This chapter has addressed some of the connection methods and the idiosyncrasies of the most commonly used NetWare client platforms. It has given you the opportunity to see what software your organization uses to connect the desktop machines with the network you have already investigated and protected. Now that you have the basic network and client information, you're ready to progress to the next chapter to take charge of the network.

Taking Charge of the Network

Understanding the Role of the Network

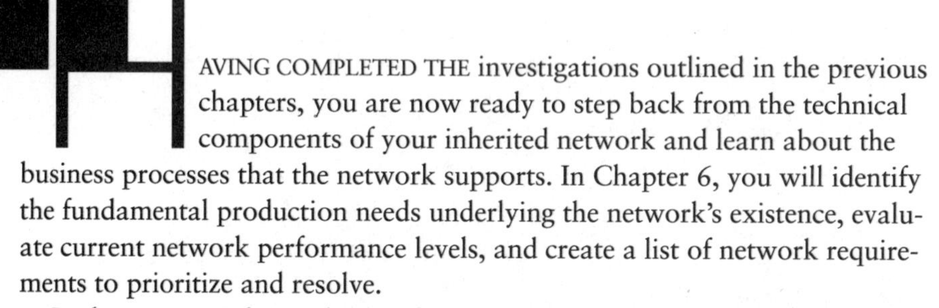

HAVING COMPLETED THE investigations outlined in the previous chapters, you are now ready to step back from the technical components of your inherited network and learn about the business processes that the network supports. In Chapter 6, you will identify the fundamental production needs underlying the network's existence, evaluate current network performance levels, and create a list of network requirements to prioritize and resolve.

In the section Asking About What Goes On in Chapter 3, you looked at documentation and talked to technical staff, managers, and production staff to understand how the network is used. In this chapter, you'll be going to the same sources and discussing similar information, but instead of determining what *is happening* on the network, your goal is to determine what *should be happening* on the network.

The Vital Information

IN INVESTIGATING HOW the network is used (and *should* be used), you'll gather information about the data being processed, the ways in which it is created and manipulated, and the network users who develop and implement the business processes. Use the following checklist to help you keep track of what you learn:

COMPLETED	TASK
❑	Identify the products or services your organization provides.

COMPLETED	TASK
❑	Locate the data generated in support of each product.
❑	Determine the procedures in use for manipulating the data.
❑	Assess how sophisticated the users who manipulate the data are.
❑	Prioritize network-related production tasks.
❑	Judge the network performance for each task.

Understanding Production Needs

THE MOST IMPORTANT aspect of the work you'll be doing is maintaining the tools that keep your organization running. Whether your network is used only for printing services and electronic mail or is a heavily utilized client/server operation with multiple users accessing data on multiple servers, you must understand the contribution of network capability—and stability—to the bottom line.

Finding this information is an iterative and time-consuming process. One way of making your search easier and more meaningful is to stratify it. Identify from the ground up each significant aspect of the business process. You should pay particular attention to the following four layers:

1. Data
2. Process
3. Personnel
4. Technology

Data is the building block on which the other aspects are founded, and its composition and handling requirements dictate the *process* used to create and deliver it. The complexity or special requirements of the process determine the *personnel* required to use and maintain the processes and data. Finally, your piece—the *technology*—is built on each of the preceding layers.

The personnel in some departments may make a case, directly or indirectly, for the importance of their activities as soon as you inherit the network. You may be approached with requests for system redundancy and increased bandwidth, or you may merely hear complaints about unreliability or sluggish system performance. In any case, the user wants a technology enhancement; the skill you need to develop is the ability to determine what the user is asking for and then to look at the data, process, and personnel to determine whether the technology in place is appropriate.

Assessing Data Requirements

Your first step in taking charge of the network is identifying the organization's business data. As a denizen of the Information Age, you'll be barraged with many competing issues, each vying for your attention. Many system administrators have a tendency to focus solely on technology; they incorporate new technology that seems useful or improved, but they lack an understanding of what the users need to store their data on or what kind of data they need to transmit over the network. Remember that you need to have a grasp of what appears on the lowest layer of the Systems Analysis Pyramid shown in Figure 6.1 before you can move on to the higher levels…let alone before you can begin to determine suitable technology.

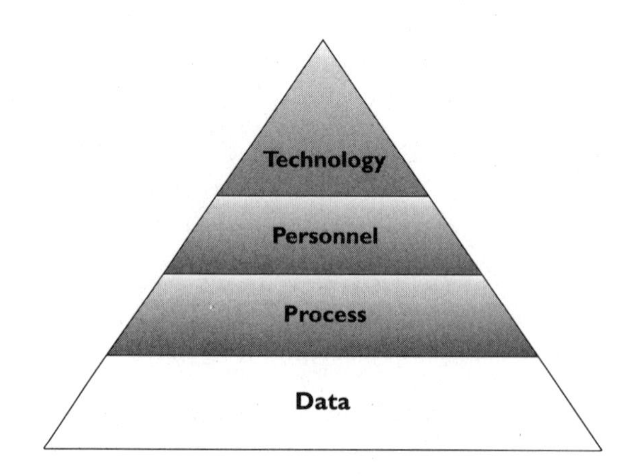

FIGURE 6.1
A network administrator must understand the data produced and used by an organization in order to tailor the technology to suit the business needs.

Data is a vague term in this context, but that's the nature of business. In some organizations, the data is easily identified as the result of research or the output of production staff. In other organizations, the nature of the data is somewhat more elusive. Customer contact information, repositories of programming code, accounting databases, and even resume files may be critical data that your organization processes and stores. Some managers are able to clearly explain what their data requirements are. Others won't even talk to you until they have a problem that keeps them from creating, accessing, or delivering their data.

Finding the Data

Because you cannot rely on the groups working with the data to proactively help you understand their requirements, you may have to use some of the information you've already gathered to launch your data analysis program. A server volume map like the one shown in Figure 6.2 can be a good place to start, because it helps you identify data already on the network.

Use the NDIR command in NetWare to display directory contents and view the login names of the users who created the data.

Some of the best people to talk to about the important data are executives. In many organizations, the executives know little about the details of procedures, personnel, or technology involved in the everyday production and manipulation of data, but they have a keen grasp on what comes in and goes out of the company and what contributes to the bottom line. If you can arrange interviews with upper-level management, you may find that their high-level understanding of what is important helps you focus on the low-level data that is most vital. Depending on your organization, of course, you may not be able to steal 30 minutes of time from upper management or you may irritate those in your chain of command if you do. Step carefully, and be sure to read the section Adjusting to the Support Organization in Chapter 7.

One of the easiest ways to find data and to gain a greater understanding of how your organization works is to read a list of products or services offered by your organization. Talk to the personnel in the marketing department about what they offer customers. See if you can find revenue figures broken

FIGURE 6.2
A server volume map can be a useful starting point for data analysis because you can use it to determine the origins of the data you have identified and keep track of it.

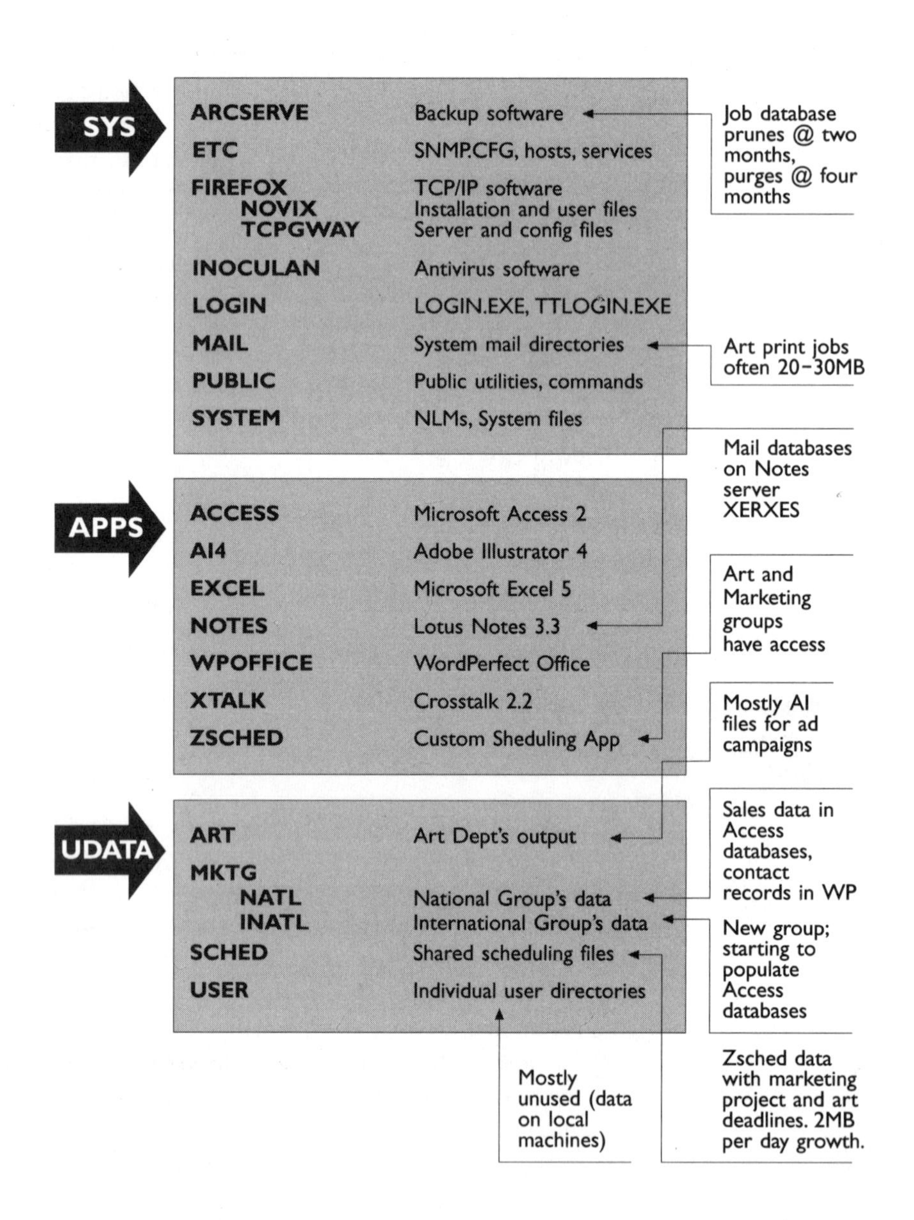

down by group and product line. This information may be difficult to obtain in private companies, but you should be able to find someone who can give you *relative* revenue information. You don't need to know how many billions of dollars your company's magnetic widgets bring in, but it would be useful to know that they generate over two-thirds of the company's revenue.

Improving the Handling of the Data

Your options for enhancing the business processes used to manipulate data are rather limited. Identification and prioritization of the data are mostly useful for determining which processes should be improved or tuned first. Use what you learn about the data to check your disaster prevention and recovery plans. Be certain that you are appropriately caring for the data that is most fundamental. Since your understanding of the business processes will evolve over time, you probably will eventually need to bolster system redundancy or add some spares in certain areas. Making these kinds of changes is normal so you shouldn't be wary of it.

The network is always going to be developing. Whether technology development or internal changes prompt network alterations, networks are dynamic creations that require ongoing understanding of both the latest gadgets and the business processes that make use of them. Stay in touch with industry news and the strategic changes in your organization by paying attention to plans and initiatives—and by keeping your ear to the ground.

Observing Business Processes

The next layer of the Systems Analysis Pyramid, illustrated in Figure 6.3, is business processes, which are performed by people and machines to create or manipulate the data you've already identified. Several factors influence how important a business process is to an organization, but no factor is more significant than the fundamental issue of how vital the data is. You should continue to ask this question of others and of yourself, because it ultimately prioritizes every issue.

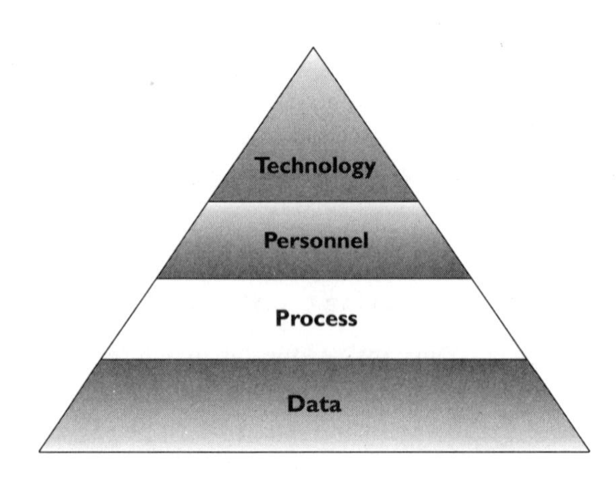

FIGURE 6.3
The processes used to create, manipulate, and deliver corporate data play a major role in determining the functions a network must support.

The procedures built around important data are often ready for improvement. You'll want to acquaint yourself with the processes involved in creating products or delivering services. Observe how the staff manipulates the data, noting any inefficiencies that you may be able to eliminate by improving the network structure or operation.

Pay particular attention to:

- Time spent on each process
- Environment and layout of each group involved
- Interaction between groups
- Problems and their resolutions

These factors have the most impact on how the network should work to support the business processes. Look for as much information about these factors as possible.

Understanding Production Cycles

You don't need to be an expert on the finer points of the production process, but you should know which groups do which refinements to the data processed in the company. If the data is information related to the manufacture of an antenna, for example, you might expect several groups to be involved in the different processes. The functional specifications need to be developed.

Then the layout documents are created. Functional changes are likely to be made, so engineering change orders (ECOs) are being created for incorporation into the layout. Prototyping will lead to tests being developed and test results created. Meanwhile, acceptability procedures such as calculating MTBF may be going on. Documentation and installation manuals are written. Customers are contacted, contracts are written, and revenue is generated.

Each of these steps is related to the same product, but each step involves different processes and some involve different kinds of data. Each kind of data is handled by a different group.

DATA	PROCESS	GROUP
Specifications	Development	Product Management
Layout	Creation	Engineering
Specifications	Modification	Product Management
Layout	Modification	Engineering
Prototype	Creation and testing	Engineering
Layout	Modification	Engineering
Product	Assembly	Manufacturing
Product	Testing	Quality Assurance
Product	Reliability determination	Quality Assurance
Product	Documentation	Technical Publications
Specifications	Marketing	Sales
Revenue	Creation	Sales

Believe it or not, this list is a simplified version of the processes involved in creating and selling the antenna. Dozens of different kinds of data may be stored in different areas of the network. Knowing how the pieces relate to one another helps you determine how to support the processes. For each set of related data, keep a simple flow chart that helps you understand what is happening to the data and where it needs to go next. A sample chart for the antenna manufacturing processes is shown in Figure 6.4.

FIGURE 6.4
This process flow shows the critical data and the processes involved in developing an antenna from concept to product.

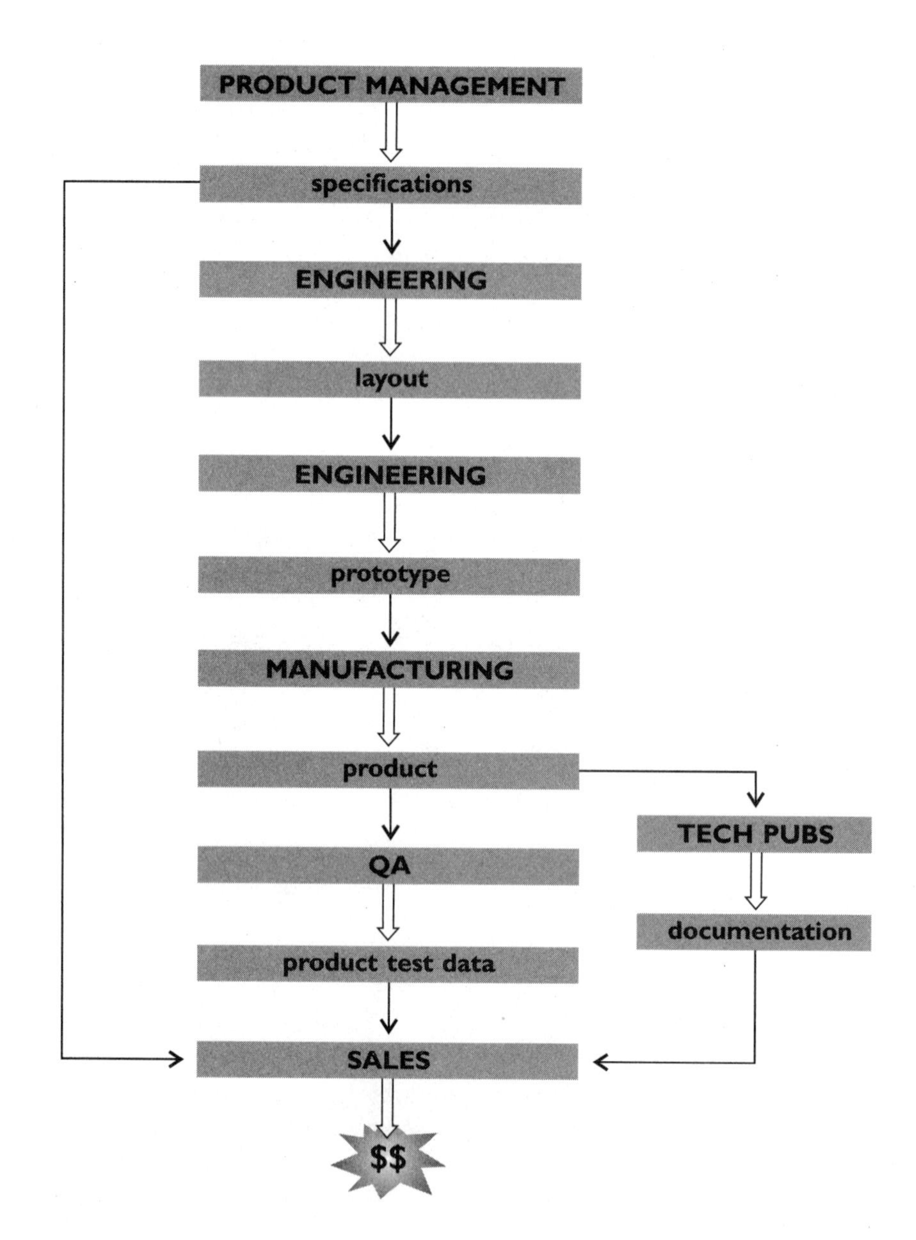

Determining the Location and Environment of the Process

Location refers to the departmental and physical locations in which processes take place. *Environment* refers to the technology and tools available within those departments and locations.

Each time data moves from one process to another, a demand is made on the technology. If the product specifications are delivered to the marketing group via sneakernet, there is obviously room for improvement in how the data is transmitted. If the specifications and the layout diagrams are stored in different database formats and cannot be electronically cross-referenced, there's potential for enhancement in this situation, too. If the ECO system runs on a proprietary standalone system, you can make a change for the better.

In each of these cases, however, the problem has a different source. If the sales group is connected to the same network as the product management group, you can resolve the technology use problem by creating a network directory accessible by the project management people and readable by the sales people. Tighter integration is certainly possible, but even a quick and dirty solution yields time and efficiency savings. If the sales staff is at a remote site, a connectivity solution may be in order. If linking the sites results in a savings of only one FedEx charge each quarter, however, most remote connectivity solutions would not be cost effective in this case. An understanding of your organization's data sources and processes helps you determine the most appropriate approach.

Using two closely related types of data in similar processes does not mean you'll have closely related tools to manipulate that data. Migration to client/server structures and software often involves significant changes, and changes occurring at different times may result in multiple software solutions. In the case of specifications and layouts residing in dissimilar databases, you'll have to determine how difficult it will be to find and implement a solution meshing the data. Balance that difficulty with the amount of time wasted looking in two places for related information. Don't forget to add the cost of maintaining two databases rather than one.

In the example I gave earlier of developing the ECOs on a proprietary standalone system, a non-networked system is a vital part of the production cycle. Since the payoff of a networkable solution is likely to be significant for the engineering staff, the question concerns implementation. Can the proprietary system be networked? Is that a better solution than moving the ECO system to another repository? Is it an effective short-term solution?

The Productivity Paradox

Some people question the value of investing in information technology (IT). One of the more famous expressions of these misgivings came from Morgan Stanley economist Stephen Roach, who was one of the first to discuss the belief that the money companies were spending on computing technology was not yielding the expected return on investment (ROI).

Results of a study of 400 large companies by researchers at MIT's Sloan School of Management indicate that capital investment in IT averages a 68 percent ROI. This compares quite favorably with the 10 percent ROI generated by other kinds of capital investments.

The return is not simply the result of automation; it stems from the business changes made possible by the technology. IT investment allows some of the traditional barriers from intraorganizational communication to be broken, providing the basis for unprecedented information-sharing and improved teamwork.

The researchers emphasize that business and technology planning must go hand-in-hand for IT investment to pay off. Although it is possible to make a situation more confusing by investing in IT, proper planning makes spending capital on computer technology a wise investment with quick return.

You're not likely to have the last word on the solutions to these kinds of problems. Nonetheless, you'll need to decide on the best plan of action, and you should be able to elaborate on why your plan is preferable to others. Gathering data and process information helps you make these kinds of decisions.

Understanding Departmental Interaction

Another aspect you should understand about the business processes is the way in which the departments associated with the same processes interact. Departments that are closely linked, such as the management and engineering groups developing the same products, are more likely to have process synergy that makes close network ties and similar software solutions preferable.

Keep an organization chart handy until you are familiar with the structure of a company. Note any dotted-line relationships or gather additional information about the interactions of the various departments within your organization.

Unfortunately, the different status of management and production staff often causes a dichotomy in the kinds of technology implemented. One of your initiatives should be to enhance communications between groups that handle the same data or work on the same processes. You may move toward this goal, for example, by simply adding appropriate groups or bulletin boards to your electronic mail systems. Enhancing communications may require the synchronization of hardware and software. Use your common sense and your knowledge of the products available, because however you achieve it, improved communications facilitates the production process.

Making Up Your Mind

Now that you have a handle on understanding the procedures that are most important to your organization, you're going to have to determine how you will deal with critical situations in the future. Your production cycle information tells you when the various procedures are supposed to occur, but what happens when something goes wrong? If the network goes down for a time and you cannot adhere to the production schedule, what do you do?

This question has to be answered according to the unique circumstances of each situation. Certain factors can help you make the right decisions. First, determine your production priorities. Consider the relative importance of the tasks confronting you, and then think about the specifics of the emergency at hand. Most importantly, know how to put your foot down once you've selected the best course of action.

PRIORITIZING PRODUCTION TASKS Determining production priorities in a vacuum is no problem. After you've figured out how much revenue is dependent on each product or service being handled correctly, you *know* what's most important. However, other factors, such as the ones listed below, can influence the order in which you prioritize production tasks.

- Most important products
- Availability of resources

- Processing time
- Likelihood of success

Before you decide which problem process to handle first, consider your window of opportunity for each process. If you need to make a delivery on a secondary product before a remote host shuts down at 8:00 p.m., you may want to defer delivery of the primary product, which doesn't need to be received until later in the evening. Another resource you may want to consider is human specialists. If your programmer is in the office until 6:00 p.m., you may want to give his partially tested production process a try before he goes home so he can make changes if necessary.

The processing time for each product or group of data should also be considered when you're addressing a problem. Jobs that run quickly are the ones you should take care of immediately. After they're out of the way, you can focus on other processes. On the other hand, processing time may cause problems with the resource window of opportunity. You may need to run the longer process first. Your understanding of the procedure itself comes into play when you make this decision.

You may also want to think about which processes are most likely to be completed successfully. Since the goal is to complete *all* the procedures, you should complete the ones that can be accomplished as quickly as you can. The rest of your organization will have little admiration for how long you spend attempting to resolve a situation; they are much more likely to want to know which data has been processed properly and which is still a problem. Try to get as much in the first category as you can.

Considering User Situations

Personnel appear on the next level of the Systems Analysis Pyramid, as pictured in Figure 6.5. Just as the processes are based on the data requirements, the kind of people you find creating and performing the production processes are determined by the processes themselves. At one extreme is the department in which many of the users have as much computing experience as you do. At the other extreme is a low-level data entry situation in which the user performs little analysis. Three of the aspects of user situations you'll want to consider are the hours and shifts the employees work, the various levels of user sophistication, and the availability of user resources.

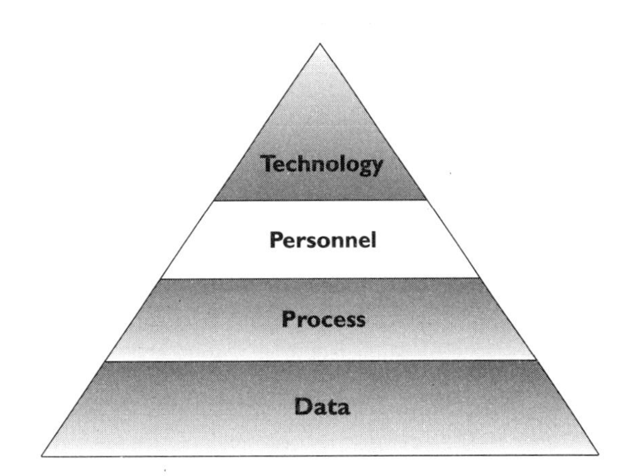

FIGURE 6.5 The nature of the underlying data and the data-manipulation processes determine the type of employees who create and perform the processes.

Work Shifts

The presence of users has two major ramifications for the network administrator. First, users mean network load. If your company runs shifts around the clock, the network is more likely to run into trouble. This isn't because problems occur more frequently at 2:00 a.m., although this sometimes appears to be true. A hub hanging and dropping users on a 24-hour network is *guaranteed* to stop processing, whereas a hub hanging on a network that's only in use for 12 hours a day may not cause a problem at all.

Another ramification of the presence of users is that it is preferable to be able to plan on some scheduled system downtime. If users are expected to be off the system from midnight to 6:00 a.m., that's six hours you have to attend to problems without interrupting anybody's work. A 24-hour workday requires advance notification or a workaround. Or it results in worker downtime, which means process downtime. And that costs money.

If you are in a situation in which users are on the system at all hours, consider enhancing your network's fault tolerance features to prevent costly downtime.

User Sophistication

User sophistication is of interest for two reasons. A user's procedural sophistication, that is, how well a user understands the process she works on, determines the kinds of changes you can make to the process without unduly disrupting production. A user's technical sophistication dictates how complex a technology solution can be and still be beneficial. Ascertaining a user's technical sophistication is usually somewhat easier than figuring out, as an outsider, how well users understand the processes they perform.

User Resources

The training and problem resolution resources available to the users should also be considered when you're planning on implementing a network-based enhancement to the production system. Users who have trouble logging into the network and remembering their passwords can be expected to have problems with a new system. If training is an option for these users, you may be able to successfully employ high-level solutions. Even simple resources, such as documenting procedures and including example screens and simple step-by-step instructions may be adequate.

If your organization has an established help desk or other assistance provider, such as a departmental tech guru, you may be able to explain the changes to the support staff, who in turn can help those who have problems. The more aid that can be given to users, the better. One of the primary payoffs of the Age of Easy Data is supposed to be the sharing of information; implementing that theory in your organization will make the network run that much more smoothly.

Determining Performance Levels

THE PERFORMANCE OF the network is measured in this chapter by the qualitative impressions of the users and by the thorough analysis you are able to provide because of your detailed understanding of the data, processes, and users in the organization. The Technology level of the

Systems Administration Pyramid is influenced by these underlying factors, as shown in Figure 6.6. To some extent, you must still rely on the users to provide you with information about what are acceptable performance levels, but you should be developing enough familiarity with the system and the business to enable you to see where the glaring problems exist. Or at least you should be able to determine the legitimacy of a claimed problem after you investigate it.

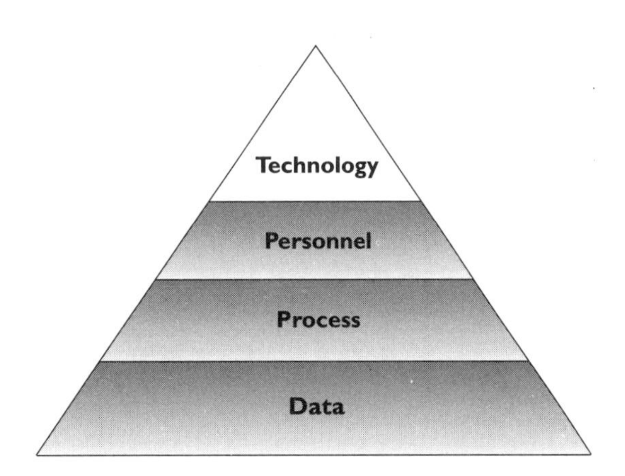

FIGURE 6.6 The technology used in an organization serves the needs of the users who perform the processes on the vital corporate data.

Develop a strategy for identifying or verifying network problems. Then establish a procedure for resolving problems in a reasonable period of time. You'll want to go beyond problem resolution, however, and develop a method for identifying areas that can be improved before a problem arises. Being proactive like this keeps the business running smoothly and keeps you interested in the job by allowing you to explore new solutions.

Identifying Problems

Problem identification is a technique that you'll need to develop and adapt to your particular organization and circumstance. The key is to actively and passively gather information that can help you locate network problems that affect data and processes.

One way of gathering this information is to keep tabs on the network itself. Look at each server periodically to see how many users are logged in, as shown in MONITOR's Connections in Use line in Figure 6.7. Make a note if the number of users connected is near or equal to the number of user licenses available. Check the processor utilization to make sure the server isn't struggling under the process load. Make use of more sophisticated tools (some of which are discussed in Chapter 14), if appropriate.

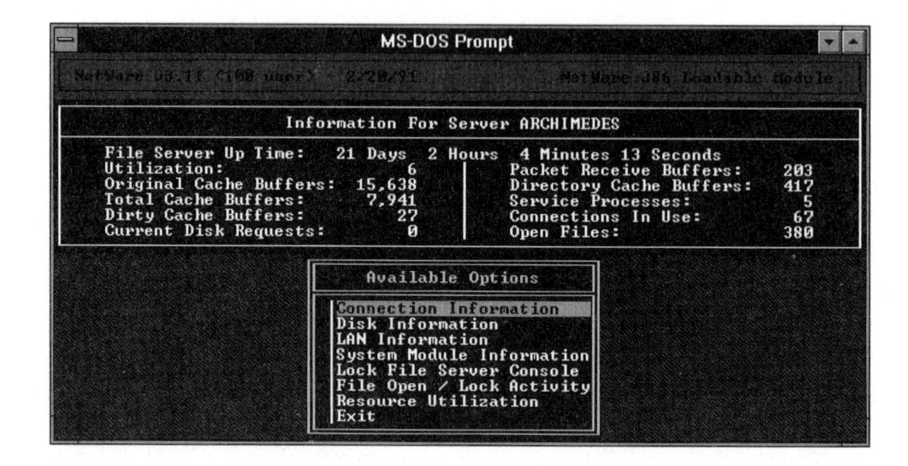

FIGURE 6.7 The MONITOR screen shows the total number of user licenses and the number of connections in use.

Another way to gather information about problems and potential problems is to check with the other members of the support staff. Communicate closely with other network administrators to ensure that you don't each hold a piece of information useful to the others. Check with the help desk staff to see what kinds of problems the users are reporting. Talk to the computer center personnel to see whether they've noticed unusual behavior. When you hear suspicious-sounding information from these sources, check any problems that could be widespread. If the reports indicate possible problems with important data or procedures, be sure to investigate further.

Finally, you can approach users for ongoing system information. If you make a change to a process or system, follow up with the affected users to ensure that the change is functioning properly.

In the end, your list of problems should indicate the source of information, the nature of the problem, and the relative importance for resolution, shown in Figure 6.8.

FIGURE 6.8
Maintain an ongoing list of production-related network problems that provides the information source, a description of the problem, and the priority of the solution.

Server	Production Problem	Priority	Technical Problem
SNYDER	Users can't run central database applications on Monday	High	Recurring problem with .DDL corruption
SMITH	ECO database keeps losing data	Vital	Server crashes trash open database files
WALDORF	Department can't access network several times each week	Vital	Engineering users thrown off periodically
THEDER	Belinda doesn't like beeping when logging in	Low	Fire Phasers too loud on her PC

Beyond Survival

McConnell Consulting's 1994 study, *Shifts in Enterprise Management Perspectives,* indicates a move in Fortune 1000 companies from responding to network emergencies and problems to enhancing the usefulness and efficiency of the technology. Technology managers at the 51 surveyed organizations indicate that they are spending three-fourths of their time on planning and enhancement functions. Eighty-one percent of the respondents believe that integration of business processes with network management would improve network value.

Problem Resolution

Your approach to problem resolution must take into consideration the relative importance of the problems, the relative complexity of the problems, and the availability of workarounds. Since production can be interrupted by something as easy to fix as a damaged patch cable or by something as complicated as an intermittent motherboard failure, you can't take a blanket approach to repairing problems.

You can take a blanket approach to applying the triage principle to the network, however. Always use your triage skills to resolve the problems that need immediate attention, and defer the problems that can wait. I'll extend that maxim in this case to add that workarounds, if available, should be applied if a full fix is not a reasonable option. For example, if your server is restarting itself periodically because the motherboard is partially fried, don't focus your attention on finding the problem…or even on getting the service contract fulfilled. Find another server with some disk space free, and store the relevant data. Then log the users into the alternate server. When resolving problems, find an alternative appropriate to your circumstances and resources.

As you resolve the problems you identify, indicate the resolution measures on your problems log, as illustrated in Figure 6.9. When time permits, you can review the problems and resolutions and determine whether alternate approaches would work better or whether a change in the network configuration or management would prevent the problem in the future. Add the finished log to your ongoing documentation.

FIGURE 6.9
Add problem-resolution information to your ongoing list of production-related network problems. Consider alternate approaches when you review the list later.

Server	Production Problem	Priority	Technical Problem	Past Response	Possible Solution
SNYDER	Users can't run central database applications on Monday	High	Recurring problem with .DDL corruption	1. Marked files Read-Only 2. Updated DLLs 3. Limited user rights to volume to Read and File Scan only	Replace SCSI disk adapter
SMITH	ECO database keeps losing data	Vital	Server crashes trash open database files	1. Lynne backs up DB files after lunch	Add database task to make backup
WALDORF	Department can't access network several times each week	Vital	Engineering users thrown off periodically	1. Reset hung hub 2. Swapped out hub	Replace old NIC connecting to hanging hub with new standard
THEDER	Belinda doesn't like beeping when logging in	Low	Fire Phasers too loud on her PC	1. Removed FIRE PHASERS from login script	

System Response Time

One area to keep tabs on is the system response time for the various network-intensive processes you encounter. Determine when network response time is unacceptable, and identify the users affected. The symptom may be perpetually sluggish performance from a single system, performance degradation when multiple users in a group connect to a network resource, or intermittent slowdowns. You may not get to decide that a remote site requires its own server rather than dial-in access, but by documenting the network behavior and how it affects the users, you can intelligently address the situation and make a recommendation. If you can pinpoint the area to troubleshoot when the problem is localized to a single user or group, you'll have a good start to resolving the problem.

Technology Status

You should have a process-oriented view of technology. In your professional capacity, your aim should be to maximize efficiency and stability while minimizing cost. Being a processor level behind the leading edge should not make you anxious unless the processes running on the year-old server are pushing the hardware to its limit. Similarly, the software you run needs to help the users do their jobs, nothing more.

Quite honestly, the process-oriented perspective on network administration is rather dull. However, it is the only reasonable way to approach the situation. Technology will continue to develop, and you will always be ogling the newest, fastest, sexiest toys at trade shows and in trade journals. The point is to find applications for the cool tools in your own situation. If you have production problems to solve, you will have a much greater chance of getting buy-in from those who develop your budget if you adopt the process-oriented perspective.

Network development is by necessity an aspect of business development. Understanding how the network tools are used by an organization's employees to create and manipulate the data that builds products, supports services, and issues paychecks should be a major focus for the administrator of an inherited network. In Chapter 7, we address the organization that provides technical support for the vital business processes investigated in this chapter.

Understanding the Network Administrator's Role

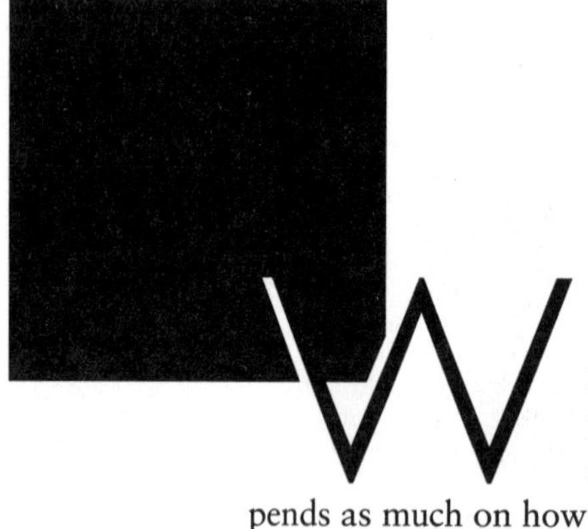

WHILE CHAPTER 6 considered the role of the network, this chapter focuses on the network administrator's position itself. The full description of what you do depends as much on how you interact with users, your peers, and your managers as it does on your job description. Maximizing the rewards of the position and minimizing its frustrations is a worthwhile goal.

For some administrators, the support role is the most difficult aspect of the job. Some people who take a network administrator's job have a background in independent, project-oriented work. In most organizations, the network administrator's role is not nearly as cloistered and quiet.

Other administrators have trouble fitting into the IS department within the organization that hires them. Centralized operations can be unnerving for those who have never experienced them, and the near-chaos of a distributed system can be frustrating for new administrators.

Finally, the network administration position is particularly visible to management, in part because so much typically depends on the smooth and speedy operation of the network. This visibility can be a heavy burden but can also be beneficial when used to your advantage.

The Vital Information

THE MOST IMPORTANT issues covered in this chapter are those relating to your department's structure. Understanding the kind of support group you're a part of is necessary for you to make the best use of your time. The composition of the IS group dictates the level of interaction you have with users, the responsibilities you are given, and the problems you're likely to encounter.

COMPLETED	TASK
❑	Define the central point of support.
❑	Develop a method for handling hardware and software requests.
❑	Develop a standard system configuration.
❑	Create a list of supported applications.
❑	Identify executives and high-maintenance users.
❑	Prioritize problems and assign appropriate response times.
❑	Distinguish central IS tasks from distributed IS tasks.

Adapting to the Support Role

IF YOU HAVE made it to Chapter 7 without knowing with absolute certainty that you're in a support role, you're either not employed as a network administrator or you're reading very rapidly. User issues arise daily in all but the simplest of networks, and they're not uncommon even in the simple ones. Not everyone springs from the womb ready to be at the beck and call of every nitwit and numskull in the company.

All the same, network administration is about providing a service for your company's employees. Fortunately, you can use certain techniques to keep from being driven to distraction on a daily basis. An important aspect of managing the support role is creating guidelines for handling interactions with users. Another important aspect of managing your role is determining support levels appropriate to the network functions in place and the business needs using those functions.

Defining Interactions with Users

Very small organizations and very isolated networks may support few enough users that most network administrators could handle all the client systems and configurations, answer all questions about the software in use, and still have time to run, tune, and expand the network. If you have more than 30 users, don't even bother trying to do it all alone. You need help, even if it's just an administrative assistant queuing up the service calls and questions and passing along the most important requests.

One of the most important skills to learn and practice is that of delegation. If your network is large enough to merit an assistant for you, give him the tasks you prefer not to do and that don't require your personal involvement.

Most organizations take a more stratified approach to technical support, as we will discuss later in this chapter in the section Adjusting to the Support Organization. Regardless of the specifics of your organization, you'll want to make sure that the channels of communication are clearly defined so that the users know where to call and what to expect. You'll also want to cater to the particular needs of any corporate executives in your purview. Finally, you need to determine an approach to supporting the whiny or perpetually angry users who seem to grace every organization.

Defining Channels of Communication

You may already have a defined role with respect to your network users. Kudos to your organization if that's the case, but don't get too comfortable yet. Even if your network doesn't change in the time you manage it (and let's hope it does), your users are changing, and there's nothing you can do about it.

Take a trip through your local computer superstore some Saturday afternoon. Oh, you'll find plenty of geeks and cybercowpokes who look a powerful lot like you do, but you'll also see kids, retirees, and even a middle manager or two. In short, technology is starting to reach out and touch everyone. And whether Newt Gingrich puts a laptop in every pot...er, lap, declining prices and increased exposure are going to bring computer technology to even more people.

What does this have to do with your users? Take a look at them. They're seeing OS/2 commercials during football games. Their children are programming in Pascal. They want Web browsers and Usenet. They've become aware of technology outside the scope of memo writing, order entry logging, and budget spreadsheet calculations. Some of them are as interested as you are in the new technology that's out there, and if they see you as a resource, you can expect they're going to ask you about it.

All of these factors are positive. The problem is distinguishing the technology that is personally interesting from the technology that is professionally useful. One of your responsibilities as a network administrator is to make that distinction. The process of determination will be easier if you can consider the issues rationally rather than being badgered by users, which means you need to determine the "rules of engagement" before problems arise rather than afterward. Here are some suggested guidelines:

- All support calls must be made to one location.
- Requests for hardware or software must be made in writing.
- New client systems will use standard configurations.
- Only approved applications will be supported.

CENTRALIZED USER SUPPORT Having a single point of contact for the network users is beneficial to both parties involved. As shown in Figure 7.1, the users need to remember only one phone number and one process, while you and any other support staff personnel do not have to answer each client's call and redirect it to appropriate channels. Instead, you can spend your highly valued time on keeping the data flowing quickly and efficiently. If you have a multitiered support organization, all levels of support calls should be routed through the single source. Just be sure to compensate the central support person properly. First-level support is generally neither fun nor terribly rewarding, but quality support at that level makes life easier for you and your users.

WRITTEN REQUESTS FOR PROCUREMENTS You should also insist that users submit their requests for computer products in writing. A common-sense step provided to ensure accountability in the event that someone haphazardly requests hardware or software, it also ensures that you won't be confronted with any surprises in your network's future—new servers nobody told you about or unusual client configurations. Be sure to familiarize yourself with your company's procurement and return procedures.

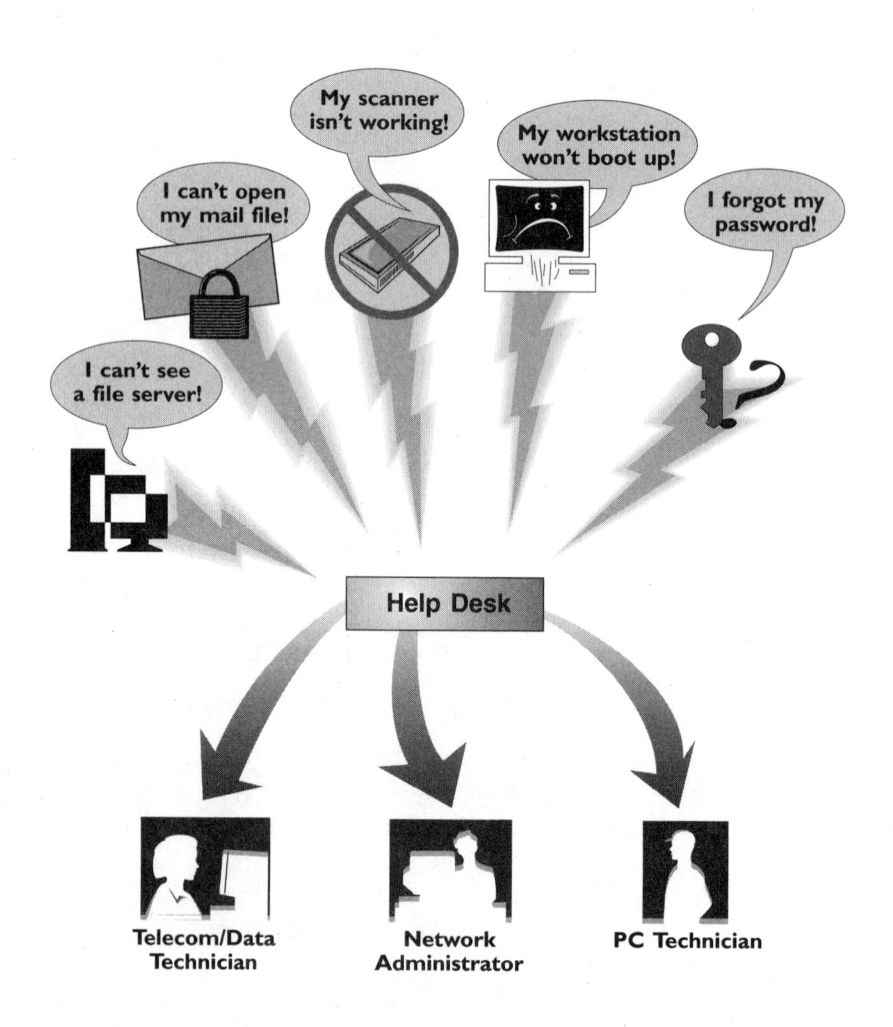

FIGURE 7.1
Centralized user support makes resolution of system problems easier for users, who need to remember only one telephone number, and for support personnel, who can concentrate on their areas of specialization.

STANDARD CLIENT SYSTEMS When users need to obtain new hardware to connect to the network, make sure they order standard configurations. This guideline naturally requires that you determine a standard configuration. If your organization already has a standard computer description, take a look at it. Look at the price per unit, and find out about the service included. See if the components are ones you have used before or have heard positive comments about. Check to see that adequate amounts of memory and hard disk space are being obtained.

A common system standard is a PC with a DX/2 or DX/4 processor running between 66 and 100 MHz, with 8MB of RAM, a 340MB hard disk, and a 15" monitor. This configuration is rather skimpy, especially considering the declining hard disk and microprocessor prices. A 75 MHz to 100 MHz Pentium system with 16MB of RAM and a 500MB hard disk, equipped with a solid NIC like 3Com's 3C509, is a better bet.

If your organization does not have a system standard, consider your options. Check with local vendors to see whether you can negotiate favorable service contracts and pricing if you standardize on their products. Look at the price and performance of some of the widely distributed systems. Pick up a copy of an ad-riddled publication such as *PC Magazine* or *Computer Shopper*, and look at the prices and components available from mail-order firms.

Whether or not the approved configuration is new, make sure the appropriate people in the IS group—client service management, help desk management, and IS management—review it and distribute it to departmental managers.

Standardized servers and other networking equipment are discussed in Chapter 17, The Hard Stuff: Hardware Upgrades to Consider.

SUPPORT FOR APPROVED APPLICATIONS This step may seem a little extreme, especially if you have a relatively small or relatively unsophisticated user pool. Unfortunately, one of the by-products of the new awakening to technology is that people have their own tools of preference. If you're primarily supporting users running a custom-designed production application in Windows, the last thing you want is to be configuring workstations for the oddball Macintosh user or Norton Desktop aficionado. You don't want to be so inflexible that you won't consider alternative software, but you need to make it clear that you cannot support operating systems or applications that aren't on the approved list.

The standardized desktop is not a necessity in most organizations, but a certain level of homogeneity is advantageous for you and your users. You can avoid the frustration of dealing with very unusual system configurations, and your users can take training sessions, share productivity tips, and work with the output their colleagues provide.

Generating the approved list requires that you select applications that are suited to the business needs you identified in Chapter 6. Since most of the mainstream packages offer the same feature set with minor differences, select the applications that make the most sense to you. Remember, too, that file format compatibility between *types* of applications can be useful. This is one reason that suites are so popular; integration between suite packages is generally better than the interaction you can coax from a mixture of applications from various vendors. Keep in mind the installed base for each of the software packages you specify, and arrange training for users who want to migrate to the "approved" tools. Your specifications for approved applications could look like the following:

FUNCTION	APPROVED APPLICATION
Word Processing	WordPerfect
Spreadsheet	Excel
Database	Microsoft Access
Electronic Mail	cc:Mail
PIM	Lotus Organizer
Page Layout	QuarkXPress
Drawing	Adobe Illustrator
Presentation	Freelance Graphics

I am not suggesting that these particular applications are the ones you should purchase; these are popular packages that may or may not be appropriate for your organization.

THE NEEDS OF EXECUTIVES Considering special executive needs is not to be confused with kissing up. Whether you like them or get the willies when they're nearby, you almost always need to treat executives differently than you treat your other users. On the most basic level, this means you shouldn't roll your eyes when they ask a stupid question. In general, an approach that is respectful of an executive's time and computing needs will be well received.

The Peter Principle holds that workers are promoted to their level of incompetence. In other words, you continue to be promoted until you're no longer doing a good job. Some companies battle this phenomenon by adding one more promotion...to a "special projects" role in which the Peter Principled employee can do no harm.

Not every executive reciprocates with respect, and like other users, many find ways to irritate or befuddle you. Do not expect a high level of technical sophistication from the average executive, but don't assume that lack of computer savvy means a general lack of intelligence or common sense. As I've mentioned before, the strategic level of thinking and planning most executives are engaged in can be useful to you, so try to learn which business aspects concern each executive and what their collective needs entail.

Greasing Squeaky Wheels

My first response to people who are always agitated and griping is to ignore them. I have to suppress this urge on a daily basis when dealing with coworkers whose basic approach is confrontational. The best way to deal with these users is to give them the attention they need until they are quiet. Most of the tirades and fits thrown in the workplace stem from genuine frustration rather than a need for attention or separation anxiety. By recognizing this general principle, you can avoid exacerbating problems with users who are accustomed to raising a stink.

The Biblical admonition that "a soft answer turns away wrath" is often useful when dealing with a noisy user. When you've been around for a while and have gotten to know the personalities involved, you may find that there are crackpots who should be ignored. Initially, however, you should assume that users are not interested in excuses, they want results.

I was once supported by a tech who would happily agree to do anything I asked and then wouldn't return to help me and wouldn't leave a voice mail or send e-mail. If I cornered him at the coffee machine, he would look apologetic and promise to get back to me. I would have been much happier if he had told me he had no time, inclination, or ability to help me. I just wanted my problem solved. Having found myself with the shoe on the other foot, I try to keep my users up to date on the status of their requests.

Another way to make use of loud users is to involve them in a feedback process. Consider them for usability surveys and pilot projects. Be sure to solicit their input on the state of network support. Quite often, the realization that they are being heard quiets the outburst-prone users.

Providing Appropriate Support Levels

Another aspect of the support role that can be difficult to adjust to is the prioritization and turnaround aspects of the work. Regardless of whether you're new to the service role, the prioritization, response, and resolution process is your friend. The system allows you to track incoming and ongoing problems, communicate resolution status to the users, and ensure complete resolution of the problems.

Prioritization and Turnaround Times

The most important aspect of the support-level system is prioritization. To implement the system, you need to first determine the appropriate response times for the problems that are reported. Your response categories may look like the following Priorities list:

LEVEL	DESCRIPTION	TURNAROUND TIME
1	Critical Work Stoppage	3 hours
2	Process Hampered	1 day
3	Upgrades, New Installations	3 days
4	Projects	Varies

If you can support faster turnaround times, go for it. But make the turnaround time something reasonable—an amount of time you can be held to. Determining the priorities of user-reported problems involves some of the skills described in Chapter 6, such as weighing the time required to resolve a problem against the importance of the process being held up by the problem.

Response

After you create and distribute your Priorities list and the calls for assistance start rolling in, you'll have to assign each problem a priority level. Next, you'll need to contact the user who reported the problem to let her know you're aware of the problem and the time frame in which you anticipate it being resolved.

If you cannot resolve the problem in the time frame you specified in the Priorities list, be sure to inform the user. Try to avoid this situation by realistically assigning priorities, but when it happens, have the courtesy to inform the user of a delay. Then get cracking on resolving the problem.

Resolution

After you have fixed the problem, make a note of the completion date and time, and inform the user that you have eliminated the error. Ask the user to check back with you if the repair does not work so that you'll know the problem still exists. Ideally, you'd like the user to test the process while you're still around to ensure that it runs properly.

Adjusting to the Support Organization

INTERACTING WITH USERS is not the only sticky part of an IS job. As a network administrator, you have to figure out how your work relates to the tasks performed by the other members of your IS organization. The single largest factor contributing to the atmosphere in your organization is the degree of centralization implemented by the IS department.

Long before personal computers arrived on the scene, business used computers for calculations and other processes too complicated or lengthy to efficiently be completed by humans. The hardware itself could be delicate, and the software was anything but user-friendly. Although the NetWare console prompt can be an imposing sight to a new operator, it is much more accessible as an interface than the punch cards, tapes, and wire recording devices found on early computer systems.

The combination of the black art of running a system and the relative sensitivity of the computer equipment itself made a centralized computing center desirable. Since most users requested output from computer operators and programmers and since many processes had to be programmed each time they were run, end-users had no need for—and no interest in—direct access to the computers. An example of a centralized computing center is illustrated in Figure 7.2.

FIGURE 7.2
Centralized computing centers typically include mainframes or minicomputers, programming staff, and operations staff.

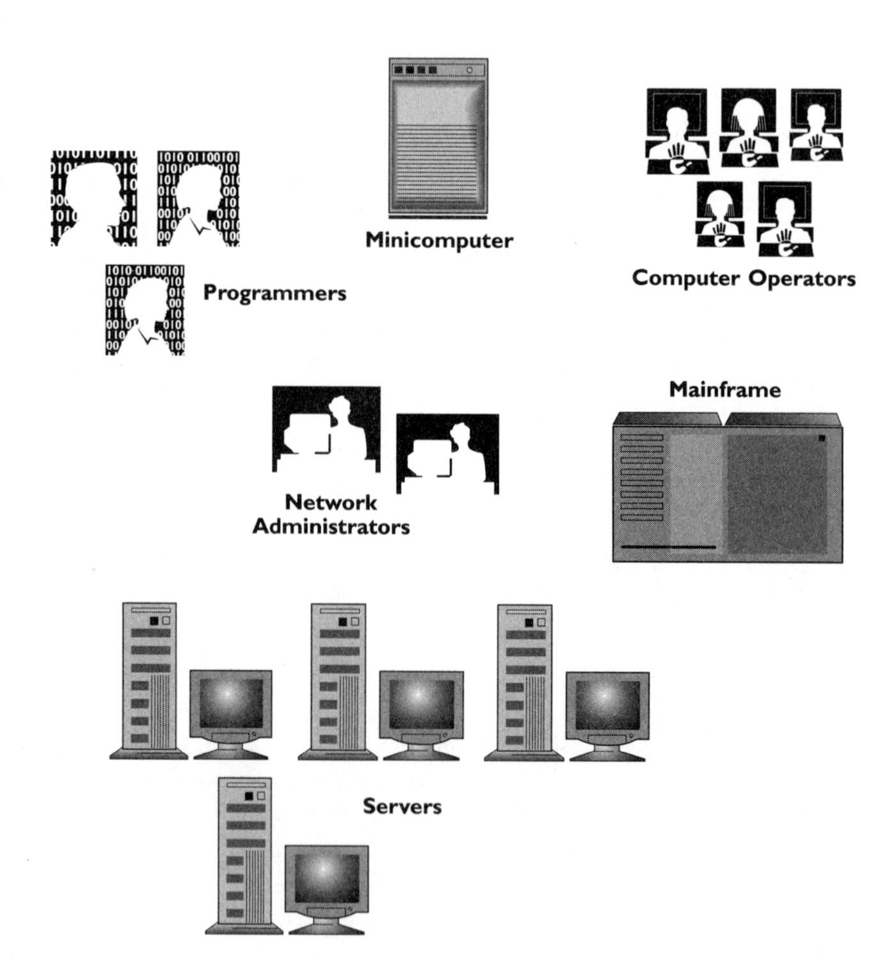

Even when terminals began appearing on users' desks or in central areas, they were used for entering data or directly requesting reports to be run on central databases. Output was generally created on line printers in the computer center, which remained the heart of systems management.

When the personal computer became more widespread in the corporate environment and when users began to define their own reports and print their own memos, tables, and graphs on their own printers, the nature of centralized computer management did not often change. Personal computers were a sideline for many IS departments—and PC support personnel often fell under different management than that of the operators of the heavy metal in the computer room.

The advent of PC networks has merged the two areas of technical support and has brought back certain aspects of the "glass house" enveloping computer equipment. Many of the mainframe and minicomputer systems that remain in use have been linked to networks and act as data repositories or still retain their original functions as legacy systems. A typical computer system structure is shown in Figure 7.3.

More importantly for most system administrators, users once again rely on systems that are beyond their control. When applications are stored on disk volumes that cannot be written to by end users, the applications have moved out of the control of the PC user and back into the domain of the computer center. One advantage of this move is central management of application usage (for licensing purposes, for example). Another advantage is that many applications can be efficiently run from the network, saving megabytes of space on users' local drives. These advantages come at the cost of greater responsibility for the network administrator, who now must ensure that appropriate access is maintained for the users who rely on the applications.

Many organizations have relatively few local printers because high-capacity networked printers can efficiently serve many more users. Additional advantages of this move are fewer points of potential mechanical failure and fewer configuration problems. On the other hand, more users cannot print when a single unit fails.

These examples demonstrate the trade-offs of the centralized systems, but the traditional centralized IS department involves more than the distribution of hardware and access rights. The organizational structure of a business that has been served by a centralized technical operation is of particular interest to the new network administrator.

FIGURE 7.3 Modern computer networks often include servers, superservers, and minicomputers or mainframes in a central location.

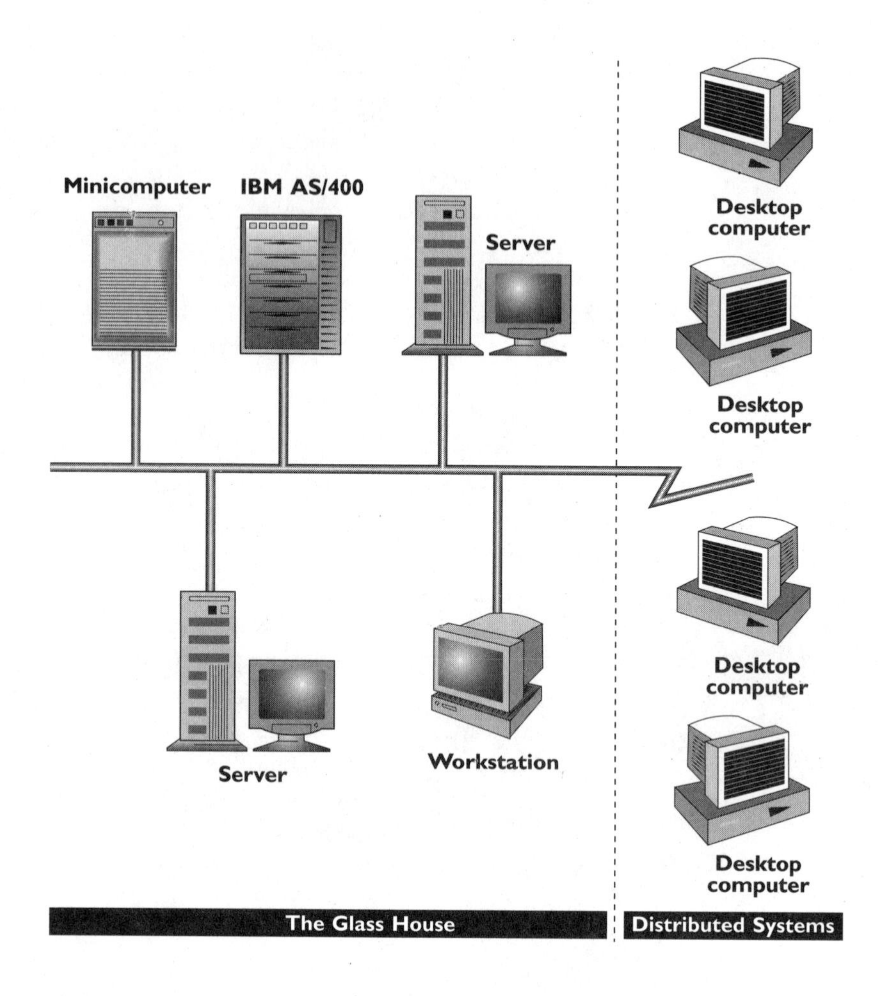

Fitting into a Centralized IS Department

I have yet to encounter a centralized IS group running a NetWare network that has not been somewhat decentralized by the advent of user access and other client innovations. Old-school shops are still out there, their glass houses still intact, but they're now the exception. Despite concessions to the new technology and the emergence of some distributed support methods, many of their centralized systems still exist.

The glass house offers some advantages. Certain security issues are avoided simply by preventing user access. Centralized management allows better strategic oversight for technology development as a whole. Centralized location of technical support resources encourages cooperation, sharing, and functional redundancy.

Naturally, cooperation and sharing are goals to be worked toward rather than guarantees. Network administration sometimes fosters a selfish or self-serving attitude in which some employees do all the work in a particular area, attempting to remain vital and powerful without regard to the greater needs of the organization. Others want to work only on pet projects and get you to do the tedious tasks. Don't be one of these maladjusted network administrators.

On the other hand, a centralized support staff has a more difficult time understanding the unique needs of different operational groups. Central standards may prevent small groups with unique needs from getting the most from available technology. And a cloistered development staff generally takes longer to understand user needs and problems than a staff divided among process-oriented groups.

Making Use of Centralized Resources

If you work in a centralized system, you may have much to be thankful for. A computer center is generally staffed with computer operators who can perform any tasks you can document step by step. Thus, you can offload tasks such as labeling tapes and running backups. The operators are often in-house around the clock. If properly trained, they may be able to identify problems and contact you before a problem gets out of control.

In both these cases, the network administrator is obliged to provide documentation and training. Since tasks such as labeling tapes and running backups are appropriate ones to offload to staff members, the investment of time and effort in documentation and training is worthwhile. Changing backup tapes doesn't take long, but the time adds up if you label and change tapes every day. Operators can perform other tasks as well, so get to know the operators and find out which ones know the most (and therefore need the least training).

Another handy feature of a centralized computing operation is the presence of a help desk. A properly staffed desk can make your life much easier by eliminating the blatant user-error calls, routing the calls best handled by somebody else, and helping you determine the priority of the network calls. The help desk is also a reliable resource for information about the organization, its employees, and its production processes.

Yet another benefit of a centralized system is the IS structure itself. As long as you're reporting into a structure, make use of it. The IS standards and procedures can help you CYA (take care of yourself) and can ward off blame. Instead of having to say, "I'm sorry, I don't support that," you can say, "I'm sorry, we don't support that." A fine point, perhaps, but quite useful for brushing off unmerited abuse from angry users working on nonstandard systems.

Avoiding Bureaucracy Bog

The IS structure can come back to haunt you, unfortunately. Like the character in the movie "Brazil" who is literally killed by paperwork, you may find yourself awash in a sea of forms and procedural issues. Avoid getting caught in this situation by discussing the job requirements with your manager. Eliminate excessive paperwork and offload what remains to a departmental administrative assistant.

Avoid having your system enhancements and changes slowed to a standstill within the organization by soliciting management buy-in before the project gets too large. Make departmental politics planning a part of your normal routine if it's necessary. Take comfort in the hope that someday your organization will become enlightened.

Bureaucracy can be your friend if you know how to play the game. If your company is devoted to a process-oriented—rather than goal-oriented—operation style, make sure you fortify your position with appropriate processes. Write and distribute policy documents and document standard operating procedures to define your role and the role of the network in your organization.

Managing a Distributed Network Structure

The client/server architecture supported by NetWare and other networking products has forcibly altered the state of network computing by placing the data—and the power to manipulate data—in the hands of the users. In many organizations, the advent of PC networks has spurred major changes in the ways support is provided. In newer businesses, the common phenomenon is that of networks that evolved in separate corporate units and have been interconnected as network links became more affordable and more important to the flow of data through the business.

If you're an administrator in a central IS structure providing oversight and backbone support for a distributed network, you'll want to know about how the distributed network is currently managed, and you may want to make changes in the way your organization works. If you have been hired to oversee a single group's networking endeavors or have become your group's technology manager, you'll want to determine the extent to which you'll need to (and be able to) look to a central IS organization or to peers in other business units for help.

The most important management tasks for the manager in a distributed network setting are determining the responsibility and authority of your position and identifying the best uses for the tools and people in your group.

Gaining and Maintaining Authority

Most organizations of any size continue to support a centralized IS department. Despite the move of data management to *logical process* units, the expertise required to interconnect and maintain wide area and enterprisewide network links is typically more useful in a central location. Although there are plenty of fiefdoms to fight over, authority over centralized and distributed IS systems can be logically divided.

The integration of technology into business has been shown to provide a substantial return on investment. When business processes and tools are developed or modified in concert, the return is even more substantial. Maintaining network support within business units allows corporate technology to be tailored to the logical processes taking place within the units.

CENTRAL RESPONSIBILITIES Central IS management should be responsible for the development of network interconnections, network installations, corporate standards, electronic mail systems, and fundamental business tool decisions. Business tools include corporatewide databases or technologies that can be accessed and leveraged by multiple groups. Centralized databases are one example. Additional specific duties that are best handled centrally include maintaining efficient routing, fast backbone transport, and network operating system version control and patching. Legacy systems and other traditionally heavy-metal hardware are also most reasonably managed by the central IS system that previously supported them.

DISTRIBUTED RESPONSIBILITIES While the central IS folks have a corporate view of the network, tools, and data, managers along the distributed network should be more concerned with the processes and data flow within their own departments. This does not preclude providing input to the central IS organization; in fact, it is vital that systems administrators in the trenches discuss their needs and experiences with the central network managers. Your needs in distributed networks may be similar to needs in other networks, making the issues of importance to the corporation as a whole, not just to your department.

The task of providing input and feedback to the central systems staff is only one responsibility of the distributed network administrator. Other duties include specifying hardware and software requirements based on business needs, performing server installations (or assisting, as appropriate), managing users and peripherals on your department's servers, maintaining applications on your servers, and safeguarding the department's data. You may also need to work with your department's programmers or consultants to ensure proper custom application development and operation.

DISTINGUISHING YOURSELF The single best way to make your mark in your organization, carve out a niche, and make the job what you want it to be is to do your job well. Put in the time required to solve problems that arise. Give as much consideration to the business needs and issues as possible. Diligently and tenaciously pursue additional knowledge about the technologies already in place and about the new products that may be useful in your group.

Don't feign knowledge of products or technologies. You run the risk of losing credibility with anyone who knows you're bluffing, but even worse, you'll be limiting your opportunity to learn. Few network administrators have all the answers; be someone who can find the answers rather than fake them.

Communicate with other network administrators in your organization in whatever fashion makes the most sense. If a biweekly bull session over donuts and coffee is the most comfortable approach, suggest it, and keep it going as long as it's productive. If formal meetings are more appropriate to your organization or personal style, create a list of attendees, develop an agenda, and keep the meeting as painless as possible by not letting it degenerate into a whine-in.

Making Use of Distributed Assets

Your distributed assets include staff, end users, and tools that can make your job easier and more effective. Since your job is to make your staff, tools, and end-users more effective, this can create good synergy.

WORKING WITH DISTRIBUTED SUPPORT STAFF If you manage or work closely with support staff members, you'll want to make sure that they're reasonably suited to and happy with their job duties. You may find that some of your support staff are more creative than others; make use of the more creative members for newer and more experimental tasks—installing and testing new software, for example—and use the less creative for more straightforward tasks, such as installing new network workstations. Distributing the tasks to your support staff in this manner ensures that each kind of task is completed as effectively as possible. It also prevents the creative staff from becoming bored and the others from becoming confused.

You'll probably be developing opinions about the competence of staff members as you have more experience and interactions with them. Avoid the temptation to write anyone off as worthless; some workers who seem to be lazy simply need more challenge, while others who appear to be slow merely need task-oriented duties rather than work that requires creative thinking, such as troubleshooting.

WORKING WITH TECHNICAL USERS The technically skilled user can be a hassle to manage and support. It can be tiresome to sort out the network connection problem on a system so tweaked and packed with beta software it's likely to spontaneously reboot at any moment. On the other hand, these users are a wonderful asset, both because they usually have a good grasp of the technical aspects of the business process you're supporting, but also because they can more easily be taught new procedures. If you have new applications, new network access scripts, or other system changes, you can approach a technical user to help test and debug the changes. Once the process itself is ready for mass use, the technical users can be of assistance in training other users, answering questions, and building consensus behind the new activities.

I once worked with a person whose ego knew no bounds. He was a self-proclaimed expert on every subject, and he was rather frustrated that I did not accept his every word as gospel truth. The times we came closest to getting along generally occurred when we were both exploring a new technology, providing tips and challenges for one another. By channeling our competitive feelings into something constructive, we were able to accomplish more.

On the other hand, a technical user often wants to know more than you're comfortable or able to tell them. They ask questions that are penetrating and difficult. And of course, they're likely to be the ones asking the world of you. Be certain not to dismiss their concerns and queries out of hand. Give them reasons that situations are the way they are and can't be changed. Or listen to them and initiate changes that make sense.

PROCESS-ORIENTED INFRASTRUCTURES The process-oriented infrastructure is the network you inherit that is already serving the business needs of your operation. Maintaining a happy user base and keeping the fun in your job depends on making sure that the directions you take the network follow the needs and the changes of the business you support. Constant input from users and managers is part of the equation; information from these sources allows you to more fully understand the evolving organizational requirements and goals. Consult outside sources of information, through professional organizations, user groups, online forums, publications, and technical resources. These sources allow you to find technology suited to the applications your business needs.

Accommodating Management Philosophy

THE FINAL STEP in determining your role in administering the network is to determine the management philosophies that influence business decisions and technological development. As you carve out your niche, supported by a developing understanding of the company's goals and by an ongoing familiarity with trusted and emerging technologies, you'll be in a better situation to pitch your plans to management in terms that can be understood and accepted.

Always begin by identifying the issues that are important to your audience. Then use your understanding of those issues to persuade management to accept your ideas and fund your initiatives.

Identifying the Important Issues

By this point, you may be tired of finding out about the business you're in. It's true, you have been pressed rather hard to identify what goes on in your organization. This step is so vital to success as a network administrator that it bears repeating once more.

Your role is to make the business run consistently and efficiently. Your charges are the network and its assorted accoutrements. You must avoid being perceived by users as yet another know-nothing who steps into the job with grandiose schemes that have little to do with what's really happening. This kind of prejudice is common, and it's normal. Head it off at the pass by making yourself available to input and by soliciting ideas from business managers.

Identify the products and services that make the most money for your organization, and determine how your network is involved in the process. Do all you can to ensure that the network continues to perform these functions reliably, and do what you can to improve the speed of the process. Then learn more about the processes from start to finish. Try to determine how technology can be used to improve reliability, speed, and efficiency. Then prepare to sell your idea to the managers.

Accessing Paths of Persuasion

There's more than one way to skin a cat, and there's more than one way to gain approval from decision-makers who are involved in accepting or denying your requests for changes and enhancements. Each of the techniques comes down to a single principle, however. Always address the issues that are most important to your audience.

You've gained an understanding of the issues that are important to your business. Catch phrases like *time to market* and *data for the dollar* indicate premiums placed on turnaround time and cost reductions. If you hear managers employing phrases like these, you may be able to target the kinds of issues they address in their rhetoric. Fortunately, even if you're totally unfamiliar with a particular person's attitudes, you can still make an effective presentation of your ideas.

Make a list of the business processes that would be altered or enhanced by the changes you wish to make. Then show how each item would be influenced by the change you're considering. Shaving a day from the production time of your magazine could be important to management. Reducing the costs of production by 15 percent would also be appealing. Eliminating existing problems can be compelling. For example, you would probably be able to sell management on a plan to improve a network so the primary server no longer crashes once a week.

When you have a list of the business improvements resulting from your change, order them in order of strength. When you make your presentation, order them in the strongest way possible. Unless another order is obviously better, put the strongest reason first. Then make the weakest argument second, and list the other arguments in increasing order of strength, making the second-best reason the last one on your list.

Unless your company is swimming in cash or has an end-of-year surplus that needs to be spent (for example, if you have a government job and can't let my tax dollars lie fallow), don't bother developing proposals you can't justify to yourself within the context of business needs. It's not worth your time or the potential damage to your credibility.

Opening the Purse Strings

Most organizations are not as free with their money as their network administrators would like them to be. If you're in a free-spending situation, enjoy it. Use the lure of additional sales to entice resellers into giving you training, demonstrations, and other sweetened deals. Go ahead and gamble some of the company's money on solutions you're not certain about. Equip your networks with the finest, most reliable configurations available.

Meanwhile, the rest of us will be attempting to spend our money wisely. As with most of the network administrator's problems, the best guiding light is your understanding of the business and its needs. It's okay to buy expensive, big-name manufacturer servers and peripherals for the systems that require reliability and rapid response in case of failure. Just be wise enough to pass on the nouveau technology where it's unnecessary.

You may not know what kind of spending was considered normal before you arrived; you'll want to find out, if you can. Consult requisitions, purchase orders, and packing slips. See if you can find departmental budgets from previous years, and pay particular attention to the amount of capital expenditures (both budgeted and actual). Try to find out how much equipment and software is purchased through your department's budget rather than through the other business units' budgets.

Now you've got the required information: you know what the organization needs, what it can afford, and what it has spent in the past. Make your case to management as strong as possible. If you get buy-in from other departmental managers, you may be able to reduce or eliminate the amount you have to pay from your own budget.

The scope of the network administrator's role is largely in your hands, even if your job is relatively well defined and structured. By expanding and applying your understanding of the important business processes and goals and by making the most of the support structure you are a part of, you can distinguish yourself as someone whose ideas and solutions merit attention, respect, and dollars.

Lock the Door Behind You: Resolving Network Security Issues

IF YOU'RE LIKE most network administrators, network security doesn't exactly turn your crank. Security is one of the issues that you want to be low profile because the only time anybody makes a fuss about it is when problems arise. Whether or not you're excited about security, an important step in managing your inherited network is making sure it allows access only to those who are supposed to have it.

One reason many administrators don't care much for network security issues is that the process typically forces you to consider yourself a potential victim, which isn't the most pleasant business task you may have on your plate. One way of thinking about network security is from the predator's point of view. Think about what you've learned about your network, and consider what the potential points of interest or entrance might be.

The easiest way to conceptualize your network assets is to consider the value of the equipment you've installed. The hardware and software itself can be quite valuable, and much of it can be easily resold. Another major network asset is the data stored on it. Think about the business plans your executives store in their user directories on the network. Consider the marketing databases and the engineering designs that are stored or transmitted on the network. Imagine the prying eyes of curious employees, disgruntled workers, or those heading for new jobs at competitive organizations. Then consider the possible routes of access to the sensitive or vital data available to nosy *crackers* or business rivals. Finally, consider the potential damage should a destructive program be intentionally or unintentionally set loose in your network.

Although media sources outside the computer industry refer to those who gain unauthorized access to computer systems as hackers, the term preferred by many computer professionals is crackers. Many highly proficient programmers and computer systems experts consider themselves hackers, reserving the term to describe adept users of computer technology.

Consider each asset and each potential mode of entry, and shut the door so that entry cannot be made or repeated. If you learn of previous security breaches, find out what steps have been taken to prevent future problems. When possible, duplicate entry methods yourself. When you're satisfied that you haven't left any gaping holes, document what you've done to ensure network security.

The Vital Information

THIS CHAPTER PROVIDES a three-part approach to enhancing network security. Physical access to the network must be limited to prevent theft and unauthorized access. Network accounts must be protected on unconnected networks and internetworks alike. And virus protection must be installed on clients and servers to avoid infection and possible loss of data.

COMPLETED	TASK
❑	Locate the servers in a locked room with limited access.
❑	Lock up spare equipment and original software.
❑	Secure the server console.
❑	Implement security features on desktop computers whose users have network connections.
❑	Set NetWare account defaults.
❑	Use the SECURITY command to identify potential security problems.
❑	Install antivirus software for client systems.
❑	Install antivirus software for network servers.

Limiting Physical Access to the Network

ALTHOUGH YOUR FIRST impression of criminals who want to tweak your network may be Doritos-munching, red-eyed hackers sitting in fluorescent-lit university computer labs, the ordinary thief presents a very real threat. Look over the lists of equipment you created as you worked through Chapter 1. Consider the total value of what is described there. It's probably significant enough to be an enticement to somebody.

In addition to the threat of physical removal of assets from your network, you have to worry about invaders on the premises gaining access to your network. A copy of SERVER.EXE on a bootable DOS diskette is sufficient for somebody who wants to get Supervisor access to the network. A more mundane but far more common means of access is through employees' workstations while they're away from their desks.

The success of all three of these potential security risks depends on physical access to the network. This common factor means you can take steps to limit—to control, if not eliminate—the risk your network runs from unauthorized physical access.

Protecting the Network's Physical Assets

If you take a look around your server room or wiring closet, you probably won't see much that would appeal to thieves or kleptomaniacs. Running servers are generally very bulky, sporting heavy FCC-compliant chassis, power supplies, and a complement of boards and drives. The systems are also hitched with cables to their peripherals, the network, and the power sources. Unless you've got so much high-end equipment that robbers might be inclined to tie up your operations staff, back a truck up to your building, and abscond with your network, it's not likely that you'll come in some Monday to find your network cupboard bare.

Preserving Network Components

Although major thefts occur, it's much more likely that components or smaller devices will be taken. In several publicized cases, armed intruders have opened file servers and removed the high-density SIMMs inside. Those 32MB memory modules for which you paid $1,500 each are easily concealable, practically impossible to trace, and easily repackaged and resold as new. The same goes for your Pentium chips, conveniently located in Zero Insertion Force (ZIF) sockets, which also require zero extraction force.

Component Theft and Collateral Damage

If you've ever had your car stereo stolen, you are probably aware of one of the additional complications that can be introduced when somebody wants something you've got.

When your car stereo is lifted, you can generally expect a broken window or a lock cylinder has been rendered useless by a screwdriver. When parts are removed from your server, don't expect the thieves to gently wiggle the case where that tab rubs across the SCSI cables—they're going to wedge and pry and force the case open.

When your stereo is taken, you may find that your dashboard has been damaged by someone prying it with a screwdriver. Sometimes the thief has cracked neighboring instrument faceplates, severed or damaged wiring for other systems, and exposed a power wire in which you may now have a short. When a server is raided for parts, you may find that the memory cards or SIMM slots were damaged when the memory was removed. If access to memory or processors is obstructed by other cards, the cards may have been broken rather than removed. In one instance, a Power Macintosh was apparently smashed on the floor several times because the thief did not want to bother with the irritating task of opening the case and removing the motherboard with a screwdriver to access the memory banks. When a server is raided for parts, the motherboard, backplane, or add-in boards may have sustained hidden damage in the form of broken traces that were flexed during the theft.

Finally, a car thief may also take that nice denim jacket in the back seat, the CDs in the glove box, and the expensive pen on the map shelf. A computer thief will be on the lookout for equivalent items—small, valuable, and useful or sellable. Pocket modems, cellular phones, external print server units, and other devices may be attractive to the discriminating thief.

Protecting your servers and components from theft and damage can be difficult. Determined criminals can defeat most protection schemes, especially if the criminals aren't above threatening or resorting to physical violence. Keep the network equipment in locked rooms; temperature-controlled server rooms containing wiring and hubs as well as servers and administrative workstations are best, but even in highly distributed networks, servers should be tucked into locked offices.

Knowing that even locked rooms and security guards may not keep your equipment from being stolen, make sure the disaster recovery plan you created in Chapter 4 takes a major theft into account. If not, update the plan. Make sure your organization's insurance covers theft.

If your building has security personnel, check to see how frequently they patrol and whether they check the server rooms. Consider requesting that they ensure that the doors are locked and that the room is not in disarray. Tell the security staff that you're in charge of the network and identify the other people who may have business in the secured areas. Have the staff report anyone else it sees there.

Protecting Your Spares

The components already installed in your network are certainly potential targets, but the most likely candidates for disappearance are your extras and spares. Unless you keep (and check) a strict inventory, you may not notice that something is missing until long after one of your colleagues has taken a "five-finger discount." Some people consider anything that isn't currently in use as surplus, and whether they take the item for business use, personal use, or resale, the effect on you is the same: you'll need to spend money replacing the part, and even worse, you may not have a part you expected when an emergency strikes.

The moral of the story? Lock up your software and spares. You should maintain an inventory yourself if that's practical; if not, offload that task to a subordinate or an assistant. Make sure to do another inventory periodically to ensure that you're not missing anything critical to planned expansion or disaster recovery.

Preventing Physical Access to the Servers

Intentionally or unintentionally, a person can do quite a bit of damage from a file server console. Whether someone is dropping connected users, unloading vital NLMs, dismounting volumes, or performing other operations at the file server, he can cause disruption, corrupt data, or even down the server. Of course, if he's got physical access to the server, he also has access to the server's power switch.

In any event, you don't want the people who can achieve this level of access to be sociopaths, angry users, or simply confused tech staff. If you find incidents in which people who have access demonstrate a lack of sense (let alone a destructive instinct), consider changing the lock on the server room door and re-issuing keys as *you* see fit. Don't accept user access as part of your inheritance; you should have the freedom to limit access to ensure the safety of the network and its data.

Server Room Access: The Final Battle

ARCHIMEDES, my first network server, sat in a server room and wiring closet shared with a sister organization. The other organization had no servers in the room but had installed several patch panels and hubs. Because we did not know the members of the other organization's support staff, we did not issue keys to them and asked that they gain access by talking to me or my administrative assistant. This arrangement kept our server room keys from circulating throughout another organization, and it also meant we knew whenever somebody from their organization was in the room. Unfortunately, it opened another can of worms.

The other organization's technicians would request access to the server room to plug someone in and would leave the door open so they could return if there was a problem. When we asked that they not leave the door open, they obliged—and left the door unlocked instead of open. Finally, we worked out an arrangement by which the other organization's help desk kept a copy of the key, which was given to the techs when they needed access. The help desk would notify my department when work needed to be done. This arrangement made the technicians happy, added an inconsequential amount of work to their help desk staff's load, and allowed ARCHIMEDES to run with minimal risk.

Securing the File Server Console

If somebody does gain access to your server room, she can load NLMs that alter, damage, or copy network files and data. One way of limiting this access is to limit the file server's access to the local drives and operating systems. The SECURE CONSOLE console command disables DOS on the server, preventing an intruder from downing the server and accessing files stored on the local DOS partition.

```
:SECURE CONSOLE
```

The REMOVE DOS console command also removes DOS from the server's memory. Instead of leaving a DOS prompt on the server when the EXIT console command is issued, the server executes a warm reboot.

The SECURE CONSOLE command also keeps NLMs from being loaded from directories other than the SYSTEM directory on the SYS volume. It helps ensure that time-based security measures (intruder detection and login time restrictions, for example) are not defeated by alteration of the system date and time. Since a user with *Console Operator* or Supervisor rights can still run the RCONSOLE command from a workstation to change the time and date, access to these user accounts needs to be controlled.

To make the SECURE CONSOLE command more useful, enable the hardware password on your server hardware. This step allows you to prevent access to someone who brings the server down and restarts it. This password can generally be disabled by setting a jumper or toggling a DIP (dual inline package) switch inside the server, but that kind of access can be more difficult to obtain without being noticed and caught. It's also more time consuming, which may be a deterrent.

If you have a secured building with guards on duty, make sure they know what to do when service people or other non-employees come to visit. Do your part by informing them when you expect someone. If you carry a pager or cellular phone, leave the telephone number with the guards so you can be contacted when someone claims she needs access to the computer systems area. There are always going to be special circumstances in which the guards must make judgment calls about providing access, but you should do what you can to eliminate the security risk.

Avoiding Harmful Access from Network Nodes

Although extensive mischief can be wrought via access to file servers and similar systems, a much greater threat comes from access via network nodes. A central computer center is easier to keep an eye on than the dozens or hundreds of individual workstations connecting to the servers. The distributed nature of modern networks allows access to the data from cubicles and offices as well as the heart of the computer operations department.

A determined intruder with physical access to your network workstations can install software that records the keystrokes the user enters. This is often made unnecessary by users who leave notes posted on their monitors with their various login names and passwords. Encourage users to log out when they leave their computers for any period of time. Screen savers with password protection provide slightly more security, but many can be relatively easily bypassed.

Some screen savers for Microsoft Windows can be disabled simply by pressing Ctrl-Alt-Del while the screen saver is in operation. Windows sees the keystroke combination as a request to end the current task and in some instances displays a blue screen instructing you to press Enter to quit the current task. Press Enter, and you're in—and won't be bothered again by the screen saver, which has obediently been removed from memory by Windows.

Even open network ports that are active (patched to a live network hub) can be troublesome. An intruder placing a network analysis tool on the network may be able to capture and view network traffic.

Managing User Login and Access Rights

SEVERAL SECURITY MEASURES are built into NetWare at the user level. These measures can be set using the SYSCON utility from DOS or the NETADMIN utility from Windows on a NetWare 4.x network. Some settings are considered more secure than others, and the SECURITY command is particularly useful for identifying potential problems on inherited networks.

Using the SYSCON utility to Set Network Access

The SYSCON utility is a primary utility for the NetWare Supervisor. It provides server, group, and user information along with some valuable network management tools, including access to the file server error log and the system login script. Of particular interest are the **Intruder Detection/Lockout,** the **Group Information,** and **User Information** options.

Setting Intruder Detection/Lockout

The Intruder Detection/Lockout setting can prevent unauthorized access to a file server. This feature requires the administrator to set the acceptable number of login attempts, after which the server assumes the user is an intruder and locks the account for a period of time determined by the administrator.

Follow these steps to enable **Intruder Detection/Lockout.**

1. Type `SYSCON` at the workstation's DOS prompt.
2. Select **Supervisor Options** from the **Available Options** menu.
3. Choose **Intruder Detection/Lockout.**
4. Set the **Detect Intruders** option to Yes.
5. Under **Intruder Detection Threshold**, set the acceptable number of **Incorrect Login Attempts** (the default is 7).
6. Set the **Bad Login Count Retention Time,** which is the period of time in which the number of login attempts is counted (the default is 30 minutes).
7. Set the **Lock Account After Detection** option to Yes.
8. Set the **Length of Account Lockout,** which is the period of time the account is locked after the acceptable number of login attempts is exceeded (the default is 15 minutes).

The **Intruder Detection/Lockout** window is illustrated in Figure 8.1.

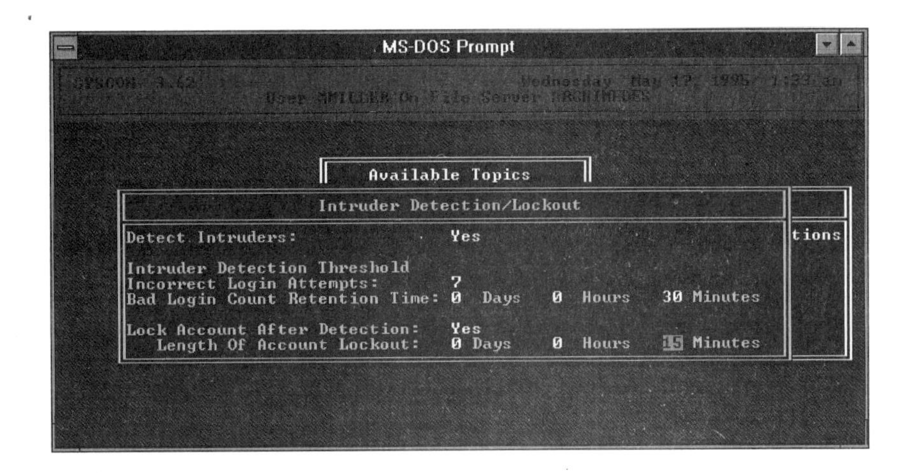

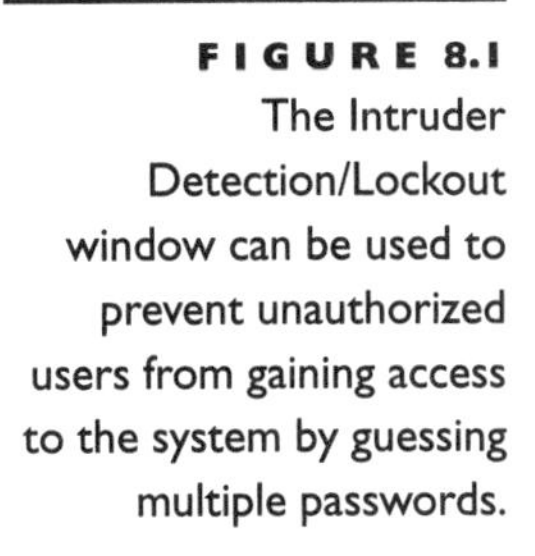
FIGURE 8.1 The Intruder Detection/Lockout window can be used to prevent unauthorized users from gaining access to the system by guessing multiple passwords.

Checking and Setting User Information

User accounts contain several important security settings. These settings can be viewed and altered by running SYSCON from a DOS prompt. Useful information includes user account restrictions, full name, groups belonged to, intruder lockout status, login script, security equivalencies, station restrictions, time restrictions, trustee assignments, and volume restrictions. To access user account information, select **User Information** from the **Available Options** menu in SYSCON. Then pick the name of the user account you wish to access. This portion of the SYSCON utility is shown in Figure 8.2.

ACCOUNT RESTRICTIONS Account restrictions determine the status of an account and its password requirements. Figure 8.3 shows a restrictions window.

A disabled account cannot be used; you can set an expiration date to make an account temporary. The number of times a user can be logged in under the same account name can be set at the **Account Restrictions** window, as can the password options.

For most user accounts, you'll want to allow the user to change the password, which should be required. A length of at least five characters is recommended (five is the default). Periodic password changes can be set at intervals you determine, and the number of times a user can log in after the password change is requested can also be configured here. Unique passwords must be different from each other and from the user account name. Since NetWare remembers eight previous passwords, users can cycle through nine unique passwords if they wish.

FIGURE 8.2
The User Information window in the SYSCON utility lets you access a wide variety of information about user accounts, much of which can be useful when checking network security.

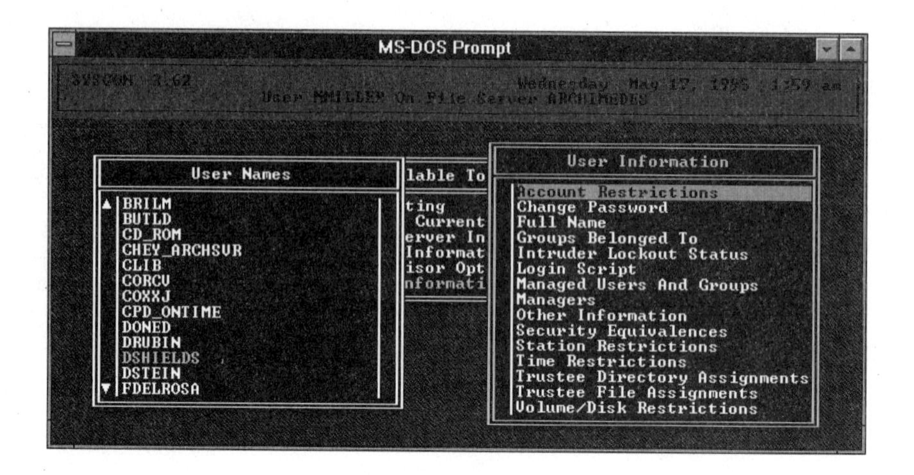

FIGURE 8.3
The SYSCON Account Restrictions window allows modification of account status and password settings.

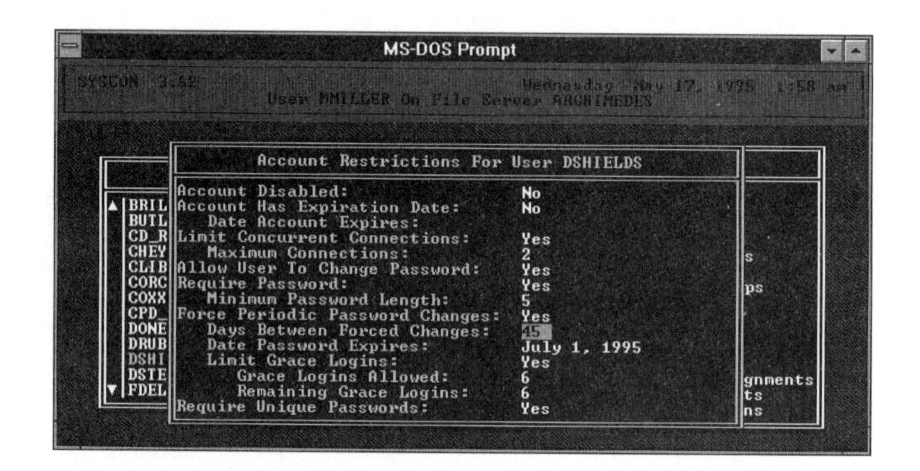

If you force users to change their passwords periodically, many have difficulty remembering them. You'll have to weigh the value of the information they can access against the time and effort you will have to spend unlocking and changing passwords. By forcing users to change passwords periodically, you also may indirectly encourage them to record their passwords at their desks or to use simple passwords, like the name of the month, which could easily be guessed by an intruder. Consider whether all users need to have the same password alteration schedules.

CHANGE PASSWORD While NetWare's tools won't tell you a user's password, they do allow you to change the account's password to something new. Simply select the **Change Password** option in the **User Information** window of the SYSCON utility, enter the password, retype it to confirm it, and the new password is ready to roll. Users can also run SYSCON from their client stations to change their own passwords.

FULL NAME This isn't a security issue in the usual sense, but it helps you keep track of the users associated with various account names. Include a full name for every user you add, and fill in blank entries when you can.

GROUPS BELONGED TO Although trustee rights can be assigned to individual users, they are often granted to groups of users who need similar access to network applications and data. Select the **Groups Belonged To** option from the **User Information** window of the SYSCON utility to see which groups a particular user account belongs to.

INTRUDER LOCKOUT STATUS When you select the **Intruder Lockout Status** option, you can see whether the account has been locked because of too many incorrect login attempts. Other information displayed on this screen includes the number of incorrect logins currently being remembered by the system, the time the account will be unlocked (or the time the incorrect login count will be reset to zero), the time remaining until the account is accessible, and the last network address of someone who entered an incorrect password or locked the account.

LOGIN SCRIPT You can check to see that a login script exists from the **Login Script** entry at the **User Information** window of the SYSCON utility. To prevent someone with network access from creating personal login scripts for other users, each user should at least have the following comment:

```
;Blank login script file
```

MANAGERS AND MANAGED USERS AND GROUPS The **Managed Users and Groups** entry in the **User Information** window of the SYSCON utility shows the user accounts and group names that this account can modify. This option gives the managing user the ability to modify settings and group members. Be sure there aren't surprises here. The **Managers** entry in the **User Information** window indicates the user accounts that can modify the selected account.

SECURITY EQUIVALENCIES These entries include group memberships and rights set to correspond to those of other users. This feature is most commonly used to provide Supervisor access, which can be granted by pressing the Insert key and selecting the Supervisor user. You'll probably be more interested in removing Supervisor rights, which involves highlighting the **Supervisor** entry and pressing the Delete key.

STATION RESTRICTIONS These settings indicate the network addresses from which the selected account can log in. If this table doesn't contain any entries, the account can be accessed from any address. This restriction can be particularly useful for processes running on dedicated machines or for Supervisor-equivalent accounts that are used only in a central computer center. If the boss has access to sensitive directories or files, you may want to limit his account to work only on his workstation.

If you set station restrictions, remember to alter them if you move the user, replace her network card, or connect her client system to a different hub.

CREATING TIME RESTRICTIONS If you want to limit your users to logging in during business hours, you can set the **Time Restrictions** option to kick the user off at a certain time and enable login later. In Figure 8.4, the user will be logged out of the network at midnight and won't be able to reconnect until 5:30 a.m. This option can be handy for ensuring that files are not open during network backups, and it can also help avoid attempts to gain access during the times when no legitimate business is planned.

TRUSTEE ASSIGNMENTS Trustee assignments are the rights that user accounts or groups are given to particular directories or files. By looking at the rights assigned for each user or group, you can identify potentially problematic situations. The best rule of thumb is to avoid giving the Supervisor right to anyone. Limit Access Control rights as much as possible. Look for inappropriate Erase or Create rights assignments. Remember that Read and File Scan rights allow users to run programs, and don't forget about software licensing obligations. Select **Trustee Directory Assignments** in the **User Information** window of the SYSCON utility to view the user's specific trustee rights for directories, and select **Trustee File Assignments** to see user rights for individual files.

VOLUME/DISK RESTRICTIONS Select **Volume/Disk Restrictions** to pick a volume and view any space restrictions that may have been imposed upon the account for that volume. Pay particular attention to the SYS volume, and set limits where necessary to avoid overuse of space. This screen also indicates the amount of space a user has in use on each volume.

FIGURE 8.4
The asterisks in the Time Restrictions window indicate times the user can be connected to the network.

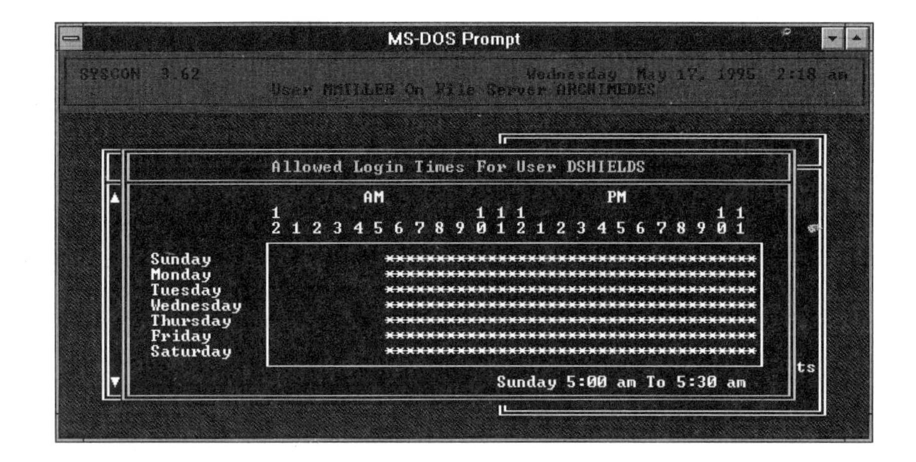

Checking and Setting Group Information

Since groups are blocks of users, the access rights and managed users they support are often even more important than those in place for individual users. Although the options work the same for groups as they do for users, fewer options are available. Each group has the following options:

- Full Name
- Managed Users and Groups
- Managers
- Member List
- Other Information
- Trustee Directory Assignments
- Trustee File Assignments

The Other Information group indicates whether the group can operate the file server console remotely, and it also shows a group identification number.

Setting Default Account Restrictions

Use the SYSCON utility from DOS to set the default access for new user accounts:

1. Type `SYSCON` at the DOS prompt.
2. Select **Supervisor Options**.
3. Select **Default Account Balance/Restrictions** to get a list of the settings that can be set to an administrator-determined default:
   - Account expiration date
   - Concurrent connections limitations
   - Home directory creation
   - Password and password length requirements
   - Periodic password change settings
   - Password uniqueness demands
   - Default accounting information

Using the SECURITY Command to Check Network Access

The SECURITY command works from a DOS prompt. The SECURITY.EXE file is found in the SYS:SYSTEM directory, so on most networks, Supervisor access is required to run this command. SECURITY identifies such mundane items as users without full name entries but also flags more important issues, including users who do not need passwords or do not need to change passwords. It also indicates levels of trustee rights that seem inappropriate for users.

The SECURITY command consults the NetWare bindery and identifies the problems it sees. Since the list that SECURITY generates is often quite long, you may want to redirect the output to a file, as shown in the following command line:

```
S:\SYSTEM>SECURITY > X:\SECURE\S0601.TXT
```

SECURITY flags the following potential problems:

- Accounts without assigned passwords
- Accounts with non-unique, short, or infrequently changed passwords
- Accounts with Supervisor equivalency

- Accounts or groups with rights to root directories
- Accounts without login scripts
- Accounts with excessive rights in the standard SYS directories

Accounts without login scripts are insecure because all users have Create rights in user mail directories. This means any user could insert a login script into another user's directory unless a script file is already there.

Controlling Alien Rights and Connections

ALIEN RIGHTS IN the NetWare sense are fairly limited. If you have a wide area network that is somewhat decentralized, you may encounter the situation in which people outside your local area network want access—to look at files you produce, to deliver files they produce, or to use other network resources. For example, you may have a remote group in your organization that produces a report they'd rather print to one of your printers than mail to you. There's nothing wrong with establishing network accounts for these users, but you should remember to treat these accounts carefully, because you have no control over how they are used at the user workstation.

Be certain you understand the purpose of the alien account. If only a means of delivering files is required, you may want to consider the *dropbox* configuration, in which the user is given Create rights only. The user can see the destination directory but can't see the files inside it. If you'll be leaving files to be picked up by the outside users, you probably need to provide only Read and File Scan rights for the alien login name.

If other account restrictions are appropriate, implement them. Remember to factor in distance (and therefore time zone differences) when setting time restrictions on users. Be certain to place disk space limitations on users who have Create rights, lest they waste space and network bandwidth pumping unnecessary files onto your servers.

Finally, be sure to run the SECURITY command periodically to identify users who have not recently logged in. If accounts are no longer useful, remove them. They can always be recreated if they are needed again.

Run the BINDFIX command from a DOS prompt to check the bindery objects in a NetWare 3.1x network. You can use this utility to remove mail directories and trustee rights for users who no longer exist.

Isolating Dial-In Connections

DIAL-IN CONNECTIONS are steadily growing in popularity, especially with the current trend toward people working at home. With more users needing access to their business data, the unscrupulous have more opportunities to use the dial-in infrastructure to access the network for their own purposes.

One common network cracker tool is a dialing system that telephones a series of telephone numbers, looking for a modem connection on the other end. These dialers can be programmed by someone who wants to target your company specifically to look at all the extensions in your company's prefix. The dialers can also be set to dial numbers randomly. Either way, they look for a response that indicates a live system on the other side.

If your network includes systems that broadcast a welcome screen when you dial in to a network connection, you've got a potential opening for intrusion by crackers. Additional tools can be used to run through a series of commonly used passwords.

Securing Network Management Dial-In

Even a dial-in connection that does not provide a user connection to the network can be problematic. If your hubs are configurable via an RS232 port and you have a modem connected, someone who finds the number can view your network traffic and can certainly alter your configuration.

One way to reduce the chances of your becoming the victim of a random attack is by setting your modems to answer after a relatively long period of time. With Hayes-compatible modems, you can use the following s register setting to make your phones answer after seven rings, which causes a 40-second delay between the time the call started and the time the connection is made.

```
ats0=7
```

Since most automatic dialing systems are set to look for a connection in the first four rings or so, they should bypass your modem line altogether. For Hayes-compatible modems your business uses only for dial-out purposes, prevent the modem from answering calls by setting the response time to zero rings:

```
ats0=0
```

Securing Remote User Connections

Find out which users use remote-control software (Carbon Copy or pcAnywhere, for example), and make certain that they are using password protection on their systems. It is important to ensure that access to the network—whether via local machines or remote systems using remote-control software—is understood to be your bailiwick. If your organization has a telephone switch, check with the telecom manager to obtain a list of the direct inward dial (DID) phone lines. Make sure that the users have implemented safeguards on whatever systems are attached to the lines, and if they haven't, help them secure their connections.

Finally, remote-access software generally has as high a degree of security as your ordinary network users have. Dial-in access to your system will be easy to obtain if the login names and passwords used in your system are known. And if any names or passwords are known, more can be determined or found via brute-force password generators. Be sure you follow the guidelines discussed earlier in the section Managing User Login and Access Rights.

Securing Internetworks

NOW WE'RE TALKING about some fun. If you've got UNIX systems on your network and a connection to the Internet, you're sailing in some very exciting waters. Mind the pirates and sharks, though. UNIX itself is riddled with security holes, and if you connect yourself to the whole wide world out there, you may be asking for trouble.

Tightening UNIX Security

Although UNIX systems vary in many ways, the similarities in most versions can be useful to those trying to access your network. One common approach a cracker may take in accessing a UNIX system is by making use of common user IDs, especially those that are required by the system or by particular applications running on the network.

Common login accounts are not unique to UNIX. The account names you may want to worry about most in your NetWare network are the standard ones: Supervisor and Guest. Make sure you change the Supervisor password when you start your job. Don't use a simple or common password that may easily be guessed. If someone with malign intent accesses the Supervisor account, you might as well start making copies of your resume. The Guest account is not generally allowed access to any sensitive data, but with a tool like the SYSCON DOS command, it can be used to identify other potentially useful account names.

Once a user ID is identified, the cracker can attack the system using a tool that feeds hundreds of common passwords to the system, looking for one that works. Names of sports teams, the user ID name itself, names of months, and common first names are all likely to work on one ID or another. Even if a single user ID doesn't have access to any "interesting" files, the ID can see the /etc/passwd file, which contains the system passwords in encrypted form.

After the password file has been copied to a file, its contents are compared to an encrypted version of the list of common passwords—or even an electronic dictionary with thousands of entries—until a match is found.

The way to prevent these kinds of tools from succeeding easily is to eliminate default passwords, make sure the password file is shadowed so that users cannot read it, prevent users from attempting to log in unsuccessfully more than two or three times, and encourage users to choose unusual passwords.

Approaching Internet Security

Internet security is an enormous issue, in part because of the huge number of sites that are connected into one internetwork, but also because security was not a primary design issue for the Internet. Sharing information and limiting access to information are generally competing priorities, and in many cases, the ability to share information far outstrips the ability to prevent people from accessing it.

For many companies, a *firewall* is the best way to address Internet security. A firewall is a protective barrier that insulates your network from the rest of the Internet. It is a bit like a one-way mirror, keeping traffic from the outside from penetrating into your network, while allowing your users to access sites outside the firewall.

Unfortunately, the Internet is considered a great marketplace, which means that your company will probably want to display its goods and services on a World Wide Web home page and a series of supporting pages. This is both useful and informative (in some cases, anyway), and it certainly makes your company look cool. You want to make sure your Web site is outside the firewall, which ensures that even if your Web system is invaded and turned into a graphic advertisement for an obscene 900 number, the pirates won't be able to get into your primary business system.

If you don't have a firewall, the next best thing is to provide access control by configuring your Internet router to reject all but a set of "legitimate" IP addresses. This arrangement theoretically prevents access from users or sites who have no business poking around in your network, while allowing your users or customers to FTP information or perform other Internet tricks. Sadly, hotshot cybervandals may set their systems to claim to be an acceptable IP address. To limit the success of this technique, which is referred to as *spoofing*, you have to configure your router to determine *where* the information is coming from (in other words, which side of the wall) as well as *who* the information claims to come from (the source IP address). Users claiming to be located on your network who are identified as being outside the network can be denied access.

The Security Administrator Tool for Analyzing Networks, commonly referred to as SATAN, is a widely distributed tool that allows administrators of Internet-connected networks to identify security flaws. The program, which has been distributed on the Internet and runs on UNIX systems, seeks out network weaknesses so that they can be secured. Of course, you've got to think that any utility named SATAN could be trouble, and in this case, the trouble is that Internet-connected networks can be probed by SATAN users who are looking for access routes. The Lawrence Livermore National Laboratories has countered with a utility—called Courtney—that can identify SATAN investigating your network.

All of this highlights the central issue with Internet connectivity. Getting on the Information Turnpike has many advantages, but in any network, the more access you want to provide to those on the outside, the more opportunity there is for problems to be introduced from the outside. And the higher profile your company gets, the more interest focused on it by the information banditos.

Identifying and Removing Viruses

DEALING WITH VIRUSES in general is a bit like dealing with lice. As you lather up with kerosene, you wonder why modern science hasn't devised a method for dealing with the pesky little critters. The good news is that network-aware viruses are still relatively uncommon. The bad news is that boot-sector viruses are all over the place, and those rare network viruses can really be painful to treat.

Although many tools are available to help the deranged and morally destitute create new viruses, tools are also available that can identify many families and strains of viruses. Some can identify the *characteristics* of the viruses and don't need to be familiar with the particular viruses themselves. Some antivirus software can also remove viruses when they are found. All of these features are valuable, but they need to be implemented and updated to be practical.

The Virus Primer

Viruses are programs that make duplicates of themselves without user knowledge or intention. Viruses in their most benign forms typically display just a message, but some attempt to delete files or destroy disks. Whether or not the virus is intended to cause permanent system damage, it can be dangerous because its behavior may not be benign on any given system.

A virus that attempts to hide in the boot sector on a DOS-based FAT (File Allocation Table) file system may end up trashing an OS/2 HPFS (High Performance File System) volume. Even if the virus' intent was harmless, its effect can be deadly.

Other Viral Strains

A *stealth virus* often includes a portion that resides in RAM and is invoked when the file system attempts to open an infected file. Before the file can be opened, the stealth virus disinfects the file. The file is infected again when it is closed. A *worm* uses its reproductive cycle to use up system resources. A worm makes multiple copies of itself, taxing the processor, RAM, and often disk space. A *Trojan horse* masquerades as a legitimate program. When the user executes the Trojan horse executable file, the virus goes into action, possibly infecting the user's disk or destroying files.

Many viruses are concentrated in the boot sector of the disks they infect; they may alter or replace the original boot sector and execute when the system is booted with the disk or diskette. Other viruses attach to files, usually executable files, so that the virus runs before the executable starts.

A more recent kind of virus, sometimes called a *polymorphic virus*, changes its appearance to avoid detection. Viruses are usually identified by a unique set of instructions that identify their types or at least the families they belong to. These *signatures* may not be the same each time a polymorphic virus infects a file. In fact, these kinds of viruses actually mutate into many variants of the original. Some viruses even encode themselves to cloak their signatures from antivirus software.

Identifying Viruses

Virus identification can involve several different approaches. At the file level, cyclic redundancy checks (CRCs) can be used to compare the expected size or other characteristics of a file with the actual characteristics found before the file is opened. If the new check does not match the result stored in a database, the file has been changed, possibly by a virus. Files may also be scanned for the presence of known virus signatures, the code that identifies each unique strain.

Another way of identifying viruses is by noticing their operation. Rather than looking at the passive files for evidence of virus infection, this approach requires that a memory-resident task search for the kind of behavior exhibited by viruses. The search can identify stealth and polymorphic viruses. This kind of software typically intercepts the activity that appears suspicious and either follows a preset list of isolation and removal techniques or waits for user input on how to proceed. The process may finger a program or file that isn't infected at all, and the memory-resident software may steal resources from other processes, but it is the only way to get ongoing protection from viruses.

Identifying Viruses from the Network

The network can be a resource as well as a liability when you are at risk of virus infection. The network login script is a good place to include a command performing a virus check on your client systems. It can also be a central place to locate the latest virus identification software. However, the network can also increase the spread of viruses. Your users can now transmit viruses from their own machines to your servers, where the viruses, even if they do not harm the network operation, can spread to other users.

In any event, you'll want to prevent viruses from infecting both your local client workstations and your network systems. You may need to implement procedures that can chew up a minute or two when your users log in, and you may need to take a small hit on network performance to keep your virus shield operating all the time. Consider your possible routes of infection and the potential damage that viruses could do, and weigh these factors against the time, bandwidth, and cost of a solution. I've met few people who consider antivirus measures too big a hassle.

Finding Viruses on Client Systems

Most of your DOS-based systems may already have antivirus software installed. The latest versions of MS-DOS include Central Point Software's antivirus program. Called Microsoft Anti-Virus, the DOS and Windows versions of this utility allow users to scan their disks for viruses. From DOS, run the MSAV.EXE file to start the antivirus software. The opening screen is shown in Figure 8.5.

```
C:\>MSAV
```

When the utility starts, it offers several choices. **Detect** looks for viruses on the **Work Drive** (displayed in the lower right portion of the screen). It

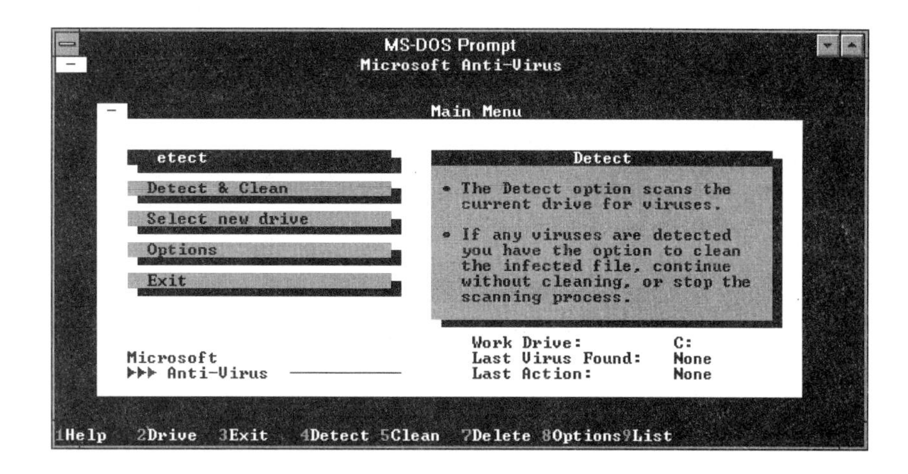

FIGURE 8.5
The Microsoft Anti-Virus utility comes with MS-DOS 6.x and allows you to find viruses and eliminate the files they have infected.

prompts you for its next move when it finds a virus. **Detect & Clean** automatically attempts to clean the infected files. **Select new drive** allows you to inspect another drive (including network drives). **Options** allows you to set the following parameters:

- Verify Integrity
- Create New Checksums
- Create Checksums on Floppy
- Disable Alarm Sound
- Create Backup
- Create Report
- Prompt While Detect
- Anti-Stealth
- Check All Files

The **Verify Integrity**, **Create New Checksums**, and **Create Checksums on Floppy** options are used to create a CRC file and ensure that files are checked against their CRC results in the future. The **Create Backup** option creates a renamed version of each infected file before cleaning the file. This option leaves the virus on your disk, which may be your only alternative if you need to keep the file for some reason. The **Anti-Stealth** option slows the virus check, but it may find more viruses. Use it with the **Verify Integrity** option. Microsoft Anti-Virus scans only executable files unless **Check All Files** is selected.

Using the **Create New Checksums** *option can cause one irritating side effect: it creates a number of files that you might not have room for on your drive. Those checksum files are stored in each directory on the drive you scan. Each file is named CHKLIST.MS, and they help the antivirus software identify changes made to files—possibly by viruses. If you don't mind losing this feature, you can uncheck the* **Create New Checksums** *box.*

Similar options are available in the Windows version of the product. After you select a drive to inspect, you can press the **Detect** or **Detect and Clean** buttons shown in Figure 8.6. Microsoft Anti-Virus first checks memory for signs of viruses, then begins scanning the selected drive's files.

If you decide you don't like the CHKLIST.MS files littering your drives, you can use the Windows version of the product, and select the drives where you want to eliminate the files. Then select **Scan...Delete CHKLIST files***, and press the* **Delete** *button when you're prompted.*

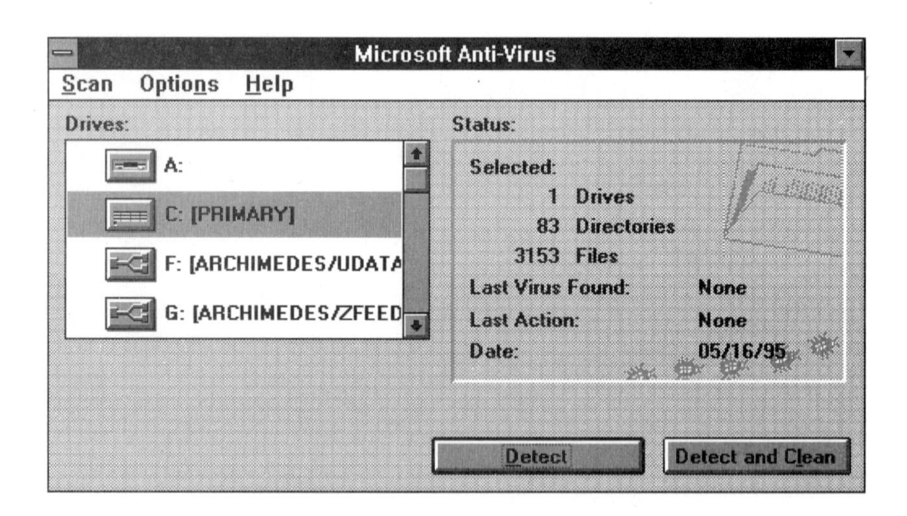

FIGURE 8.6
The Microsoft Anti-Virus product bundled with MS-DOS 6.x includes a Windows-based virus scanning and removal utility.

Both versions of the product work reasonably well, and if they're not the most complete or fastest products on the market, they are certainly a good deal and include an extensive list of known viruses, as shown in Figure 8.7. They're also a much better alternative than *nothing*.

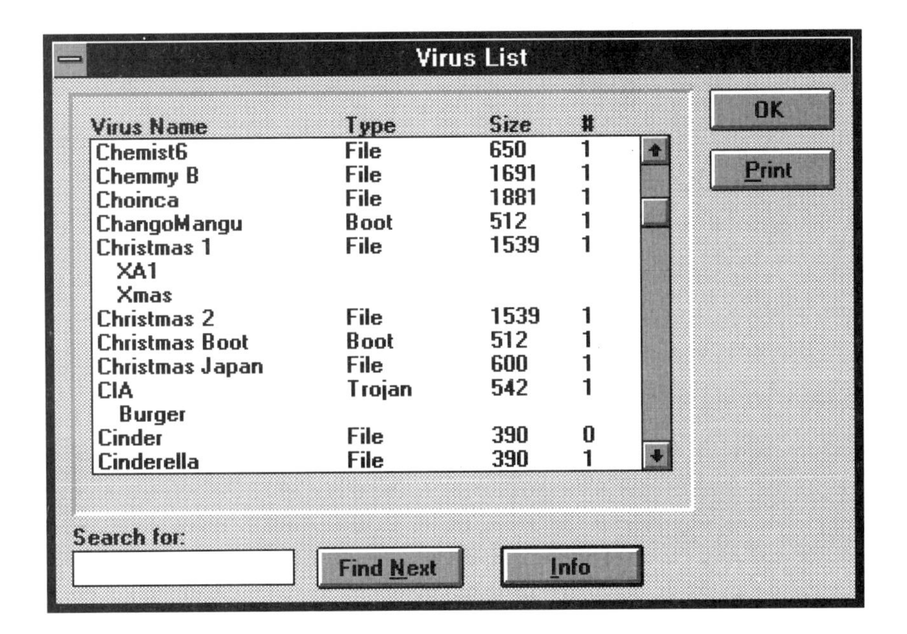

FIGURE 8.7 Antivirus packages typically include a long list of known viruses, including variants and virus aliases.

Microsoft Anti-Virus, which comes with later versions of MS-DOS, does not work with Windows 95. Viruses that install themselves from CD-ROMs can be particularly problematic with the Windows 95 AutoPlay feature, which may allow viruses to be copied to your system without your knowing to check for them.

If you want to know more about a virus you find, most antivirus products include information about the viruses in their databases. Microsoft Anti-Virus is no exception; an example of the information it provides is shown in Figure 8.8.

Although Microsoft's offering is nearly free, you may have access to or may want to consider obtaining other products. If you use two Symantec

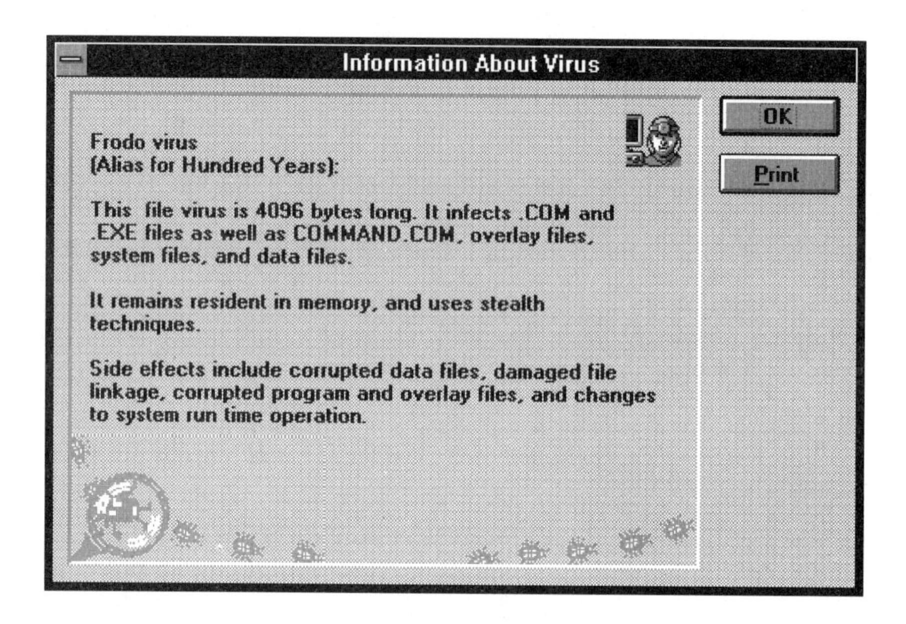

FIGURE 8.8 Antivirus packages often include information about known viruses, including the name, characteristics, methods, and damage done by each virus.

desktop products for Windows, the Norton Desktop or Central Point's PC Tools (both Norton and Central Point are owned by Symantec), you have access to the Norton and Central Point antivirus products. IBM's PC-DOS also includes antivirus software. If you're looking for a standalone antivirus package for the desktop, two of the highly rated contenders are McAfee's VirusScan on the PC platform and Datawatch's Virex on the Macintosh.

Locating Viruses on the Network

Relatively few viruses are network-aware. Unfortunately, the ones that exist can be quite a bit of trouble, and viruses that are not network-aware can still strike network drives and memory. Typical antivirus packages intended for network use allow scanning of user workstations upon network login. Network antivirus packages run as NLMs and are particularly useful against stealth viruses.

Symantec's Central Point Anti-Virus for NetWare is easily configurable by administrators, runs rapidly, and is a pleasure to use. S&S Software

International's Dr. Solomon's Anti-Virus Toolkit for NetWare is adept at finding viruses that have infected a network, but it can scan only disk drives; it has no intercept mode for real-time virus checking. Symantec's Norton AntiVirus for NetWare is another excellent program with good management tools. Cheyenne Software's InocuLAN performs well, but it's not as good at catching viruses as some of the other products. It can be configured to automatically update its virus definition tables from Cheyenne's electronic bulletin board system.

Your network won't run as quickly if you have real-time virus scanning installed, but the performance hit may be worth the peace of mind you gain.

Dealing with Viruses You Find

Once you have located a virus, you'll want to remove it. Some programs claim to be able to repair certain files from virus alteration, but in most cases, expect to lose some files. The network products often isolate the infected file by creating a special directory with no user access; the Supervisor can then identify the culprit virus strain and collect more information.

Other products rename the file or simply delete it. In any event, you should find out what action your software takes, and then decide how to follow up. You may want to perform a scan of the network volumes on the server that was affected; if significant traffic flows between your network servers, you may want to run a scan on some of the other systems, too.

If you can find a source of infection, do so. If you know who owns the file (doing an NDIR in the directory before the file is moved or renamed provides this information), you may be able to locate the file's source. If you know what the directory or volume's purpose is, you may also be able to tell the likely source of the infection. Likely sources of infection include bulletin board systems (BBSs), other companies, especially those outside the United States, and users' home computers.

You can also use the FILER utility from DOS to see who has rights to the directory containing an infected file. Check with the users themselves to see where new files or data may be coming from, and investigate any promising leads.

Ensuring that Virus Protection Is in Place

You can take three steps to ensure that your organization has ongoing virus protection. The first is to create and enforce antivirus policies and procedures. The second is to install and update antivirus software on the client systems. We just discussed the third, which is to invest in network-based antivirus software.

Each of these steps is vital in the efficient protection of your company's data and in saving your own time and effort. If users cannot be bothered to check the disks they bring in or wait for their client workstation virus scans to run each morning, you pay the price with the blame and the hassle of repairing the damage.

Implementing Antivirus Policies

Your antivirus policies need to address the introduction of foreign files into your network environment. Users feel an understandable ownership of their client systems, but they need to understand—and you should tell them—that their business computers are not their own. You need to have some control over what happens on their desktops.

The most likely sources of infection are diskettes, which often contain boot sector viruses. Diskettes sneakernetting around the office may be infecting multiple PCs; oftentimes, users who access various online services at home bring a file to the office from home, only to find that it is accompanied by an unwelcome clinger-on.

If your users have modems or Internet access, they can connect to a large number of BBS systems or FTP sites that may contain infected files. Even though most online systems and major bulletin boards virus-check their software, any alien files should be considered possible sources of infection.

Insist that your users virus-check the floppy disks they introduce into the network environment. Have them download files from online sources to floppy disks and then virus-check them. This process prevents the viruses from infecting anything else before they can be eliminated.

Another way to avoid the spread of viruses, control software distribution, and save money is to use diskless workstations. These client machines lack local hard disk drives and boot from a floppy drive or from logic on the NIC. They use network-based applications and data.

Maintaining Client Antivirus Software

The simplest way of installing client antivirus software is to include a command in the AUTOEXEC.BAT file to run MSAV.EXE, the Microsoft Anti-Virus, or to run some other software. This method has two major flaws. The first is the evolutionary nature of viruses, which develop very quickly and elude virus checkers that are not updated with new information about the latest strains and variations.

The second problem is that users have a tendency to tweak their machines and may not leave the antivirus ritual intact. If their virus scan routines require three minutes each time they reboot their machines, they may find it an irritating waste of time.

Both of these limitations can be overcome by placing antivirus software on the network. Run the program from the login script so that users can't avoid it. Then make sure you update the virus definitions as frequently as you can to ensure currency.

Network security includes three major components. Physical access to equipment can result in theft or access to critical data. Network login accounts may allow users to access data they shouldn't, or the network accounts may be easily used by network crackers seeking entry into your domain. Viruses are a problem for all computer users, and viruses can be particularly easily transmitted, but also easily identified, over a network.

Cleaning the Augean Stables: Streamlining the Network

IN GREEK LEGEND, one of Heracles' twelve labors was the cleaning of King Augeas' stables. The stables held enormous herds of oxen and goats and had not been cleaned for 30 years. Heracles performed the feat by diverting the Alpheus River to flow through the stables. Cleaning up a mature network's baggage can also be a quite distasteful and gigantic undertaking, and you need to be similarly clever to accomplish it efficiently and effectively.

Each NetWare network has its own unique ox debris, the amount of which depends on how the administrator approaches network development and growth. The most common problems are user accounts that are out of date, user and group trustee rights that are too broad, user home directories that are strewn across the network, SYS volumes cluttered with extraneous files, and login scripts that have been thrown together and modified haphazardly.

In every case, network cleanup is a task that requires your care in making changes while understanding the ways in which users may be affected by your changes. Modifications to user accounts, rights, and especially login scripts should not be made haphazardly. You need the force of the Alpheus, but you've got to make sure that you're removing the dung and not the oxen.

The Vital Information

IN THIS CHAPTER, the baggage you're looking for includes nonstandard user accounts and home directories, garbage cluttering the SYS volume, and spaghetti code in the system login script. The following checklist includes the items you should be giving the most attention.

COMPLETED	TASK
❑	Design standard user profiles.
❑	Reflect standard profiles in default user definitions.
❑	Modify existing users to reflect standard profiles.
❑	Standardize form and use of NetWare groups.
❑	Create a centralized user directory location.
❑	Move existing user directories to new locations.
❑	Find and remove large waste files in SYS volume.
❑	Unravel and comment system login script.
❑	Eliminate active use of user login scripts where possible.

Supervising User Accounts

USER ACCOUNTS ARE the most basic source of trouble with network trash. The section Managing User Login and Access Rights in Chapter 8 discusses some of the user account restriction issues of interest from a network security standpoint. These concerns are also of interest from a network homogeneity standpoint. You should have a standard network access profile that defines and constrains the type of network access the default user receives. The default user profile may vary depending on the type of user, but every utilization of a standard profile brings you closer to maintaining a network that is easy to monitor and understand.

You need to define and standardize certain user account parameters. Standardize login names to a particular format; if you need to diverge from this format, follow backup guidelines so that you—and anyone who inherits the network from you—can understand why the variations exist and how to interpret them. Similar information, such as the full names associated with users and the names of groups, print queues, and print servers should follow a reasonable set of guidelines.

Finally, you should ensure that you are providing standard access to all the tools—and only the tools—your users need. Inspect each user account to ensure that the rights assigned to it make sense. This requires you to also investigate the way in which rights are assigned through NetWare groups.

NetWare 3.x and 4.x differ somewhat in the ways they handle the relationship between users and the network resources available. Where the differences are significant, both versions are illustrated and explained.

Your goal when approaching user accounts and their associated restrictions should be to limit access to the data that is vital while standardizing access through the use of common user profiles and appropriately named groups of users with assigned rights. You want to know where to look to find out who a user is and where he needs to access network resources.

Making Standard User Profiles

The fact that you're managing an inherited network should not prevent you from defining your own standard user profiles. Some network administrators find themselves shackled to the implementations of their predecessors and feel powerless to make changes. Although it is true that converting users to newly defined standards can be time consuming, it is worthwhile because user rights and access are such an important part of NetWare management. Whether your network is large or small, one of the major ongoing factors in network management is sharing resources with the appropriate users. The appropriateness of access is dynamic because every organizational, procedural, and network change has potential trickle-down ramifications for user access. Making changes to users' access rights or methods is much easier if your users have default definitions.

Before you begin defining the user profiles, concentrate on designing the ways in which you want users to access the network. Determine the different kinds of users in your network environment, and think about the different ways in which they need network access. Map common issues for all users or for the different kinds of users you identify. Once you've prepared your "common denominator white paper," you'll be ready to use NetWare's tools to implement your design.

Creating a Network Access Philosophy

Your network access philosophy needs to incorporate your organization's structure and its use of the network resources, especially server volumes and networked printers. If you have a highly decentralized organization and a network that shares its structure, you probably should look at individual servers separately and modify access defaults accordingly.

In NetWare 4.x, individual servers are not necessarily the basis for the distribution of network assets. Container objects divide your network into logical structures called organizations and organizational units. Servers still exist as organizational units, but NetWare 4.x NDS attempts to reflect business structures and makes it possible to manage users by organization rather than by network layout.

Consider several issues when designing your default user access configurations. You'll want to have standards for:

- Login account restrictions
- Login time restrictions
- Login station restrictions
- Login intruder detection and lockout

ACCOUNT RESTRICTIONS Although account restrictions were discussed in Chapter 8, Lock the Door Behind You: Resolving Network Security Issues, they're worth revisiting in the context of standard user login accounts. Think about each of the account restriction options with respect to your inherited network to determine how it might apply to your situation.

For example, setting an expiration date for each account can be a major undertaking, but if you're working in an organization that hires only temporary or contract employees, it may be the best way to avoid leaving user accounts open to abuse. If you need to set account restrictions for most new and existing users, you have to integrate feedback about project scheduling and contract details into your administration routine. You need to get data from project managers or human resources personnel to ensure that you've got dates to input for each user account. You also need to make sure you stay "in the loop" to get information about changes in scheduling.

Even if you do not set account expiration dates, you should get lists of new hires and terminations from your human resources department so you can create and delete user accounts as necessary.

Concurrent user connections are multiple uses of a login account at different workstations. If some of your users log into several machines at once—a desktop machine used for mail and applications and another computer used to test software under development—you may want to limit most accounts to two or three concurrent connections. If your users have no business being logged into the system on multiple stations, set the default limit to one connection. Some organizations use a single login to provide access for multiple users. In this case, a whole department might use a single user account. Think twice about setting concurrent connection limits in these situations.

Don't forget that each connection counts against the user license. Logging multiple users in under the same account name does not prevent your running out of connections on a NetWare server.

As hard disk prices continue to drop, it makes sense to provide centralized network storage space for users. NetWare allows the creation of network home directories for each user, and you should consider using this feature. Network disk space is generally more easily managed, backed up, and replaced after failure than local disk space. If your network users are not supposed to use network space to store files, however, you should definitely not create user home directories. The section Tidying Home Directories, later in this chapter, discusses these user directories in more detail.

You already know that user accounts should require passwords by default, and in most cases, users should be prompted to change their passwords every two or three months. Passwords should also be unique—they should not be the same as the account name or as previous passwords. But although most network administrators allow users to change their own passwords, you may want to consider centralizing password changes. The situation described earlier in which many users log in using the same account is an example of an account for which you should centralize password changes. You don't want one rogue user changing the password, preventing other users from logging in.

Finally, one way of limiting the damage that users can do to a network is to limit the amount of disk space users can take up on the server volumes. Space limitations can be important if your network is space-starved. Although your goal should be to provide users with the knowledge and power they need to police their own use of network space, you may need to encourage them with a gentle application of a space limitation brick wall. Consider in particular the necessity of limiting space on the SYS volume and any server volumes that contain production data.

Once again, your understanding of what happens on the network comes into play in a big way. To intelligently consider any of the issues discussed in this chapter, you need to know what the average user does. Use of disk space, in particular, requires an understanding of where the vital data is located so you can avoid problems.

TIME RESTRICTIONS You have already considered restrictions on the times an account can access the network. Previously, you were concerned primarily with the security of the network and the integrity of the backup. These concerns are going to be the driving forces behind the limits you establish for your default account. Another issue to consider is the power of the accounts with respect to their time restrictions. Allow me to explain.

Many network administrators find that the accounts with the most access rights also need to access the network at all hours. Whether the accounts are used for processes that manipulate data while the users are snuggled in their beds or by the workaholic who works until midnight and comes back at 4:00 a.m., you're going to have to consider the exceptions to your login time rule. Make sure you know the reasons for time restrictions (if time restrictions are necessary). If exceptions must be made to the time restrictions rules, work out a way of satisfying the needs that required the restrictions in the first place. If you're worried about unauthorized access taking place late at night, make sure the security settings on the nonstandard accounts are set conservatively. If you think users will leave files open and prevent a solid backup, consider options for making copies of the critical files that will be open. These copies can then be backed up in the usual manner.

STATION RESTRICTIONS If your users have designated workstations, you may want to establish station restrictions for each user account. Talk about pain, though—choosing this as a default part of your user configuration requires a great deal of additional work, because the station restrictions are determined on the basis of the NIC address for each workstation. If your users have computer problems, they won't be able to use spare systems or even spare NICs without having their accounts modified.

However, you should think about special cases in which accounts have to be tied to particular workstations. For workstations acting as mail routers or print servers in a physically secured area, you could limit the login accounts and dispense with passwords so the machines could easily be restarted. User accounts with Supervisor rights could also be limited to particular stations in a secure area. In any event, the most powerful accounts—the accounts with the most access rights—should be the most likely candidates for station restrictions.

INTRUDER DETECTION AND LOCKOUT It's almost always a good idea to activate the intruder detection feature, but it may not be appropriate in some instances. If many users share one login name, you may not want to lock the login name when somebody forgets the password and enters the wrong one too many times. Are you noticing that the "many users, one login account" approach has some potentially hazardous ramifications? You're right.

Implementing an Access Philosophy

After you have developed your access philosophy, you're ready to implement it. You can start with the easy part, which is setting your system to default to the appropriate options where that is possible. You may need to alter other settings on a case-by-case basis, and you'll have to alter existing users separately.

SETTING UP NEW USERS When you create new users, you have the luxury of starting with a clean slate, which means you can control the way the account works and the users won't know an account could work any other way. You should avoid introducing change whenever possible. An additional benefit of creating new users is that you can configure the account defaults to reflect your network account philosophy. Not all the settings can be customized in your default user template, but every little bit counts, right?

NetWare 3.x account creation is generally performed in the SYSCON utility, which is run from a DOS prompt at a client workstation. To set your default account restrictions, complete the following steps:

1. Type `SYSCON` from a DOS prompt on a client system.
2. Select **Supervisor Options**.
3. Select **Default Account Balance/Restrictions.**

The account restriction options for which you can set defaults are shown in Figure 9.1.

FIGURE 9.1 Default restrictions for user accounts can be set in the SYSCON utility from the Default Account Balance/Restrictions window.

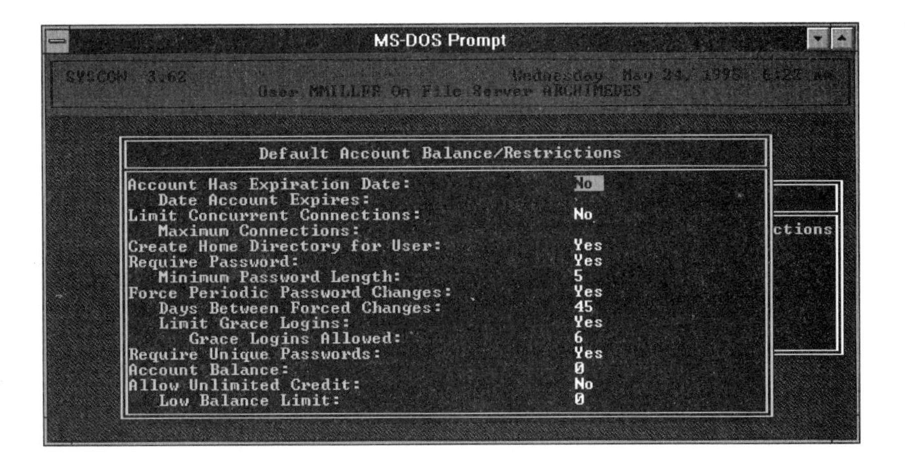

Account balance settings are for networks with the Accounting feature installed. You install this feature using SYSCON, and it stores information about the time users spend on the system, the amount of network disk space they use, and the load they place on the server's processor.

You can also use SYSCON to set default restrictions on access times. This option is also available from the **Supervisor Options** menu. As shown in Figure 9.2, the **Default Time Restrictions** window looks just like the one used to set individual user time restrictions.

Since SYSCON's ability to set account options globally is rather limited, you have to implement the other defaults when new users are created. NetWare 4.x does not use SYSCON, and it is not subject to the same limitations. The NetWare 4.x utilities for managing users and other NDS objects are NETADMIN, a DOS utility, and NWADMIN, a Windows utility. Most administrators seem to prefer NWADMIN's graphical interface.

NetWare 4.x allows you to define default user settings for each organizational unit. The user settings can be defined in NWADMIN in several ways:

- Create a user object named User_Template.
- Choose **Define User Defaults** when creating organizational units.
- Highlight an organizational unit's name, go to the **Object** menu, and select **User Template.**

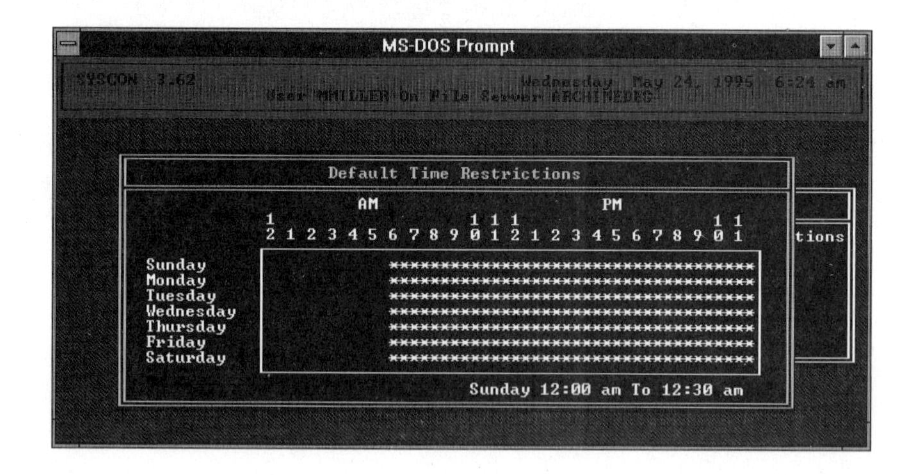

FIGURE 9.2
The Default Time Restrictions window in the SYSCON utility uses asterisks to represent the times user accounts can access the network.

NetWare 4.x NDS Components

NetWare 4.x replaces the NetWare 3.x bindery database with a new structure called NetWare Directory Services (NDS). The NDS uses a tree structure to organize all the servers, organizations, users, and other network *objects*. NDS is based on—but does not strictly adhere to—the International Standards Organization (ISO) and International Telephone and Telegraph Consultative Committee (CCITT) X.500 Directory Recommendations.

Here's a simple NDS tree.

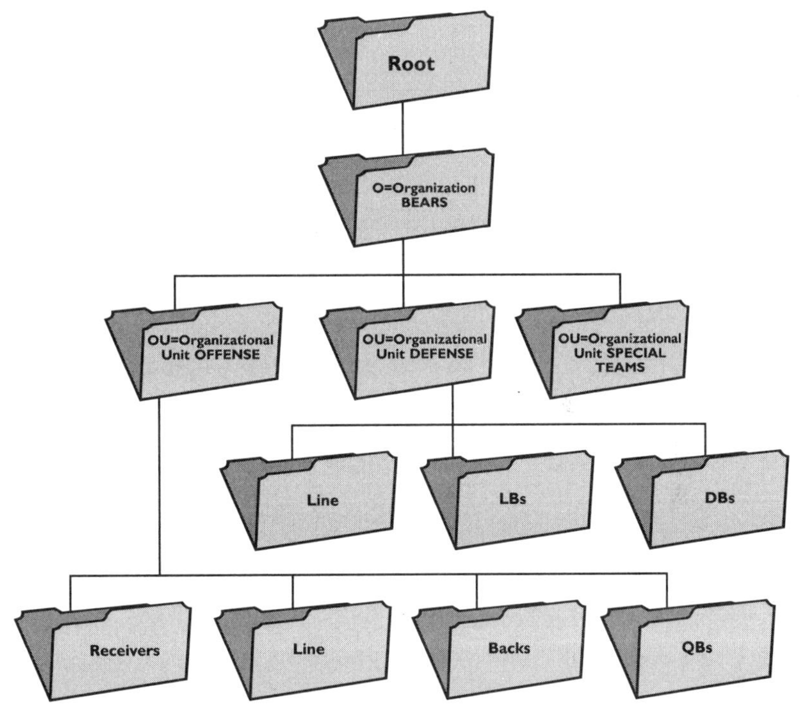

Each type of object in the NDS tree has associated properties. Each particular object has values associated with those properties. For example, the user object has a number of properties, including a login name, a given name, telephone and fax numbers, an electronic mail address, and login and password restrictions. Each user is given specific values for these properties.

(continued)

Properties	Values
Login Name	*mknife.SHARKBITE*
Given Name	*Mac T. Knife*
Telephone	*(555) 867-5309*
Fax	*(555) 867-5310*
Email	*mknife@SHARKBITE*
Account Disable?	*No*
Has Expiration Date?	*Yes*
Expiration Date & Time	*10/01/96 5:30 p.m.*
Limit Concurrent Connections?	*No*
Maximum Connections?	
Last Login?	*11/01/95 1:35 a.m.*

NDS objects include *organizations*, which are usually associated with company names, *organizational units*, which often represent different corporate locations, operating units, and workgroups, and *leaf objects*, which are the physical and logical objects that make up the network—users, print servers, and print queues, for example.

The top of the tree is called *[Root]*. Giving rights to this object provides rights for the subordinate objects. By default, NetWare 4.x creates a user called "admin" with rights to [Root], but the "admin" name is not special the way Supervisor is in NetWare 2.x and 3.x. Admin is created by default, but it can be renamed or replaced with an equivalent object. You can also create a Supervisor user in 4.x if you wish.

The NWADMIN Windows utility uses buttons on the right side of the screen to control the portion of the object information being displayed. In Figure 9.3, the user template is being edited to set a default limit of three concurrent connections. Other buttons allow the creation of default login scripts, print job configurations, security equivalencies, and more.

To create an icon for NWADMIN in Windows, select an appropriate group to place it in (or create a new group called Network by selecting **File...New...Group** *from the Program Manager). Then create an item called NWAdmin by selecting* **File...New...Item** *from the Program Manager. Use Z:\PUBLIC\NWADMIN.EXE as the program name, and click OK.*

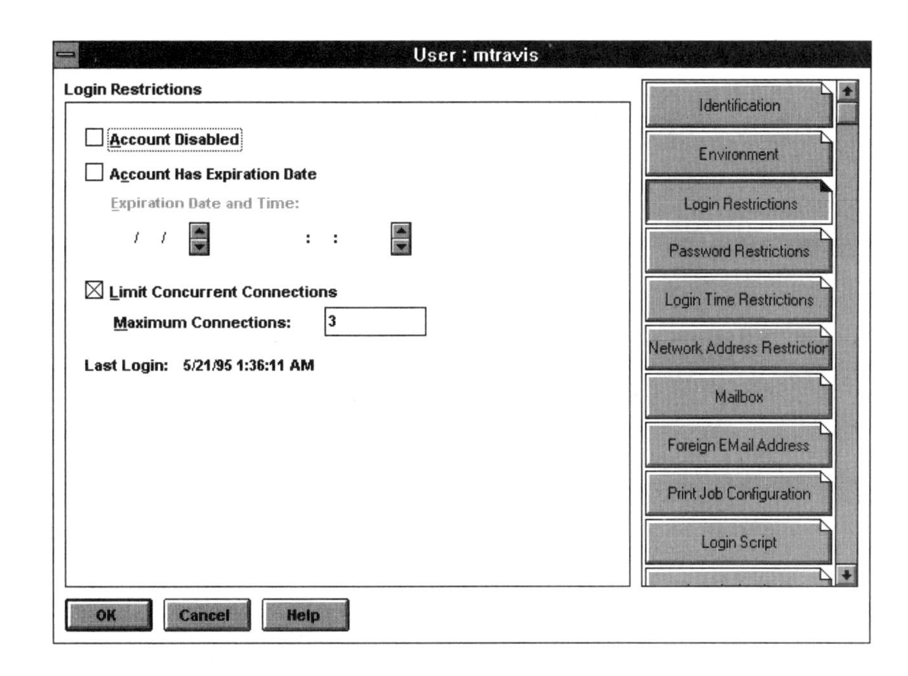

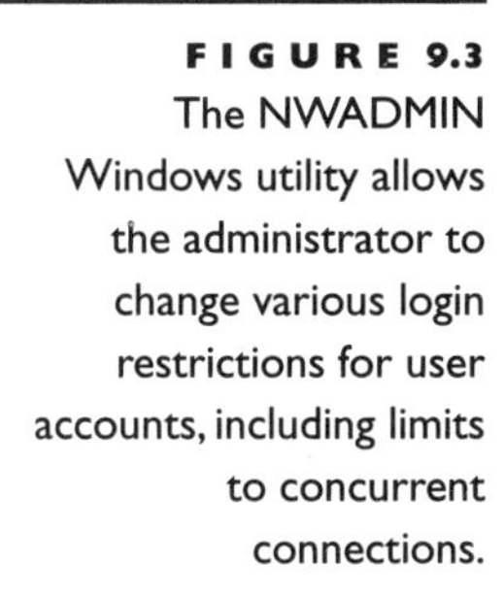

FIGURE 9.3
The NWADMIN Windows utility allows the administrator to change various login restrictions for user accounts, including limits to concurrent connections.

NetWare 4.x makes your implementation a much easier job than in versions 2.x and 3.x because 4.x gives you the power to standardize more settings. You can even set mail addresses and the language NetWare uses for each organization.

CONVERTING EXISTING USERS NetWare 3.x can cause you some grief when you expand your implementation of the standards you created to existing login accounts. The good news is that you can use SYSCON to set account restrictions, station restrictions, and time restrictions for multiple users.

1. Enter `SYSCON` at a DOS prompt on a client workstation.
2. Select **User Information.**
3. Press F5 to select multiple users, and highlight the ones you want to change.
4. Press Enter to bring up the **Set User Information** window.

Creating Large Numbers of New Users

You can also create users in the MAKEUSER utility. This utility allows you to create a user account definition file, called a .USR script, which specifies user creation details such as passwords, account restrictions, and group memberships. One limitation of this utility is that it cannot assign trustee rights to specific files.

Another utility that builds on MAKEUSER is the USERDEF utility. This utility creates a temporary .USR file and creates accounts with the usernames you specify. Some idiosyncrasies of the USERDEF utility are its creation of user login scripts for each user and its appropriation of the Supervisor account's print job configurations for the users it creates.

Neither utility is generally of much use for a manager of an inherited network, but if you do get a large influx of users, you may want to consider these tools to automate the account creation process to some extent.

The **Set User Information** window is shown in Figure 9.4. It allows you to duplicate the restrictions you set for new users and apply them to existing users.

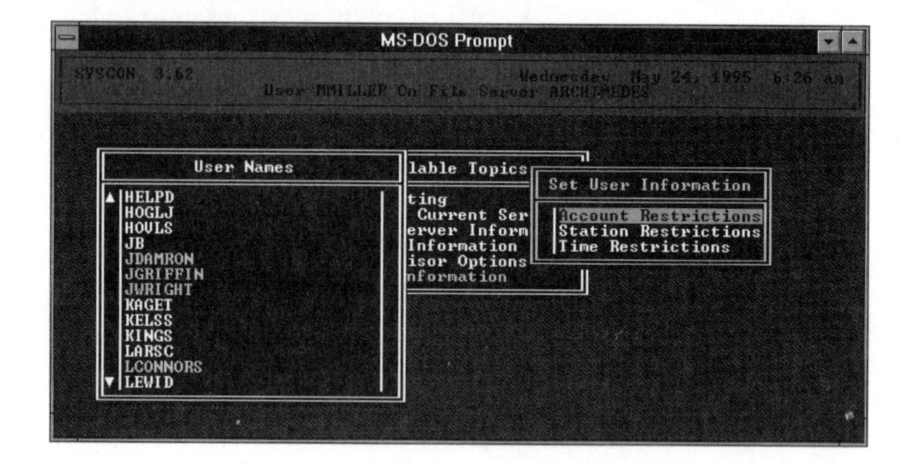

FIGURE 9.4
The SYSCON utility allows administrators to select multiple user accounts and standardize their restrictions using the Set User Information window.

Part of the network administrator's job is diplomacy, and one of the major complaints users have is that the network is changed without their input or knowledge. You've been collecting their input directly and indirectly, but you also need to inform them when you make alterations that affect them. Limiting their access times and requiring password changes definitely fit in this category, so tell your users before you make the changes.

NetWare 4.x, alas, makes your task even more painful. After your users are created, they'll need to be altered manually. This is one reason you should make sure you carefully plan a migration to NetWare 4.x. Many issues that are easily resolved in the planning stage are difficult or impossible to reconcile after an implementation is in place.

Creating Standard Forms of Entry

The name you give each of the objects in your network configuration, whether they are NetWare 2.x or 3.x bindery objects or NetWare 4.x NDS objects, should perform two functions. Each name should convey information about what the object is or does, and each name should help distinguish the object from other objects.

The most prolific object type is typically the user. NetWare usernames should follow a standard that allows administrators and other users to determine who the real-life user is. Group names should convey the way in which the group members are associated. Print queues should indicate the location and type of printer they serve. The names of NetWare 4.x *containers*, which are the countries, organizations, and organizational units that logically divide the *leaf objects*, which are users, servers, printers, and other objects that do not contain other objects, should be short and easily distinguishable.

Username Formats

Usernames appear in many different formats in different networks. In my experience, the most common format combines the user's first initial and last name, so Joe Schmoe would log in as "jschmoe".

If you use this approach, be aware of one problem in particular. NetWare includes a variable that is quite handy for creating a drive mapping to the user's personal directory. This variable, *%LOGIN_NAME*, is set to the user login name, so the if the user directory name is set to the login name, a single

MAP command in the login script associates a drive letter with the home directory. The problem arises when you have a user login name longer than eight characters. Because the DOS directory name limit is eight characters plus a three-character file extension, the home directory mapping does not work. The simple solution is to truncate the username to eight characters. Thus, Ian Anderson would not log in as "ianderson", but as "ianderso".

Some administrators prefer to bypass this problem altogether by using a different naming scheme—often one that involves shorter names. The following are other suggestions:

- First initial, middle initial, first three letters of the last name—for a total of five characters
- First name, last initial—up to eight characters total
- First four letters of last name, first initial—five characters total

Your major concern in each case is uniqueness. Decide what to do if two users receive the same login name before it happens so you can consistently apply your rules.

PC Magazine is run by a fine man named Michael Jeffrey Miller. His first name, last name, and middle initial are all the same as mine, which made mail addressing a bit of a problem when we were both working for companies in the Ziff empire. In fact, we still occasionally receive electronic mail intended for the "other" Michael Miller. And beware...we're everywhere.

Changing NetWare 3.x usernames requires that you create a new user and then delete the old user with the original name. So you may want to retain the existing standard (if one exists), even if it's distasteful to you, as long as it's workable. Otherwise, you'll have a time-consuming task ahead of you. If you create the new user accounts after you make your new defaults, you'll be in good shape.

Changing NetWare 4.x usernames is much easier than doing so in version 3.x. Novell was kind enough to include a tool that allows you to make the change quickly and easily. Simply follow these steps:

1. Start NWADMIN by double-clicking on its icon in Windows.
2. Single-click on the username you wish to change.
3. Select the **Object** menu.

4. Pick **Rename.**

5. Enter the new username.

6. If you wish, you can check the **Save Old Name** box to preserve the old name as an *other name* for the user, allowing other users to search on the old name to find the new name.

Group Formats

Group names are a little bit different than usernames. While login names are typically associated with people with names like "Jim" and "Lisa," groups are typically associated with concepts like "people who need access to the payroll databases." Since group names are also less frequently used to create drive mappings, the eight-character limitation is not usually a concern.

Standard group names formats are difficult to create because groups serve so many different purposes. The idea is to stay away from names like TEST, which convey a small amount of information but not enough to distinguish the group purpose at a glance. ORACLE_TEST would be a better choice, for example. If the reason for the group is still not readily apparent, use the **Full Name** entry in SYSCON or NWADMIN to define the group name further.

Print Queue Formats

Print queue names should indicate the location and type of printer they feed. In very small networks, simple names such as HP4M or even QA may be sufficient. As the network expands, however, names like these become confusing. As awkward as the name 355_DOWN_ETEXT_HP4M seems, it is easy to remember that the printer it serves is an HP LaserJet 4M located in building 355, downstairs in the electronic text processing department. If most users capture to their printers via the login script, they won't have to type the bulky name themselves.

Container Formats

Containers are primarily used to differentiate parts of the NDS tree in your organization. Since they are usually referenced to identify the *context* of another container or of leaf objects, container names should be short. This way, when you describe the location of a particular printer, you don't have to append several long character strings beforehand. In the organization illustrated in Figure 9.5, the user "mtravis" is in the context Line.DEFENSE.BEARS.

FIGURE 9.5
Part of a directory tree showing a user object in the context of its organizational units and organization.

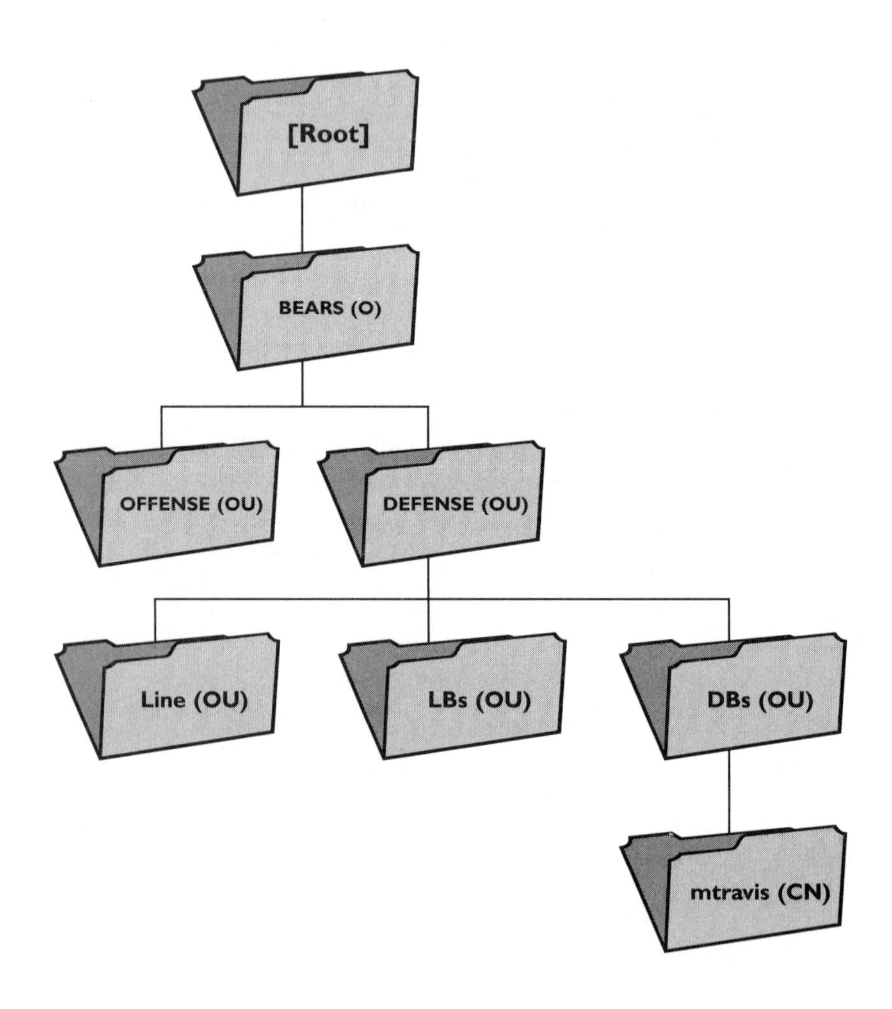

The context is used when describing the *complete name*, which is mtravis .Line.DEFENSE.BEARS in the example shown in Figure 9.5, and when showing the *distinguished name*, which is CN=mtravis.OU=Line.OU=DEFENSE.O=BEARS. The complete name and distinguished name are both derived by taking the common name of the object and appending the organizational units and organization in ascending order as you move up the tree. The complete name identifies the object uniquely in the NDS, and although the distinguished name does the same, it is rarely used. Either one helps identify an object that may be located in a remote part of the NDS tree.

Using NetWare Groups

NetWare groups are generally used for three purposes:

1. Assigning trustee rights to files and directories
2. Allowing access to print queues
3. Executing commands in the login script

The last item in the list will be addressed later in this chapter, in Handling Login Scripts. For the first two purposes, however, you should standardize on the sensible use of groups.

Assigning Trustee Rights via Groups

The fewer trustee rights you can assign directly to NetWare users, the better. You should avoid directly giving multiple user login accounts access to the same areas; instead, you should create groups, add the appropriate users to the groups, and assign the appropriate trustee rights to the groups themselves. This process makes changing the rights (especially removing them) faster and easier. It also reduces the amount of searching you must do to find trustee rights tucked away here and there.

Assigning Access to Print Queues via Groups

You can manage printer access in two ways. One way is to give the group EVERYONE access to all your print queues and then capture print jobs manually. If you have a sophisticated group of users and a wide variety of printer types, this approach may be appropriate.

Most administrators find that the other solution is more effective. Assign access to print queues to a NetWare group, and then use the login script to establish print capturing when users log in.

This approach prevents users from pumping out forest-clearing amounts of paper to printers they shouldn't even be using. It also makes network printing transparent to users, which is very desirable.

Assigning Trustee Rights

Each user has at least two specifically assigned trustee rights, generated automatically when the user is created. One is to a subdirectory on the SYS volume under the MAIL directory. This directory contains the user's personal login script (if any) and print job data. It is also used by some NetWare-aware electronic mail applications.

To make sure that each user has a directory in the SYS:MAIL directory on a NetWare 2.x or 3.x server, run BINDFIX from the DOS prompt. This utility, which is found in the SYS:SYSTEM directory, eliminates mail directories for users who have been deleted. It also repairs other bindery problems. Since BINDFIX closes the bindery database, run it only when no users are on the system.

The second set of trustee rights assigned to each user are for the user's home directory. NetWare grants the user Read, Write, Create, Erase, File Scan, Modify, and Access Control rights by default. These rights are generally appropriate for a user directory. If you choose not to create home directories, this trustee entry doesn't exist.

Avoid maintaining other trustee rights from individual user accounts. Directories that can be accessed by only one user should be placed in that user's home directory. Directories that have shared access should be associated with a group name that provides trustee rights (and possibly drive mappings as well).

Tidying Home Directories

HOME DIRECTORIES CAN write Anacin all over a network administrator's head. If your network users already have home directories, make sure they're in the same place on each server. If your network users do not have home directories and you want to add them, you've got some major work ahead of you. In either case, ongoing maintenance of home directories can be rough because users, like Augeas' oxen, seem to spend much of their time dumping junk onto the network.

Standardizing User Directories

The dream configuration for user directories is locating them on their own volumes, where each user is limited to a certain amount of space and the total space in use does not squeeze out system data or other vital information. The dream configuration isn't necessarily something that can be done in an inherited network, in part because adding volumes typically involves adding disk space, which in turn costs money, which often can't be obtained for "housecleaning" items like streamlining home directory access.

Whether you can partition a dedicated area for your users should not prevent you from placing all your user directories in a single place, however. Check the trustee rights assigned to your individual users. If they all point to the same volume for their home directories, you're probably in good shape. Create a test user, and see where NetWare creates the home directory by default. If it's the same place as the current users directories, you're really sitting pretty. However, if you notice differences between volumes or subdirectories, you should allot some time for standardizing the user directory location.

Pick an appropriate volume, and make sure that enough space is available to add some data. It's always nice to have home directories in a directory with a helpful name such as \HOME or \USER. Follow these streamlined steps to move the home directories that are not in the proper location:

1. Type `FILER` from a network drive prompt.
2. Choose **Select Current Directory**, and move to the parent directory of the user's existing home directory.

3. Select **Subdirectory Options,** and choose **Copy Subdirectory's Structure.**
4. Copy the home directory to the parent directory you've chosen.
5. From the new directory, select **View/Set Directory Information,** and add the user as a trustee with rights RWCEMF.
6. Go back to the existing home directory, and delete it.

This process is painful, but it helps keep your login script simple, allows you to easily remove defunct directories, and helps you assist users who want to give others access to files or subdirectories in their home directories.

Adding User Directories

If your network doesn't already use home directories for users, and you think the enhancement would be useful, you can use FILER to create directories and assign trustees. Since this process could be time consuming, be sure you have a good reason for doing this before you embark on the journey.

1. Type `FILER` from a network drive prompt.
2. Choose **Select Current Directory,** and pick the parent directory.
3. Select **Directory Contents,** and press the Ins key.
4. Enter the name of the new directory (it's the same as the user account name).
5. Select the new directory name from the **Directory Contents** window.
6. Select **View/Set Directory Information,** and add the user as a trustee with RWCEMF rights.

Another way to approach the issue is to determine how many other user changes you'd like to make and create new accounts if that would be more efficient than modifying the existing ones. This involves a lot of work, but if you're going to have to alter each and every user login account for more than one reason, it might be an appropriate alternative.

Maintaining User Directories

Existing user directories may already have collected a mess. You'll need to check for obsolete user directories from users long gone and seek out extraneous files that should be removed or stored elsewhere. You should also make user directory maintenance an ongoing task.

Deleting Obsolete User Directories

When you are informed that an employee is no longer with the company, you should be sure to deactivate her network login account. Most administrators remember to do this, but many forget to clean up the residual trash left behind by the user. Check with the departed employee's supervisor to ensure that valuable data was not stored in the employee's home directory, and then delete the directory and its subdirectories.

If important data is located in the user directory, try to find out the nature of the files. Should they be moved to a replacement or coworker home directory? Another option is to create a shared directory that can be accessed by those who need to. Another possibility is to give the supervisor access to the directory so she can look at the data and move it to the appropriate locations. Be sure to communicate a date by which the data should be moved and follow up so that you can remove the defunct directory.

Reducing Gargantuan User Directories

When some users see the amount of space available on network volumes, they have a Pavlovian response of sorts. Rather than drooling, however, they start shoveling data from local directories to the network. They back up their entire local hard disks to the network. They make redundant copies of all their project, proposal, and memo files. In short, they abuse the space they can use.

If your network abounds with disk space, this may not be a problem for you. However, I've seen few cases in which users who are given the opportunity to use network space as they please can actually refrain from filling all the space available. Fortunately, you can take several steps to identify and eliminate files that should not be on the network.

- Search for particularly large files.
- Search for files that have not been accessed recently.
- Make compression utilities available to users.
- Provide access to archiving tools.

The size of a large file depends mostly on the amount of space available. If you've got multiple gigabytes of space on the network, a large file might be 5MB or larger. If your partitions aren't much bigger than 100MB, however, a 1MB file takes up one percent of the total volume space. To search for files of a particular size, use the NDIR command and filter on file size. For example, you can look for files larger than 2.5MB using this command:

```
Z:\>NDIR /si gr 2500000 /sub
```

This command instructs NetWare to look on the volume mapped to the Z drive, in the root directory and all subdirectories, for files that are larger than 2,500,000 bytes. If it finds some, look at their file names, extensions, and the last date they were accessed to find clues about what they contain and how frequently they're used. Check the username listed as the owner, and then check that user's home directory. Execute an NDIR with only the /sub option to see how much space is taken up by the user's files:

```
Z:\USER\MTRAVIS>NDIR /sub
```

You can also check for out-of-date files, which may be archived and forgotten on the network. Use the NDIR command with an access date filter to identify files that have not been used in some time:

```
Z:\USER\MTRAVIS>NDIR /ac bef 1-1-95 /sub
```

Then check with the user to see whether it's necessary that the files be retained. If the user wants to keep the files, it's possible that an archiving tool can be used to store the files offline or to compress them so they take up less space on an uncompressed NetWare volume (NetWare 4.x volumes can be compressed).

If the user needs rapid access to the files, you can keep them on the network drive as compressed files. Several tools are available to compress files into archive files or self-extracting archives. I like PKUNZIP 2.04g, a shareware package that can be found on most online services and many bulletin boards.

If the files should be saved but the user doesn't need instant access to them, make archival tools such as tape drives or writable optical disks available to preserve copies of the files that can be kept indefinitely. If the files are valuable, add them to your secured offsite storage, being sure to update your disaster preparedness inventory to reflect their inclusion.

Managing Growth in User Directories

Once you've gone to all the trouble of removing the garbage from user directories and freeing up the space for useful work, you should do what you can to restrict the messes your oxen can make on the network. If you're fortunate enough to have your home directories located on a single volume, you can easily impose volume restrictions so that users can store only a specific amount of data in their home directories and its subdirectories. If you have a single-volume configuration and its structure does not allow you to limit the users in this way, be sure to add space checks to your maintenance routines. See the section Planning a Monthly Checkup Routine in Chapter 13 for more details.

Managing the SYS Volume

BECAUSE THE SYS volume is used to store queued print jobs and system files, it's important to police the space available on the volume. Running out of space on another volume can interrupt the workflow, but running out of SYS space can crash a server.

To avoid this problem, don't put unnecessary data on the SYS volume. User directories are best placed elsewhere, for example. You should also keep track of the files you store on the SYS volume to make sure they do not get too large. For example, database files maintained by some backup software packages can grow extremely large if they are not pruned back. Mail database files can become bloated if they are not compacted or reorganized. Make efficient use of the space you have available.

You can increase the threshold at which a server issues a broadcast message warning users that a volume is out of space. By default, the message is issued when 256 blocks are remaining. If you use the default block size of 4KB, the server issues the warning when less than 1MB of space remains on the volume. You can alter this setting from the server console by typing `SET VOLUME LOW WARNING THRESHOLD=x`*, where x is the number of blocks from 0 to 100,000.*

Handling Login Scripts

LOGIN SCRIPTS ARE extremely powerful and can be quite elegant. Unfortunately, many administrators find that the login scripts they inherit are convoluted, difficult to understand, and inconsistent. Since the scripts tend to evolve, you shouldn't judge your predecessors by the state in which they leave their login scripts.

Three kinds of login scripts come into play on NetWare servers: the default login script, user login scripts, and the system login script. As the Apostle Paul might say, "but the greatest of these is the system login script."

Default Login Script

The default login script is intended to be used temporarily. It executes after the system login script finishes, but it executes only if no user login script exists. This is one reason to include a one-line user login script containing only a comment, because the default login script is defined by Novell and isn't likely to work well with your configuration. The default login script sets the COMSPEC command interpreter variable to point to the second *search drive* mapping, assuming that this drive points to a network installation of DOS. Since the drive often does not point to a installation of DOS in many networks, you may find that your users lose their DOS directories from their paths and can't execute basic commands unless they bypass the default login script.

User Login Scripts

One way of bypassing the default login script is to define a user login script for each user on your network, which you can do using the SYSCON utility.

1. Enter `SYSCON` from a client workstation DOS prompt.
2. Select **User Information**, and pick a username.
3. Choose **Login Script**, and create a new file if prompted.
4. Enter a semicolon.
5. Press ESC, and save the file.

The semicolon isn't really necessary, but it gives you visual reinforcement of the existence of the user login script if you need it. If you've got dozens of users, though, you're probably tired of making changes to each login script. In fact, you'd just as soon never select the **User Information** option again. Fortunately, since the system login script can also be instructed to bypass the default login script, the only reason to add individual user login scripts is to seal the security breach discussed in the section Managing User Login and Access Rights in Chapter 8.

System Login Script

The system login script is the bad boy you want to be playing with. It's your one-stop shopping source for establishing drive mappings, network printer captures, and displaying messages to users. You can also run files, update client workstation files, or cause the client workstation to beep. Which, let's face it, is why you wanted to be a network administrator in the first place, right?

The system login script is the first to execute and is started when the user successfully logs into the network. The login script is a small program that uses NetWare variables, DOS environment variables, login script commands, DOS commands, and IF...THEN...ELSE logic to configure the user's network environment.

Variables in the Login Script

You can refer to environment variables set in DOS simply by entering their names. The following standard NetWare variables are useful:

VARIABLE	RETURNS THE VALUE
AM_PM	AM or PM
DAY	Numeric day of month
DAY_OF_WEEK	Name of current day
FILE_SERVER	File server name
FULL_NAME	User account full name value
GREETING_TIME	Morning, afternoon, or evening
HOUR	Hour on 12-hour clock
LOGIN_NAME	User login name
MEMBER OF "*group*"	TRUE if user is member of group, otherwise FALSE
MONTH	Number of month
MONTH_NAME	Name of month
NETWORK_ADDRESS	IPX number of attached network
STATION	Connection number
YEAR	Year number

Logic in the Login Script

The logic contained in login scripts is very simple. The only support provided is for IF…THEN…ELSE structures. (NetWare 2.x doesn't include the ELSE clause, but I already told you to upgrade, didn't I?) You can *nest* up to ten levels of IF…THEN clauses, but this won't make a terribly elegant or easily understood script.

Use the IF test to determine whether a condition is true, and if it is, use the THEN clause to indicate what should happen. Use the ELSE clause if you want another event to take place when the IF test is false.

Although you can refer to individual usernames in the login script, doing so is usually bad form and can create cumbersome scripts. If you have several individuals with unique configurations, you should consider rethinking their situations, and come up with a standard access method. If they simply cannot use the same commands as the other users, you may want to grudgingly create user login scripts for them and record them as exceptions.

Commands in the Login Script

The most frequently executed commands in login scripts are drive mappings, printer captures, server attachments, and login script exits. Other commands can be useful but less frequently so.

Although Novell claims that you need to map a search drive to an installation of DOS sitting on the server, this is not true. Managing multiple DOS versions on the server and in the login script can be a real hassle. Unless you have diskless workstations, dispense with mappings to server-based DOS directories.

MAPPING DRIVES One of the fundamental design features of NetWare is the way it represents network drives with familiar drive letters. This allows DOS and Windows users to view network volumes and directories in the same ways they view local drives and directories. Network drives are defined for users with the MAP command.

There are two kinds of drive mappings. *Standard* drive mappings define the server, volume, and directory associated with a particular drive letter. *Search* drive mappings provide additional functionality. On standalone DOS machines, the operating system searches the current directory for an executable file when a command is entered at a DOS prompt. If the corresponding file is not found, the DOS *path* is consulted. Typical installations search the \DOS directory and then the \WINDOWS directory for the correct executable file.

NetWare search drive mappings are added to the DOS path. In fact, if you use the MAP command to display the current drive mappings on a network-connected workstation, you will find that the DOS path is included in the search drive list, as shown in Figure 9.6.

```
MS-DOS Prompt
C:\WINDOWS>map

Drive  A:   maps to a local disk.
Drive  B:   maps to a local disk.
Drive  C:   maps to a local disk.
Drive  D:   maps to a local disk.
Drive  E:   maps to a local disk.
Drive  F: = ARCHIMEDES\UDATA:MMILLER  \WINCOLL
Drive  G: = ARCHIMEDES\ZFEED:  \
Drive  L: = ARCHIMEDES\ZFEED2:  \
Drive  M: = TEST01\SYS:  \CCMAIL\CCWIN20
Drive  O: = ARCHIMEDES\CD5:  \
Drive  P: = ARCHIMEDES\CD3:  \
Drive  Q: = ARCHIMEDES\CD4:  \
-------
SEARCH1:  = Z:. [ARCHIMEDES\SYS:  \PUBLIC]
SEARCH2:  = Y:. [ARCHIMEDES\APPS:  \]
SEARCH3:  = X:. [ARCHIMEDES\UDATA:  \MMILLER\DATA\NOTES]
SEARCH4:  = C:\WINDOWS\APPS\NOVIX\LANWP\BIN
SEARCH5:  = W:. [ARCHIMEDES\UDATA:  \APPS\ONTIME\OTCLIENT]
SEARCH6:  = C:\DOS
SEARCH7:  = C:\WINDOWS

C:\WINDOWS>
```

FIGURE 9.6
The MAP command shows that directories in the DOS path are included in the list of search drives.

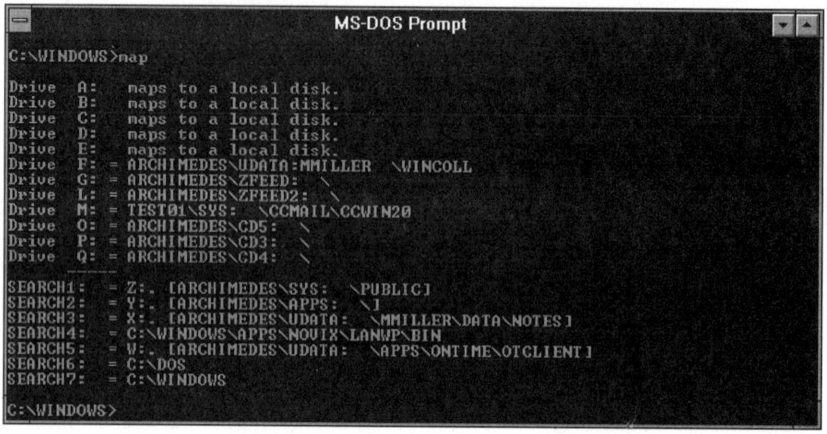

The DOS path itself is altered when search drive mappings are created; the search drive mappings are included first, with the original directories specified in the DOS path appended to the end of the search drive list:

```
C:\>PATH
PATH=Z:.;Y:.;C:\NET\NWCLIENT;C:\DOS;C:\WINDOWS
```

In this example, the original DOS path looked in the C:\NET\NWCLIENT, C:\DOS, and C:\WINDOWS directories when it could not find a command or file name in the current directory. The subsequent network search drive mappings have been added at the beginning of this list, so DOS and NetWare look at where the directories Z, Y, and X point to before looking for files on the local hard disk.

The only drive mapping that is required by NetWare is a mapping to the SYS:PUBLIC directory. You can create a user account that doesn't get this mapping, but after logging into the network, the user won't be able to execute any network commands, including drive mappings, printer captures, or even the LOGOUT command. A command like this one should appear at the beginning of your system login scripts:

```
REM Required map for network commands
MAP INS S1:=SYS:PUBLIC
```

To create a network drive mapping, include a command like the following, which maps the F drive to each user's personal directory on the UDATA volume:

```
REM Map to user's home directory
Map F:=UDATA:%LOGIN_NAME
```

You can also create a *fake root* mapping, in which the drive letter points to a subdirectory, but the user cannot see the parent directories. This type of mapping can provide additional security or can fool applications that want to be run from a root directory:

```
REM Create fake root on G for the DOS
REM Scheduling program
MAP ROOT G:=APPS:SCHEDULE\DOSSCHED
```

CAPTURING PRINTERS The CAPTURE command is a DOS command that routes output intended for one of the printer ports to a network queue. Since the command options can be somewhat convoluted and your printer queue names can be rather complicated, the CAPTURE commands are typically integrated into the login script. The CAPTURE command must be preceded by a pound sign (#) because it is not a native login command. You can specify the queue name and a printer port, but you may also want to suppress the *banner*, a page that identifies the print job and its owner, extra form feeds at the end of print jobs, and automatic tab conversion:

```
REM Capture electronic text group
REM To their HP and Tektronix printers
IF MEMBER OF "ETEXT" THEN BEGIN
  #CAPTURE q=355_DOWN_ETEXT_HP4M nb nff nt l=1
  #CAPTURE q=355_DOWN_ETEXT_TEK nb nff nt l=2
END
```

These commands would redirect output for LPT1 and LPT2 to the HP and Tektronix printers, respectively. Notice the use of the group name (ETEXT) for the printer CAPTURE command.

ATTACHING TO OTHER SERVERS If your users connect to multiple servers, you may want to automate these connections by including them in the login script. The ATTACH command can be run from DOS or from a login script:

```
REM Map electronic text group
REM To incoming data volume
REM On server STEIN
```

```
IF MEMBER OF "ETEXT" THEN
  ATTACH STEIN\%LOGIN_NAME
  MAP I:=STEIN\INCOMING:
END
```

EXITING THE LOGIN SCRIPT The EXIT command is easy to use; the only complication is making sure it isn't executed too early. You can also specify a file to run upon exit from the program, although the path and file name specified must be 14 characters or fewer.

```
REM Return to C: drive
REM And exit to Windows
DRIVE C:
EXIT "WIN"
```

This example also includes the DRIVE command, which sets the current drive to the drive letter specified.

WRITING TO THE SCREEN You can provide users with information about the progress of the login script, network news, or frivolous greetings by using the WRITE command. The following example also includes the PAUSE command, which stops the execution of the login script until the user presses a key.

```
REM News and chitchat
WRITE "The network will be down this Saturday"
PAUSE
WRITE "Good %GREETING_TIME, %LOGIN_NAME"
```

FIRING PHASERS Even less useful than the WRITE command, but somewhat more fun, is the attention-getting FIRE PHASERS. Unfortunately, this command is irritating at worst and ignorable at best. Still, it's fun to play with. You can fire the phasers up to nine times per command.

```
FIRE 5
```

UPDATING FILES Much more useful is the WSUPDATE command, which, surprisingly, is used infrequently. WSUPDATE is a DOS command that compares a specified version of a file to another copy of the file and replaces the second copy if it is older. This command can be very handy when you want to update network drivers or other files. The following example compares versions of the 3C5X9.COM file on all local hard disks and subdirectories to a copy stored in the SYS:PUBLIC\UPDATE directory:

```
REM Update to latest 3Com driver
#WSUPDATE Z:\PUBLIC\UPDATE\3C5X9.COM /LOCAL:3C5X9.COM /S
```

Structuring the Login Script

You want your login script to flow smoothly, with all the commands that should execute for all users located at the beginning of the file. Login scripts accept comments preceded by REM, REMARK, an asterisk, or a semicolon. Follow the programming prime directive: explain what you're doing in the script. For example, you might explain a drive mapping:

```
REM Map the electronic text group members
REM To their shared directory
IF MEMBER OF "ETEXT" THEN
  MAP S:=ETEXT:SHARED
END
```

After the users have executed the standard mappings and worked through the IF...THEN statements, include the EXIT command to allow them to bypass their user login scripts or the default login script. If users employ a menu utility or wish to start Windows or another application when exiting from the login script, include the appropriate file name in quotation marks. If you need to run a file with multiple options, be aware of the 14-character limitation on the EXIT command, and run a batch file with the correct command line instead.

This chapter has addressed three issues, two in a direct fashion and one in a roundabout way. You have been asked to think about the design issues that make user accounts difficult or easy to manage. These design issues include the name format, the way groups provide access rights and mappings, and the way users handle the files in their home directories. You have also looked at specific ways in which you can standardize your network configuration and eliminate the inconsistencies and trouble areas that have cluttered your network stables. Finally, you have just been introduced to some of the utilities that are used to provide consistent, seamless access for users on your networks. Time to get cleaned up and move on to document your shiny, enhanced network.

Cleaning House: Documenting the Network

NOW THAT YOU are painfully familiar with your inherited network, its use, and its idiosyncrasies, it's time to create documentation that will serve you and posterity. You have enough to worry about without keeping track of every bit of information you have collected over the course of the past nine chapters. It's important that you have complete and current documentation because everything you do from this point on depends on your knowledge of what is happening and where it happens.

Furthermore, as you continue your tenancy of the network administrator position, you're likely to drift farther away from some of the information you have recently uncovered. Your carefully designed business recovery plan shouldn't go to waste because the document is gone and forgotten. Your default user configurations should be recorded so that your associates, assistants, or replacements will be able to understand the sense and the beauty of the network they see.

Does network documentation sound a bit more glamorous than it did before? Well, there's more good news. In addition to being important and sexy, documenting a network can be easy—if you've been recording the information as you've been finding it as you should have been. If not, don't exacerbate the problem by moving on to other projects without recording this information on paper. Use this chapter as a guideline, and find the information you need to document the network properly.

The Vital Information

THIS CHAPTER SHOULDN'T take long to work through. The information you have gathered already needs to be collected and massaged slightly so that it's intelligible to other administrators. Use the following checklist to make sure you've completed each of the component documents:

COMPLETED	TASK
❑	Create a server detail document for each of your file servers.
❑	Refine your list of products and their underlying data and processes, the personnel that create the products, and how the network infrastructure supports the products.
❑	Generate a list of standard client configurations for existing systems and future purchases.
❑	Polish your network backup procedures document.
❑	Record your system redundancy measures.
❑	Map your power management device distribution.
❑	Complete your disaster recovery plan.
❑	Maintain a list of exceptions to network standards.
❑	Distribute user documentation.
❑	Begin a network operation and performance record.

Documenting Network Structure

AH, REMEMBER THE section back in Chapter 1, Inspecting the File Servers, when you were going through the touchy-feely routine with your network hardware? Now is the time to make sure that the notes you took are transcribed into a legible form. You'll want to record all the information you can about each server's hardware configuration.

You'll also want to add the information you found in later chapters, including the version of NetWare installed on each server, the number of user licenses for each server, and the applications running on each server. Indicate the kind of work being done on the servers and their interconnections. Then record information about the client systems connected to your network.

Documenting Server Information

File server information includes hardware data that may be useful for distinguishing, troubleshooting, and upgrading or replacing servers. Also include the software that's specific to each server. You may want to generate a list like the following:

- Name
    - IPX internal network number
- Make/model
- Processor model/clock speed
- NetWare version
- User licenses installed
- Bus architecture
    - Map of add-in slot contents
- Total memory installed
    - Memory SIMMs or chips installed
- Disk controllers
    - Hard disks
    - Floppy disks
    - CD-ROMs
    - Tape drives
- Partition table
    - Volume map

NICs

Driver versions

Protocols bound

Network addresses

Network modules and versions

Applications

Networked peripherals

You should also consider creating a network map showing your network and its interconnections, as shown in Figure 10.1.

FIGURE 10.1
A network map makes it easy to find network interconnections and locate routing problems.

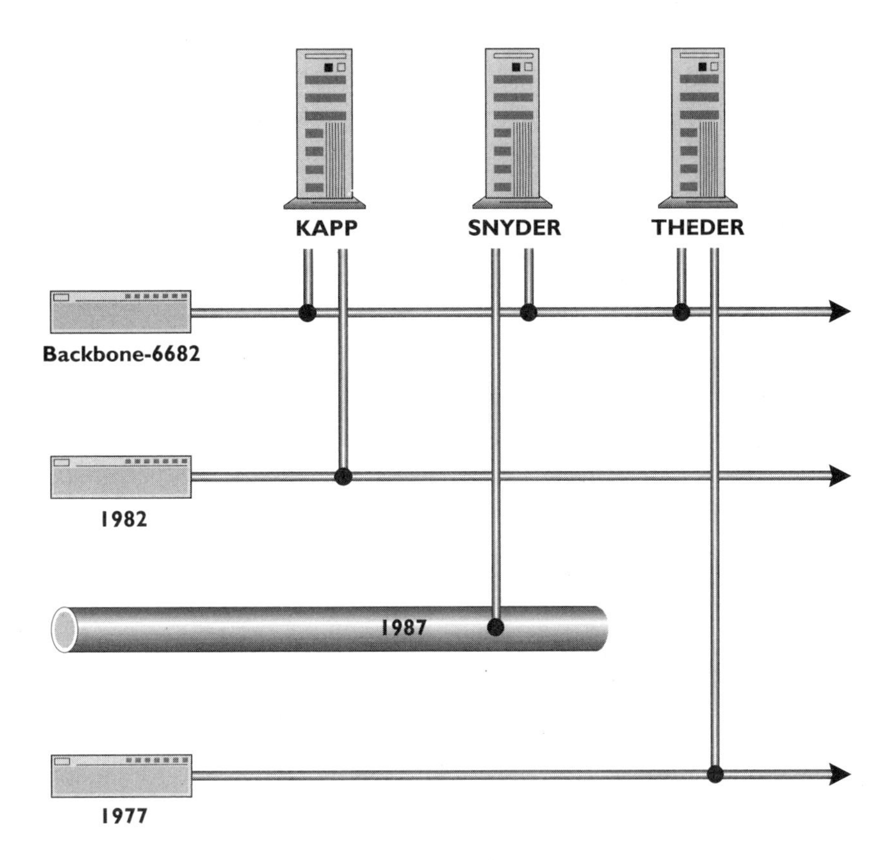

Documenting Work Distribution

To create this part of the documentation, you have to proceed in the opposite direction: rather than identifying the work done on each server, identify the work produced by the organization. Then prioritize the network functions and indicate the network resources upon which each job depends. Take a "top down" approach, listing corporate products and services and then showing the operations and infrastructure that support them. Include the following information:

- Name of the product or service
- Data generated to create the product/service
- Procedures used to manipulate the product/service
- User groups associated with the product/service
- Network resources required to produce the product/service

Documenting Client Systems

You want to know about the installed client systems: the hardware and software in use, and the hardware and software you've selected as your standard platform. You need not include extensive inventories of every client system in your inherited network; instead, record a selected few typical configurations. The age of the equipment in most companies is somewhat stratified—in most cases, hardware is purchased in cycles, so some workstations are getting old, some are only starting to be out of date, and some are new. Record the standard configuration of each "computer epoch." If you have unusual clients, such as an occasional Macintosh user in a mostly PC environment or one OS/2 user in a company of DOS users, make a reference in this part of the documentation to the Documenting Network Idiosyncrasies section later in this chapter.

If your internetwork includes bus topology networks, knowing the location of each client is important for troubleshooting purposes. Expand your network map to include each client system on the bus network. Include terminators, repeaters, and connections to ground.

You should also include the standard user profiles developed in the Supervising User Accounts and Restrictions section in Chapter 9.

Documenting Emergency Procedures

CREATING BACKUP PROCEDURES and a contingency plan were major topics in Chapter 4, Lightning Strikes: Preparing for Disaster. Be sure your documentation includes enough information that your colleagues could run the backup if you came down with mononucleosis from spending long hours in the cold server room. Document the NetWare redundancy levels installed, the safe procedure for a server shutdown, and the routine for storing backup tapes off-site. Create diagrams of the power supplies and line conditioners in use to show the load on each one. Finally, be sure you have a disaster plan that can help you recover from a partial or total disaster. Information you should provide in this plan includes:

- Identifying an off-site operations center
- Creating and distributing a document explaining how to contact you in case of emergencies
- Defining data to be stored off-site
- Distributing copies of the documents created earlier in this chapter to identify the data lost, the systems damaged, and the business functions interrupted by the disaster
- Writing procedures for replacing equipment or relocating users so they can resume work
- Listing vendors, VARs, and insurance companies
- Creating step-by-step contingency plans for the most time-critical operations
- Listing contact numbers for managers and technical staff to ensure smooth operation

Documenting Network Idiosyncrasies

THIS CATEGORY OF documentation is the grab bag for items that aren't significant enough to place anywhere else. These items stand out only because they are unique. Descriptions of highly nonstandard client configurations, server software, user restrictions, and other anomalies are all candidates for this section. You've been working hard to create a coherent and consistent network, but some situations often require a bit more explanation.

This list can be extremely useful for a new hire who joins the organization to help you—or for the person who inherits the network from you. If you identify the unique circumstances up front, you can help them see the logic you used to create whatever homogeneity exists.

Documenting the Network for Users

THE AMOUNT OF documentation you need to provide for your users depends on a variety of factors. The most important consideration is the sophistication level of your users. If your users are highly trained and are already familiar with the network operations they need to perform, your documentation responsibility extends only to changes you make or to complex processes users are starting to undertake.

If your users are unsophisticated, target your documentation to the fundamental issues that concern them on a daily basis. Don't expect to lead them to the networking promised land over night, and don't expect them to understand or remember even the simplest procedures by themselves. The major problem for the unsophisticated user arises in circumstances when something goes wrong—newer users tend to jump to the wrong conclusions and make the wrong judgments. This makes a "what to do when things go wrong" procedure a must.

Most organizations have a smattering of very technical users bringing their own special kind of joy to your heart—using too much of the network bandwidth and resources, making unrealistic demands for new features, and requesting (or taking) more power. Hapless users will pelt you with calls for help logging in, printing, or saving files. Most users fall somewhere in between—having enough knowledge in some cases to be dangerous, but not knowing enough to be completely self-sufficient.

Your network documentation task, then, requires you to make a judgment about your users and to generate material that can answer most of the stupid questions the low-end users ask, while explaining most of the reasons why the network works as it does to the high-end users.

Documenting Basic Network How-To Information

Whether or not your users already have network experience, you should generate some basic information about how to function in your network environment. These documents can make life easier for new employees or workers having trouble with a particular fundamental issue.

The most essential issues are logging in and logging out; dealing with drive mappings, directories, and files; and printing on the network. A one- or two-page document that covers these issues can provide most of the information your users need.

Keep network documentation as brief as possible, and use as many step-by-step descriptions as you can. Users aren't looking for anything complex; they don't care about network operations as a subject, but only as a means to accomplishing their goals.

Explaining Logging In and Out

NetWare security's first line of defense is forcing users to log in before sharing the milk and honey you've so graciously installed on the network. Unfortunately, this security measure can be a mine field for novice users who don't know exactly what the procedure is for getting on to the network—and can't determine if they're connected. Talk the users through these potential pitfalls by *briefly* describing the way to log in—whether the login process is done manually or executed from a batch file.

Logging out eliminates a potential entrance to the network by an unwitting or unscrupulous coworker (or outsider). Encourage your users to log out if they plan to be away from their desks for an extended period of time, and request that they save energy and ensure backup integrity by logging out and powering down their systems before they go home at night. If you have limited their connection time window, indicate the standard hours they can be connected and the message they'll receive if the system logs them out after they've been on the system during nonstandard hours.

A Sample Login/Logout User Document

How to Log into the Network

You will not be able to log in between the hours of 12:00 midnight and 5:00 a.m.

Turn on your computer or press Ctrl-Alt-Del to reboot your computer.

When your system starts up, it prompts you for a password. Enter your password when prompted.

If you mistype your password, type `LOGIN` *`servername\username`*.

How to Change Your Password

Network passwords must be changed every 60 days.

The network password you choose must be five characters or longer and must be a password you haven't used before. Passwords are not case-sensitive.

When it's time to change, the system asks if you want to change your password. If you want to change your password, type `Y` and press Enter.

Enter your new password when prompted.

Re-enter your new password to verify it when prompted.

If you are connected to multiple servers, type `Y` when asked if you want to synchronize passwords.

If you want to change your password before the 60 days expire, type `SETPASS` from a DOS prompt while logged into the network. You will be prompted for a new password and for verification of the new password.

Logging Out

To log completely off the network, exit Windows, and type `LOGOUT` from a DOS prompt.

To log off a single server, type `LOGOUT` *`servername`* from a DOS prompt.

You will be disconnected automatically from the network at 12:00 midnight.

LOGGING INTO THE NETWORK Since it takes place first, logging into the network should be described at the beginning of your user documentation. If your users connect to the network automatically when they log in, your documentation can be shorter because the users won't be running the network client files themselves. Tell the users which files they need to execute, if any—a NET.BAT or STARTNET.BAT file are commonly executed, though most users prefer to have these files called in their AUTOEXEC.BAT files because they always want to connect to the network.

Macintosh clients have the option to automatically log in and add network volume icons to their desktops. Although it is easy to set up the Macintosh to remember its user's login name and password, it is advisable to force the password entry during each start-up to prevent unauthorized access to the network.

SETTING PASSWORDS If you set user account passwords to expire, you should document the password change process after the network login process. Since the user encounters the password change information immediately after logging in, discuss it immediately after the login information in your user documentation. Include information on setting the password between password expiration intervals using the SETPASS command. Also refer to any password restrictions you have in place. The default minimum length for a NetWare password is five characters; include your minimum character length if it's different. Note that NetWare passwords are not case-sensitive. And if you have password uniqueness set, mention that the passwords cannot be the same as the usernames and that they have to be different each time they are changed. Don't mention the eight-password memory in NetWare.

LOGGING OUT OF THE NETWORK Logging out of the network isn't terribly difficult; in fact, your users are likely to encounter only two problems. One is the situation in which they attach to multiple servers and wish to disconnect from only one. In this case, they'll need to issue the LOGOUT command with an additional parameter: the server they wish to log out from.

```
Z:\PUBLIC>LOGOUT THEDER
```

The other potential pitfall comes when a user attempts to use the LOGOUT command from the DOS shell in Windows. Older versions of the NetWare client software cause the system to lock up in this circumstance.

Altering the DOS Shell Prompt in Windows

You can help users remember they have shelled out to DOS by setting the DOS prompt in a Windows shell so the prompt reminds them they're still in Windows. Make sure you have a line specifying a unique prompt by adding something like this to the AUTOEXEC.BAT file:

```
SET WINPMT=Windows DOS Shell$_$p$g
```

This line changes the standard DOS prompt to a two-line prompt reminding the users that they are in Windows.

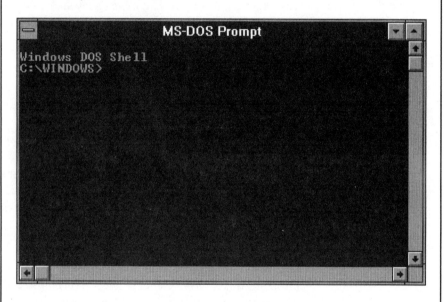

Discussing Drives, Directories, and Files

Now that you've got the steady patter of users logging in and out of the network to keep you company, you're ready to move on to meatier issues. Users are going to be concerned next with files that sit on the network and the drives and directories that act as containers for them.

Remember that the concepts of network volumes—and perhaps even network servers themselves—are not terribly intuitive. If you have users who are barely able to run a standalone workstation, you may want to take a little time to explain how the network files are stored and accessed. But don't do that here. The documentation you're in the process of creating is an ongoing reference, one that facilitates the work of the organization. You can expand the technical horizons of the users later.

A Sample Document Explaining Drives, Directories, and Subdirectories

To find out which drive letters correspond to network connections, type `MAP` from the DOS prompt. The network lists the drive letters and the corresponding file servers, volumes, and directories.

```
MS-DOS Prompt
C:\WINDOWS>map

Drive  A:    maps to a local disk.
Drive  B:    maps to a local disk.
Drive  C:    maps to a local disk.
Drive  D:    maps to a local disk.
Drive  E:    maps to a local disk.
Drive  F: = ARCHIMEDES\UDATA:MMILLER  \WINCOLL
Drive  G: = ARCHIMEDES\ZFEED:  \
Drive  L: = ARCHIMEDES\ZFEED2:  \
Drive  M: = TEST01\SYS:   \CCMAIL\CCWIN20
Drive  O: = ARCHIMEDES\CD5:  \
Drive  P: = ARCHIMEDES\CD3:  \
Drive  Q: = ARCHIMEDES\CD4:  \
       -----
SEARCH1:  = Z:. [ARCHIMEDES\SYS:  \PUBLIC]
SEARCH2:  = Y:. [ARCHIMEDES\APPS:  \]
SEARCH3:  = X:. [ARCHIMEDES\UDATA:  \MMILLER\DATA\NOTES]
SEARCH4:  = C:\WINDOWS\APPS\NOVIX\LANWP\BIN
SEARCH5:  = W:. [ARCHIMEDES\UDATA:  \APPS\ONTIME\OTCLIENT]
SEARCH6:  = C:\DOS
SEARCH7:  = C:\WINDOWS
SEARCH8:  = C:\BATCH

C:\WINDOWS>
```

To determine the amount of disk space available to you on a server, type `CHKVOL *`. This command displays the server volumes and a list of volume statistics, including the total volume size, the space used by files, and the space available to you.

EXPLAINING NETWORK DRIVE MAPPINGS Don't assume that your average user is going to understand how drive mappings work. Most people don't think of their data being on *servername\volumename:directory\subdirectory*. They think of their data being on *F:*. That's why drive mappings exist in the first place—so users don't have to worry about the underlying storage structure.

A Sample Document Explaining Volumes and Directories

When you log into the network, several drive letters are accessible to you. These drive letters point to disk space on the network.

The network hard drives are divided up into different areas called *volumes*. Volumes are like boxes in that they have a set size. We cannot increase the size of a volume without adding more drives to the servers.

Volumes are divided into spaces called *directories*. Directories are like balloons in the volume boxes. They do not have fixed sizes; they hold as much as they need to, but combined together, all the directories on one volume can use only as much space as the volume contains. Directories are divided into *subdirectories*, which are like balloons within balloons. There can be many layers of directory and subdirectory balloons inside the volume boxes.

Your access to the network is limited by which volumes, directories, and subdirectories you can see, write to, and remove files or directories from. It is also limited by how much information you can place on any given volume. This restriction keeps the volumes from being filled by a few users.

Your access to volumes, directories, and subdirectories is made possible by mappings of these locations to drive letters.

Unfortunately, you're not likely to have the same drive mappings as your users do. Even if you have the time to check the system login script and the individual login scripts to see what the mappings might be, you can't rule out drive mappings taking place via batch files or manual mappings from the client station. The bottom line is that you must explain drive mappings to your users, tell them how to determine what their drive letters are currently mapped to, and how to create or delete mappings of their own.

You can probably save search drive mappings for the more experienced users; instead of trying to explain that concept to novices, give them some explanations of commonly used terms, such as *volumes*, *directories*, *root directories*, *subdirectories*, and *default directories*. You have my permission to use the definitions in the Glossary, but when you speak of me, speak well.

Describing Printing Issues

Most users do not need to know how to set up their own print jobs. If your network login scripts automatically capture users to the printers they want to use, there's no point in documenting the procedures involved in configuring the print jobs. Explain the term *capture* so that nobody gets confused when you use the term, but don't worry about listing options for the CAPTURE command.

Instead of concentrating on the underlying NetWare print issues, you can focus on the print utilities your users are likely to need help with. If you have DOS users, you may want to describe how to use the PRINT command from DOS to copy files to a printer port. If your DOS users will always be printing files from an application, however, you shouldn't have to tell them even that much.

If you have Windows users, introduce them to the Print Manager. Show them how to select a network printer if they capture to several. For the most part, however, printing should be an issue users take for granted. Make sure they're set up properly to begin with, and as long as they keep logging in, they should be just fine.

Documenting Basic Network Concepts

You may already have defined some network concepts for your users: logging in and out, capturing, and network volume mapping. In some cases, it is helpful for the users if you create a simplified map showing the network. You do not need to include IPX internal network numbers, IP addresses, or other technical information. Instead, include the server names. Tell the users what kind of equipment you're using and the total amount of disk space on each server. Show network printers if it makes sense to do so.

Don't give away any secrets; what you want to be doing is increasing awareness about the tools in use. People tend to disregard or downplay the importance of things they don't understand, and if they trivialize your job, they may develop unrealistic expectations of you and the network itself. Try to head that tendency off at the pass by briefly sharing the scope and nature of your network.

Notifying Users of Updates and Changes

One way to make users hopping mad is to make system changes they notice without telling them. The changes can be subtle—altering login time restrictions slightly or setting space restrictions—or more noticeable—deleting files or taking servers down. Either way, you're likely to find at least a handful of users who get bent out of shape because you didn't hold their hands and talk them through it.

All they really want to know, actually, is what's going on and how it affects them. That's not unreasonable, and you should accommodate them. Since there are several ways of going about this, you can pick the method that seems best suited to the situation at hand.

One approach is to inform managers whenever a change may affect their departments. You can let the managers decide how to disseminate the information to their subordinates. One advantage of this approach is that you may find out about a problem with your plan *before* the users have been notified.

Another approach is to inform the individual users affected by the change you're making. If you're making a minor change, this approach is probably a reasonable one. This approach may also be acceptable if an entire organization is affected. You should consider creating lists of users in your electronic mail package so that you can send a mass mailing to announce scheduled downtime or a new policy.

A third approach is to send a network broadcast message or an overhead page on the public address system. Consider these options when you need to bring a server down suddenly—or when a server crashes. It's good form to inform the users that the system will go down (or has gone down), and even better form to notify the users when the system is available again. Public address messages are often an appropriate choice for these situations, especially when a server has gone down and a network message won't work. If you opt for a network message, by using the BROADCAST console command or the SEND command from DOS, for example, don't forget that some users may execute CASTOFF or CASTOFF ALL commands to avoid receiving these messages.

Explaining Network Utilities

You may not want to explain any network utilities at all. However, the SESSION DOS utility is a tool that includes useful information and isn't likely to cause much trouble for you. SESSION allows users to perform the following operations:

- Attach to additional servers or view information on other servers.
- Check current drive mappings and add or remove drives.
- Send network messages.
- View and set search drive mappings.
- Select the current drive.

The advantage of SESSION is that its interface is easy to use and navigate. The disadvantage of SESSION is that most network commands that run from the DOS prompt perform the same tasks much faster. You decide whether it makes more sense to use the SESSION utility or the SETPASS, USERLIST, SEND, NDIR, NCOPY, ATTACH, MAP, CASTON, and CASTOFF commands.

You may also want to include instructions for users who wish to use NWUSER (the NetWare User Tools utility) in Windows. However, many users who want to use the user tools won't really need your information because the tools are easy to use and come with online help.

Recording User Information

A different flavor of user documentation involves recording a user's current configuration information, such as drive mappings, start-up file contents, rights lists, and disk space in use. You can incorporate this kind of information into automated routines that are periodically updated to reflect current configurations. These issues are addressed in Chapter 13: Net R_X: Network Checkup Routines.

Documenting Network Performance

YOU WILL DEVELOP this section of the documentation as you work through the following chapters. You'll want to record ongoing operation and performance information, such as problems and their resolutions, enhancement installation reasons and dates, network checkup routines, output from your administration tools, proposals for upgrades, and contract details arranged with vendors, VARs, or support suppliers.

There now, that wasn't so difficult, was it? Don't you feel better with that big stack of paper in front of you? Your network is a dynamic beast, to be sure, and you're going to make some changes, but you now have an up-to-date status report that leaves you free to consider more important issues, like how to solve the problems you're encountering. We'll discuss troubleshooting issues in the next chapter.

Taking Care of the Network

Looking for Trouble: Common Network Errors and Fixes

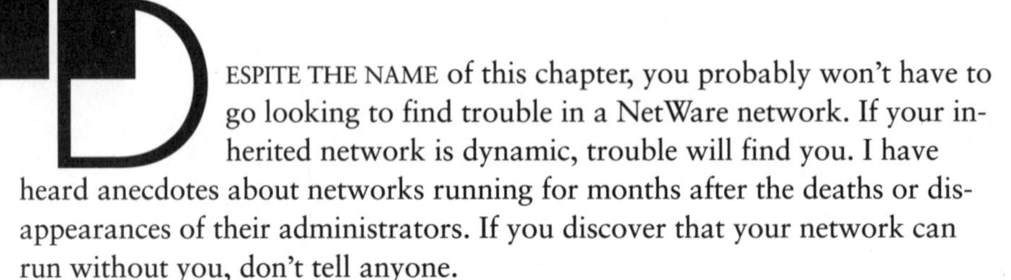

DESPITE THE NAME of this chapter, you probably won't have to go looking to find trouble in a NetWare network. If your inherited network is dynamic, trouble will find you. I have heard anecdotes about networks running for months after the deaths or disappearances of their administrators. If you discover that your network can run without you, don't tell anyone.

If you're like the rest of us, you have changing business demands, user turnover, internal systems under development, or simple disasters such as power outages and disk drive failures. You'll be busy identifying and repairing problems appearing on your network and won't have time to spread apocryphal stories, which is just as well.

The most important troubleshooting for you to be able to perform takes place on the file servers. As long as the servers are operational, centrally stored data is safe, and users can access it when they need to. Of course, your network connection equipment needs to work for the clients to continue working, and the client workstations themselves need to run properly.

Even if your network hardware is functioning, you may find that your users encounter problems with applications running on the network. These problems can be more difficult to troubleshoot because they often involve application design issues rather than network configuration or operation issues. If you cannot troubleshoot the application yourself, you should at least make yourself available to the developer attempting to identify the problem.

The Vital Information

THE FOUR VITAL components of the troubleshooting process are finding evidence of the problem, tracing the problem to its source, eliminating the problem, and documenting the solution to the problem. As your familiarity with the network grows, your ability to troubleshoot the network also grows. In the meantime, consult the flow chart in Figure 11.1 to be certain you're thinking logically and methodically about your network problems.

FIGURE 11.1
Approach network troubleshooting methodically to find problems and solutions quickly and easily.

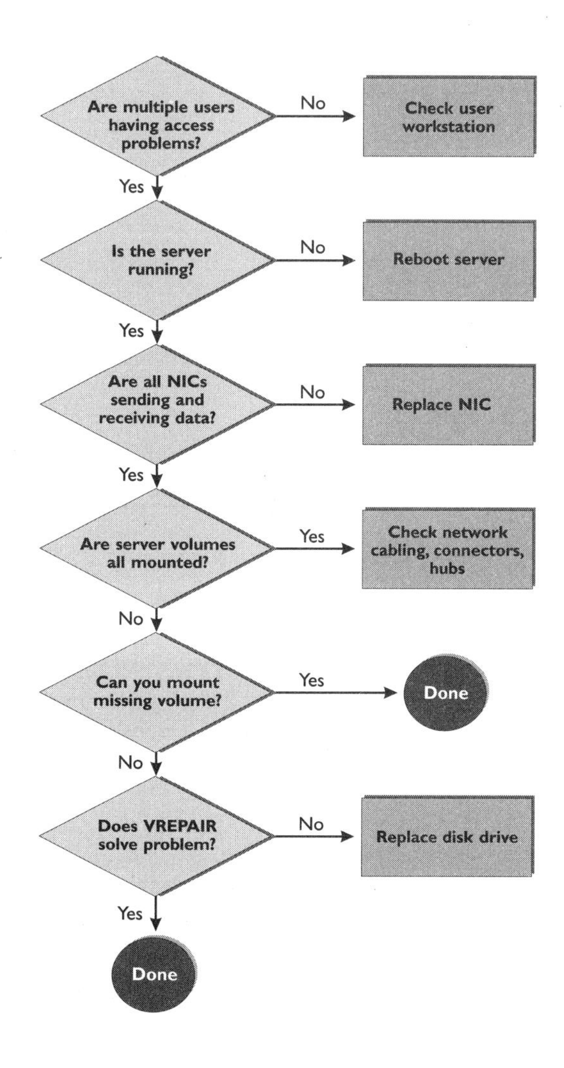

Network troubleshooting often requires quite a bit of investigation, but relatively few problems are truly complicated. More often, the answer is simple but obscured by other problems or incomplete information.

Troubleshooting Server Errors

ERRORS ON THE file servers are squarely in your sphere of responsibility and generally affect a large number of users. Unfortunately, one common problem is that users can no longer "see" a file server or a particular volume they use frequently. When you encounter a problem that appears to affect multiple users, first look for a common network resource, and that resource is often a file server.

Knowing where to look to find the information you need to troubleshoot a problem is the first step. Knowing what to do when you've identified the problem is the next logical step. The bonus step is learning from the problem. If you encounter a hardware conflict that causes a problem on one server, make it a priority to check for that conflict elsewhere. If you update an NLM that doesn't work properly with a server module, be sure to update the NLM wherever it is used.

These common-sense steps will help you locate the problem, solve it, and avoid similar problems elsewhere. For additional information about particularly complex problems, you may need to turn to your VAR, a user group, or an online service.

Using the file server console, the MONITOR console utility, the file server error log, and the INSTALL console utility, you ought to be able to identify most of the problems you encounter. You may be able to use INSTALL, the VREPAIR console utility, and the BINDFIX utility to repair problems you find. Information about INSTALL and VREPAIR is provided later in this chapter. BINDFIX is discussed in the section Checking Security and Bindery Status in Chapter 13, where you'll also find information about DSREPAIR, a console utility available in NetWare 4.x, that you can use to resolve problems with NDS.

Uncovering File Server Problems

When your users or help desk staff call you with problems, check to see whether other users are experiencing the same ones. If you're getting 10 calls from users describing the same kind of problem, you're more likely to be dealing with a server or network cabling problem than with user workstation failures.

Widespread workstation failures do occur; for example, you may encounter a case in which repeated brownouts—temporary sags in AC power levels—cause component failure on multiple workstations at about the same time. These cases are extremely rare, fortunately. If multiple users are having problems, check the server and then the cabling systems they use.

Armed with information about the users experiencing the problems, you'll be able to narrow the field of possible problem servers. In most NetWare networks, users in the same departments log into the same file servers, so you'll know which server to look at as soon as you know who is reporting the problem. Take a look at the file server that appears to be the common source of the problem. Check the following:

Is the server running?

- Is the monitor showing information?
- Does the server respond to keyboard input?
- Is the server console displaying an abend or other message?
- Are the server's NICs sending and receiving data? (See the Is Respiration Normal? section to learn how to use MONITOR to determine this.)
- Are the server's volumes mounted? (See the Missing Vital Organs? section.)

If these items all check out, chances are that the network cabling system is the source of the problem. If the network in question uses a bus topology, you may have some extensive troubleshooting ahead of you. If the users experiencing problems are on a physical star, look at the hub or MAU to see whether it's powered up and running properly. If the connection equipment itself is in good shape, check its physical connection to the server.

Is There a Pulse?

Although there have been many television shows and movies about hospitals and doctors, I defy you to come up with a single TV show or movie about network administrators. Oh, you'll see a smattering of geeks and an occasional sprinkling of cybercriminals, but network administration doesn't seem to appeal to Hollywood as a very exciting topic for TV shows or movies. When you're troubleshooting a NetWare server, you do many of the same kinds of things a doctor would do to a patient. First you see whether there's a pulse.

As soon as you ascertain that multiple users are experiencing a problem, go to the server console to check on the patient. If the monitor is displaying any information, that's one good sign. Press Alt-Esc to switch between various console utility screens (if they're loaded), or execute a console command, such as CONFIG, to see whether the server responds to keyboard input. If it does, your patient shows signs of life.

Keeping up with Packet Receive Buffers

One common problem occurs when the server runs out of network communications buffers. Since this shouldn't happen very frequently, it may be an indication of a problem with a NIC, but it may just be the result of a server setting that is too low for current usage.

Troubleshoot this problem by using the MONITOR utility to check the number of packet receive buffers in use. Then check the setting for the maximum number of these buffers. Packet receive buffers hold requests from clients until the server's file service processes can respond to them. If the maximum number of packet receive buffers is reached, client requests are no longer accepted by the server. If the maximum was reached because the load on the server has increased since the maximum was set, it's a simple matter to increase the number of buffers. If the maximum was reached because another problem exists, however, there's still work to be done.

To check the number of packet receive buffers and increase it, if necessary, follow these steps:

1. Type `LOAD MONITOR` at the console prompt.
2. Look at the current value for Packet receive buffers.

(continued)

ssing Alt-Esc to cycle through active screens.

enter `1` to look at the communications

Receive Buffers.

n value, increase the maximum value by `PACKET RECEIVE BUFFERS` mpt.

and find that the number currently in use (displayed on the MONITOR console utility's main screen) begins climbing, you may need to further increase the value. Repeat step 6 as necessary. If the current value continues to climb up to the maximum value of 2,000 buffers, you probably have a hub or NIC problem. Down the server, bring it up again, and see whether the packet receive buffers value remains stable. If it doesn't, it's time to check your network connections.

Check the **LAN Information** screen in the MONITOR console utility, and look at each NIC to see whether the Total packets received value is increasing very rapidly for one of the NICs. Check the network cabling or connection device attached to the NIC in question to ensure they're intact and operational. Make sure an IRQ conflict isn't affecting one or more of the network cards, and change settings if necessary. Wishful thinkers can unload the NIC drivers and reload them. Finally, replace any NICs still exhibiting unusual behavior.

If there's no response to keyboard input, an abend may have occurred. If NetWare has identified the source of a server crash, it displays an error message. Abend messages are often helpful because they indicate the module in which the problem occurred. Unfortunately, not every abend message gives you a clear idea of what caused the problem. And not every crash generates an abend message. In any case, you have to power down the server and restart it to resume operation. A cold reboot works on a file server very much in the same way as a defibrillator works in a hospital drama on TV.

ABEND MESSAGES NetWare's *System Messages* manual contains descriptions of many system error messages, including abends. Be sure to accurately copy the message you see on the server console so you can find it in the *System Messages* manual or another troubleshooting information source.

The manual is organized so that the exact wording of the message is important. The messages are alphabetized starting with the first word of the message. If the error message is "The file server name has NOT been set," look in the T section of the System Messages manual.

If the error is not listed in the NetWare documentation, you should look for it elsewhere. You can find troubleshooting information on many online services (see Chapter 19 for more information these services), and your VAR may be able to help you.

WHEN THERE'S NO ABEND MESSAGE If the server does not respond to keyboard input but is not displaying an error message, check to make sure the keyboard connection is working. Be sure the keyboard cable is firmly seated in its connector, and toggle the switch on a keyboard sharing device if you have one installed. Although it sounds silly, it's also worth checking to make sure you're using the correct keyboard. If the problem doesn't appear to be communication between the keyboard and the server hardware, power down the server, and restart it.

Watch the server as it powers up to note any unusual error messages. You may see information about file length differences as the server program begins; this is normal. NetWare's Transaction Tracking System (TTS) may want to alter database files to roll them back to the last fully completed transactions; this is also normal.

If the server returns to operation in good shape, log in from a client workstation, and check the server error log for error messages. You can look at the error log from the SYSCON or NWADMIN utilities. To use SYSCON, follow these steps:

1. Type `SYSCON` from a DOS prompt.
2. Select **Supervisor Options.**
3. Select **View File Server Error Logs.**
4. Scroll to the end of the file to view recent errors.

To use the NWADMIN utility to view the server error log, follow these steps:

1. Double-click on the **NWADMIN** icon.
2. Double-click on the name of the server you're concerned about.
3. Click the **Error Log** button for that server.

An example of a server log in NWADMIN is shown in Figure 11.2.

The details in a file server error log may indicate the last operations performed on the server before the crash or may include other clues that can help you find the problem.

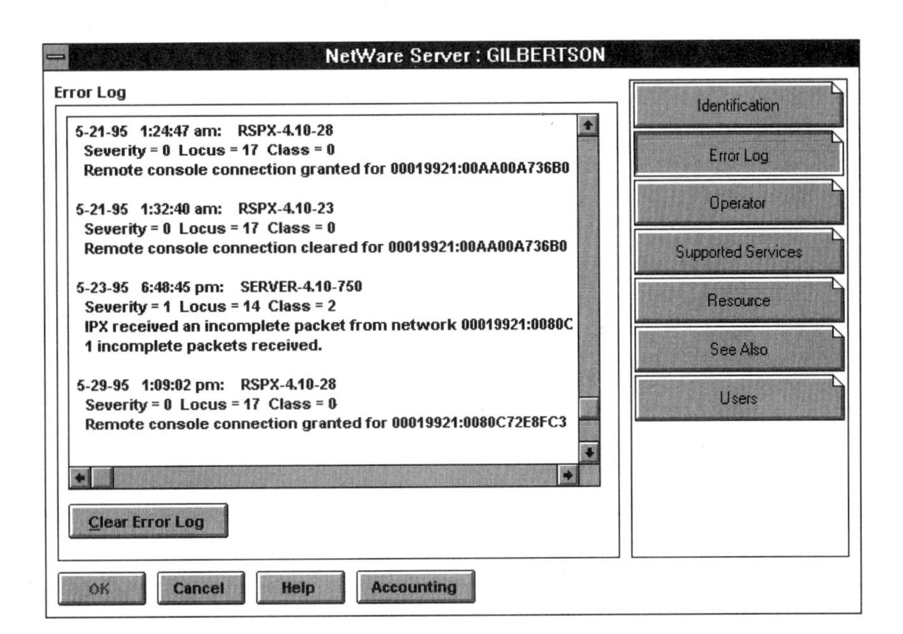

FIGURE 11.2 The NWADMIN utility can be used to view a file server's error log.

Is Respiration Normal?

If your patient's heart is still beating, make sure it's getting air. In our line of work, that translates to getting and receiving data via the NICs. You can check to see that the correct protocols are loaded and bound to the NICs, that the NICs are set to the correct network addresses, and that the NICs are sending and receiving packets. The remainder of this section provides information on how to check for this information.

PROTOCOLS IN PLACE You may find that some users in a multiprotocol environment aren't able to communicate with—or through—a server that has lost one or more of its network protocol bindings. This doesn't happen accidentally very often, but it's certainly a possibility if there's a problem with the NIC or its driver. This would be more likely to happen if someone changes the server settings or does an UNBIND of a protocol. Normally, you'll want each protocol that runs on a server's NIC to be bound to the NIC when you start the server. If you have a routing problem or want to reset the NIC, these protocols can be individually unbound from the NIC.

To make sure the correct protocols are running, type `CONFIG` at the console prompt, and look at the frame type and LAN protocol bound to each network board. Multiple protocols bound to the same board display as separate entries.

Type `PROTOCOL` at the console prompt to see the protocols and frame types registered on the server.

Check the results of the CONFIG command against your network map or server documentation. Be sure what you see now matches what you saw when you created the documentation.

CORRECT NETWORK ADDRESSES Use the results of the CONFIG command to check the IPX and IP addresses on your network. Compare the IPX network number reported for each NIC running IPX with the IP address reported by the same board. Make sure the results are consistent.

If the addresses reported by the network boards are internally consistent, check your current network map to confirm that they're also externally consistent. If you administer an internetwork, an incorrect IPX network number may cause other servers to display error messages on their consoles, indicating that a server is claiming an incorrect IPX number.

PACKETS SENT AND RECEIVED Use the MONITOR console utility to check the flow of data through each NIC installed in the server.

1. Type `LOAD MONITOR` at the console prompt.
2. Select **LAN/WAN information** from the **Available Options** menu.
3. Choose the first installed LAN driver.

4. Make sure both the Total packets sent and Total packets received values are increasing.

5. Check the various error lines under **Generic statistics** to see whether errors have been reported.

The Total packets sent and Total packets received lines, as well as other LAN driver information, are shown in Figure 11.3.

If you see a large or growing number of errors or if packets aren't flowing in both directions, you may need to restart the server or replace the NIC.

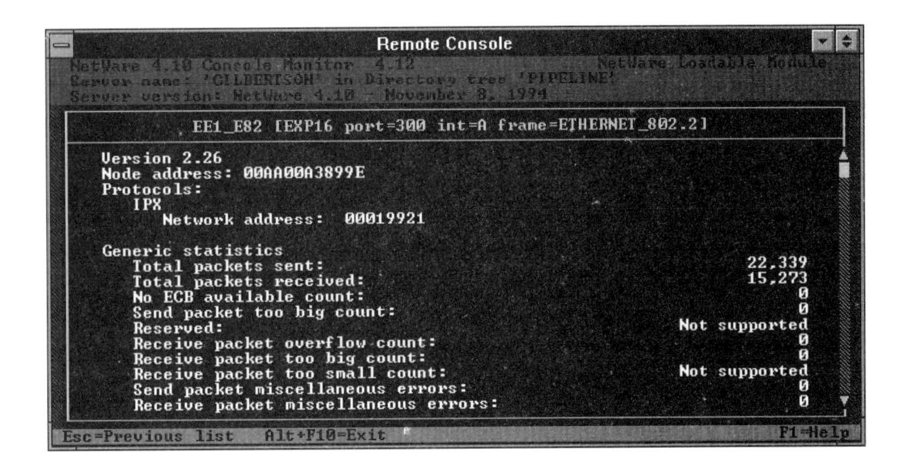

FIGURE 11.3 Each LAN driver entry displayed in the MONITOR console utility indicates the packets sent and received by the NIC.

Missing Vital Organs

Once you've assured yourself that the patient is breathing and has a pulse, it's time to check for the other typical problem. Network volumes sometimes disappear from sight on a NetWare server, and even if the server is running properly, it won't do your organization much good unless users can access the applications and data stored on it.

Problems with disk drives are the usual culprits in these cases, but volumes may also be dismounted due to errors introduced by another problem. For example, your server crashes because its NIC went bad. When you replace the card, the server starts but does not mount all its volumes. This problem is a common one and has a simple and effective solution.

The VREPAIR console utility is an effective way of dealing with many volume-related problems. VREPAIR is easy to use, but it can take a long time to run on a large volume. You may need to apply it several times before it solves all the volume problems, but you will be able to mount the volume once VREPAIR runs without finding any errors.

UNMOUNTED VOLUMES The INSTALL console utility makes it easy to check for volumes that are not mounted. To check the server volumes using INSTALL, follow these steps:

1. Enter `LOAD INSTALL` from the console prompt.
2. Select **Volume Options** from the **Installation Options** menu.
3. Select a volume and check its status.

Each of the server volumes should be mounted. If the status line indicates that the volume is dismounted, you'll want to try to mount it.

MOUNTING VOLUMES To mount a volume you have identified as missing, simply type `MOUNT` *`volname`* at the console prompt. If multiple volumes are missing, type `MOUNT ALL` to mount every volume that isn't already mounted. MOUNT ALL is also a way of checking for unmounted volumes; you won't hurt anything if you execute this command when all volumes are already mounted. It may be prudent to identify the missing volumes before you attempt to mount them.

RUNNING VREPAIR If you are not successful in mounting the missing volumes, it's time to turn to VREPAIR. This console utility is the solution to most volume-related problems; you should check each error message in the *System Messages* manual, but you'll find that the solution to most of these errors is predictable. The volume-related error messages in *System Messages* all reference VREPAIR.

You may also need VREPAIR to solve a problem on a volume that is currently mounted. If an error message indicates that you need to run VREPAIR on a mounted volume, first use the DISMOUNT console command to deactivate the volume.

To start VREPAIR, follow these steps:

1. Enter `LOAD VREPAIR` from the console prompt.

2. Select Option 2 to check the VREPAIR options.

3. Return to the main menu, and select Option 1 to repair a volume.

The VREPAIR options are shown in Figure 11.4. Notice that the current selections are shown at the top of the screen, while the other options are listed at the bottom of the screen.

FIGURE 11.4 The VREPAIR console utility options control the way the utility handles name spaces, changes, and deleted files.

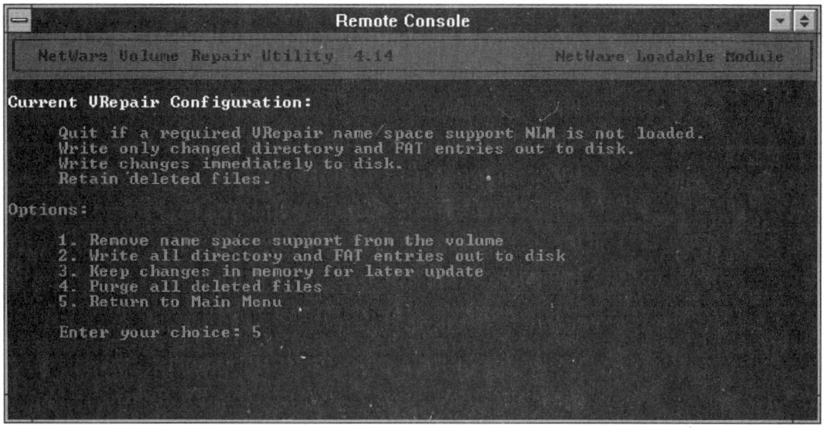

```
Remote Console
NetWare Volume Repair Utility 4.14                NetWare Loadable Module

Current VRepair Configuration:

    Quit if a required VRepair name space support NLM is not loaded.
    Write only changed directory and FAT entries out to disk.
    Write changes immediately to disk.
    Retain deleted files.

Options:

    1. Remove name space support from the volume
    2. Write all directory and FAT entries out to disk
    3. Keep changes in memory for later update
    4. Purge all deleted files
    5. Return to Main Menu

    Enter your choice: 5
```

The first option can be used to remove additional name space support from a volume. The second and third options control the way changes are written and cached, and the fourth option indicates what happens to files deleted during the volume cleanup.

Once you begin volume repair by selecting Option 1 from the main VREPAIR menu, you can check several additional options. By default, VREPAIR pauses when it encounters an error and does not store the error information it records in a file. To change these settings, you can select the other options from the **Current Error Settings** screen, as shown in Figure 11.5.

When you are satisfied with the settings (my preference is not to pause between errors, and I log errors to a file only when I'm not sure why the volume is having problems), VREPAIR checks the volume's FAT entries, mirroring, directories, files, trustees, and free blocks for errors. If you encounter errors

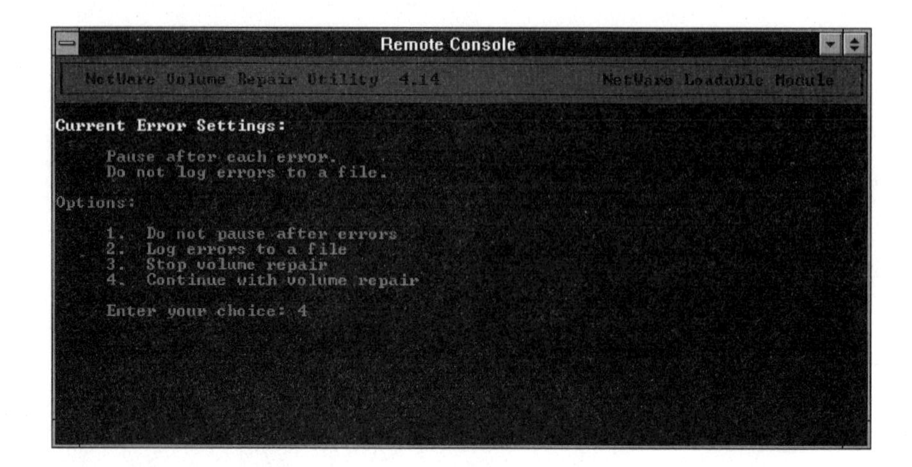

FIGURE 11.5 VREPAIR allows the network administrator to control how the utility responds when it encounters volume errors.

running VREPAIR, run it again. Novell recommeds you run VREPAIR repeatedly until it reports no errors, and then once more, but in practice, you can omit the final VREPAIR to save time. Then you should be ready to mount the volume!

Common Sources of Trouble

NetWare file servers are generally quite stable, but they're particularly prone to three kinds of problems. The first problem is not NetWare's fault—it's due to configuration changes. Whenever you alter the setup of a NetWare server, be sure you document the date and the changes you have made. Most administrators find that the ramifications of changes they make cause them the most grief.

The second kind of problem that occurs relatively frequently on a NetWare server is a component failure. NIC and disk controller failures are the most common, but you may find everything from keyboard ports to SIMMs going bad, even on high-quality servers. These experiences can be traumatic, but they shouldn't be long-term problems if you keep an adequate supply of spares and stay on top of your VARs and vendors to fulfill their warranty obligations.

Finally, NetWare servers can run into problems because the NetWare operating system does not protect memory as carefully as it might. NLMs are not always prevented from using memory they shouldn't access, which puts the burden on NLM developers to write modules that behave well. Since problems with NLMs are often quickly identified and resolved, updating to the latest versions can often eliminate or prevent problems.

Configuration Changes

You have two effective tools to deal with problems initiated by configuration changes. The first tool is planning, and the second is documentation.

Every alteration you make to the server's hardware, start-up files, and loaded software can affect the server's operation. By planning changes before implementing them, you have a chance to review the ways in which the server may behave differently.

The most common configuration-related problems occur immediately after you make the change. Ill-behaved NLMs usually start causing conflicts shortly after the change occurs—and certainly surface as soon as you have a demanding user load. Hardware problems typically manifest themselves immediately, but, as I mentioned earlier, you may see only intermittent problems with SCSI devices.

Some problems do not appear until later, which is why your documentation needs to be complete. When you plan a configuration change, indicate implementation steps as necessary. When you implement the changes, be sure to indicate the changes you made that are different than the changes you planned. Don't forget to indicate the date and time you made the changes.

When you have a record of the modification you've made, you can consult it when problems appear for the first time. Compare the recent changes you've made with the appearance of the first symptoms. These comparisons can indicate which changes may have caused problems, but they may also show that an alteration *didn't* result in problems, which can be equally useful.

Component Failure

Component failure is a fact of life in NetWare networks. Even the highest rated, most reliable equipment available eventually fails, which is why NetWare supports multiple levels of system fault tolerance. When part of a server goes bad, you have two options. One option is to replace the part, which is usually the appropriate response, especially if the dead component can be replaced with a spare from your hoard.

The other option is to upgrade the component, which is a reasonable course of action only when the component is getting old or has been the source of repeated problems.

One lesson to learn from your troubleshooting is to identify components that fail more frequently than others. If you can single out the parts that cause the most conflicts or are the least reliable, you can change your inherited network in a way that tangibly increases reliability. Noticeable improvements always make you look good.

If you're having problems with your disk controllers, you should consider changing models or brands. Even better, you may want to upgrade to a controller with better functionality. For example, replace your existing controllers with RAID controllers that allow hot swapping and improve performance. The incremental increase in cost is easier to justify to those who hold the purse strings when the old controllers have proved unreliable.

Problems with NLMs

The best way to handle NLM conflict is to avoid it altogether. Read about the software you use in trade publications or online user forums to identify problematic modules and any patches that exist. Involve your VAR or a systems integrator before making large-scale changes that would involve several new NLMs. And watch for updates to the NLMs that are most likely to cause problems:

- Disk drivers
- LAN drivers
- NLMs used by other NLMs

You can find these updates on online services, FTP sites, WWW pages, BBS systems, and at your VARs. Disk drivers and LAN drivers are usually developed by the manufacturers of the disk controllers and NICs used in your servers. NLMs used by other NLMs are common modules that are used widely and frequently enough that they may be a source of problems. New NLMs may require specific versions of these common NLMs or may uncover limitations of these NLMs.

The most extreme example of an NLM used by other NLMs is the CLIB.NLM module, which is a library of routines used by other programs. Updates to this module are posted quarterly to Novell's online sites, which are discussed in more detail in Chapter 19.

Identifying Connection Problems

A VARIETY OF PROBLEMS may appear on your physical network. Cable and connector degradation, electromagnetic interference (EMI), and cable length limitations are the most common sources of physical network problems. Connection equipment, such as patch panels, hubs, and routers, can also cause problems.

Cables and Connectors

One common problem with cabling is that it is exposed to the environment. Users can damage cables and their connectors, especially when users move client workstations or inadvertently kick their wiring boxes and separate their network patch cables from their connectors. Most of these cable problems can be identified by inspection or by using a cable tester.

A cable tester connects to both ends of a cable and identifies reversed wires, which are not likely to be found on an inherited network. You may find your cable supplier gave you some faulty new cables. A tester also checks the cable integrity from connector to connector. One way to check an entire cable run on a 10BaseT client is to connect one half of the tester to the connector that sits in the user's NIC, and connect the other half to the connector that sits in the network hub. The tester indicates if a fault exists anywhere along the entire intervening length of cable.

You should also be checking the cable itself to ensure that it's the proper type for the network in place. The connectors should be the correct size and shape, and terminators should have the correct resistance.

Avoiding Interference

The rat's nest of cabling that populates most wiring closets can be the source of physical network problems because of EMI. Although crosstalk (interference) between the strands in a UTP cable can be problematic, external sources such as power supplies and power cables can also cause trouble. Using high-quality category 5 UTP cable can minimize the effect of crosstalk, but if you work in a 10BaseT environment, be careful about how your cabling is routed to avoid external sources of interference.

Coaxial cable inherently resists EMI much better than UTP cabling because of the former's electromagnetic properties. STP's shielding reduces the effects of interference, but fiber optic cabling is virtually immune to the effects of EMI.

Cabling within the Lines

The maximum cable lengths supported by your network depends on the topologies and access methods in use. You need to understand your network's physical layout to be able to determine the total network length and the length of each network segment.

Ethernet Cabling Restrictions

Your Ethernet networks employ either bus or star topologies, depending on the implementation. Thick and thin Ethernet use a physical bus topology, with a limit on each LAN of five segments, four repeaters, and three segments supporting workstations. Table 11.1 indicates the maximum total length, segment length, and workstation limits for each flavor of Ethernet.

TABLE 11.1 Ethernet cable restrictions depend on the cable type and topology in use.

	10Base5 Thick Ethernet	10Base2 Thin Ethernet	10BaseT Ethernet
Overall Length Limit	1,525 feet	3,000 feet	N/A
Segment Length Limit	1,625 feet	600 feet	325 feet (hub to NIC)
Client Systems Limit	100	30	N/A

Token Ring Cabling Restrictions

Token Ring networks pass tokens around logical rings in their MAUs, which also act as the center of their physical star topologies. Token Ring networks are very stable, in part because Token Ring NICs take themselves off the network when they fail, allowing the token to be passed to other stations on the ring. A NIC that does not shut itself off may prevent the token from being passed, but this event is relatively uncommon.

Token Ring cable is typically Type 1 or Type 2 STP or Type 3 UTP. Fiber optic cable is also used but is less common. STP and UTP cable limits are shown in Table 11.2.

TABLE 11.2 Token Ring cable restrictions are different for shielded and unshielded twisted pair networks.

	Token Ring over STP	Token Ring over UTP
Single MAU Length Limit	975 feet	325 feet
Multiple MAU Length Limit	325 feet	145 feet
MAU Separation Limit	650 feet	390 feet
Network Node Limit	240	72

ARCNet Cable Restrictions

ARCNet networks generally use RG-62 coaxial cable, which is less expensive and not the same as the RG-58 cable used in thin Ethernet networks. Be sure the support personnel installing your ARCNet or thin Ethernet cabling know the difference. ARCNet networks wired with UTP cable are not uncommon, but as you can see from Table 11.3, the cable limitations are rather more severe for twisted pair ARCNet networks.

TABLE 11.3 ARCNet cable restrictions are more limiting on UTP networks than on the more common coaxial networks.

	ARCNet over Coaxial	ARCNet over UTP
Overall Length Limit	20,000 feet	20,000 feet
Length Limit Between Active Hubs and NICs or Other Active Hubs	2,000 feet	6 feet between NICs
Length Limit Between Passive Hubs and NICs or Other Passive Hubs	100 feet	N/A
Network Station Limit	255	255 per ring

Resolving Client Errors

Client workstations on NetWare networks can experience a variety of problems. If you're the primary technical support person for an organization or department, you have to troubleshoot client machines as well as servers. If you have a larger, more centralized support organization, you may need to respond only to problems that are network related.

In either case, the most common problems are the obvious ones—the system is not physically connected to the network or the user has not successfully logged into the network—so it's a good idea to check the simple solutions first. If the client is getting a "file server cannot be found" error message when loading the network client software, check the network connections and cabling before you replace the NIC.

You can narrow your search for a problem on a NetWare client workstation in three ways. The first is to narrow your search based on the evidence you see. This approach is useful if you have seen the error before or if it indicates a problem with a particular subsystem or setting.

The second way of narrowing your search for the source of a client problem is to identify a change that preceded the problem. If you can identify what was added, removed, or altered before the user began encountering difficulties, you are likely to have uncovered the source of the problem.

If neither of these methods reveal the source of trouble, troubleshoot from the ground up. That is, make sure the basic components are functioning properly at the hardware level, and work your way through software configuration, applications in use, and the users themselves. You may want to use a troubleshooting checklist for these instances.

WORKING?	COMPONENT	SUBCOMPONENT
❑	Power	Power source Power cable Power supply
❑	Keyboard	
❑	Display	Monitor Monitor cable Graphics board
❑	Network connection	Cabling NIC
❑	Motherboard	Battery BIOS Other circuits
❑	Operating system	Version Executables Configuration files

WORKING?	COMPONENT	SUBCOMPONENT
❑	Network software	NetWare configuration files NetWare ODI drivers NetWare VLMs
❑	Applications	Option settings Installation
❑	User problem	Compatibility issues

User error is the most common source of problems with client workstations in most networks. Unfortunately, as soon as you react in a knee-jerk manner and blame the users, they'll uncover problems with the network and burn you. It's more professional for you to quickly eliminate possible sources of errors other than user error.

Be certain to use your troubleshooting to cover future events. If you find a particular NIC model is failing more frequently than other models, record the incidents and make a case for standardizing on another product. If your users have more difficulty with one process than with others, create a tip sheet or other documentation to help guide them or automate the process for them, if possible.

This chapter describes processes for troubleshooting servers, network cabling, and client workstations. The problems you encounter should suggest enhancements and upgrades that are appropriate for your network, but you should also consider some upgrades even if you aren't experiencing any problems. Upgrade suggestions are provided in the next chapter.

Gotta Have It: Upgrades You Need Immediately

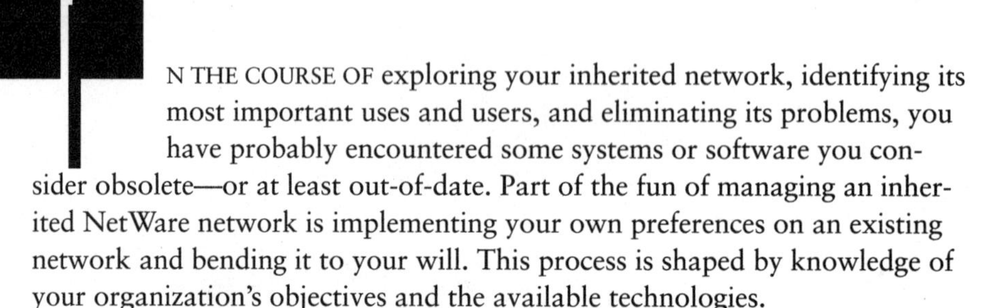

IN THE COURSE OF exploring your inherited network, identifying its most important uses and users, and eliminating its problems, you have probably encountered some systems or software you consider obsolete—or at least out-of-date. Part of the fun of managing an inherited NetWare network is implementing your own preferences on an existing network and bending it to your will. This process is shaped by knowledge of your organization's objectives and the available technologies.

Upgrading a network is an ongoing process that involves salesmanship and planning on your part. These long-term development issues are discussed in Chapters 16 and 17. At the moment, you need to consider the upgrades necessary to keep the network running properly. These may be hardware or software upgrades, although operating system upgrades are usually the most compelling. Look through the Vital Information section in this chapter to see a list of possible upgrades you can make to your network. Then consider the reasons why you should upgrade a component, evaluate the price tags for the upgrades, and decide whether you want to make a case to management for implementing a change immediately.

Whether you change right away or postpone the upgrade until later—when you have a larger budget, more familiarity with the network, or fewer fires to fight—you should not simply dismiss these options out of hand. If you think the upgrade is a good idea, schedule time to develop an implementation plan. If you believe the upgrade is unnecessary, write yourself a quick explanation outlining your reasons. If you are asked why you haven't made a change listed in Vital Information, you can respond intelligently. In addition, if you have a change of heart, you can address your former reservations.

The Vital Information

IN THIS CHAPTER, we'll be looking at upgrades you'll want to consider immediately. These are issues that may be worth addressing even if funds aren't budgeted for upgrades. Expanding the network, replacing faulty equipment, and eliminating the grossly inefficient use of resources are your immediate targets. Consider the following items, and think about whether upgrades would dramatically improve the performance or reliability of your network.

UPGRADE NEEDED?	IMMEDIATE UPGRADE OPTION	REASON
❑	Server license upgrade	Add users
❑	NetWare version upgrade	Replace obsolete/buggy version
❑	Server upgrades	Add disk space Add fault tolerance Add memory Improve inefficient routing Upgrade obsolete hardware
❑	Client software upgrade	Increase user efficiency
❑	Print server upgrade	Ensure reliable printing
❑	CD-ROM centralization	Reduce client equipment costs Free DOS memory

Upgrading Servers

THERE ARE THREE kinds of compelling server upgrades. The simplest of these is upgrading a user license. If the servers on your network are filled to capacity and need to accommodate more users, a license upgrade is necessary.

Another type of compelling server upgrade is an operating system upgrade. If you're using an obsolete or a bug-plagued version of NetWare, you should upgrade to a later version. The licensing arrangement provided with NetWare 4.x allows network administrators more flexibility in selecting the number of users appropriate to their networks, and many administrators find this a compelling reason to upgrade.

A third type of compelling server upgrade is a bit broader. Hardware upgrades are likely to take the form of disk space additions, fault tolerance measures, or system upgrades. Adding disk space is easy in a NetWare environment, especially if your servers use SCSI controllers. Adding RAID, disk mirroring, disk duplexing, or SFT III may also be a measure you want to take immediately. Finally, upgrading the server hardware itself—from a 386-based ISA system to a Pentium-based EISA or PCI server, for example—may be important if the load on the server is too great.

When you have identified the most important upgrades, identify the products you need to purchase, and estimate the upgrade costs. Then create a list of steps you need to follow to implement the upgrade. Finally, outline the advantages of the new configuration, emphasizing cost and efficiency issues.

Upgrading Server Licenses

Before you suggest spending hundreds or thousands of dollars increasing the number of user licenses, make sure that the licenses are needed. Are there other servers on the network that are running below capacity? It may be that a redistribution of users can solve the problem.

In many cases, a redistribution of users would increase network traffic because users whose client workstations connect to one physical network would be logging into servers on other physical networks. That doesn't make much sense; you want to be *decreasing* the number of connections that must be routed through the network. You may also find that adding users to other

Upgrading Your Network Topology

A network topology upgrade is neither fish nor fowl. It may require changes to servers and clients, but it could require that you only replace the network cabling. In most cases, a change in topology can be made a long-term project and a budgeted item. However, you may find that an upgrade is necessary in Ethernet networks using a bus topology.

Thick and thin Ethernet configurations are easy to understand, and coaxial cable is more resilient and resistant to EMI than UTP cable used in 10BaseT Ethernet. However, bus topologies can be difficult to maintain, especially when aging cables and connectors lead to unreliable connections.

You may not be able to convince management to pay for upgrades to Category 5 UTP cable and managed Ethernet hubs. Upgrading the cabling, connectors, and terminators on the Ethernet bus may suffice. If you hope to take advantage of switched Ethernet or some of the fast Ethernet solutions, however, you need to make UTP cabling on a star topology a priority upgrade.

servers requires copying many files between servers and forces changes to the other server login scripts. If these kinds of trickle-down changes require a lot of time to perform, test, and troubleshoot, you may be better off spending the money on more licenses instead.

If you decide to purchase additional licenses, check to see what licensing options are available for your version of NetWare. Consult your VAR for prices and for the number of users that can be added. You may find that you have to change NetWare versions to add additional users.

Adding User Licenses

To add additional users to an existing NetWare 4.x server, follow these steps:

1. Type `LOAD INSTALL` at the server console prompt.
2. Insert the new license diskette in the server's floppy drive.
3. Select the **License Options** entry. NetWare reads the license diskette and adds the number of users to your network.

Removing User Licenses

If you want to remove user licenses, you can do so in NetWare 4.x by following these steps:

1. Type `LOAD INSTALL` at the server console prompt.
2. Select the **License Options** entry.
3. Press the F8 key to delete the last license installed.

You can repeat this process until only the original user license is installed. Removing additional licenses from one server allows you to use those licenses on other servers that require more connections.

Replacing or Changing User Licenses

If you want to completely restart your licensing arrangement, follow these steps:

1. Type `LOAD INSTALL` at the server console prompt.
2. Select the **License Options** entry.
3. Press the F8 key to delete the installed user license.
4. Insert an original license diskette in the server's floppy drive.

In this case, INSTALL won't accept a user license upgrade disk. The first license installed must be an original NetWare license disk.

Upgrading NetWare Versions

If your internetwork includes servers running NetWare 2.x, you should definitely consider upgrading to a current version of the operating system. If your 2.x servers are running without problems and don't need to be expanded or enhanced, upgrading may not be your top priority, and that's fine. However, the newer products offer a variety of enhancements, and if you feel tentative about dealing with NetWare 4.x, version 3.x is mature and stable.

If you administer a NetWare 3.x network, you're not likely to need an emergency upgrade. If you want to add additional users, you may find that an upgrade is more cost effective than buying more user licenses; otherwise, upgrading immediately isn't necessary. See the section Upgrading Server Software in Chapter 18 for more information about upgrading to NetWare 4.x.

If you are using a version earlier than NetWare 4.1, you need to upgrade to version 4.1 immediately. The latest version has eliminated many of the bugs that plagued the early releases of version 4.x—4.0, 4.01, and 4.02.

NetWare Installation

You can use the INSTALL console utility included with the latest versions of NetWare to upgrade your network operating system. Run this installation program on the server you are upgrading. You can upgrade a NetWare 3.1x server to NetWare 3.12 or 4.1 and a NetWare 4.0x server to version 4.1.

Across-the-Wire Migration

Installing a new server when you upgrade NetWare is a good option for administrators of NetWare 2.x and 3.x networks who wish to upgrade from their bindery-based versions of NetWare to NDS. The MIGRATE utility runs on a client workstation and converts the bindery database on the existing server to an NDS structure on the new server.

Same-Server Migration

You can also use the MIGRATE utility to install NetWare 4.x on a server that is currently running NetWare 2.x or 3.x. This migration is achieved in several steps:

1. Back up the data files on the server.
2. Use MIGRATE to convert the bindery to NDS, and store it on a client workstation.
3. Upgrade the server system software to NetWare 4.x.

4. Restore the data files from backup.
5. MIGRATE the NDS from the client system to the server.

In-Place Upgrade

In-place upgrades convert NetWare 2.x servers to 3.x, allowing further upgrade to NetWare 4.x using the methods I described in the previous section. The process of converting from NetWare 2.x to 3.x involves a number of stages:

1. NetWare performs a server inventory to identify the contents of the NetWare 2.x file system.
2. NetWare analyzes each disk on the NetWare 2.x server to identify blocks that need to be moved and to ensure adequate disk space for the new file system.
3. NetWare then installs the NetWare 3.x file system on the server.
4. Finally, NetWare converts the 2.x bindery to a version 3.x bindery.

Server Hardware Upgrades

By now you should be familiar with the hardware components that make up your NetWare servers, the tasks these servers are expected to perform, and the problems they encounter. Some or all of the following systems may require upgrades:

- Disk Subsystems
    - Capacity
    - Redundancy
        - Mirroring
        - Duplexing
        - RAID

RAM

NICs

Number

Type

Servers

Before you make wholesale changes to your client workstation configurations, test the new software on selected stations. Other technical support staff, sophisticated users, and users with special needs are all potential targets of the latest client software.

Beefing Up Disk Subsystems

Adding disk space is likely to be on your immediate "to-do" list. Few inherited networks have adequate space for future growth, and more space for data is a perpetual need in most organizations. If your servers use SCSI disk controllers, you can simply add disks to the SCSI chain up to the seven-drive limit. This limit is a problem on some of the servers I administer, especially those that needed the most disk space in the old days, when disk prices were high and disk densities were low. These older servers tend to have SCSI chains filled to capacity with 1GB and 2GB drives. You can currently obtain 4GB drives in a half-height, 5.25" form factor, and 9GB drives are available in full-height, 5.25" packages. If you're already at the limit of your SCSI chain, you can add additional SCSI controllers or replace some lower-density drives with newer, high-density models.

Disk fault tolerance has been discussed in Chapter 2 and Chapter 4. If you have identified mission-critical data residing on disks that are not mirrored, duplexed, or included in a hot-swappable array, you have a good reason to upgrade immediately. Budget redundancy of some kind for all your servers, but spend money immediately if vital data is unprotected.

Adding RAM

If you're adding additional disk space, your users are likely to fill the space with directories full of files. The more files and directories your users create, the more memory your servers need to provide effective file caching. Heavy user loads and processor-intensive NLMs also increase server memory requirements because the additional service processes running on the server take up additional memory.

If some of your servers run database programs, such as Oracle, they may need even more memory. Check with your database administrator to determine whether additional memory needs to be installed.

Enhancing NICs

If you're adding users to your networks or if your network users are accessing files or resources on multiple servers, you should consider adding NICs to your servers. These new NICs might directly connect servers to existing physical networks to reduce network traffic. They might also connect to entirely new physical networks that support new groups of users. Either way, adding NICs to your servers may improve your network's efficiency.

If your server NICs are troublesome or underpowered, you should think about upgrading some or all of them to faster, more reliable models. Your ARCNet network may be fine for your users, but its 2.5 Mbps throughput is probably inadequate for your server backbone. Upgrading to 100BaseT or 16 Mbps Token Ring—even if it's just for the backbone—may be a good move. Look at the distribution of work and users to find likely bottlenecks.

Upgrading Servers

Time is unkind to servers as well as humans. Although computers don't tend to wrinkle, they show their age by becoming slower and less reliable than new equipment. If your file servers have 386 processors, ISA bus designs, or IDE drives, they may be ready to be put out to pasture. Upgrading individual components rather than entire server units may seem a reasonable option, but servers push their hardware to the limit, and older designs are indicative of older equipment that may develop other problems. Years of heat, dust collection, and the insertion and removal of adapters can conspire to cause failure. Retire the really old equipment, especially if it gives you any trouble.

Implementing Client Upgrades

THE OLD CLIENT software for NetWare networks is a drag. The software for DOS and Windows users, in particular, has improved in the latest versions of NetWare. Many users in evolving network environments retain the original client software installed when they were first connected to the network.

Updating your client systems to the new NetWare DOS Requester software is easy if you have NetWare 3.12 or 4.x software installed, and you can automate the installation process to ensure that the latest files are copied to each network user's workstation. An automation procedure is described in the section Automating Checkup Routines in Chapter 13.

If you copy the client software installation program to a network volume, you can install the DOS Requester on the network for client systems that are already connected to the network. Since the INSTALL console utility also allows you to create installation diskettes, you can configure new systems with the latest software. Client systems equipped with CD-ROM drives can use the original NetWare CD-ROM to load the client software. Many NICs come with configuration utilities that install the DOS Requester software on client stations.

If you have OS/2, Macintosh, or Windows NT users on your NetWare network, consider upgrading the client software on these systems as well. NetWare 4.1, in particular, includes the improved NetWare Client 2.11 for OS/2 and NetWare for Macintosh 4.1. Windows NT users should have the NetWare Client for Windows NT, which expands NetWare support for NT users.

Before you make wholesale changes to your client workstation configurations, test the new software on selected stations. Other technical support staff, sophisticated users, and users with special needs are all potential targets of the latest client software.

Solving Problems with Peripherals

TWO KINDS OF peripheral problems might require your immediate attention. Networked printers can be the source of problems, especially in older networks that are not yet taking advantage of the latest dedicated print server devices. CD-ROM drives can be a problem in your organization—by not being connected to the network. Many organizations purchase multiple CD-ROM drives for their networked users, who connect the devices locally and access one or two CD-ROMs regularly. Local CD-ROM connection can be expensive because of the cost of CD-ROM drives, the value of the client workstation memory their drivers occupy, and the price of purchasing multiple standalone copies of CD-ROM software. NetWare 3.12 and 4.x include software that allows CD-ROM drives attached to file servers to be mounted as NetWare volumes.

Networking Printers

NetWare includes support for three kinds of network printing. One way to connect network printers is to attach them to client systems. These systems run software that makes the printer available to NetWare users. Another way to connect network printers is to attach them to the file servers themselves. The third method is to connect the printers to dedicated computers or special add-on devices that run the NetWare print server software. Each of these methods can be reliable, but if you notice problems with a particular method in your inherited network, a new print server unit is a wise investment.

Problems with Remote Printing

Networked printers in older environments are sometimes connected to a client workstation running a memory-resident program called RPRINTER.EXE. This program allows printers connected directly to user workstations to be accessed via NetWare print queues—and other users. The print jobs are managed by a module called PSERVER running on the file server. This configuration is illustrated in Figure 12.1.

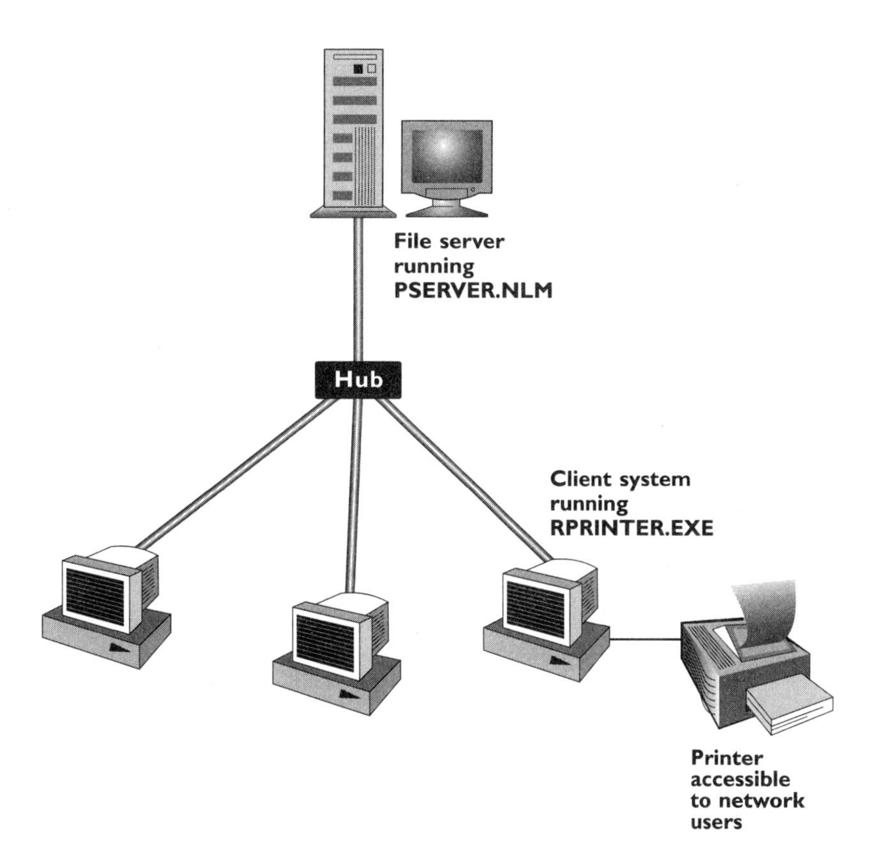

FIGURE 12.1
Network users can send print jobs to printers connected to client workstations running RPRINTER.EXE.

This configuration isn't often a dream scenario for the user whose printer is churning away with other users' print jobs, and it can also be a problem for the other network users, especially if the workstation they rely on to provide printing is slow or tends to crash frequently.

Problems with Server-Connected Printers

The RPRINTER memory-resident software isn't the only potential printing pitfall in a NetWare environment. Another way of connecting printers to the network is to run the PSERVER module on the file servers and connect the network printers directly to the servers. This configuration is somewhat more efficient than routing print jobs through a user station, but it can sometimes be the source of a security problem. If your file servers are not secured because users need to be able to access their printouts, consider an immediate upgrade to an external print server unit.

Problems with Print Servers

Print servers are network-connected devices that run software to handle the print jobs and control the printer. The old way of performing this task was to connect printers to dedicated computers. These computers would run the PSERVER.EXE utility to control the printer and handle the print jobs. If this method works acceptably on your network, don't change it.

However, the computers used as dedicated print servers in many networks are old systems that are not necessarily reliable. They also take up a fair amount of room for the single purpose they serve. If you don't leave a monitor attached, you may not notice that there's a problem with the system. If you do leave a monitor attached, you're draining energy and taking up space to display very little information. If these issues concern you, consider using a print server device.

Dedicated Print Server Devices

A good alternative to all three traditional methods of connecting printers is the dedicated print server unit. These devices are typically external boxes that run the print server software and can control one or more attached printers. Intel's NetPortExpress XL, Hewlett-Packard's JetDirect EX, Lantronix's EPS-2, Emulex's NetQueue, and Digital Products' NetPrint/200 are examples of external units that can provide printer access on multiprotocol networks. HP also offers internal JetDirect boards for its LaserJet 4 line of printers. These boards are optional on most models and can connect to Token Ring or Ethernet networks.

All these devices are reliable, easy to use and reset, and come with management software that helps you create and manage print queues.

Networking CD-ROMS

CD-ROM sharing took a major step forward with the release of NetWare 3.12 and 4.x, which both include support for network-attached CD-ROM drives. Other solutions are available, including third-party software that allows CD-ROM sharing from file servers, and CD-ROM server units that connect as network nodes and can be accessed by multiple users. These solutions are more expensive than using the built-in NetWare functionality. If you are running NetWare version 3.2 or 4.x, the CDROM server utility may be the most expedient option.

CD-ROM drives connected to client systems are often inefficient. If many of your users are accessing the same data—a large marketing database burned onto CD-ROM or a commercial reference package such as an "electronic yellow pages" product—it may be prudent to move the software to a network-connected CD-ROM drive. This way, you have to update only one CD-ROM, your users won't need to load the memory-resident CD-ROM drivers on their local systems, and you can obtain a limited number of the very fastest CD-ROM drives rather than providing them for each user accessing the data.

Loading the CD-ROM software is not difficult; you'll need a driver for your SCSI adapter (NetWare wants to use only SCSI CD-ROM drives) and the ASPITRAN.DSK, ASPICD.DSK, and CDROM.NLM modules. The last three drivers are included with NetWare 3.12 and 4.x; your SCSI adapter may be included, but you may need to get the NetWare driver from the vendor. Load the modules in this order:

1. SCSI adapter driver
2. ASPITRAN.DSK
3. ASPICD.DSK
4. CDROM.NLM

Access to a networked CD-ROM drive goes to the EVERYONE group by default. You can change this or add groups using the CD GROUP console command. To add a group, enter the name of the group you want to give access and a group number. This command assigns the group number 1 to the group TACKLES and allows access to a CD-ROM drive.

```
:CD GROUP TACKLES 1
```

To delete a group, enter DEL and the group number:

```
:CD GROUP DEL 1
```

To mount a CD-ROM as a NetWare volume, follow these steps:

1. Enter `CD DEVICE LIST` from the console prompt. Note the device number of the CD-ROM(s) installed.
2. Enter `CD MOUNT` *`devicenum`* `'/G=`*`groupnum`*`'`.

The '/G=*groupnum*' option indicates the number of the group you want to allow to access the CD-ROM device.

Additional information about the CDROM module options can be displayed by entering `CD HELP` *at the console prompt when CDROM is loaded.*

While you are considering immediately making upgrades, keep in mind that you are trying to eliminate existing problems and avoid emergencies or downtime. Look at the way you're spending your time on a daily basis to see if any network components are screaming to be replaced or upgraded. Look at the workflow your users create, and decide whether data on the critical path is at risk, can't be accessed, or is being handled inefficiently. Fine tuning can take place later; for the moment, deal with the issues that have the greatest detrimental impact—and that provide the greatest reward once they are addressed.

Net R_x: Network Checkup Routines

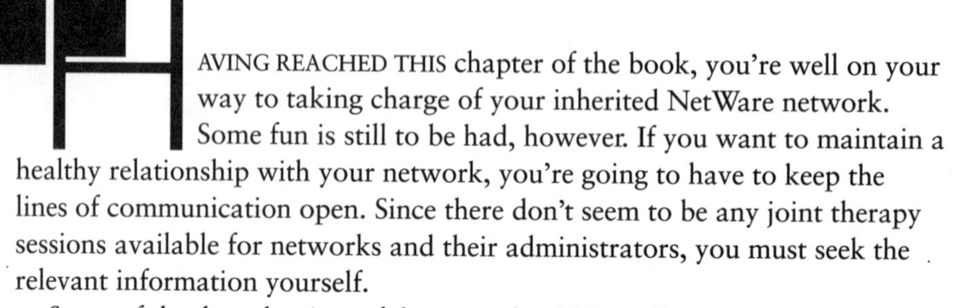

HAVING REACHED THIS chapter of the book, you're well on your way to taking charge of your inherited NetWare network. Some fun is still to be had, however. If you want to maintain a healthy relationship with your network, you're going to have to keep the lines of communication open. Since there don't seem to be any joint therapy sessions available for networks and their administrators, you must seek the relevant information yourself.

Some of the data that is useful to you should be collected daily. Dynamic information about the status and health of your servers falls into this category. Some of this information is easily collected, but other data is more difficult to extract. Since some issues do not need to be addressed on a daily basis, a monthly routine is also useful to develop. A monthly maintenance routine is a bit like changing the oil in your car because it helps keep the network running smoothly so that major changes can happen when you or your users dictate, not when the network seizes up from lack of attention.

The Vital Information

FREQUENCY	ACTIVITY
Daily	Check volume space on each server.
Daily	List files created the previous day.
Daily	Find old files that can be archived/removed.
Daily	Check backup execution.
Daily	List servers on internetwork.

FREQUENCY	ACTIVITY
Daily	View server error log.
Daily	Remove old users.
Monthly	Check user account security.
Monthly	Repair bindery/NDS.
Monthly	Ensure backup integrity.
Monthly	Update server modules.
Monthly	Update client files.

Planning a Daily Checkup Routine

NETWORK INFORMATION THAT you should collect on a daily basis is the really important data that affects the daily operation of your organization. You should be keeping track of available disk space, backup routine success, and server health issues. A task that you don't necessarily need to do every day but should handle as part of your daily routine is cleaning up after users who leave the network.

Checking Disk Space

Disk space information is important because running out of space will bring your users—and possibly your networks—to their knees. Since disk space is a dynamic resource, keeping track of available space on a daily basis is essential. In fact, daily tracking may not be sufficient. If your network handles a large volume of data, you may find that a volume that had plenty of free space in the morning is broadcasting warning messages before noon, especially if it contains files created by programs as well as by users.

Filled with Phantom Files

One network administrator reported that his network was running out of volume space—for no apparent reason. At the start of the day, he had 250MB free on a volume running a production database. Since the normal increase in size for the database was never more than 10MB per day, he was startled to get a message indicating that the volume was low on disk space.

He was just executing a VOLINFO command when he received another message indicating that the volume was out of space. He immediately performed an NDIR with filters set to find files created in the past day.

When that didn't return any sizeable results, he executed an NDIR and looked for files 1MB and larger. When he didn't find anything unusual, he checked the size of the production database. It was normal.

He checked the volume and found some archive files he could delete and some reference files he could move elsewhere. This freed 35MB, which he hoped would give him more time to identify the source of the problem.

Next, he ran virus detection software, hoping to uncover a problem of that kind. The server came up clean shortly before the next space warning message was broadcast. The administrator removed a few more files and ran another NDIR to check for new files.

To his surprise, he found a 120MB file that had not registered previously. He checked the owner name listed by NDIR; it was an account used by automated processes. He looked at the contents of the file and was disgusted to see that most of the file was empty space. He used a compression utility to shrink the file to 1.2MB.

He then checked with the programming groups, one by one, until he found the group whose data was output to that directory. It turned out that one of the automated processes had been altered and executed that morning, and a bug had inserted over 100MB of space characters into the output file.

The file had not initially been caught by the administrator's NDIR because it was still being written to and wasn't reporting its total size. The process was aborted and repaired, and the network returned to normal operation.

Disk space reports should include the following information:

- Space available by volume
- Space filled by recently created files
- Space occupied by old files

You may be interested in other information, especially how much space each user occupies and what the volume restrictions are for each user, but this information is important only if you have users abusing disk space.

Space Available by Volume

Determining the amount of space available on each volume is not difficult. The CHKVOL command, run from a network workstation, indicates how much space is available on a NetWare 3.x file server. You can display the same kind of information using the NDIR /VOL command from a client workstation on a NetWare 4.x server. (The /VOL option tells NDIR to look for volume objects.) Both utilities indicate the following information:

- Total space on the volume
- Amount of space used
- Total amount of space remaining on the volume
- Amount of space available to the user issuing the command

NDIR /VOL reports additional information about volumes with data compression enabled.

CHKVOL Using CHKVOL has been discussed previously in the section Using CHKVOL to View Available Disk Space in Chapter 3, but it's worth revisiting the utility in the context of identifying the space available on all the network volumes. CHKVOL includes two options that can make checking disk space quick and easy. To show information about all the volumes on a server, use one asterisk:

```
Z:\>CHKVOL *
```

To show information about all the volumes on all the servers to which you are currently attached, use two asterisks:

```
Z:\>CHKVOL */*
```

If you are working on a network with a single server, the single asterisk is sufficient. If you are working on an internetwork, using two asterisks is faster. In a very large network, such as a corporate WAN, even the */* option won't be terribly effective, because you won't be able to attach to all the servers on your network simultaneously. If you need to check disk space on more servers than you can attach to at once, create batch files to perform attachments en masse.

NDIR NDIR provides somewhat different output than CHKVOL does. For each volume, it indicates the following information:

- Total volume space
- Space used
- Deleted space that can't be purged
- Space available
- Space available to the user who issued the command
- Maximum directory entries allowed
- Available directory entries
- Space used if files were not compressed
- Space used by compressed files
- Space saved by file compression
- Uncompressed space in use
- Additional name spaces loaded

Recently Occupied Space

Checking the amount of space that has been used in the previous workday is a useful way of keeping tabs on the sources of network data. It's also helpful for identifying obvious misuse or potential problems. If you're checking disk space as part of your daily routine, it's a good idea to look at the files created in the past day.

This check works the same way for NetWare 3.x and 4.x. It makes use of the NDIR command:

```
Z:\>NDIR /CR EQ date /SUB
```

If you use the previous day's date, you get a list of all the files created that day. Since this command works on only one volume at a time, you may want to run it for the more dynamic or critical volumes.

Identifying Old Files

Old files are files that have not been accessed recently. For these purposes, creation dates are not as important as access dates, which indicate the last time somebody looked at the file, ran it, or wrote to it. Since this routine also uses the NDIR command, it is the same for NetWare 3.x and 4.x:

```
Z:\>NDIR /AC BEF date /sub
```

This command identifies all of the files that have not been accessed since *date*. In many cases, it's safe to say that a file that has not been accessed in six months isn't worth retaining. This situation is another one in which knowing your network and how it's used can be critical; you should always check to make sure the data really doesn't have to be immediately accessed. If it doesn't, archive it through your backup system, and remove it from the server's hard disk.

Checking Backup Routine Success

You have spent a fair amount of time establishing and documenting your network backup routine, and it only makes sense to check in periodically to make sure it's still running properly. On a daily basis, that means checking that the backup routine executed without fatal errors. You should also check to make sure that the backups can be recovered properly, but that's a task better left for the monthly list.

Performing a quick check of the backup system also ensures that you are aware of problems when they appear rather than later, when you need to recover data that was not backed up properly. You should be checking the server console to make sure the backup tasks have been completed, the backup database to make sure that the job did not encounter errors, and the backup units themselves to see that they're powered up and not displaying failure messages.

Ensuring the Backup Is Completed

Most backup utilities display a monitoring screen on the server console. One of the tasks that you should perform daily is checking that monitoring screen to make sure that the backup has not been aborted or delayed and isn't still in progress. Backups can use quite a bit of processor power, so if the backup process is running all night and into the next workday, it's time to consider a new backup strategy, with higher-capacity media or higher-speed equipment.

Checking the Backup Log for Errors

The backup log takes different forms, depending on the software you are using. Most programs have at least a simple log file that is opened each night, and any error conditions that are identified are appended. This basic functionality is sufficient for ongoing checks. Some of the errors you might be concerned about are indications that files could not be backed up because they were open, complaints from the software that the backup device could not be found or opened, and messages indicating that the file tracking database could not be read.

If your software includes a more detailed log—perhaps a backup job database that indicates all the files that were successfully archived—you may want to check it for more information. Be particularly aware of the size of these databases, which can sometimes become corrupted and either continue to grow without ever purging database entries or not record any information at all.

Watching the Backup Devices for Warning Signs

Device failure is relatively rare, even with mechanical devices like tape drives. However, these failures can occur, and although they are likely to be indicated by the backup software, it's a good idea to do a "sanity check" and make sure that the backup devices are powered up and are not registering unusual information on their displays or LEDs.

Checking Server Status

Checking the server status should also be part of your daily routine. You should make sure that the servers are running, can be seen by users, and have not announced significant errors. You can accomplish the first two tasks by performing an SLIST in NetWare 3.x and NLIST in NetWare 4.x.

Using SLIST to Locate Servers

If you are administering a NetWare 3.x network, the SLIST command is a fast and easy way to check the servers on an internetwork to make sure they're still running. If you are administering servers on a large WAN, you may find that too many servers are listed to isolate your own servers. In this case, you should consider running a batch file that looks for your servers by name:

```
SLIST THEDER
SLIST SNYDER
SLIST KAPP
```

Using NLIST to Locate Servers

NetWare 4.x includes the NLIST command in place of SLIST. NLIST is a more generalized tool that allows you to view information about groups, users, print queues, and other network objects, including file servers. To view a list of the servers that can be seen on the network, specify server objects:

```
Z:\>NLIST server
```

Checking the Server Error Log

The server error log records information about situations that it finds noteworthy. These events include bindery open requests, remote console sessions requested, incomplete packets received, and device deactivations. Some of these events may interest you, others may not, but the only way to stay on top of these issues is to check the log. In NetWare 3.x, the error log can be viewed using the SYSCON utility:

1. Enter `SYSCON` from a DOS prompt.
2. Select **Supervisor Options.**
3. Select **View File Server Error Log.**

When you have finished viewing the error log, you can press Esc to exit. SYSCON asks you whether you wish to clear the error log; if no errors are reported, you can eliminate the log's contents.

NetWare 4.x administrators can view the error log by using the NWADMIN utility in Windows:

1. Double-click on the **NWADMIN** icon.
2. Double-click on the server icon that represents the server whose log you want to check.
3. Click on the **Error Log** button.

A button beneath the **Error Log** text box allows you to clear the log's contents if you wish. The **Error Log** window is shown in Figure 13.1.

Deleting Old Users

Although you may not have to remove user accounts on a daily basis, you may have to delete an account on any given day. Make this account cleanup part of your daily routine so that you do not leave accounts open to access by former employees. You should also remove the files these users leave behind to prevent clutter.

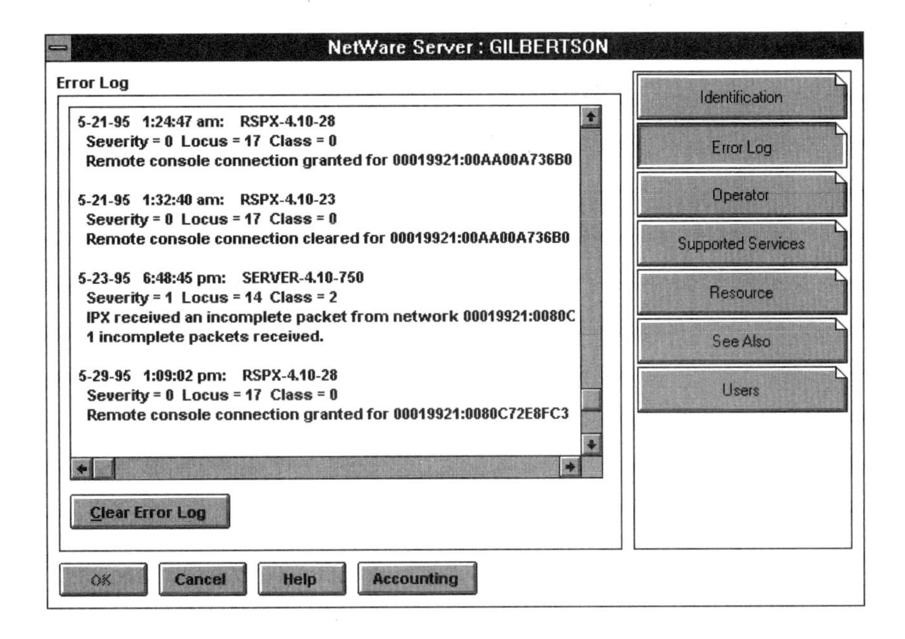

FIGURE 13.1
The NWADMIN utility can be used to view file server error logs in Windows.

Sometimes it makes sense to deactivate a user account rather than delete it completely. If a user is taking a leave of absence or is quitting but will return to work as a consultant, you can leave the account intact but inactive.

Deleting users is easy in SYSCON and NWADMIN; you just select the appropriate username and press Del. Doing other cleanup tasks should also be part of your routine:

- Check user's group membership.
- Delete account.
- Delete group if user was last member.
- Delete home directory.
- Remove specific mention of username from login script.

Planning a Monthly Checkup Routine

OTHER ROUTINES ARE more time consuming and don't have to be performed on a daily basis. Create a list of monthly tasks, and set aside time to perform them. One way of approaching this is to take one day per month to perform these checks and any periodic maintenance that may be necessary. A day in which the network isn't being used for production is the best time to schedule these checks; that allows you the greatest flexibility to run programs that would require users to log off, or even to down servers if necessary.

Most of these tasks have already been discussed in this book. They include:

- Checking security
- Running BINDFIX
- Finding new server files
- Finding new client files

Checking Security and Bindery Status

The SECURITY command generates a list of users on a server running NetWare 3.x. It indicates accounts that have not been used in a long time, Supervisor equivalents, and other conditions that may be security problems. NetWare 4.x doesn't contain an equivalent to the SECURITY command, but you can view information about security in the NWADMIN utility.

BINDFIX runs from a client workstation in a NetWare 3.x network and resolves problems with the NetWare bindery database. NetWare 4.x replaces this approach with the DSREPAIR console utility. DSREPAIR runs from the file server and includes more functionality to deal with the more complex NDS structure used by NetWare 4.x.

Finding New Files

The process of updating server and client files should be ongoing. Your network should make use of the enhancements in the incremental updates of the individual modules that are added to the network operating system. Even if you have recently upgraded your NetWare version, you are still likely to find new files that eliminate bugs and improve operation.

These files are available in a variety of places, but VARs and online services are the best places to find them. Check Novell's online sites and your hardware vendors' BBS and FTP sites to make sure you're using the latest drivers and modules.

Automating Checkup Routines

IT'S A GOOD idea to automate as many of your checkup routines as possible. You may be able to use a scheduling utility to execute your checkup routine batch files automatically, and then you can check the output of the routines over coffee when you arrive in the morning. Some tasks are not well suited to automation, but you may be able to find utilities to help you execute the tasks more easily.

The following is a sample batch file that checks the space on a small internetwork's servers and outputs the results to a file called DAILY.TXT. This file could be scheduled to run daily.

```
REM Daily routine for NetWare 3.x network
REM
REM Login and attach to network servers
LOGIN THEDER\SUPERVISOR
ATTACH SNYDER\SUPERVISOR
ATTACH KAPP\SUPERVISOR
REM
REM Map drives
MAP I:=THEDER\SYS:
MAP J:=SNYDER\SYS:
MAP K:=KAPP\SYS:
```

```
REM
REM Prepare to point output
REM to THEDER\SYS:DAILY.TXT
I:
CD\
DEL DAILY.TXT
ECHO Daily Routine > DAILY.TXT
REM
REM Check volume space on each server
ECHO Volume space on each server >> DAILY.TXT
CHKVOL */* >> DAILY.TXT
```

Another batch file could add a list of large files created the previous day to the results in the DAILY.TXT report. You would have to manually alter this batch file each day to reflect the correct dates:

```
REM Check for large files created previous day
REM
REM Create explanation line in output file
ECHO Large files created yesterday >> DAILY.TXT
REM
REM Replace old date with new date
I:
NDIR /CR EQ 7-21-95 /SI GR 1000000 /SUB >> DAILY.TXT
CD APPS:
NDIR /CR EQ 7-21-95 /SI GR 1000000 /SUB >> DAILY.TXT
CD UDATA:
NDIR /CR EQ 7-21-95 /SI GR 1000000 /SUB >> DAILY.TXT
CD SYS:
J:
NDIR /CR EQ 7-21-95 /SI GR 1000000 /SUB >> DAILY.TXT
CD APPS:
NDIR /CR EQ 7-21-95 /SI GR 1000000 /SUB >> DAILY.TXT
CD UDATA:
NDIR /CR EQ 7-21-95 /SI GR 1000000 /SUB >> DAILY.TXT
CD SYS:
K:
NDIR /CR EQ 7-21-95 /SI GR 1000000 /SUB >> DAILY.TXT
```

```
CD APPS:
NDIR /CR EQ 7-21-95 /SI GR 1000000 /SUB >> DAILY.TXT
CD UDATA:
NDIR /CR EQ 7-21-95 /SI GR 1000000 /SUB >> DAILY.TXT
CD SYS:
REM
REM Find old files
I:
NDIR /AC BEF 1-1-95 /SUB >> DAILY.TXT
CD APPS:
NDIR /AC BEF 1-1-95 /SUB >> DAILY.TXT
CD UDATA:
NDIR /AC BEF 1-1-95 /SUB >> DAILY.TXT
CD SYS:
J:
NDIR /AC BEF 1-1-95 /SUB >> DAILY.TXT
CD APPS:
NDIR /AC BEF 1-1-95 /SUB >> DAILY.TXT
CD UDATA:
NDIR /AC BEF 1-1-95 /SUB >> DAILY.TXT
CD SYS:
K:
NDIR /AC BEF 1-1-95 /SUB >> DAILY.TXT
CD APPS:
NDIR /AC BEF 1-1-95 /SUB >> DAILY.TXT
CD UDATA:
NDIR /AC BEF 1-1-95 /SUB >> DAILY.TXT
CD SYS:
I:
```

These files could be refined and could use third-party utilities to automate the identification of yesterday's date and an "old" date. An automated approach makes ongoing maintenance much easier.

Remember that all the routines described in this chapter are examples of the kinds of issues you should be concerned about. Do not simply apply these routines without thinking about the unique characteristics of your network structure and use. If you notice trends in structure or usage that you can make use of or need to emphasize in your ongoing collection of information, do so. The network is yours now, so make sure you keep tabs on it.

The Tool Belt: Network Administration Utilities

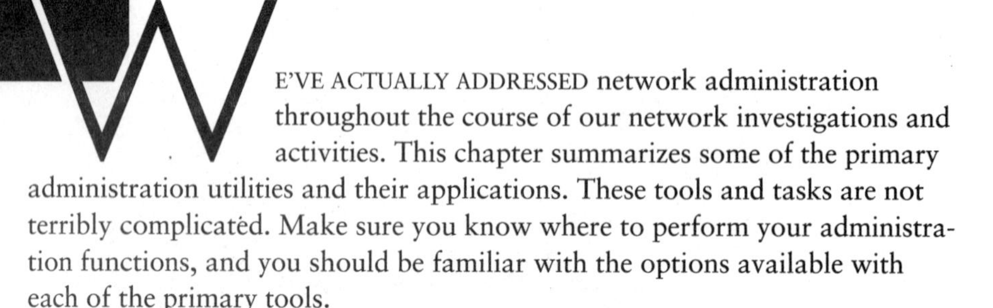

WE'VE ACTUALLY ADDRESSED network administration throughout the course of our network investigations and activities. This chapter summarizes some of the primary administration utilities and their applications. These tools and tasks are not terribly complicated. Make sure you know where to perform your administration functions, and you should be familiar with the options available with each of the primary tools.

The most difficult task for many administrators to take on is determining what tools to use to solve problems. What do you need to do that requires the use of the NetWare administration tools? Which tool is best suited to that task? The most common issues are ones that deal with the important network objects: users, groups of users, print queues, files, and directories. Many administration tasks fall outside these areas, but if you familiarize yourself with the functions of the NetWare tools available, you'll be able to pick the correct utility for the job at hand.

This chapter includes a discussion of the network utilities included on the CD-ROM that accompanies this book. Most of the programs included on the disk are utilities that can make your network administration tasks easier to perform. One of the utilities is shareware, which means you can install the program and try it before you purchase it. The other utilities are freeware programs that other network administrators or programmers have developed and are willing to share without charge. Of course, if you find their products useful, the developers almost always cheerfully accept thanks or contributions.

Most of the important administration tasks are ones we have identified in previous chapters. Among the most important tasks are: adding and removing users, setting and revoking trustee rights, setting volume space limitations, modifying system and user login scripts, salvaging unintentionally deleted files, changing user passwords, and managing print queues.

Vital Information

THIS CHAPTER FOCUSES primarily upon the NetWare commands used to manage a network and on the installation and use of the programs on the CD included with this book. The top issues to be aware of are:

- Commands that perform the SYSCON functions
- Commands that perform the FILER and SALVAGE functions
- Console commands new in NetWare 4.x
- Installation of Computer Select Trial Edition
- Installation and use of DispBind
- Installation and use of Netalk
- Installation and use of NET-ALERT
- Installation and use of Nice Capture
- Installation and use of Nice Login
- Installation and use of LOG.EXE

NetWare Administration Tools

YOU CAN PERFORM system management tasks in SYSCON, the file management tasks in FILER and SALVAGE, and other important administrative tasks with the file server console commands. Most of the tasks associated with utilities can also be completed using commands from network drive prompts in DOS. In this section, we'll look again at the primary utilities and describe the related command-line tools.

SYSCON Tasks

SYSCON is a real Swiss army knife of a utility. It allows you to manage server, accounting and network security features, to administer user groups and users and to execute special Supervisor commands. The NetWare 4.x implementation of SYSCON is NETADMIN in DOS and NWADMIN in Windows. These NetWare 4.x utilities offer additional functionality, especially with respect to DNS management, which doesn't exist in a NetWare 3.x environment.

In addition to being able to execute the SYSCON functions via NETADMIN and NWADMIN, you can use the following DOS commands to accomplish the same tasks. Notice that some of the commands in version 3.x remain the same in NetWare 4.x, while others change:

NetWare 3.x	NetWare 4.x
ATTACH	LOGIN
GRANT	RIGHTS
REMOVE	RIGHTS
REVOKE	RIGHTS
RIGHTS	RIGHTS
SETPASS	SETPASS
SLIST	NLIST Server
TLIST	RIGHTS

NetWare 4.x uses fewer commands with more command-line options to perform these tasks than NetWare 3.x does.

Using the SYSCON-Equivalent Commands

Running a DOS command-line program to perform a function that can be handled by a menu-driven or graphical utility may seem odd, but these commands offer one compelling advantage: they're fast. Instead of working your way through menus or dialog boxes to find or change the information you need, you can tell the computer exactly what you want it to do. These commands are also easily automated because they can be included in a batch file to execute frequently performed tasks.

ATTACH The NetWare 3.x ATTACH command allows you to connect to additional file servers after you have logged in. You do not execute the system or personal login scripts when you use ATTACH to get onto a server. The ATTACH command specifies a server name and a user account name:

```
F:\>ATTACH KAPP\MPAWLAWS
```

In this example, the user "mpawlaws", who is already logged into a server, is attempting to connect to the server KAPP. ATTACH requests are handled with the same kind of network security used with LOGIN, so after "mpawlaws" enters his ATTACH command, he is prompted for his user password for the account on KAPP. If he enters his password correctly, he is attached to KAPP and can map drives, capture to print queues, and do the other voodoo that NetWare does so well.

GRANT The GRANT command is useful for setting file or directory trustee rights for users and groups. The command can quickly set whatever combination of trustee rights is appropriate. The command uses a surprisingly efficient syntax to set or remove multiple kinds of rights. Rights can be assigned using the ALL BUT, ONLY, and NO RIGHTS options. In the following example, the user "wtrance" is being granted the Read, Write, Create, Erase, Modify, File Scan, and Access Control rights to the MMILLER directory and its subdirectories on the UDATA volume:

```
F:\>GRANT ALL BUT S FOR UDATA:MMILLER TO USER
WTRANCE /S
```

GRANT involves several options. The rights package being granted to the user or group is specified using the one-letter abbreviations of the trustee rights shown in the list below:

GRANT Abbreviation	Rights
ALL	All rights
N	No rights
S	Supervisory rights
R	Read
W	Write
C	Create

GRANT Abbreviation	Rights
E	Erase
M	Modify
F	File Scan
A	Access Control

The rest of the GRANT options specify the path of the file or directory to be accessed, the user or group to be given access, and /S to grant access to subdirectories or /F for access to files.

LOGIN In NetWare 3.x, LOGIN clears current network connections, attaches a user to a server, and executes the appropriate login scripts. In NetWare 4.x, LOGIN performs both logins and server attachments. The following example illustrates how "jbauman" would log into ARISTOTLE under NetWare 3.x:

```
F:\>LOGIN ARISTOTLE/JBAUMAN
```

Under NetWare 4.x, the same command would work in the same manner as it does in this example. However, NetWare 4.x includes command-line options for the LOGIN that weren't previously available:

LOGIN Option	Description
/B	Performs a Bindery login.
/NB	Suppresses the "Welcome to NetWare" banner at login.
/NOSWAP	Disables LOGIN swapping to disk, EMS, or XMS.
/NS	Does not log user out of currently attached servers and does not execute a login script.
/PR=*Profile_name*	Runs a Profile object's script at login.
/S *path_or_object*	Specifies a login script by file name or object name.
SWAP=*path*	Specifies a DOS swap path for external commands.
/TREE	Logs into a tree.

NLIST NLIST is a NetWare 4.x command that searches for and displays object information for NDS objects such as servers, volumes, groups, and users. It can also show information about certain bindery objects. The following table shows the objects that can be listed by NLIST:

Object Database	Object Class
Bindery	User
Bindery	Server
Bindery	Queue
Bindery	Group
Bindery	Volume
NDS	AFP Server
NDS	Alias
NDS	Computer
NDS	Country
NDS	Directory Map
NDS	Group
NDS	Organization
NDS	Organizational Role
NDS	Print Server
NDS	Printer
NDS	Profile
NDS	Queue
NDS	Server
NDS	User
NDS	Volume

You can use NLIST to list these objects or obtain more detailed information about them, but most of the time, you'll be interested in the same kind of information you found using SLIST, USERLIST, and the other NetWare 3.x commands. You may want to view lists of servers that can be seen by your workstation, or users currently logged in, or printer status. In the following example, NLIST is being asked to list servers in the directory tree:

```
F:\>NLIST SERVER /S
```

REVOKE The REVOKE command allows you to remove a user or group's trustee rights from a file or directory. REVOKE partially or completely undoes the trustee assignments created using SYSCON or GRANT. REVOKE has several options, in the same form as GRANT. You must indicate the rights to be removed, the file or directory they applied to, and the person to remove them from. In the following example, Supervisory, Access Control, Create, Modify, and Write rights are being taken away from "lhanson" in the MMILLER directory and its subdirectories on the UDATA volume:

```
F:\>REVOKE S A C M W FOR UDATA:MMILLER FROM USER
LHANSON /S
```

Specifying that "lhanson" is a USER is not really necessary unless there is also a group named LHANSON.

REVOKE Abbreviation	Rights
ALL	All rights
S	Supervisory rights
R	Read
W	Write
C	Create
E	Erase
M	Modify
F	File Scan
A	Access Control

REMOVE is another DOS command that can be used to manage trustee rights. REMOVE completely eliminates a user or group as a trustee of a file or directory, while REVOKE is useful for narrowing an existing list of trustee rights.

RIGHTS The RIGHTS command is used in NetWare 3.x to display a user's effective rights for a file or directory. The command syntax is simple; the user can simply issue the command with no options to return her effective rights in the current directory as shown in Figure 14.1, or she can specify the path for which she wants to see her effective rights.

FIGURE 14.1 The RIGHTS command displays the user's effective rights for a file or directory.

```
MS-DOS Prompt
H:\SYSTEM>RIGHTS
NIRVANA\SYS:SYSTEM
Your Effective Rights for this directory are [SRWCEMFA]
    You have Supervisor Rights to Directory.    (S)
  * May Read from File.                         (R)
  * May Write to File.                          (W)
    May Create Subdirectories and Files.        (C)
    May Erase Directory.                        (E)
    May Modify Directory.                       (M)
    May Scan for Files.                         (F)
    May Change Access Control.                  (A)

* Has no effect on directory.

    Entries in Directory May Inherit [SRWCEMFA] rights.
    You have ALL RIGHTS to Directory Entry.

H:\SYSTEM>
```

The Read and Write rights apply to the files in the directory rather than to the directories themselves.

In NetWare 4.x, RIGHTS is used to view and to modify the rights a user or group has for files, directories, and volumes. The NetWare 4.x RIGHTS command is used to perform the same tasks that GRANT, REMOVE, REVOKE, and TLIST serve in NetWare 3.x. In the following example, RIGHTS is used to remove "swragg" from the MMILLER subdirectory on the UDATA volume, performing a task that REMOVE would be used for in NetWare 3.x.

```
F:\>RIGHTS SNYDER\UDATA:MMILLER REM /NAME=SWRAGG
```

The NetWare 4.x version of the RIGHTS command has more complicated command-line options. You must specify a path to a file, directory, or volume. If you wish to add or remove rights, you need to indicate which ones.

The following rights can be assigned or revoked:

RIGHTS Abbreviation	Assigns
ALL	All rights
N	No rights
REM	Removes the user or group as a trustee
S	Supervisory
R	Read
W	Write
C	Create
E	Erase
M	Modify
F	File Scan
A	Access Control

RIGHTS also supports several command-line options, as shown in the list below:

RIGHTS Option	Use
/C	Continuously scroll output.
/F	Display the Inherited Rights Filter (IRF).
/I	View where inherited rights came from.
/NAME=*name*	Display or alter rights for a specified user or group.
/S	Display or alter rights for subdirectories.
/T	View directory trustee assignments.

SETPASS The SETPASS command works the same way in NetWare 3.x and NetWare 4.x. In both products, it is used to set a user account password for a particular server. A user can simply type SETPASS to change the password for his current login name, or the user can specify a server or another username. If you have Root or Supervisor rights, you'll be able to change someone else's password. In the following example, the user changes his password on the server KAPP.

```
F:\>SETPASS KAPP
```

Note that if you are logged into multiple servers and change the password for a single server, NetWare asks if you wish to synchronize passwords for the accounts on all servers.

SLIST This command lists the file servers on an internetwork that can be seen by a particular workstation. SLIST also displays each server's IPX internal network number, the server's node number on the network, and whether the user is currently attached to the server, as shown in Figure 14.2. The attachment status column shows Default for the server that the user is logged into and Attached for servers the user has attached to since then. By entering the following command, the user displays only the server names that start with the letter R:

```
F:\>SLIST R*
```

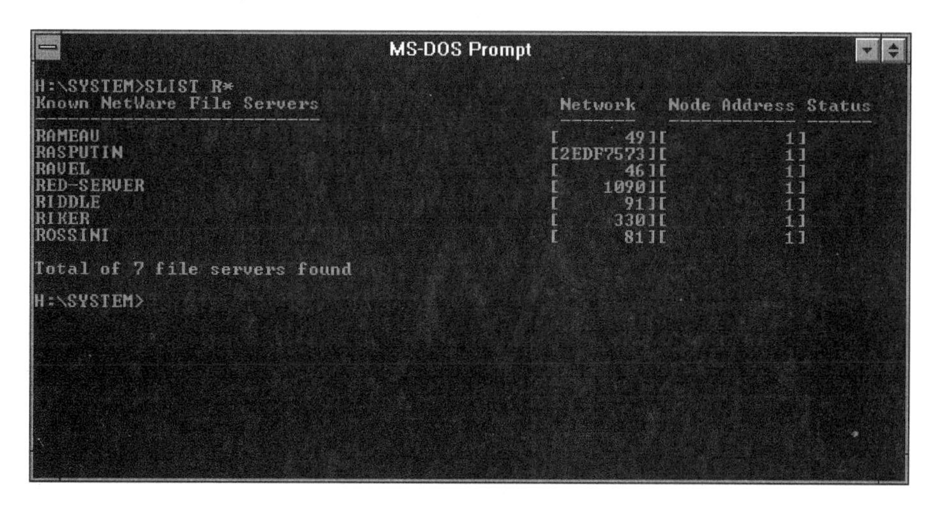

FIGURE 14.2 The SLIST command provides information about the file servers on an internetwork.

The FILER/SALVAGE Tasks

While SYSCON focuses on network objects, FILER and SALVAGE work with files and directories. FILER is used on "live" files, while SALVAGE is used to purge or recover deleted files. FILER runs under NetWare 3.x and 4.x. The following NetWare 3.x and 4.x commands duplicate the functions available in FILER:

NetWare 3.x	NetWare 4.x
FLAG	FLAG
FLAGDIR	FLAG
LISTDIR	NDIR
NCOPY	NCOPY
NDIR	NDIR
RENDIR	RENDIR

Running the FILER-Equivalent Commands

Though you may prefer in some instances to use the FILER utility to perform file- and directory-related tasks, most administrators find that command-line instructions are faster, and they are certainly easier to automate because they can be placed in batch files. There is less change in the FILER-related commands between NetWare 3.x and NetWare 4.x than there was in the two versions of the SYSCON-equivalent commands. There are some differences, however, and it's worth having a look at how each of these commands can be used.

FLAG The FLAG command allows you to manipulate the file and directory attributes on your network volumes. These attributes control the ways in which you manage your network files and directories. The FLAG command is similar in NetWare 3.x and 4.x. The differences can be seen in the list below, which provides the FLAG command attributes:

File/Directory	Option	Description	NetWare Version
F/D	ALL	Sets DI, H, IC, P, RI, and SY attributes for a directory or A,CI, DI, H, IC, P, RI, RO, SH, SY, and T attributes for a file.	3.x, 4.x
F	A	Archive Needed: file changed since last backup.	3.x, 4.x
F	CI	Copy Inhibit: prevents Mac files from being copied.	3.x, 4.x
F/D	DC	Don't Compress: prevents file or directory from being compressed.	4.x
F/D	DI	Delete Inhibit: prevents file or directory from being deleted or overwritten.	3.x, 4.x
F/D	DM	Don't Migrate: prevents a file or directory from being migrated to a secondary backup system.	4.x
F	DS	Don't Suballocate: prevents suballocation of a particular file, usually those that are added to frequently.	4.x
F/D	H	Hidden: prevents a file or directory from being seen by the DIR command in DOS; prevents copying or deletion of files.	3.x, 4.x
F/D	IC	Immediate Compress: requests compression of a file or directory as soon as possible.	4.x
F/D	N	Normal: sets no attributes for a directory or the RW attribute for a file.	3.x, 4.x

File/Directory	Option	Description	NetWare Version
F/D	P	Purge: purge the file or directory immediately upon deletion.	3.x, 4.x
F/D	RI	Rename Inhibit: prevents renaming of files or directories.	3.x, 4.x
F	RO	Read Only: keeps a file from being deleted or written to.	3.x, 4.x
F	RW	Read Write: allows a file to be read and written to.	3.x, 4.x
F	SH	Shareable: allows several users to access a file at one time.	3.x, 4.x
F/D	SY	System: prevents copying or deletion and hides a file or directory from the DIR command in DOS.	3.x, 4.x
F	T	Transactional: uses TTS to back out of incomplete transactions for a file.	3.x, 4.x
F	X	Execute only: prevents .EXE and .COM files from being copied; the X attribute cannot be removed.	3.x, 4.x

Two other NetWare 3.x attributes, Read Audit and Write Audit, can be set with FLAG but do not have any function in NetWare.

FLAGDIR This command displays or modifies the attributes of the subdirectories hanging off the current directory. The FLAGDIR command is used only in NetWare 3.x; its functionality is contained in the FLAG command used in NetWare 4.x. The FLAGDIR command can set attributes to Delete Inhibit, Hidden, Normal, Purge, Rename Inhibit, or System.

In the following example, all subdirectories of the current directory are flagged with the Purge attribute, which sets the directories to be purged as soon as they are deleted:

```
F:\>FLAGDIR* P
```

The asterisk is a wildcard character that indicates all subdirectories should be included.

LISTDIR LISTDIR is a NetWare 3.x command that shows a directory's subdirectories and can display additional information about each subdirectory. The options for the LISTDIR command are described in the list below:

LISTDIR Option	Description
/All	Displays all the information specified by the other options.
/Rights	Shows each subdirectory's IRM.
/Effective Rights	Shows the effective rights in each subdirectory.
/Date	Shows each subdirectory's creation date and time (identical to /Time).
/Sub-directories	Displays all levels of subdirectories beneath the specified directory.
/Time	Shows each subdirectory's creation date and time (identical to /Date).

The following command displays all information about the EXPORT directory's subdirectories:

```
G:\>LISTDIR G:\EXPORT /ALL
```

The results of this LISTDIR command are shown in Figure 14.3.

NCOPY NCOPY is used in NetWare 3.x and 4.x to copy files between directories. FILER's interface to this operation is somewhat more accessible than the NCOPY command line, especially if you're dealing with multilevel directory trees, but we're not talking about brain surgery here. NCOPY needs a path for the source file or files, a path for the intended destination (if you

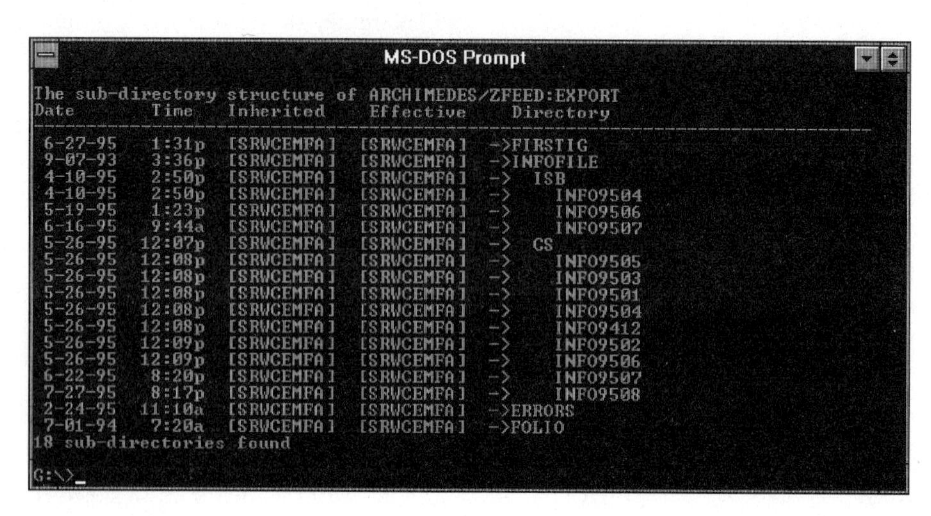

FIGURE 14.3 The LISTDIR command can show creation time, inherited and effective rights, and a complete subdirectory tree.

leave this out, the files are copied to the current directory). Here's an example of a simple NCOPY command line:

```
F:\>NCOPY Z:\PUBLIC\LOGIN.EXE TO G:\ARCHIVE\OLDPUB
```

In this example, the LOGIN.EXE file from the PUBLIC directory on the Z drive is copied to the OLDPUB subdirectory under the ARCHIVE directory on G. NCOPY also supports more complicated options:

NCOPY Option	Description
/A	Copies only files with the archive attribute set.
/Copy	Copies without preserving file attributes and name space information, which are preserved by default.
/Empty subdirectories	Copies empty subdirectories of the source directory.
/Force sparse files	Forces NetWare to write to sparse files.
/Inform	Notifies you if attributes or name space information is lost during the copy process.
/M	Copies files with the archive attribute set, and removes the archive bit from the source file.

NCOPY Option	Description
/Subdirectories	Copies subdirectories of the source directory.
/Verify	Checks that the source and copy are exact duplicates.

Sparse files are files with one or more empty blocks. NetWare does not save the empty space when it saves these files; instead, it saves only the portions of the file that contain data, conserving disk space. If a program attempts to read from part of the file that it expects to exist and it contains zeros, NetWare returns zeros to the program. NCOPY won't write to sparse files unless the /F option is used.

NDIR NDIR can tell you almost everything you want to know about a directory and its contents. We've discussed NDIR previously in Chapter 9 and Chapter 13, but for your convenience, a list of the options available with the NDIR command is included here.

The sorting commands sort on the following key values:

NDIR Option	Secondary Option
/SOrt	/ACcess
	/ARchive
	/CReate
	/OWner
	/SIze
	/UPdate
/REVerse SOrt	*same options as /SOrt*

For example, to sort by creation date with the most recently created files first, you'd use the reverse sort feature with the CReate argument:

```
F:\>NDIR /REV SO CR
```

The informational options display the content of the NDIR commands and provide the format in which the NDIR command lists its output:

NDIR Option	Displays
/DATES	Dates of creation and last modification, archive, and access

NDIR Option	Displays
/RIGHTS	Inherited and effective rights and file attributes
/MACintosh	Macintosh files and subdirectories in long name format
/LONGnames	Macintosh, NFS, and OS/2 extended file names

The attributes options include or exclude files and directories flagged with particular attributes (precede with the /NOT option to exclude an attribute):

/Archive needed

/Copy Inhibit

/Delete Inhibit

/Hidden

/Indexed

/Purge

/Read Only

/Rename Inhibit

/Shareable

/SYstem

/Transactional

/eXecute only

Restriction options restrict the NDIR results by limiting the output to files, directories, or subdirectories, or by using Boolean logic expressions to limit the relevant files. NOT, GReater than, EQual to, LEss than, BEFore, and AFTer can be combined with dates, names, values, and these restriction options to limit the results.

/ACcess

/ARchive

/CReate

/OWner

/SIze

/UPdate

/Files only

/Directories only

/SUBdirectories

RENDIR RENDIR renames a directory by changing the directory's name. Trustee rights are not affected because they are carried to the new directory name. Explicit mention of the old directory name in a login script or batch file has to be changed manually. To rename a directory, simply indicate the old directory name and the new one, as shown in the following example:

```
F:\>RENDIR GILBERTSON\UDATA:WTRANCE TO WMILLER
```

In this example, the WTRANCE directory on the UDATA volume of the server GILBERTSON is being renamed to WMILLER. You may find this command particularly useful for changing user directories to reflect married names.

Running SALVAGE

SALVAGE is a DOS utility in NetWare 3.x and 4.x that allows you to view or restore files that have been deleted but not yet purged. Once a file is deleted, it remains on the disk until the server needs to use the space it occupies. Unless the server is set to purge files immediately after deletion or the files themselves are flagged with the Purge attribute, all files are retained until the space they use is occupied.

If you delete files, they remain in the directory they lived in before being deleted. If you delete directories, their files are stored in the hidden directory DELETED.SAV, which exists on each NetWare volume.

SALVAGE's main menu has four options, as shown in Figure 14.4.

- The **Salvage from Deleted Directories** option allows you to restore files from directories that no longer exist.
- The **Select Current Directory** option allows you to select the server, volume, or directory you wish to view.

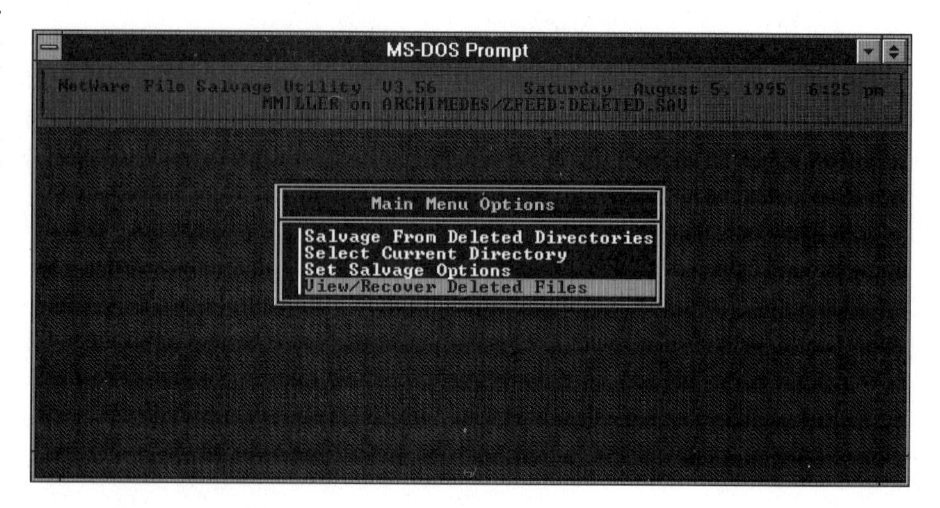

FIGURE 14.4 The SALVAGE utility allows you to change directories and sort order and recover or purge deleted files.

- The **Set Salvage Options** entry allows you to change the sort order SALVAGE uses.
- The **View/Recover Deleted Files** option lists the salvageable files in the current directory for recovery or purging.

SALVAGING FROM DELETED DIRECTORIES If you select **Salvage from Deleted Directories**, you can select a volume from the current server. If you wish to change the current server, press Esc to go to the main menu, and select **Set Current Directory**. Otherwise, highlight one of the volume names, and press Enter. SALVAGE prompts you with a box asking for the name pattern to search for. The default is the wildcard character *, which displays all files. You can enter a specific file name or combine characters and wildcards. Once you've entered the appropriate combination, press Enter to see a list of deleted files matching the file name pattern you've specified.

If you find the file you want to restore or purge, highlight its name in the list of salvageable files. Then press the Delete key to purge the file or Enter to recover the file. Purging is used less frequently, but it can be useful, especially if you want to remove all traces of a file you don't want restored. Whether you purge or recover the file, SALVAGE gives you the deletion date, the last modification date, the file owner, and the filer deletor. It then prompts you to continue, as shown in the file recovery illustrated in Figure 14.5.

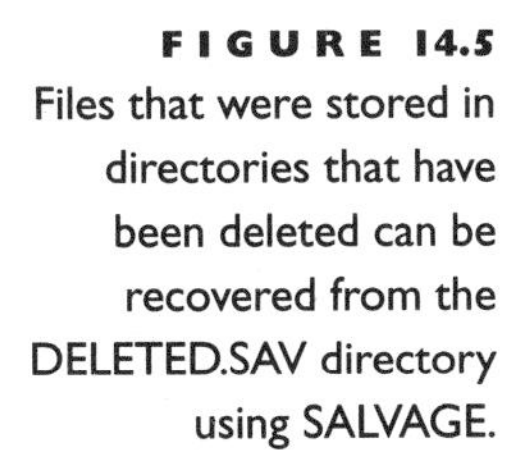

FIGURE 14.5
Files that were stored in directories that have been deleted can be recovered from the DELETED.SAV directory using SALVAGE.

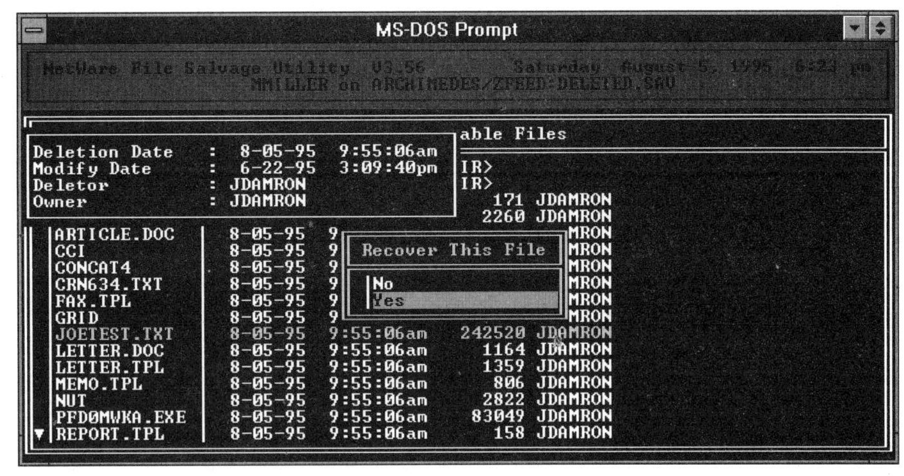

SELECTING THE CURRENT DIRECTORY To select the current directory path, choose the **Select Current Directory** option from the **Main Menu Options**, and enter the path you wish. To be guided through the available server, volume, and directory structure, press the Insert key and select a subdirectory or choose the .. entry to move to the next higher level.

SETTING SORT OPTIONS The **Set Salvage Options** entry on the **Main Menu Options** screen allows you to sort the SALVAGE lists of files. The options are:

- Sort by deletion date
- Sort by file size
- Sort by file name
- Sort by owner name

The default is to sort by file name, which is usually fine. If you're looking for particularly large files to purge or for a particular person's file out of a list of hundreds, or if you know you're looking for a recently deleted file, the other options may come in handy. Simply highlight the order you want, and press Enter.

VIEWING DELETED FILES If you wish to salvage or purge files that have been deleted from directories that still exist, select **View/Recover Deleted Files** from the **Main Menu Options** screen. SALVAGE prompts you for a file name

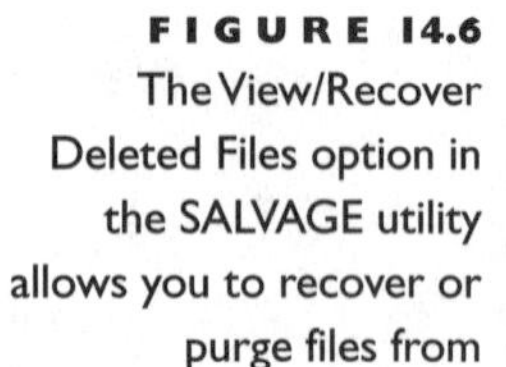

FIGURE 14.6 The View/Recover Deleted Files option in the SALVAGE utility allows you to recover or purge files from directories that still exist.

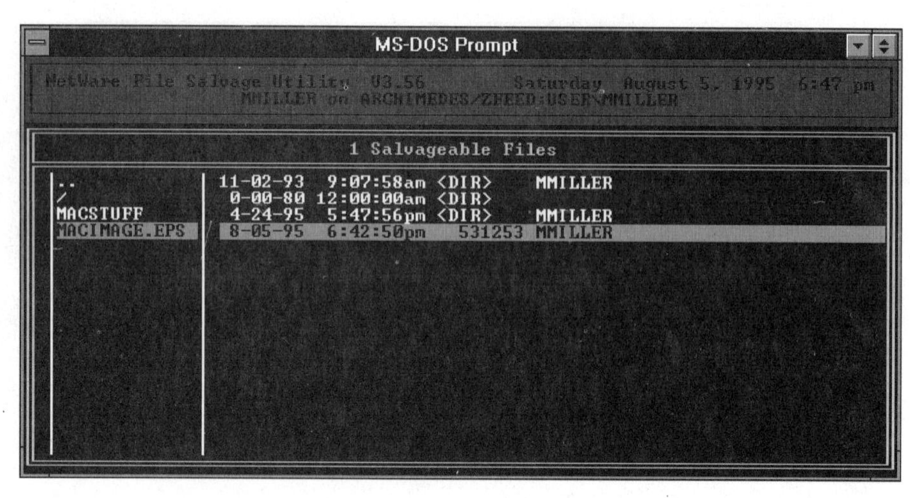

pattern, defaulting again to *, which displays all deleted files in the current directory.

You can navigate through the directories and subdirectories on a volume by highlighting the forward slash (/) entry, which takes you to the root level of the current volume, and the .. entry, which takes you to the current directory's parent directory, but you cannot look at another volume without going to ***the Main Menu Options*** *to select a new current directory.*

If there is a salvageable file in the current directory, its name is displayed as shown in Figure 14.6. You can highlight it, and press Enter to restore the file, or press Delete to purge the file.

The Console Commands

Most of the file server console commands used in NetWare 3.11 are carried over to NetWare 4.x. These common commands are listed below and are briefly explained in the Appendix.

Console Commands in Netware 3.x and 4.x

ADD NAME SPACE
BIND
BROADCAST
CLEAR STATION
CLS
CONFIG
DISABLE LOGIN
DISMOUNT
DISPLAY NETWORKS
DISPLAY SERVERS
DOWN
EDIT
ENABLE LOGIN
ENABLE TTS
EXIT
INSTALL
LOAD
MEMORY
MODULES
MONITOR
MOUNT
NAME
OFF
PROTOCOL
REGISTER MEMORY
REMOVE DOS
RESET ROUTER
SEARCH
SECURE CONSOLE
SET
SET TIME
SPEED
SPXCONFIG
TIME
TRACK OFF
TRACK ON
UNBIND
UNLOAD
UPS
UPS STATUS
UPS TIME
VOLUMES
VREPAIR

NetWare 4.x includes several new console commands:

Console Command	Purpose
MIRROR STATUS	Shows mirrored partitions and mirroring status
REMIRROR PARTITION	Initiates remirroring
ABORT REMIRROR	Cancels remirroring
INITIALIZE SYSTEM	Executes the NETINFO.CFG file from the AUTOEXEC.NCF file to enable multiprotocol routing
REINITIALIZE SYSTEM	Incorporates changes made to the NETINFO.CFG file
LANGUAGE	Determines the language used by server message files
LIST DEVICES	Shows server's disk device list
SCAN FOR NEW DEVICES	Finds added disk devices

The DSMERGE and DSREPAIR NLMs are also new to NetWare 4.x. DSMERGE allows you to rename an NDS tree and, more importantly, merge roots of NDS trees, which is important if you're integrating the networks of two separately configured organizations. DSREPAIR is similar to NetWare 3.x's BINDFIX, except that it repairs NDS problems, such as damaged database records or incorrect object references, rather than bindery problems. It also searches for time synchronization problems between servers on your network.

The Utilities Included with This Book

THE UTILITIES ON the CD-ROM included with this book can make your life as a network administrator much easier. These utilities have been selected because they are typical of the kind of programs available in the public domain as shareware or freeware. The authors of these programs work hard to make their tools useful and remove bugs; in fact, even some freeware authors promise support and bug fixes for their creations.

The seven software products included on the Companion CD that comes free with this book are:

- Information Access Company's Computer Select Trial Edition
- ITI's DispBind
- Montauk Software's Netalk
- NETMan's NET-ALERT
- K.F. Soft's Nice Capture and Nice Login
- Sexwax Software's LOG.EXE

Using Computer Select Trial Edition

The trial edition of Computer Select contains the full set of data from a single month's Computer Select subscription CD-ROM. That means one year's worth of computer and technical publication articles and text, plus hardware and software product specifications, company profile information, and computer term definitions from two industry dictionaries.

Computer Select is a monthly subscription product, so each month regular subscribers are sent a new CD-ROM, containing the most recent articles, specifications, and definitions available. Each CD-ROM contains over 70,000 articles and a year's worth of publication data. Important graphics from the text are also included for several publications, and the utilities and macros accompanying many articles are included as well.

The trial edition won't allow you to print or copy and paste information from the articles. It doesn't include the utilities and macros files, and it only runs five times after you install it. However, it can give you a good idea of how the product works and what it contains, and more importantly, you might find it useful.

More information on the content and operation of Computer Select is included in Chapter 19. To install the trial edition for DOS or Windows, follow the steps in the next sections.

Installing from DOS

Follow these steps to install the DOS version of Computer Select Trial Edition:

1. Put the CD-ROM in your computer's CD-ROM drive.
2. From any non-CD-ROM drive letter, enter `n:CS`, where `n:` is the CD-ROM drive letter. Computer Select displays a license agreement, installs software to your hard disk, and starts its DOS version.

Installing from Windows

Follow these steps to install the Windows version of Computer Select Trial Edition.

1. Put the CD-ROM in your computer's CD-ROM drive.
2. Start Windows, and select **File...Run**.
3. Enter `n:SETUPW`, where `n:` is the CD-ROM drive letter. The Setup program displays license information and prompts you for a destination for installed files. It creates a Computer Library group in Windows with a **Computer Select** icon.
4. Double-click the **Computer Select** icon to start the trial edition software.

Using ITI's DispBind

DispBind is a very simple utility that allows you to display the account restrictions for the currently logged-in user. It shows the same information you can get by starting SYSCON, selecting the correct user, and choosing **Account Restrictions** from the **User Information** menu. However, expecting a user to do this is a little unreasonable. By simply typing `DISPBIND` from a DOS prompt, the user can find the same information, as shown in Figure 14.7.

One way of using this command is to remind the users of their account restrictions when they log out. If their passwords are about to expire or have expired and they're running out of grace logins, they may notice and change

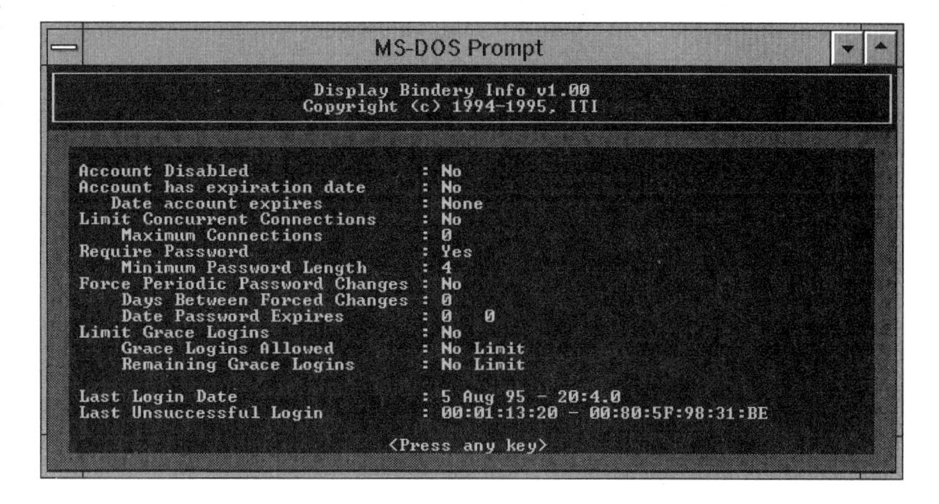

FIGURE 14.7 The DISPBIND command displays the account restrictions for the currently logged in user.

them before having to call you to unlock the account. To accomplish this, you should do the following:

1. Copy DISPBIND.EXE to SYS:PUBLIC.
2. Rename the LOGOUT.EXE file in SYS:PUBLIC to LOGOUTNW.EXE.
3. Create a file called LOGOUT.BAT.
4. On the first line of LOGOUT.BAT, type `DISPBIND`.
5. On the second line of LOGOUT.BAT, type `LOGOUTNW.EXE`.
6. Save LOGOUT.BAT.

When the users log out, they'll actually be running the batch file, so they'll see their account restrictions before they disconnect from the network. You may be able to think of another use that's more appropriate for your network.

Using Montauk Software's Netalk

This program can be useful for carrying on short conversations on a local network. It allows two users to open a connection and chat with each other. Although Netalk uses the SEND command to "open hailing frequencies" (inform the other user that you wish to have a Netalk conversation), its communications abilities are more robust.

To run Netalk, follow these steps:

1. Place Netalk in the SYS: PUBLIC directory.
2. Type `NETALK` from a DOS prompt.
3. Select the connection number for the user you want to chat with.
4. When the other user receives the network SEND message, they also run Netalk.
5. To chat, just type what you want to say.

There are a couple of limitations to the program. Netalk won't notify the other user of your desire to communicate if the user has issued a CASTOFF command. If the user is in Windows and isn't running NWPOPUP.EXE, she won't receive the SEND message until she exits Windows. This prevents the program from interrupting vital processes with those pesky SEND messages.

For a commercial product that offers this kind of functionality in Windows, with many more features (fonts, printing, archiving, and categorization, While You Were Out forms, and multiple conversations), check out E Ware's eNote, a pop-up messaging program for networked Windows users.

Using NETMan's NET-ALERT

NET-ALERT is the one shareware network utility included with this book. A full-featured version of the product is commercially available, and the most recent version of the NET-ALERT shareware version can be found on the WWW at `http://www.acs.oakland.edu/oak/SimTel/msdos/novell.html`. The current file name is NETALE22.ZIP. Future versions will be at this site under different names, so look around.

This program runs on a PC and monitors up to three servers (with the shareware version—more are supported with the registered product). When it senses that a server isn't responding, it sends a preset numeric page to the pager numbers of your choice. (Alphanumeric pager support can also be obtained if you purchase the full product.) This program, running on a Windows 95 machine in your locked office, can be a very handy way of avoiding a morning surprise.

Setting up the program is simple and flexible, and the online help is detailed. NET-ALERT runs in DOS, but it runs very nicely as a task under Windows 95. To set up the utility, follow these steps:

1. From a DOS prompt, type `D:\UTILITY\NETALE22\NETALERT\INSTALL`. Use your CD-ROM's drive letter.
2. When the NET-ALERT 2.2 welcome screen appears, press Enter to continue.
3. Read the installation instructions, and then click OK to move on.
4. Select your CD-ROM drive letter and the UTILS\ALERT directory in the **Installing From** box.
5. Select C:\NETALERT or another directory in the **Installing To** box.
6. Select the first network drive letter (the one that points to the LOGIN directory before you've logged in) in the **Network Drive** box.
7. Click OK to continue to the **Communications Setup** screen.
8. Select your communications port (COM1 or COM2 only).
9. Enter your modem initialization string.
10. Select the dialing method (ATDT is the default for tone dialing).
11. Select the maximum modem speed (300 to 19,200 bps).
12. Click OK to continue to the **File Server Setup** screen.
13. Enter the first file server name.
14. Enter the number of minutes you want NET-ALERT to wait before it is sure the server is down (to prevent high utilization from generating false messages).
15. Type `N` in the **Pager Type** field.
16. Enter `N` in the **Page Every Hour** field. (The demo needs to page you only once, right?)
17. Enter your pager number and a dial-out code or other numbers required to send a page.

18. Enter a pause time required before your paging system's PIN number needs to be entered (if relevant). Enter one comma for each two seconds you want to pause.
19. Enter your PIN number (if any).
20. Enter the delay time from the completion of dialing and PIN number entry until the message is sent. Enter one comma for each two-second delay. You may need to fine-tune this setting by trial and error.
21. Enter the page you want to send in the **Message** field. The demo supports only numeric pagers, so something like 911 would be sensible.
22. Click the **Update** button.
23. Repeat twice to add additional servers, if you wish. Make one server name a fake so that the software will think the server is down and will try to page you for a trial run.
24. Click the Done button to begin installation.
25. Click the OK button when installation has finished.
26. From a DOS prompt, type `C:\NETALERT\NETALERT`.

The NET-ALERT program loads and continuously checks to see that the server is still active. When a server goes down (or can't be found because you put in a name that doesn't exist on your network), the program initializes the modem, calls your pager number, and leaves the message you specified. It waits momentarily and then sends a second page.

Using K.F. Soft's Nice Capture

This program is an easier way than using the CAPTURE command to connect to print queues or files. The software displays the current print capture settings and allows the user to connect to any queue she can access on any of the servers she is logged into. It can also end capture to a print queue, allowing local use of a parallel port and effectively replacing the ENDCAP command as well.

To install and run the program, follow these steps:

1. Place the NICECAPT.EXE file in SYS:PUBLIC.
2. Type `NICECAPT` from a DOS prompt.

The Nice Capture screen allows users to select from a list of print queues and parallel ports, as shown in Figure 14.8.

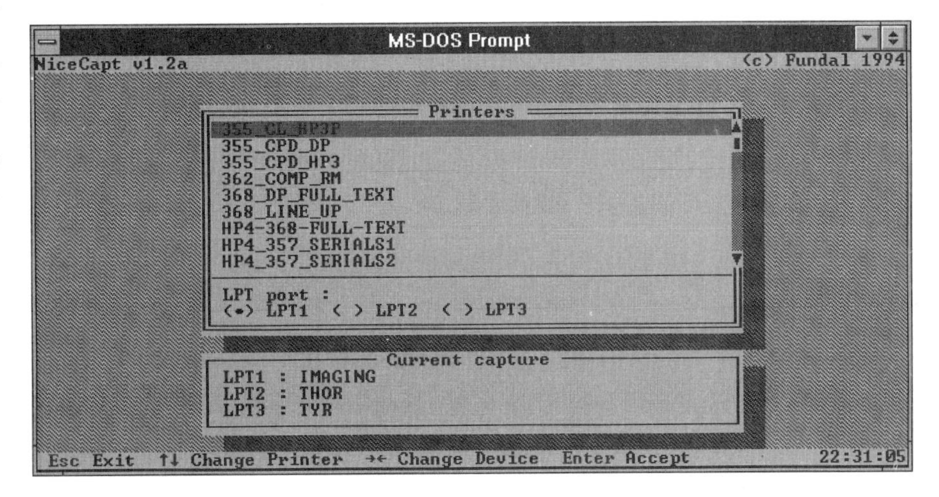

FIGURE 14.8
The Nice Capture utility makes it easier for users to capture and end capture to network print queues.

Two other handy features of the Nice Capture utility are its ability to define descriptive names for network print queues and to hide queues from users. These functions are included in the SETPROP.EXE program, which sets properties for each network queue you care to enhance. SETPROP runs from the command line and allows you to define descriptive names, set standard queue capture parameters for each queue, and hide each queue from Nice Capture.

Function	**Syntax**	**Example**
Define long queue name	`SETPROP /3` *`queue`* `IDENTIFICATION` "*`name`*"	`SETPROP /3 EXEC IDENTIFICATION "Executive LaserJet"`

Function	Syntax	Example
Define capture parameters	`SETPROP /3` *`queue`* `PARAMETERS "`*`parameters`*`"`	`SETPROP /3 EXEC PARAMETERS "/NB /NT /NFF"`
Hide from NiceCapt	`SETPROP /3` *`queue`* `DISABLE _CAPTURE " "`	`SETPROP /3 EXEC DISABLE CAPTURE " "`

Using K.F. Soft's Nice Login

This program is a real blessing if you have users who, as soon as they log in, go straight into Windows, never noticing that their passwords are expiring or that they haven't successfully logged into the network. Tools like this one can reduce the number of spurious phone calls you receive from users who just had no way of knowing that their daily login routine didn't proceed properly. It's also a friendlier way of approaching network logins than the standard LOGIN.EXE utility.

To install Nice Login, follow these directions:

1. Copy NLOGIN.EXE to SYS:LOGIN and SYS:PUBLIC.
2. Alter your network connection batch file (often STARTNET.BAT, NET.BAT, or AUTOEXEC.BAT) to run NLOGIN.EXE instead of LOGIN.EXE.
3. Rename SYS:PUBLIC\LOGOUT.EXE to LOGOUTNW.EXE.
4. Create a file called LOGOUT.BAT with `NLOGIN.EXE` as its contents.

When your users log in or log out, they will be executing Nice Login, which will log them out of the network and then present them with the login screen shown in Figure 14.9.

One problem with this program is that it does not handle multiple server attachments very gracefully. However, on a small network with users who are encountering login and logout problems, Nice Login is a very useful tool.

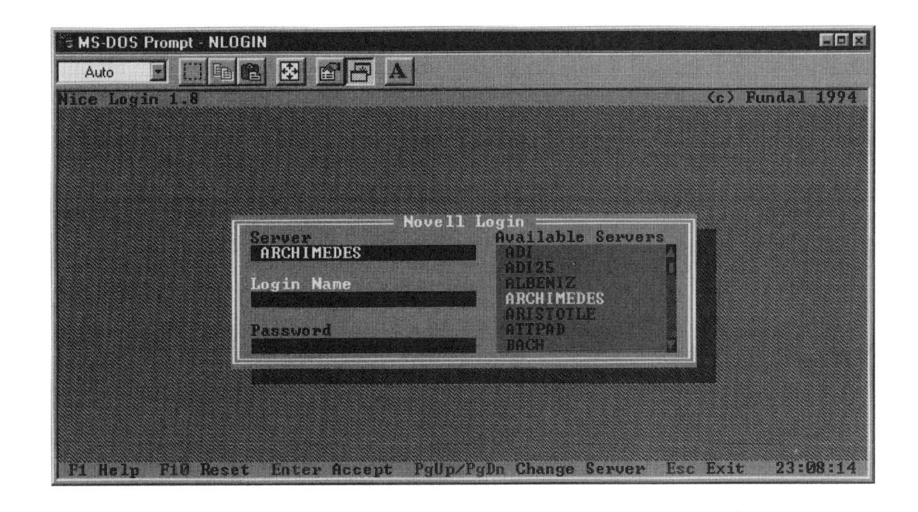

FIGURE 14.9 The Nice Login utility replaces the clumsy LOGIN.EXE command with a more helpful interface.

Using Sexwax Software's LOG.EXE

This little freeware program creates a log of user login times. The program creates a data file, called LOGFILE.DAT, in which the username, connection number, login date, login time, network number, and node address are recorded when the LOG.EXE file is run. The most straightforward way to use this program is to include it in the system login script. To maintain the LOGFILE.DAT this way, follow these steps.

1. Place LOG.EXE in the SYS:PUBLIC directory.
2. Edit the system login script to include the line `# Z:LOG.EXE`. (If you map a different search drive to SYS:PUBLIC, replace Z with the appropriate drive letter.)
3. From a DOS prompt, type the following:

   GRANT R W M F FOR SYS:PUBLIC\LOGFILE.DAT TO GROUP EVERYONE

LOGFILE.DAT is a plain ASCII text file that can be viewed or printed whenever you wish. You'll have to manually delete or prune it when it grows too large, however.

Working with the Shareware Concept

Shareware is not the same thing as *freeware*. Shareware is not free software. It is usually created by hardworking programmers who are willing to let you try before you buy. They distribute their software freely—and generally allow you to distribute it freely, too, as long as it's distributed *free*—so that potential users can evaluate the product.

If you use shareware software, look at the license agreement that comes with it. There is often a reasonable "test drive" period specified in the accompanying documentation. If you decide you don't want it, delete it. You can always download it again if you decide to give it another chance.

If you continue to use it, pay for it. Shareware authors are at least as deserving of your money as corporate geeks in Redmond or Cambridge.

We've discussed the use of several network utilities previously, in the context of network administration jobs. In this chapter, we've focused on the operation of the basic NetWare commands that allow you to perform the tasks you'll encounter on a regular basis. We've also looked at the programs included on the CD-ROM that accompanies this book and considered installation and usage issues.

In the next chapter, we'll move along to a more glamorous aspect of network administration: networking yourself. In Chapter 15, we'll consider how to build teamwork among the technical staff in your organization, work with power users, find and deal with outside help, and make use of user groups and professional associations. Let's go!

Working the Crowd: Networking Yourself

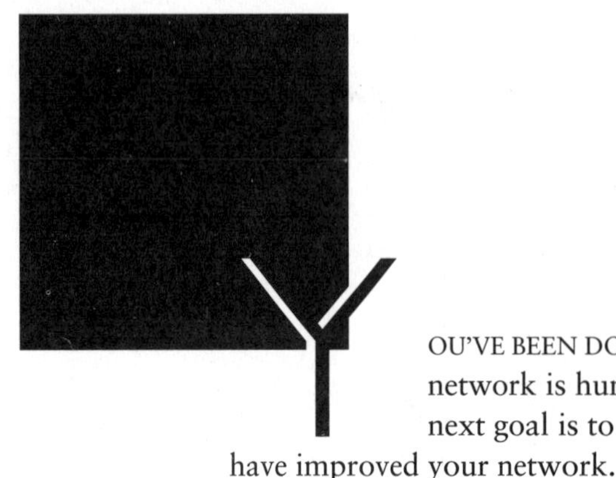

YOU'VE BEEN DOING a fine job, taking care of business, and the network is humming along. This is no time to let up. Your next goal is to improve your personal network, just as you have improved your network.

Many network managers focus so intently on the physical aspects of their management tasks that they lose sight of the other relationships that can make network administration easier and more rewarding. You do more than enhance your employment opportunities by cultivating relationships—you also improve your job performance.

The interactions you should be most interested in are those with your fellow technical staff members, your corporate power users (the more sophisticated users on your network), the VARs and vendors whose products and services you purchase, and professional associations. We'll worry more about your managers later in the Motivating Executives section in Chapter 20.

The Vital Information

THIS CHAPTER FOCUSES on some of the ways in which you can network with users, technicians, and vendors. Your ability to work constructively with others in your organization and with other professional users impacts your success as a network administrator. The following is a list of some of the ways you can network yourself:

- Build esprit de corps with technical staff.
- Cooperate with power users.

- Carefully select outside help.
- Join user groups and professional associations.

Dealing with In-House Staff

YOU PROBABLY FEEL that you are different from your fellow grunts and geeks. You may think they're more knowledgeable, more volatile, or even more attractive than you are. And you may be correct. Concentrating on your differences, however, gets you nowhere. If you are to forge alliances with your coworkers that can withstand the kind of crises that network administrators get embroiled in, you must see the value in each of your fellow IS staffers and each way-too-into-it nerd user on your network.

There's a sensible reason for all this love and understanding. You're not necessarily looking for friends to play poker with (though that would be a nice development), you're looking for people to make use of. This kind of use isn't manipulative; it's a professional utilization of the strengths and experiences of your coworkers. You should make it your business to know what your fellow staff members and coworkers have to offer.

Getting Respect from Your Users

A former colleague manages a staff of network administrators who oversee the operations of a large company's servers. He has been an excellent resource for me, and when I was managing a small network within his metropolitan area network (MAN), he was helpful to me and my department.

I was a little surprised one day when I had lunch with a coworker, and she reacted strongly when his name came up. She was angry with him because he hadn't responded to her requests for assistance, and she resented being ignored by him.

I questioned her further about the specifics of her problem, and it turned out that she had called him directly about a problem on her client workstation, completely bypassing the help desk and the client support technician who serviced her department's computers.

(continued)

As it turned out, the network manager had forwarded her calls and mail messages back to the help desk for service, and he had even called to tell her that he couldn't help her with her problem. Unfortunately, this made her even more angry.

The moral of the story, if there is one, is that you can't please everyone all the time. You can be a straight arrow and earn the respect and admiration of most of your peers and users, but there will be situations in which you can't win and people you can't win over.

Be aware that human foibles will cause conflicts between you and some of your peers and users, but never let conflict prevent you from performing your job in a professional way.

Working with Technical Staff

Your IS peers may be well trained, competent, and pleasant to work with. They may be none of the above. Most likely, they'll be somewhere in between, and you'll all suffer from crises of confidence, uncertainty about roles, and touches of moodiness. As long as you maintain a professional relationship and continue to communicate, you will get along just fine.

To whatever extent possible, take advantage of a team approach. Identify the management tasks and issues you would most like to deal with, and compare them with the preferences of the other technical staff. If you are in the position to give authority to other administrators or technicians, do so. Make the team members responsible for areas that are suited to their interests and abilities if possible.

You should also built rapport with programmers, database managers, and other technical staff that may not be in a traditional "operations" role. You rely on these coworkers to tell you what their programs and databases are doing so that you know how best to manage the network they rely on. They rely on you to keep the systems running and inform them when problems arise. Play your cards right, and you've got a rewarding symbiotic relationship rather than a territorial firefight.

Working with Power Users

Power users also want to be empowered, and providing them with power has its advantages. An empowered power user can agitate for change in the network. Managers who ignore the pleas of a network administrator sometimes listen to the arguments of the departmental techie.

On another level, you're a bit like a Jedi master attempting to keep a pupil from heading for the Dark Side. Power users can cause more damage than most other users, simply because they usually lack the fear that keeps others in check. Power users are typically quite certain that they can do no wrong, and they're not always able to distinguish a dangerous situation.

So share information with them. Throw them a bone once in a while by asking them to evaluate a new configuration or a new software package. If they cause problems for you, discuss the ramifications of their actions with them rather than immediately revoking their privileges. In short, treat them as knowledgeable and trustworthy, and tell them when they fall short.

Negotiating with VARs and Vendors

ONE AREA IN which you should become as involved as possible is purchasing. You want to be the one who specifies the products that are procured for the network. Since contract negotiations affect the installation, configuration, and maintenance of network products, you should be involved in negotiating contracts with consultants and VARs.

Selecting a Source of Support

If you want your network development projects to run smoothly, you have to put your own house in order, and you have to be able to determine whether potential support organizations have ordered their houses, too. If you are going to be specifying network upgrades, you have to know what is currently installed on the network and what needs are driving the plan for enhancement. You must be able to understand the system needs well enough to convey them to an outsider. When you're ready to select a VAR, vendor, or service provider, you must be able to clearly communicate your wishes, ensure that your wishes are understood, and then evaluate the contenders.

Cleaning Your Own House

Once you have determined the purpose, scope, and ramifications of the network enhancement plan, you should determine what role you want outside organizations playing in the implementation of a solution. Many companies have turned to outsourcing when their data processing needs exceed their internal capabilities. However, this policy erodes the control you have over your organization's production, which is its lifeblood.

Instead of outsourcing, some companies are trying "insourcing," in which an outside organization takes on a consulting role and helps re-engineer or develop the internal systems to handle new tasks and responsibilities. Although insourcing can be cost effective compared to in-house development, it also requires that healthy relationships exist between the organization's technical staff and the outside parties.

Checking Under the Rug

If your goal is to develop a healthy relationship with an outside organization, whether they are to provide systems development or applications development expertise, you need to follow these guidelines:

- Understand the project.
- Make sure the outside parties understand the project.
- Evaluate the candidates.
- Negotiate terms.

Assuming you are familiar enough with your installed systems, current network functions, and planned network functions to comply with the first guideline, you're ready to address the potential business partners. The only way for them to understand the project is for you to provide a simple model of the enhancement and compare it to the current situation. Ask the candidates to create preliminary specifications so you can make sure they understand your needs.

Investigate the organizations you've identified as being capable of fulfilling your needs. Check their referrals to ensure that their other clients are satisfied. Ascertain whether the group has experience with your particular heterogeneous system. If the project is large, check business credit reports, and ask the company for financial information. You don't want to put your eggs in a flimsy basket.

Finally, negotiate the terms of the contract. Cost is an important issue, of course, but performance guarantees, favorable rates for ongoing support, and clauses ensuring that personnel turnover does not adversely affect the project can all be as important—sometimes more so—than price.

Negotiating a Sweeter Deal

If you find a VAR that is responsive to your needs and provides acceptable service, you want to keep it happy to ensure continued satisfaction. One way to accomplish this task is to purchase items through your VAR even if you could get a better price elsewhere. On the one hand, you do not want to pay any more for your goods and services than necessary. On the other hand, you want to maintain a high profile as a valued customer.

Finding this balance should not be difficult. If you purchase a new server, buy it through your VAR, and negotiate installation in the deal. You may be able to get a better price from a superstore, but you won't find a superstore installer who knows your network, can help you install and configure the system, and can make sure it continues running. Don't buy 25 copies of WordPerfect through your VAR unless you think you'll need some help installing and configuring the software.

Taking Advantage of Associations

MANY PROFESSIONAL ASSOCIATIONS are of interest to network managers. These associations include vertical market groups that focus on the industry you work in rather than the technology you play with. You're on your own finding those groups, but here are a few professional associations and groups that may be of interest:

NAME	CONTACT
Association for Computing Machinery (ACM)	(212) 869-7440
Internet Society (ISOC)	(800) 468-9507
NetWare Users International	(800) 228-4684
Network Professional Association (NPA)	(801) 379-0330
Women in Computing	(202) 234-2111

I recommend you join the NPA in particular. You must have network administration certification to gain full membership, but associate membership is available to those who are working toward certification. The cost of full membership is $150 per year. The NPA's *Network News* publication includes articles on a variety of topics, and the association provides product discounts and previews for its members. You should also consider checking for local user groups for NetWare or other network operating systems.

Obtaining NetWare Certification

Novell has a well-established certification program that recognizes administrators who have achieved various degrees of competency with NetWare and associated products. NetWare certification currently involves four levels:

- Certified Novell Administrator
- Certified Novell Engineer
- Master Certified Novell Engineer
- Certified Novell Instructor

Each of these levels has a corresponding battery of tests and a list of associated classes. Novell Authorized Education Centers (NAECs) provide training courses and self-study kits, and Drake Testing administers the computer-based tests.

Getting along with your peers and power users is a major feather in your cap. Finding a trustworthy VAR can better than striking oil, and taking advantage of the resources that vendors and associations can offer is, if not the pinnacle of wisdom, certainly a milestone on the road up the mountain. Networking yourself with your users and outside resources will give you the respect you need to do your job properly, the resources to get large projects completed rapidly and successfully, and the information you need to make informed decisions about network development. In the next chapter, we will consider some of the ways in which you can use this information to shape your network in the future.

Taking Charge of the Future

Fire in the Hole: Anticipating Needs

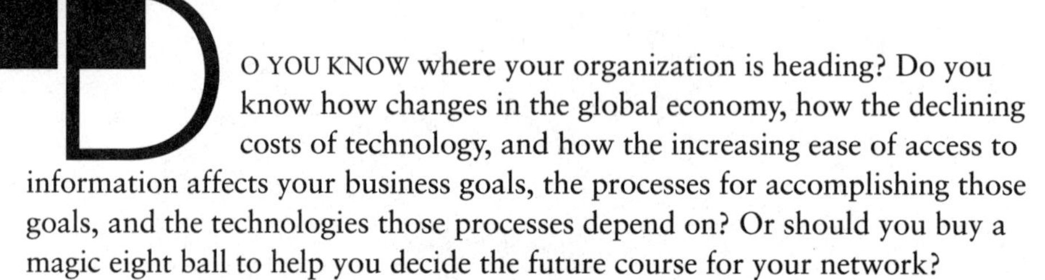

DO YOU KNOW where your organization is heading? Do you know how changes in the global economy, how the declining costs of technology, and how the increasing ease of access to information affects your business goals, the processes for accomplishing those goals, and the technologies those processes depend on? Or should you buy a magic eight ball to help you decide the future course for your network?

If you're in a position to determine long-term networking strategies, your situation is unusual. Most administrators are forced into a reactive mode by distributed decision making and the sudden changes of course that are business realities. You can create a networking philosophy, but setting your network development plans in stone based on current goals and needs is an exercise in futility. Even if you are able to keep a close eye on developments in networking and other technologies that can influence your users, expect to have the carpet pulled out from under you by changes in other quarters.

That's a rather bleak outlook on development planning. Despite my dour words, however, you can take several steps to improve your ability to respond to change and to lead your organization into new projects. When my brother was in the air force, he used to say, "The key to air superiority is flexibility, and the key to flexibility is indecision." We won't model our network flexibility on this model; instead, we'll focus on gathering information about current network loads and ongoing organizational plans and on avoiding getting locked into dead-end technologies.

The Vital Information

THE BIG NEWS in this chapter is that if you have an internetwork, you're going to need a protocol analyzer to determine your current network load and to monitor utilization changes. You'll measure your current network usage levels and identify possible trouble spots and address problems as they develop. You should also pay attention to the winds of change blowing in your organization and avoid committing yourself to a single development path.

Keeping Tabs on Network Loads

ONE WAY TO manage network development is based on the reactive method of taking steps to enhance performance when it begins to decline. Collecting baseline information about network usage is not necessarily a purely reactive measure, however. If you can identify the existing network load and potential bottleneck areas, you are well on your way to knowing where proactive measures can be taken to stave off problems.

The Infonetics research organization indicates that network capacity planning is the low task on network administrators' to-do lists. The Infonetics study estimates a 600 percent increase in losses due to downtime per company if planning continues to sit on the back burner. That's an estimated $27 million loss per company due to downtime that could be avoided by planning ahead. Ouch.

The good news is that you can ascertain network performance by qualitative observation of network response to client systems. I know some network administrators who run various flight simulation software from the network on systems where they work, primarily (they say) to collect this kind of qualitative performance data. If the simulator flies fast and responds well to the controls, all is well. If the simulation gets choppy or slows, something's wrong. I don't recommend this approach unless you've got an office to hide in and you turn the volume way down. The bad news is that this qualitative data isn't going to be much help if you're trying to establish a need for new equipment. Worse news is that you're going to have to shell out some money for a network analyzer to get really useful results.

Selecting a Network Analyzer

One of the most tempting LAN analysis products available is Novell's LANalyzer for Windows, a software product that supports Token Ring and Ethernet access methods and IPX/SPX, AppleTalk, TCP/IP, NFS, and SNA protocols. The software currently lists for $1,500, which isn't outrageously expensive for a protocol analyzer, and is easy to use. Some say that LANalyzer is too pricey. It works well, however and it's a well-known product from a well-known company, and those can be major advantages when you're justifying a purchase. If you need something less expensive, contact your VAR to see what's available.

One of the software-only alternatives to LANalyzer is Triticom's LANdecoder, a package that can identify and interpret IPX, SPX, NCP, RIP, TCP/IP, AppleTalk, VINES, and DECnet packets. It is easily installed, performs traffic monitoring, and costs less than Novell's product. Triticom offers a $595 ARCNet version, a $945 Ethernet version, and a $1195 Token Ring version.

Network General's Sniffer line of protocol analyzers provide more detailed and varied information. Most of the Sniffer products are pre-installed on notebook computers and currently retail for $10,000. Network Communications' Network Probe line of protocol analyzers were once called "LANalyzers," but Novell and Network Communications worked out an arrangement in early 1995 that left NCC with the protocol analyzer hardware and Novell with the name.

Other LAN analysis tools include Frontline Test Equipment's $3,000 Ethertest software for DOS and Network Instruments' $500 Observer software for Windows. HawkNet's $500 NetReport runs as an NLM and provides extensive network reporting.

Network Performance Snapshots

Whichever tool you select, you should collect data over a period of time. A week's worth of data collected every 30 or 60 minutes ought to give you an accurate idea of the average numbers for your network. Collecting data points over a short period of time or too frequently can generate misleading results because of unusual spikes or drops in activity. Record the following kinds of information for your network:

- Utilization
- Server activity
- Packet throughput

Measuring Network Utilization

Utilization is a measure of how busy the network is. Utilization measures the amount of data per second being transmitted on the network, and this number is conveyed as a percentage of the theoretical maximum of the access method.

Ethernet networks are more sensitive to network utilization levels than Token Ring networks are, but regardless of the access method in use, high utilization rates can indicate trouble, and increasing utilization rates should set off warning bells in your head as well as on your network analysis package.

If you have a high utilization rate of 50 percent on an Ethernet network segment, that means that roughly 5 Mbps are being transmitted on the network. Because Ethernet is nondeterministic, a utilization rate of 50 percent also means your packet collision rate is high, so quite a bit of traffic is probably attributable to Ethernet overhead.

Some protocol analyzers can report the *token rotation time* on a Token Ring network; this number indicates how frequently a station on the ring can capture a token. A low token rotation time usually indicates that relatively few stations are competing for tokens; this scenario is preferable to a high rotation time, which means lower performance because stations have to wait longer to transmit data.

Your network analysis tool should also indicate the rate at which network errors are encountered. There is a strong link between utilization and error rate, especially on Ethernet networks, but unusually high error rates may be indicative of network faults or broken equipment.

USING ERROR RATE DATA Collecting error information is one of the things a software-only network analysis package can do perfectly adequately. The errors include CRC errors reported from a single network node or from multiple workstations, fragment errors, mis-sized packet errors, and jabber errors.

CRC errors occur when packets do not contain the correct cyclical redundancy check value. These errors are often caused by EMI on cabling, network segments longer than the maximum length, improper grounding or termination, or worn cables. Failing NICs, transceivers, or other communications hardware can also cause these errors.

Fragment errors result from colliding packets, and they are typically caused by NIC problems or because the network segment is overused.

Packet errors involving oversized or undersized packets typically involve NIC drivers or the NICs themselves.

Jabber errors are oversized packets containing CRC errors and are usually caused by a bad NIC or transceiver.

COLLECTING UTILIZATION DATA Because most installed networks are Ethernet, and Ethernet performance can decline quite noticeably as the number of users increases, a heavily laden network may be a prime candidate for upgrading to a high-bandwidth or switched technology. Although you may know which networks are burdened simply by being familiar with the work done on them (and by this time, that should be true!), getting a measurement of network utilization can be very helpful.

The LANalyzer screen shown in Figure 16.1 is taken from a network with very high packet traffic and network utilization. Notice how the Dashboard window shows high ranges of values like the redline on a tachometer.

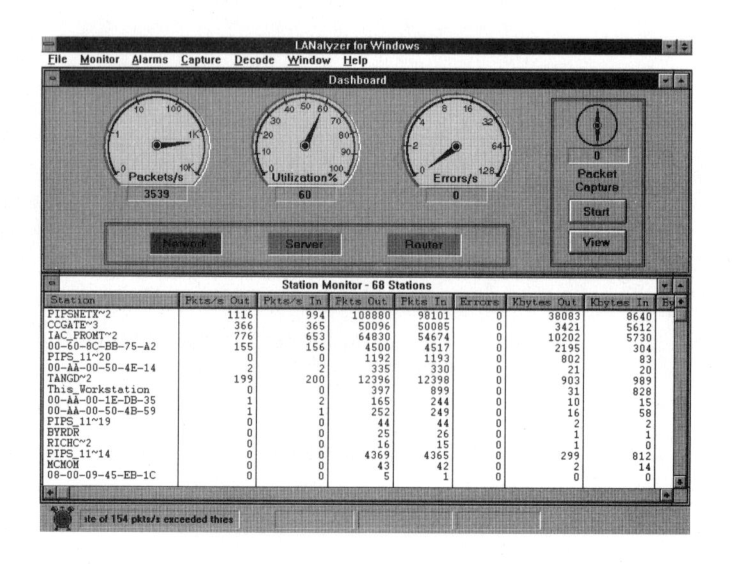

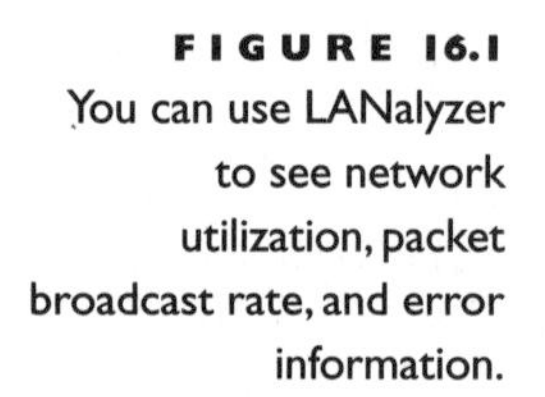

FIGURE 16.1 You can use LANalyzer to see network utilization, packet broadcast rate, and error information.

If the alarm levels you have set are exceeded, the Network, Server, or Router button turns red. By double-clicking on these buttons, you can access a list of messages that have been broadcast in response to errors. You can highlight one of the error rates shown and then start the NetWare Expert, which provides an explanation of the message and suggestions for resolving the problem, as shown in Figure 16.2.

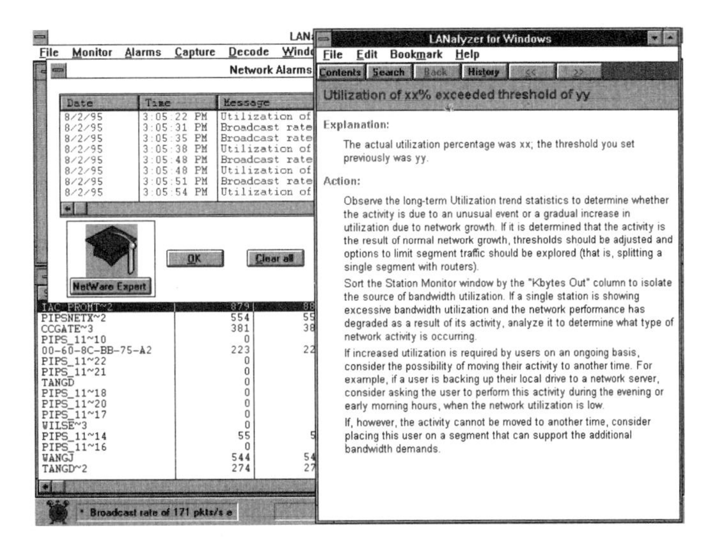

FIGURE 16.2 NetWare Expert provides an explanation of the alarm condition generated by a network and suggests courses of action to eliminate the alarms.

In the Station Monitor window in Figure 16.1, the stations on these networks appear, currently sorted in order of number of packets sent out. LANalyzer allows you to set filters to identify the portion of the total load that is attributable to certain stations. This allows you to identify somewhat difficult-to-determine problems, such as an out-of-date driver or a failing NIC.

If one or a few of the stations in the list display particularly high numbers, you can capture some packets and then view more detail about the traffic data, including the source and destination stations, the protocol in use, and other information shown in Figure 16.3.

To get an idea of how the current utilization levels fit into the network health picture, have a look at the trends view of utilization, as shown in Figure 16.4.

Server activity is important because the most active servers are the most likely to encounter performance problems. Unusual activity levels may indicate that problems caused by rapid growth or by faulty components are plaguing your network. Protocol analyzers can be set to count the number of

FIGURE 16.3 Station traffic information stored in the packet capture buffer shows where the data is going, what protocol it's using, and other information.

LANalyzer for Windows
File Monitor Alarms Capture Decode Window Help

Capture Buffer

No.	Source	Destination	Layer	Summary	Error	Size
1	PIPS_11~10	PIPSNETX~2	ncp	Req Read; Handle 6670EC300000; 615 byte		68
2	PIPSNETX~2	PIPS_11~5	ncp	Rply Unknown (Request not seen)		64
3	PIPSNETX~2	PIPS_11~10	ncp	Rply Read; 615 bytes		674
4	PIPS_11~21	PIPSNETX~2	ncp	Req Read; Handle 78AC0F440000; 378 byte		68
5	PIPS_11~5	PIPSNETX~2	ncp	Req Write; Handle 005A19400000; 1024 by		1092
6	PIPS_11~10	PIPSNETX~2	ncp	Req Read; Handle 6670EC300000; 409 byte		68
7	PIPSNETX~2	PIPS_11~21	ncp	Rply Read; 378 bytes		436
8	PIPSNETX~2	PIPS_11~5	ncp	Rply Write		64
9	PIPS_11~21	PIPSNETX~2	ncp	Req Read; Handle 78AC0F440000; 447 byte		68

```
ncp: ==================== NetWare Core Protocol ====================
      NCP Request: Read
      Request Type: 0x2222 (Request)
      Sequence Number: 19
      Connection Number Low: 11
      Task Number: 1
      Connection Number High: 0
      Function Code: 72
      File Handle: 0x66 0x70 0xEC 0x30 0x00 0x00
      Starting Byte Offset: 2702336
      Bytes to Read: 615

 0: 00 60 8C C8 16 59 00 60 8C BB 5B 5D 00 32 FF FF | .`...Y.`..[].2..
10: 00 32 00 11 00 01 13 05 00 00 00 00 00 01 04 51 | .2.............Q
20: 00 01 13 8B 00 60 8C BB 5B 5D 40 03 22 22 13 0B | .....`..[]@.""..
30: 01 00 48 00 66 70 EC 30 00 00 00 29 3C 00 02 67 | ..H.fp.0...)<..g
```

exceeded threshold of 100 ** U | Packet: 1 | Unfiltered: 969

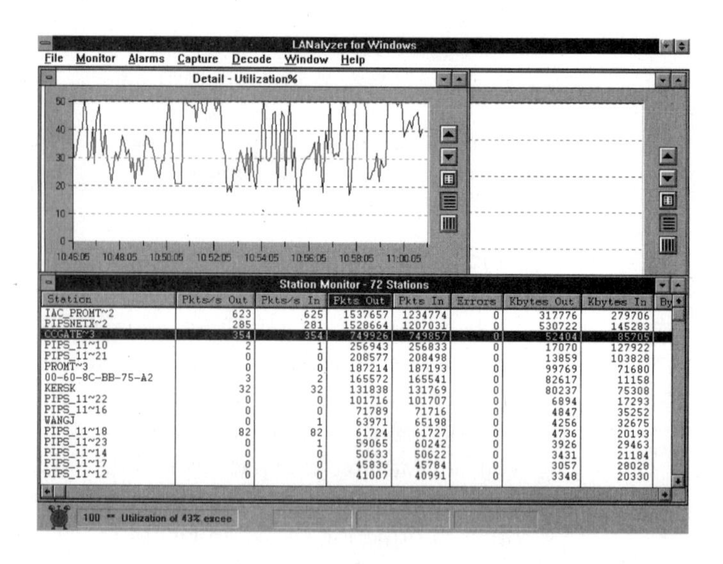

FIGURE 16.4 Network utilization displayed over time as a graph.

request being processed packets, which are packets broadcast to clients when servers are fully occupied with other tasks. Large numbers of these packets would indicate a server overload.

Heavier loads on a few servers might indicate the need for bridges or routers to reduce traffic flow across network segments. They might also imply that a high-speed or switched connection is necessary. Heavy loads can also be eliminated by redistributing users or applications.

Gauging Packet Throughput

Large networks transmit a large number of packets, including SAP and RIP broadcast packets, NCP requests or replies, and data packets. Heavy packet traffic may indicate a need for SAP filtering to reduce the load on the network.

RIP and SAP filtering reduce overhead on the network communications lines by limiting the advertisement of network services and routes. Filtering can be configured with NetWare's MultiProtocol Router software packages. Inbound filtering can cause the packets to be discarded, or even better, outbound filters limit the updates sent to each other point on the network. Other router manufacturers use their own SAP filtering software.

Anticipating Organizational Plans

KEEPING YOUR EAR to the ground is a vital part of network management. Don't be one to spread gossip in order to make use of the information you hear. In fact, one reason you should strive to get along with everyone is that you have more to gain from knowing what's going on—and more to lose if you don't know—than most of your coworkers.

Do not isolate yourself from the political and organizational struggles found in every organization; if change is afoot, you want to get wind of it so you can consider the impact on your systems before the last minute. Many companies have a tendency to develop business plans without considering the technology required to implement their plans. They make business plans now and build infrastructure later. A more effective approach molds the organizational and technology changes into a sensible and efficient re-engineering process.

Cultivate relationships with managers and administrative assistants from other departments. You don't need to milk them for information, but it makes sense to keep your eyes and ears open for any information that might be helpful to you.

Keeping Your Options Open

Ah, we're back to flexibility. Let's face it, your chances of developing a coherent development plan and sticking to it are minimal. Unless you're the president and CEO as well as the network administrator, it's not likely that you'll have enough input into planning and development to make your development paradigm stick. That's okay anyway, because technology develops, changes, and becomes obsolete in the blink of an eye. A vendor strategy you buy into one week may be abandoned next week.

That's one reason you need to maintain rapport with vendors, VARs, and other sources of industry information. These issues are discussed in further detail in the section Gathering Information about Developing Products in Chapter 19.

It's important to maintain your roots in the business realities that control your network's destiny. Now that you're thinking about where your business may be headed, you're ready to look at some of the nifty new toys that may take you where you want to go. In the next two chapters, we'll look at hardware and software products that you can use in your network environment.

The Hard Stuff: Hardware Upgrades to Consider

YOU'VE ALREADY CONSIDERED some of the most important hardware products to solve immediate problems. This chapter is intended to provide a whirlwind tour of some of the prime new products available that can improve the reliability, performance, or ease of use of your network.

We begin with a quick tour of cutting-edge server hardware, including server redundancy options and "superserver" designs that offer high performance and fault tolerance. Then we move to the client systems for a look at the latest in NICs. Next comes a quick investigation of the latest switches, hubs, and routers available. Finally, we revisit networked peripherals, including printers, CD-ROM drives, and modems.

This chapter is hardly the final word on any of these subjects. Instead, it is a starting point. Use the information sources described in the section Learning about Developing Products in Chapter 19 to collect even more up-to-date information.

Upgrading the Server Hardware

SERVER HARDWARE IS finally beginning to take care of itself. The latest server designs offer better built-in management features, hardware error checking, expandability, and fault tolerance than ever before. Excited? Well, don't answer yet, because there's more. If a hot rod server isn't adequate for you, you can pair servers to provide redundancy in case of failure.

High-Performance Servers

The Big Kahuna of NetWare file servers is the Compaq ProLiant family of servers. These servers include several features intended to prevent server downtime. The ProLiant's fault-prevention feature tracks server data and uses trend analysis to predict component failures. When the software determines that a part is breaking down, Compaq will replace the device before it fails.

The ProLiant servers use redundant power supplies, Compaq's Smart SCSI Array RAID controller, hot-swappable drives, and error checking and correcting (ECC) memory. In the event of a crash, recovery software restarts the server and can notify you that a failure has occurred. It also attempts to determine the cause of the crash. Compaq's TriFlex bus architecture employs a 64-bit processor bus, a 128-bit memory bus, and a 32-bit EISA bus, all of which are managed by data flow logic that helps make the ProLiants screaming- fast servers.

Even setting up these servers is easy; Compaq's SmartStart CD-ROMs allow you to install NetWare, Windows NT Server, or SCO UNIX and add-in packages, simply by ordering licenses.

Server Mirroring Options

We've already discussed SFT III, Novell's solution to server failure. SFT III uses nearly identical servers that are mirrored on the fly to provide total system redundancy. One of the servers can crash or be serviced, and the other takes command.

It's a great product, but there are some alternatives that are somewhat more flexible because they do not require the same degree of similarity and do not cost as much as SFT III. The cream of this crop is Vinca's StandbyServer 32, which currently lists for $3,000 and includes two adapters that can connect two file servers at distances up to 50 feet. These adapters provide 80 Mbps transfer of data between the servers, which are not required to have matching disk drives or other server hardware. A Vinca configuration is illustrated in Figure 17.1.

Since the Vinca adapters are also certified for use as SFT III MSL adapters, they provide a potential upgrade path.

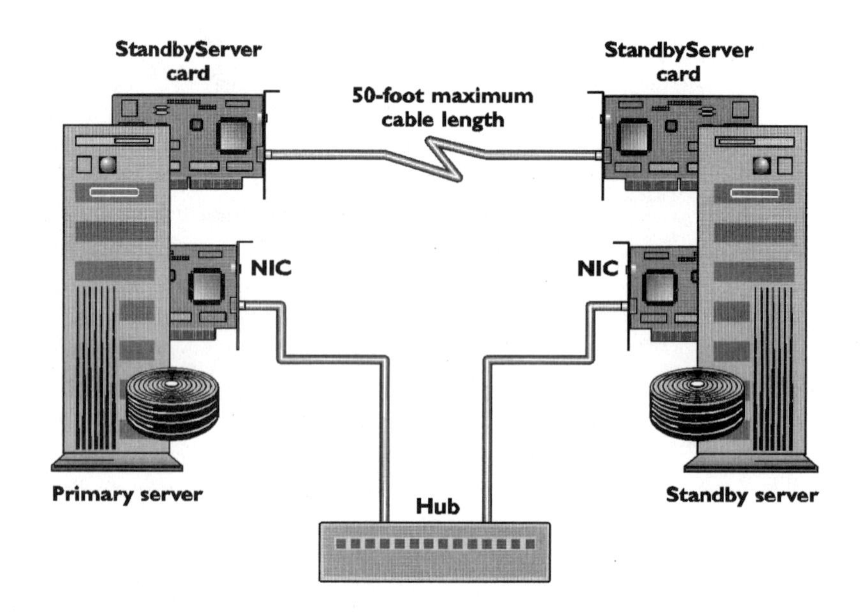

FIGURE 17.1 Vinca's StandbyServer 32 allows server mirroring between dissimilar systems connected by 80 Mbps adapters.

One drawback of the Vinca solution and most other server mirroring products is that unlike SFT III, they do not automatically switch between servers if one unit fails. The changeover must be made manually.

Other products that provide server mirroring include:

Product	Vendor
Double-Take	Network Specialists
LANshadow	Horizons Technology
LANtegrity	Network Integrity
No-Stop Network	Nonstop Networks
Off-Site Server	MiraLink

Updating Client Equipment

IF YOU HAVE client systems that pump large amounts of data on your network, you may want to take a look at Intel's EtherExpress PRO/100 NICs. These boards are available for EISA or PCI buses. Although 100 Mbps speeds may seem a little racy for client systems, the current list prices for the Intel NICs are $400 for EISA boards and $260 for PCI boards, making them a reasonable choice for high-performance network client systems (as well as file servers). The boards automatically sense the speed of the ports they are plugged into, so whether you're using a 10BaseT hub or a 100BaseT hub, the EtherExpress PRO works admirably.

Improving Connectivity Equipment

IN THE PREVIOUS sections, we have discussed specific hardware products that are among the best of their breeds. It's difficult to distinguish the absolutely best connectivity products, however. Differences in price and features can be trivial or pivotal depending on your network configuration and needs, so instead of recommending particular products, let's look at the kinds of products to consider.

Asynchronous Transfer Mode is looking like the high-speed transport technology of choice ... soon. ATM products and services are not universally available and are still quite expensive, but they will be vital to network data transfer in short order. In the meantime, 100 Mbps technologies may satisfy your need for network speed. Finally, direct Internet connections can add a high degree of complexity to network management, but they open a door to a world of information.

Preparing for Asynchronous Transfer Mode

The first class of connectivity equipment to consider is ATM switches and connections. Although ATM service between sites is not universally supported, transmission speeds in excess of 150 Mbps are already attainable, and as ATM gains momentum, the addition of multiple additional switches can push this throughput rate even higher.

ATM is not a mature or terribly stable technology at the moment, but its scalability offers a bright promise for future networks. If your organization needs to be moving buckets of data for complex calculations, video, or other bandwidth-hungry applications, preparing for ATM is a good idea.

Move your clients to 16 Mbps Token Ring or 10 Mbps Ethernet and connect them to switching hubs to take advantage of all the bandwidth available on each access method. Install high-end Ethernet hubs and Token Ring MAUs that can handle high-speed, switched data communications.

When ATM is ready for you, you'll be ready for ATM, with hubs that can be connected to a lightning-fast backbone to provide each user with a 10 Mbps connection to all points on your WAN. And if that's not fast enough for your multimedia applications, investigate the 25 Mbps NICs being developed for microcomputers. These adapters will run on Category 3 twisted-pair cabling, which is found in many organizations and is relatively easy to install, so they may integrate well into your existing environment. Adaptec is working on this kind of NIC, and UB Networks offers the GeoLAN/500 hub, a modular ATM hub that supports 155 Mbps connections to servers and 25 Mbps connections to the desktop.

Fast Interim Connections

Although FDDI has been considered the king in high-speed networking, its price tag has prohibited most network administrators from implementing it on the desktop. And while its dual counter rotating rings provide a stable backbone topology, they aren't really necessary for user stations.

FDDI design includes single attachment stations (SASs), which use only a single connection to a concentrator. The costs of fiber cabling and FDDI adapters are more responsible for the lack of FDDI on the desktop than is dual attachment design. Twisted Pair Physical Media Dependent (TP-PMD) is a specification for running FDDI on Category 5 twisted pair wiring, which may make FDDI more widely useful.

Even though statistics indicate that FDDI is not used in many LANs (many estimates place the figure at one percent), that is in part because it is typically used only as a high-speed backbone in internetworks that need its high performance and stability. Of particular interest are such features as FDDI Full-Duplex

Technology (FFDT), which allows simultaneous transmission and receipt of data by nodes on an FDDI ring. FDDI handles high levels of traffic with relatively low performance degradation, but it takes a heavy toll on server processor utilitization.

100BaseT Fast Ethernet and 100VG-AnyLAN are two solutions to the bandwidth problem; unlike Ethernet switches, which provide the full 10 Mbps bandwidth to each node on the network, these products actually increase the theoretical bandwidth of an Ethernet network tenfold. Both technologies are more affordable than FDDI, and both can use standard Category 5 UTP cabling.

100VG-AnyLAN is an HP invention that includes a priority request mechanism that allows nodes to designate high-priority packets. 100VG provides very good throughput, even over Category 3 and Category 4 wiring (though it requires four pair of these wires rather than the usual two). However, 100VG recently lost its bid to become the IEEE-designated 100 Mbps Ethernet, losing out to the lower-performance but more clearly Ethernet 100BaseT.

100BaseT isn't as fast as either FDDI or 100VG, but it's somewhat less expensive than 100VG and much less expensive than FDDI. For smaller organizations, or distributed networks with no need for a bulletproof backbone, 100BaseT is a good choice because of its speed and similarity to 10BaseT. If your network already uses 10BaseT Ethernet, as most do, 100BaseT offers higher bandwidth and greater performance without forcing you to learn a new network topology or access method.

Direct Internet Connections

Depending on your organization's size and location, you may be able to secure direct access to the Internet via ISDN, T1, T3, or frame relay communications. If your organization plans to offer goods or services on the World Wide Web or wants an Internet gateway for electronic mail, switched or dedicated Internet connections may be an appropriate choice.

Your NetWare network needs to route IP in order to allow users to access the Internet's resources; although NetWare includes the software to perform this task, some administrators prefer to use Firefox's NOV*IX, which routes IPX internally and IP externally. This reduces the management load associated with adding IP to the network, which would ordinarily require administration of IP addresses and DNS support.

Internal IP routing, combined with WWW browsers, can make distribution of internal corporate documents and information simple. If you expect to be developing Web pages for access from external users, creating internal Web documents can be a good way to iron out some of the complications of page layout, design aesthetics, and browser configuration. The result is experience with the technology that is the hot item du jour in the computer industry, and that's always a good idea for a network administrator.

At the moment, the best platform for a Web server is a UNIX system, though Windows NT Server systems are becoming popular and are easier to manage for administrators without UNIX experience. If you're willing to work with UNIX systems, however, more Web server software is available to you.

Enhancing Peripherals

YOU WANT ENHANCED peripherals? We got 'em. Specifically, we've got network printers that can service a workgroup flawlessly, CD-ROM drives that spin at four times "normal" speed or higher, and modems that can operate at 28.8 Kbps. These devices are not as glamorous as some of the high-speed transmission products available, but they have the advantages of being relatively inexpensive and frequently used. If your network includes heavy loads on these peripherals, take a look at these products.

The Latest in Network Printers

From color printers to high-capacity network printing workhorses, there are excellent networkable printers available in every description. Three of the best are the Tektronix Phaser 340 color laser printer, Lexmark International's high-resolution Optra L, and HP's 4Si MX.

Color Output from Tektronix

If you need color printing on the network, one option is the Tektronix Phaser 340 color laser printer, a 600 dots-per-inch (DPI) device that can print 2 pages per minute (PPM) at its highest resolution. The printer can be equipped with an LocalTalk, Ethernet, or Token Ring NIC, and it accommodates a 500-sheet paper tray.

Fine Detail from Lexmark

Lexmark International's Optra L printer can print at resolutions up to 1,200 DPI, comes with PCL5 and PostScript Level 2 emulation modes, a 500-page paper tray, and two NIC slots. The standard LocalTalk, Ethernet, and Token Ring NICs are available. The printer can accept up to 64MB of RAM and prints 12 PPM (less when printing at 1,200 DPI).

High Speed and Capacity from HP

The network printer to beat is HP's LaserJet 4Si MX, which generates 600 DPI output using PCL5 and PostScript Level 2. Its bidirectional parallel port contributes to outstanding print speed (the printer is rated at 17 PPM). LocalTalk, Ethernet, and Token Ring JetDirect NICs are easily configured and support multiple protocols simultaneously.

The Finest in CD-ROM Drives

Although Toshiba's 3501 and Plextor's 4PleX quad speed CD-ROM drives are inexpensive and fast, they are put to shame by Pioneer's DRM604x, a six-disk CD-ROM jukebox that uses fast quad speed drives and provides the convenience of multiple disk storage and retrieval. The Pioneer device isn't an appropriate choice if your users need to access different drives because the jukebox takes a few seconds to swap CD-ROMs, but for archival data or installation procedures, the DRM604x is a dream.

Great Remote Connections

Shiva's NetModem/E 28.8 and LANRover/2E Plus allow dial-in, dial-out, and LAN connections at 28.8 Kbps speeds. The LANRover also supports ISDN, X.25, or switched 56 Kbps links. The LANRover remote-access router includes Shiva's LANConnect package for connecting networks.

These hardware options are products worth considering. Any number of other hardware packages are worth investigating, but the ones described in this chapter are some of the best server and client upgrades, connectivity equipment, and peripherals available.

In the next chapter, some software packages worth considering are highlighted.

The Soft Sell: Software Upgrades to Consider

IN CHAPTER 17, we considered some of the better hardware products available. In this chapter, we briefly describe some of the software you can obtain to add features to your network or to make it run better.

The version of NetWare you are running may not be in dire need of upgrading, but you could probably be enticed into upgrading by the features in the latest versions of NetWare, some of which we discussed previously, such as performance enhancements, distributed NDS databases for WAN management, and simplified user access.

Whatever version of NetWare you use, you can add other Novell products to your servers to provide additional features, such as video services and print and file sharing with UNIX users.

On your client workstations, the hot software to consider is that which provides Internet access. Access to the Internet will enable you and your users to find news and information on FTP sites and the WWW.

Novell offers several network management packages, and third-party software companies also provide some products that offer a wide range of features. Most administration packages are somewhat uneven, containing tools that are useful and others that are less effective.

Vital Information

THIS CHAPTER DISCUSSES several kinds of network software to consider. Naturally, you should keep your eyes and ears open for late-breaking news about new software, but the following checklist is a good starting place when you're deciding what software you need to procure or budget for.

DESIRED?	SOFTWARE TYPE
❑	NetWare Upgrade
❑	NetWare Add-In Products
❑	Internet Dial-Up Access
❑	Network Management Tools
❑	Network Utilities

Upgrading Server Software

WE DISCUSSED VERSION upgrades in the section Upgrading Servers in Chapter 12. Although you may not have thought a NetWare version upgrade was necessary at the time you were reading Chapter 12, consider the benefits of an upgrade before moving on.

Reasons to Upgrade
Add user licenses
Upgrade from old version (2.x, 3.11)
Add NDS features
Attach network CD-ROM drives
Use better server memory management
Expand network dramatically

Upgrading NetWare Versions

If you're using a version of NetWare earlier than 3.12 or 4.1, you're missing many of the additions made in these recent releases. Again, if your network is stable and functioning properly, you don't need to change a thing. However, some administrators still using versions of NetWare earlier than 4.1 may be surprised to find that many of their users are confused logging into multiple servers or that management of resources across the internetwork is becoming far too complicated.

As a network grows and multiple business units access the same data, users have to connect to more servers than they used to. Drive mappings that once were suitable for everyone become problematic for groups of people logging into different servers and attaching to others.

It's not likely that the NetWare world will convert from 2.x and 3.x to 4.x soon. But surveys indicate that more users are planning on upgrading to 4.x in the near future, and a time will come when you'll need to pack your bindery bags and head for NDS.

Other Server Software

In addition to NetWare, Novell offers quite a number of other products, some of them a little surprising. Consult the list below for some examples:

Name	Description
NetWare Video	Stores video files on a server and runs them from multiple client stations. This NLM includes support for Microsoft's Video for Windows, Intel's Indeo, JPEG, MPEG, and QuickTime. The product requires high available network bandwidth to prevent clients from experiencing poor performance.
NetWare Telephony Service	Integrates NetWare with telephone public branch exchange (PBX). The product includes modules to route messages between network workstations and a PBX, route requests for PBX features, and handle communications between the PBX and the server.
NetWare Multiprotocol Router	Bridge/router software that runs on a NetWare server or dedicated PC. MPR routes IPX, TCP/IP, AppleTalk, and SNA and can connect networks via asynchronous communications links, frame relay, SMDS, X.25, ISDN, switched 56 Kbps lines, and leased lines.

Name	Description
NetWare FleX/IP	Provides printer and file sharing between NetWare and UNIX users. This product sits on a NetWare server and defines the UNIX hosts that can access NetWare print queues and files. It also can be configured to route requests for UNIX print and file services for NetWare clients.
NetWare for SAA	Connects NetWare and IBM AS/400 or mainframe systems that use IBM's System Application Architecture. This product allows a file server to act as a gateway to IBM systems, supporting up to 2,000 simultaneous accesses of mainframe information. NetWare for SAA makes use of NDS, has load balancing features, and can be set up in a mirrored server configuration.
NetWare for LAT	NetWare for Local Area Tranport is a protocol gateway that allows communications between NetWare clients and DEC VAX and OpenVMS computers. The clients can run IPX/SPX, AppleTalk, TCP/IP to the server, which handles the communications to the DEC machine.
NetWare Connect	Remote access and control software. This product allows simultaneous dial-in and dial-out support for up to 128 users, and in networks with NDS installed, users can log in once to access all resources they can access. The ConnectView management module allows graphical network traffic monitoring and provides cost accounting data.
NetWare Navigator	Software distribution tool that uses a central server as a distribution point to other servers that act as staging points for the installation. These secondary servers send the software and instructions to the clients on the distribution list. Navigator provides electronic software distribution (ESD) to DOS, Windows, and OS/2 client workstations.

Providing Internet Access

If you aren't able to add a direct Internet connection to your network, you should investigate dial-up access. Many national and regional service providers, some of which are listed below, can provide access. Some charge flat monthly fees, which are usually preferable to being billed according to the amount of usage.

Internet Provider	Telephone Number
CERFnet	(800) 876-2373
DATABANK, Inc.	(913) 842-6699
Digital Express Group	(800) 969-9090
Exodus Communications	(408) 522-8450
NetworkMCI	(800) 955-6505
NETCOM Online Communications	(800) 353-6600
Performance Systems International	(800) 827-7482
US Cyber	(715) 387-1700

Even if you don't provide access for your general users, you should definitely get access to the Internet somehow. CompuServe, Prodigy, and America Online also provide Internet connections and WWW browsing. However you can get access, just get it. It's important to be able to find answers from vendors to questions asked by technical users, and more often than not, you'll find cheaper and faster help through the Internet than through telephone support lines. It's also important to be able to FTP software and drivers from sites that may not be accessible through other routes.

The following list shows the kinds of software that network administrators can readily find on the Internet:

Software
NIC drivers
SCSI host adapter drivers
Video drivers
NLM updates
Product demonstrations
Shareware and freeware network utilities

Network Management Software

NETWARE'S BUILT-IN management tools handle many jobs in a reasonably straightforward manner. However, many additional network management tools are available, and many of these tools are developed by Novell itself. The Novell products include ManageWise, a package developed with Intel, and the NetWare Management System. Other network management tools for NetWare networks include Frye Computer Systems' Frye Utilities for Networks, Symantec's Norton Administrator for Networks, and McAfee's BrightWorks.

Management Tools from Novell

ManageWise was developed by Novell and Intel and is built on Intel's LANDesk product and NMS. It includes a laundry list of tools and controls, supports SNMP management, and features a Windows interface.

Some of ManageWise's best bells and whistles are its mapping features. The product's logical and physical maps are nicely related, so you can view a device in its logical location and then determine its physical location. The program's alarm configuration is very flexible and can be set to run batch files when certain alarms are triggered. The look and feel of this product is very good, with excellent reporting features and a visually appealing interface.

ManageWise's alarms are triggered when certain administrator- or software-created conditions are met. Examples would be high utilization or error rates on a vital network or high CPU utilization on an overloaded production server.

The NetWare Management System is an older product that allows you to set alarm conditions throughout the network, collect network configuration and utilization data, and manage hubs using the NetWare Hub Services add-on package. The Hub Services product gathers data on hubs, hub add-in cards, and ports, but it also allows network administrators to perform configuration locally or remotely.

SNMP is supported by both these products, which means that the basic network management tools specified by the Simple Network Management Protocol can be used by both. SNMP agents, which are built into SNMP hardware or run as software processes, report activity in network connectivity devices. The data is stored in a Management Information Base (MIB) that determines the data that is saved and which settings can be modified.

Management Tools from Third-Party Developers

Although some administrators prefer to run an all-Novell shop, buying all their network tools from NetWare's maker, many third-party products are available. Among these, the Frye Utilities for Networks, the Norton Administrator for Networks, and BrightWorks are worth discussing.

Frye Utilities for Networks

The Frye Utilities for Networks (FUN) has a bland DOS interface, but it performs admirably when providing inventories of client workstations, updating client software, scheduling execution times for NetWare commands, and metering software usage. The DOS interface is similar to the NetWare interfaces in DOS and performs snappily. The FUN utilities are a suite of products, including NetWare Management, NetWare Early Warning System, NetWare Console Commander, Statistics Display Rack, and other tools.

Software metering is a way of gauging the usage of the software programs your company has installed. Software metering can monitor locally or centrally stored executable files to see how many concurrent and how many different users access the files to run the programs. This information can help you determine usage levels to comply with software licensing agreements.

NetWare Management shows server status and statistics and allows server settings to be changed from the utility. The Early Warning System checks for error conditions such as problems with low memory, communications, files, or print queues. It can page you or invoke other Frye utilities. The Console Commander is a scripting language for scheduling jobs to run at the console. Statistics Display Rack is a Windows program that graphically illustrates network and server statistics.

Norton Administrator for Networks

The Norton Administrator for Networks (NAN) can also inventory client workstations, including Macintosh and OS/2 systems. It attempts to identify the PC manufacturer, installed memory, and even BIOS settings. It performs server and client station software metering, and as an extra bonus, it allows remote control of client stations via network or modem when used with pcAnywhere. This allows you to perform network management functions from a remote site. The Norton Antivirus for NetWare package can be used in conjunction with the Norton Administrator for Networks.

This integration with other Symantec packages is one of the most appealing aspects of NAN. If you already use some of the Norton tools, NAN fits in nicely. The workstation inventory software is excellent, running from a Windows agent without any DOS memory resident software. The client software scans the system and transmits data during periods of inactivity, lessening the agent's impact on system performance. DOS and Mac client stations are not inventoried. The software metering program listing includes over 1,500 pre-inventoried software packages.

BrightWorks

BrightWorks is McAfee's integrated network management tool. It incorporates a central network management console with server monitoring, software license metering, electronic software distribution, workstation inventory tools, and help desk features.

The help desk module is the LAN Support Center (LSC), a McAfee product integrated into BrightWorks. LSC is a database of end-user support requests that assists help desk staff in collecting and managing contact data. LSC can access the inventory information stored in the LAN Inventory module's database records.

BrightWorks also includes the NetTune module, which maps memory and monitors server configuration and performance. The module can monitor utilization patterns and dynamically modify server settings to maximize performance. McAfee claims that performance can be increased by 25 percent using NetTune.

Mind the NetWare Product Certification!

NetWare-compatible products are currently labeled with two types of certification. The certification descriptions themselves don't tell you much, and since vendors are not likely to volunteer information to clarify the issue, I will.

The Yes, NetWare Tested and Approved symbol indicates that Novell Labs has tested the product and approved it.

The Yes, It runs with NetWare certification is given to products that have been tested by their manufacturer. Novell does not check the test results, but it does receive information about the results.

Be sure the products you use have been tested by Novell or are known to work with your NetWare network software.

You should consider all the upgrades discussed in this chapter: the latest server software, NetWare add-ons that provide additional functionality to the network, network administration tools, and dial-up Internet access software. It's not critical that you make any of these upgrades, but all of them provide benefits that can facilitate your network administration tasks.

In the next chapter, we'll talk about how to anticipate and implement new technologies and trends.

The Latest, the Greatest: Anticipating Emerging Technologies

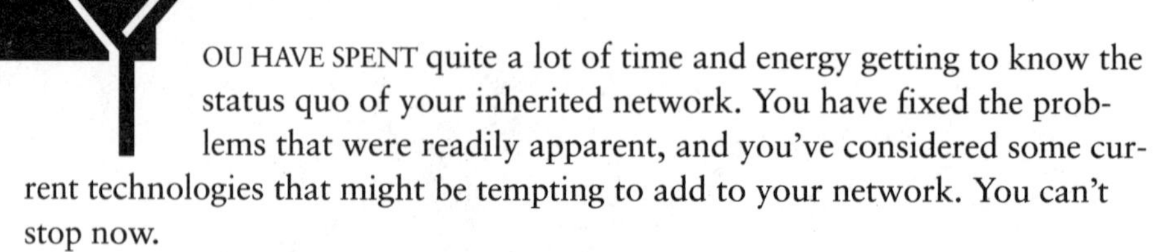

YOU HAVE SPENT quite a lot of time and energy getting to know the status quo of your inherited network. You have fixed the problems that were readily apparent, and you've considered some current technologies that might be tempting to add to your network. You can't stop now.

No, you're not getting off that easily. You've got a responsibility to yourself to stay in the technology loop and identify possible solutions to your problems as they emerge. You owe it to your users to keep their network tools as powerful as possible. And you should do your best to keep your network as healthy and responsive as you can.

For all those reasons, you need to keep your ear to the ground, which you can do in many ways. Many sources of information are at your disposal...if you have the time and inclination to find and use them. You can use the information you gather to research new products and services that could be beneficial to your organization. You can keep track of the development of industry standards to ensure that the equipment you purchase and use is compatible with other parts of your system. And you can determine the risks involved in taking the plunge with new hardware, software, and services.

The Vital Information

THE MOST IMPORTANT lesson in this chapter is that collecting information about new products and technologies is a significant and ongoing process. Many resources are available to network administrators who want to expand their knowledge of products and services that may be useful to them.

SOURCE OF INFORMATION	ACCESS ROUTE
Vendors	Mail, telephone, online service, Web site
Publications	Mail, online service, Web site, Computer Select
VARs	Telephone
Users	Online service, user group

Gathering Information about Products

NEW PRODUCTS CAN be interesting, exciting, and fun. They can also be useful. Unfortunately, they are often difficult to install, painful to configure, and impossible to manage. New products may solve your problems, and they may also create a Pandora's box of new ones. One approach to this dilemma is to try every new product that comes along, keeping the solutions that work, and abandoning those that don't. Most of us lack the patience—let alone the time and money—to baby-sit finicky software or hunt down drivers that allow a new piece of hardware to cooperate with the rest of the system.

For us, the approach is to send some scouts into the new territory before marching the whole army in. Those scouts can take different forms, and each source of information can have unique assets and liabilities. The primary sources are vendors, industry publications, resellers, and other network administrators.

Information from Vendors

Information about developing products is most likely to come from the companies developing those products. Vendors want very much for you to think about the products they offer, whether they're still under development or are mature products that are being updated.

It's in a company's best interests to do what it can to make sure that you, the potential consumer, know that it has a solution to your potential problems. That sounds pretty simple, right? Wrong. Unfortunately, few vendors can be trusted to tell you the truth, the whole truth, and nothing but the truth. Some tell you anything you want to hear to get their foot in the door, and chances are they'll say anything else they can to close the deal.

Truth, then, is not something you can depend on from vendors. There are exceptions, of course, but the trouble is that sales staff have little motivation to do anything but sell product. One doesn't get a commission by losing potential customers in a sudden fit of truth sharing. (Of course, one doesn't assure oneself a sound night's sleep by blowing smoke at people, either. I'm not saying that being a salesperson makes you disingenuous or unreliable.)

Information from Publications

Another major source of industry information is available. Go to your local computer superstore, and take a look at the magazine section. Check out the newsstand in your local bookstore. Computer-related magazines are as numerous as pornographic magazines, and that's saying there's a lot of them! Dozens of technology-related publications could be useful to you. Some are network specific, but even in the enormous group of general industry and vertical market publications, you're likely to find information that can be useful to you.

The problem with these sources is that they often have their own potential bias. Magazines published by a vendor are not likely to review competitive products. They're not going to give you information about other solutions, but they might address bugs or the limitations of their own products.

Even independent publications have been accused of bias. When you see huge advertising spreads with foldouts, don't be terribly surprised if the products advertised are also given glowing reviews. Again, I'm not saying that testers, writers, and publishers are necessarily unworthy of trust. I'm merely pointing out a potential reason for bias that you should keep in mind. An advertiser spending many thousands of dollars on advertising may well be earning a review that's a little too positive.

Information from VARs

So with those two sources and their biases in mind, we turn to the less universal information sources. The first of these is your VARs. If you have picked solid resellers and are happy with their information and support, you may have found the best source of industry information. If they have sold and installed the products elsewhere, you have the confidence of knowing that the VARs have experience with the products and have even more reasons to investigate problems and solutions than if you're the only customer using the product.

Even if you have a good relationship with a single VAR and do most of your procurement and configuration through it and obtain service from it, you might consider finding another reseller if yours doesn't have experience with a product that looks interesting. Contact the vendor for the names of local VARs.

This expertise and accountability is offset somewhat by the fact that VARs may attempt to sell you what they have experience with rather than what makes sense in your situation. If your reseller pulls this kind of maneuver and you realize it, it's time to look again at the Negotiating with VARs and Vendors section in Chapter 15.

Information from Other Administrators

Finally, other administrators are sources of information. However, they may not be any more reliable than a vendor, a magazine, or a VAR. Chances are good that an administrator can give you information about how much work is required to install, configure, and manage a product. They may also be able to pass along information about emerging products, and for this purpose, they are particularly useful. You aren't going to be able to keep tabs on every vendor, every trade publication, and every VAR, but by making use of the eyes and ears of your comrades in the trenches, you can learn a lot about emerging networking technologies and use that information to pool your information-gathering resources.

Following Standards as They Develop

THE DEVELOPMENT OF standards is very important to network administration. Adherence to standards is one of the more important aspects of a product's design. Piles of equipment are rendered useless by the fact that they did not comply with the industry standard and therefore cannot operate with the latest hardware and software. The problem with standards is that they tend to evolve or emerge from designs that catch on and are implemented as de facto standards long before any official organization gives them the stamp of approval.

One example of a de facto standard in the network world is ARCNet, which was sold and implemented for many years without an American National Standards Institute (ANSI) standard. Despite this limitation, ARCNet has been used in many networks, in part because its creator, Datapoint Corporation, licensed its chip technology and standardized components so that ARCNet parts from different vendors work with each other.

The best way to ensure interoperability on your network is to purchase products that work with the other products already in place. Check industry publications, especially if you have access to a database of periodical data such as Computer Select or Computer Database Plus on CompuServe, which are discussed later in this chapter. Search for the product by name to find indications of standards compliance. You can also search for the names of the technologies and standards themselves. If you're looking for ATM products, search for product evaluation articles that discuss ATM products. If you find anything that tickles your fancy, search for it by product name. Call the vendor for more information, and see whether your VAR has any experience with it.

Mining Sources of Industry Information

TWO OF THE SOURCES of industry information we just discussed are easily accessed by users everywhere. Vendors and industry publications are both falling all over themselves trying to put their product data and articles in places that you can see them. This is a wonderful development, because it allows you to seek products and technologies of interest to you at whatever time of day and in whatever way you want.

The major limitations of these sources of information are the biases of their creators and the limitations of access technology. Improvements have been made in the presentation of WWW pages and in online forums and CD-ROM products, but each of these delivery mechanisms still has limitations. Despite my grousing, however, I think it's a good idea to look for products that interest you using as many of these three sources as possible.

Using the WWW to Find Information from Vendors

The WWW is composed of Internet sites with servers that display pages of text and graphics that include dynamic links to other pages. The Web allows the logical grouping of information because the hypertext links on Web pages make the destination address immaterial: users need only click on the link to go to the remote site; they do not have to keep track of the Internet address they are currently pointing to.

That's the idea, at any rate. In practice, many useless home pages contain many useless links, and if I had a dollar for every overzealous would-be Webmaster with a hopelessly complicated, pointless Web site, I'd be a rich man, indeed. Fortunately, Web sites are useful for collecting vendor information because most large organizations are devoting major resources to giving their products a high profile for all the Web surfers.

If you have a direct Internet connection through your network, you need to install an IP stack and a Web browser to access WWW's wonder. Mosaic, SPRY, and Netscape are three of the most popular Web browsers; I prefer Netscape to the other products, but the distinctions are relatively miniscule. Any of the major packages should be suitable.

If your network is not Internet connected, you already should have obtained access through an Internet provider. You can use a modem connection to access the Web, and although performance isn't as snappy as a fast network connection, it's adequate for most needs.

When you're ready to check out the Web, the first place to go is Novell's site.

Big Red's WWW Offerings

Novell's home page is located at the universal resource locator (URL) `http://www.novell.com`. The page is a good one, and it includes most of the information you would want to find, including technical resources, special offers, product information, and development strategies. The Web page is illustrated in Figure 19.1.

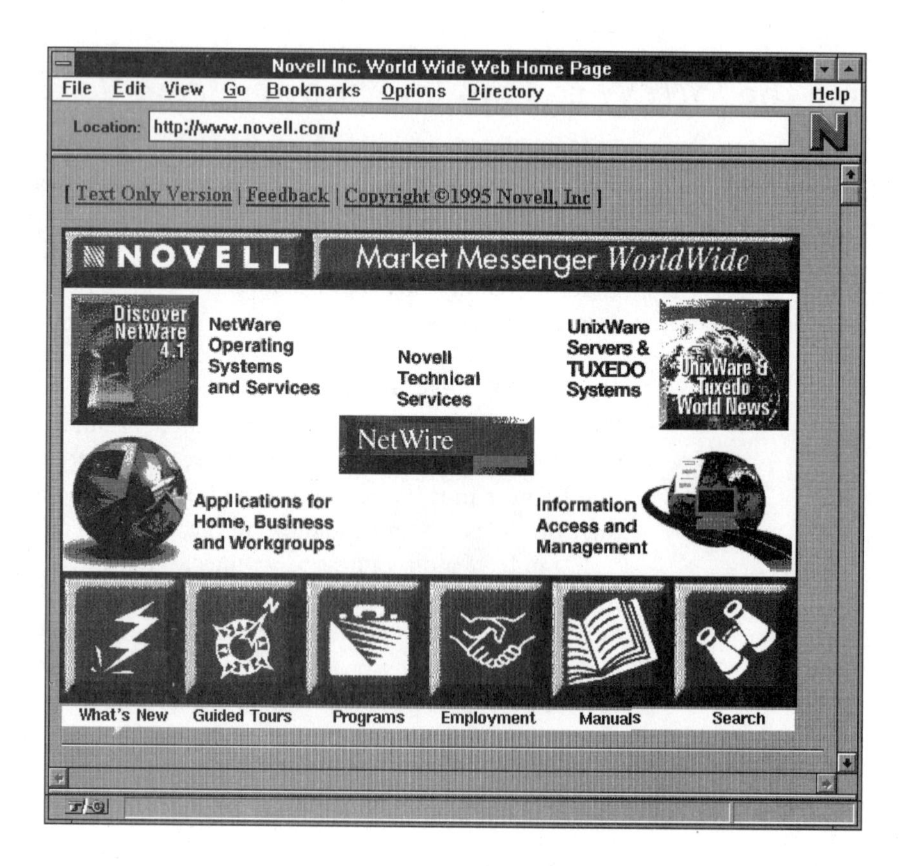

FIGURE 19.1 Novell's WWW home page includes links to information about the company's full line of products, from NetWare to desktop applications.

Investigating Other Web Sites

After you have poked around Novell's site a bit, look elsewhere for information about other products or services that might interest you. URLs for some of the sites that interest me are included below:

URL	SITE
http://thomas.loc.gov	U.S. Congress
http://www.adaptec.com	Adaptec
http://www.adobe.com	Adobe Systems
http://chocolate.pa.dec.com/bagnet.html	Bay Area Gigabit Testbed at Digital Equipment
http://www.compaq.com	Compaq Computer
http://www.irs.com	Internal Revenue Service
http://www.lotus.com	Lotus Development
http://www.mcafee.com	McAfee
http://www.netscape.com	Netscape
http://www.pacbell.com	Pacific Bell
http://www.quantum.com	Quantum
http://www.sybex.com	SYBEX
http://www.ziff.com	Ziff-Davis Publishing

If you can't find a Web site for a company, try a Web search using one of the WWW searching tools available at the following sites:

URL	SEARCH ENGINE
http://lycos.cs.cmu.edu	Lycos
http://webcrawler.cs.washington.edu/WebCrawler/WebQuery.html	WebCrawler
http://www.yahoo.com	Yahoo

Using CompuServe to Find Information about Products

Another place to find product information is the CompuServe online service. CompuServe currently offers a wide variety of options for those seeking tools and toys. CompuServe is attempting to be a one-stop online service for its users. It even allows connection to the Internet via a Point- to-Point Protocol (PPP) or Serial Line IP (SLIP) connection and a version of SPRY's Web browser, which can be downloaded from a standard CompuServe account. The CompuServe home page is shown in its own browser in Figure 19.2.

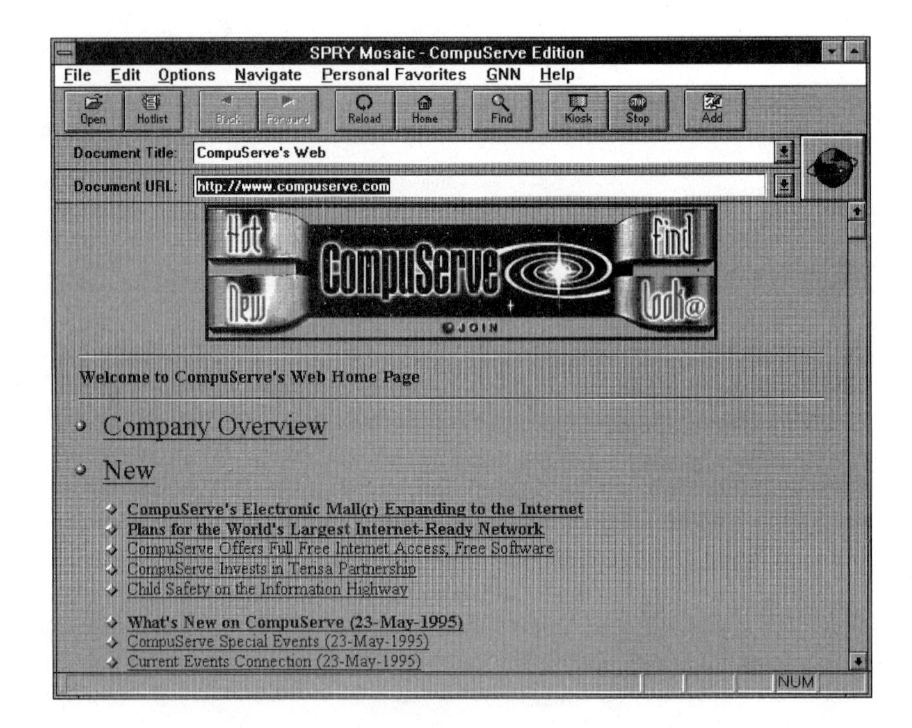

FIGURE 19.2
The CompuServe online service also allows connection to the Internet using a version of SPRY's Web browser.

One of the things CompuServe does better than the Web is store user input in its online forums. These forums are divided by vendor or subject and range from the Role Playing Games Forum to the Windows Utility Forum. Naturally, Novell has a major presence on CompuServe, and many other hardware and software vendors provide a great deal of information and support through these forums.

Using the WinCIM (CompuServe Information Manager for Windows) navigation software, you can find forums using keywords, locate information in file libraries or message sections, post requests for assistance (or provide it to others!), and send or receive files and mail. Other CompuServe navigation packages include 02CIM and Tapcis.

To access the Novell forums, you instruct WinCIM to `GO NETWIRE`. When the smoke clears, you see a screen like the one illustrated in Figure 19.3.

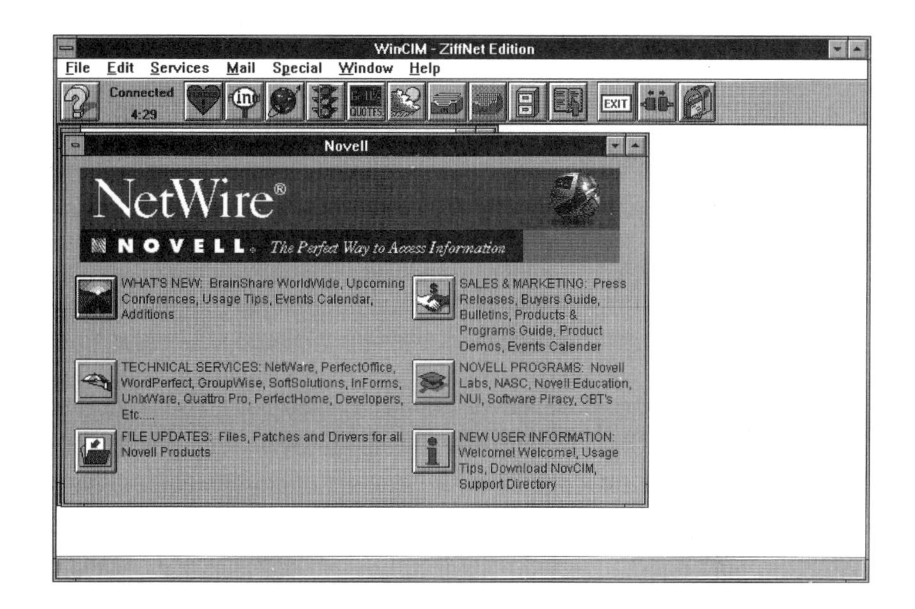

FIGURE 19.3
Novell's NetWire is the heart of its presence on CompuServe. You can go to any of Novell's forums from here.

When you explore the areas available to you in NetWire, you'll find a variety of options. Discussion forums, knowledge bases, and product information repositories abound. You can search for and download update files, look for conversation threads on subjects of relevance, or simply read about Novell's products. Technical support forums are listed in the window shown in Figure 19.4.

You can also look for direct or indirect support from other vendors in other CompuServe forums. The service is robust and mature, and if you want a single bill for your information-gathering, it comes close to meeting all your needs.

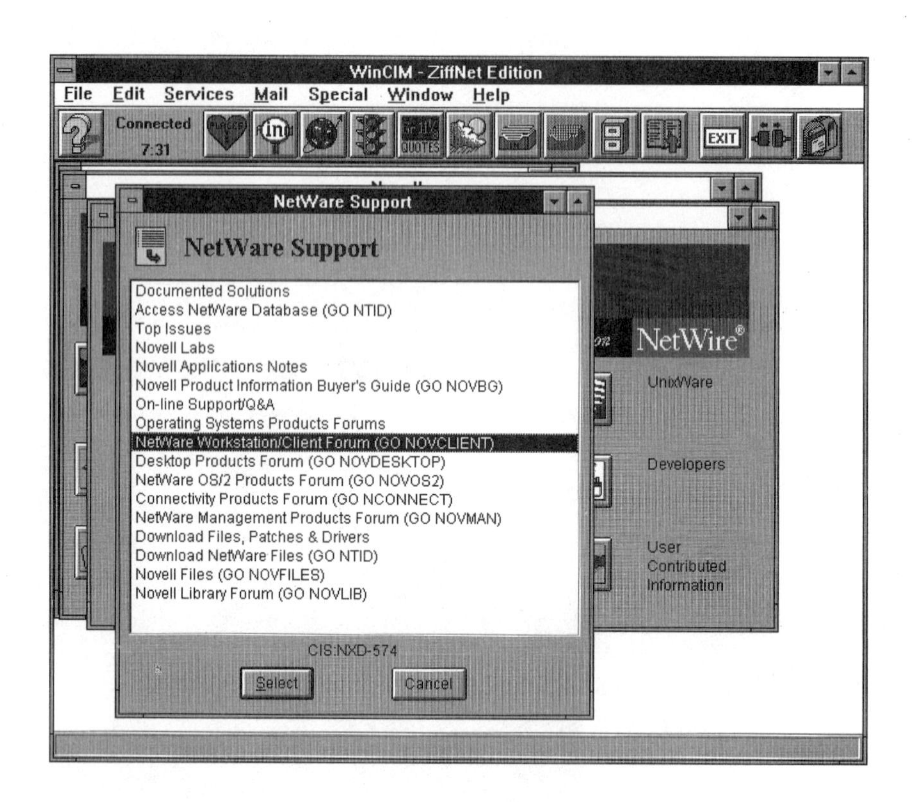

FIGURE 19.4 NetWare support forums can be accessed by selecting the desired entry.

Using Computer Select to Find Information

The WWW and CompuServe information comes primarily from vendors and users, but products are also available that allow you to search databases of articles from computer periodicals. The most successful of these is the Computer Select CD-ROM product.

Computer Select is a CD-ROM of information from a variety of computer and technical publications, including full text coverage of major magazines such as *PC Magazine*, *Macworld*, *Infoworld*, and *Network Computing*. These and other publications are divided into articles, indexed by product name, company name, and topic, and placed in a database that you can search. Most publications include abstracts of the articles, and the abstracts summarize the salient points and most vital information in the articles. Some publications include the full text of all the articles, and several include informational graphics such as diagrams, graphs, and tables.

Computer Database Plus on CompuServe

Much of the data that is on the Computer Select CD-ROM is also available on ZiffNet, a system attached to CompuServe. Computer Database Plus is one of several periodical databases on ZiffNet. It uses a character-based interface that isn't pretty, but it is updated more frequently than the CD-ROM. If you need the very latest information or can't justify the expense of a Computer Select subscription, Computer Database Plus is an option to consider. It's also another reason CompuServe is such a useful tool.

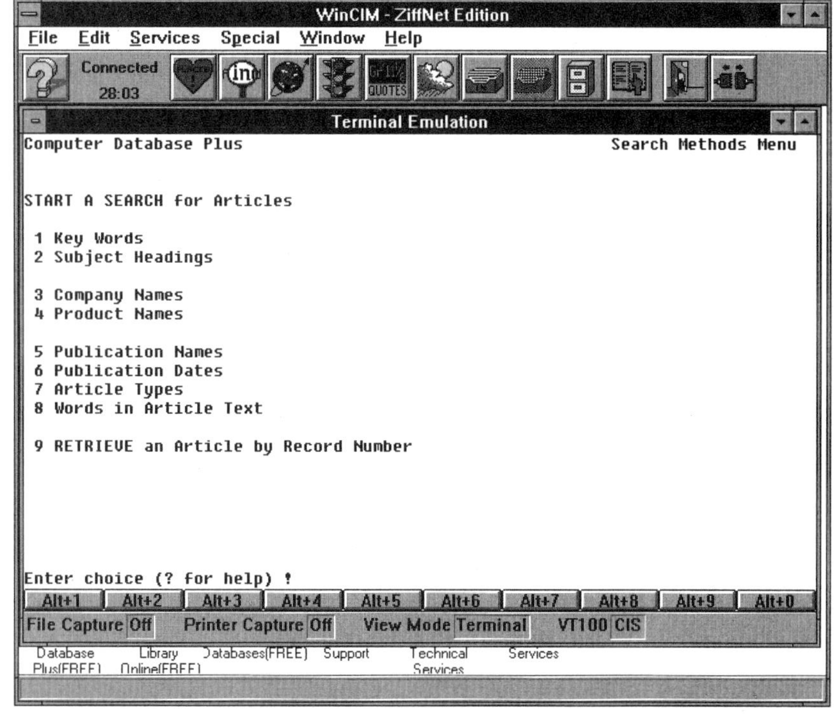

Unlike most forums, Computer Database Plus is a premium service, so you are billed a surcharge for your connect time as well as a fee for the articles you view or download.

Computer Select doesn't completely replace the magazines themselves; even though it includes the informational graphics from some of the most important magazines, it does not convey the visual information that makes written documents attractive. I suggest subscribing to a computer newsweekly such as Infoworld or PC Week and to any magazines that are particularly interesting to you even if you have a Computer Select subscription.

The Computer Select search screen includes several fields that you can use to gather information on the subjects that interest you. The entire database contains more than 70,000 articles. You could look at the articles by publication and issue, reading the articles in your favorite magazines an issue at a time, but it's more useful to search to narrow the number of documents you have to look at.

The fields shown in Table 19.1 can be used to narrow the search:

TABLE 19.1 You can search Computer Select fields to access product information.

FIELD NAME	FIELD FUNCTION
Section	Selects database: articles, product specs, company info, definitions
Words Anywhere	Searches entire documents
Words in Titles	Searches titles only
Product Name	Searches for hardware or software product name and product type
Company Name	Searches for name of company
Publication Name	Searches for name of source publication
Publication Date	Searches for issue date of source publication
Author	Searches for the name of the article's writer
Article Type	Selects type of article: evaluation, tutorial, product announcement, etc.
Topic	Searches for subjects of the article
Attachment Type	Selects type of attached file: macro, chart, table, program, etc.

These fields are available for the Articles database. The other databases on the CD-ROM include:

- Hardware Product Specifications
- Software Product Specifications
- Computer Company Profiles
- Glossary of Computer Terms

Together, these databases are useful for administrators, technicians, corporate buyers, and others who need to be able to find extensive industry information in one place.

When to Jump on the Bandwagon

KNOWING WHEN TO take the plunge is always difficult, and unfortunately, there isn't a hard and fast rule to guide you. You need to collect as much information as you can from the sources described in this chapter and determine the risks you're taking. If the scope of the problem you want to resolve with new technology is broad, you need to be more careful about the choices you make than if the scope of the problem were narrow. The more exposure your network has to uncertain hardware or software, the greater the chance you'll be putting out fires rather than developing a better infrastructure.

Before you make your final decision, consider these questions:

- What problem am I addressing with this product?
- Are any competitive products available?
- Is this product the market leader?
- Is there a standard for this type of product?
- Does my product adhere to the standard?
- Can I find someone else who has implemented this solution?
- Was his or her experience a positive one?
- Does this vendor have a reputation for supporting its products?

A Sample Computer Select Articles Search

Computer Select contains so much information, it's hard not to find what you're looking for. If you wonder if 100VG-AnyLAN might be useful for your network, for example, you can perform a search for the string *100VG*. Seeing that 272 articles discuss this topic, you would probably decide to narrow your search. You select Network Architecture from the **Topics** field to limit the results to discussions of network design. This search results in a total of 16 articles, a manageable number.

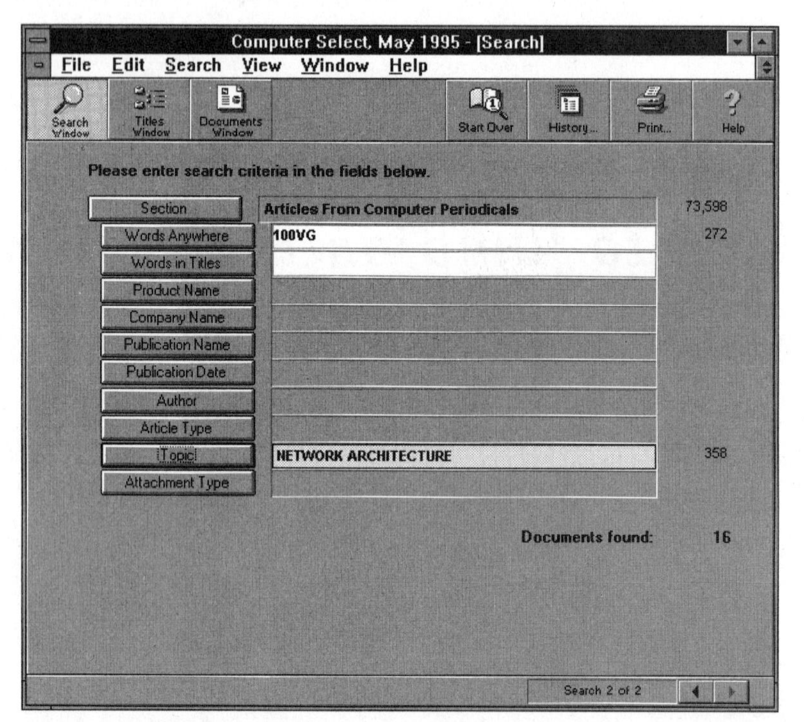

Clicking on the **Titles Window** button, you find a list of article titles and the names and issue dates of their source publications.

(continued)

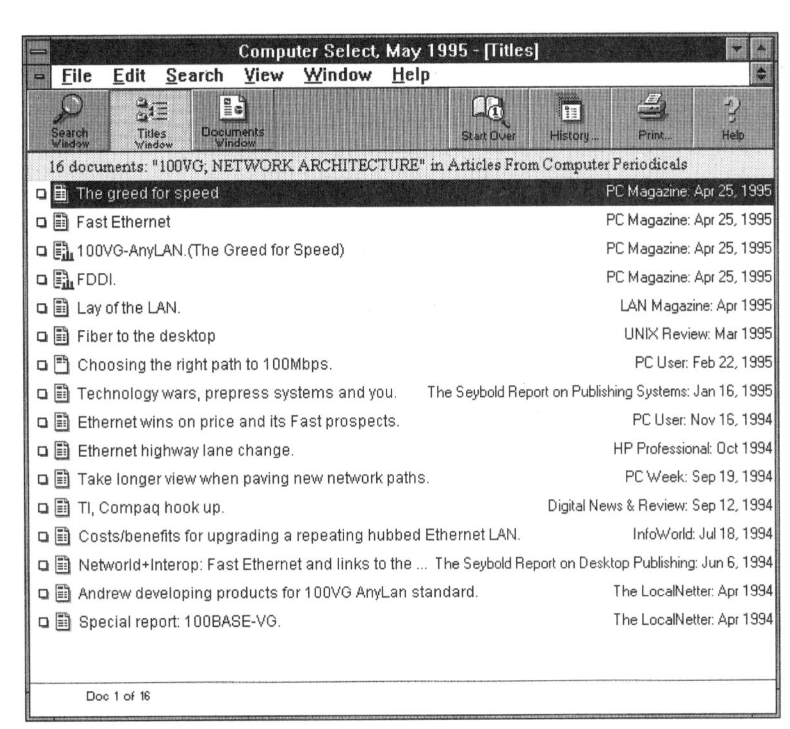

The most recent articles are from an issue of *PC Magazine*, and you can see that two of the articles contain graphics as well as full article text. You double-click on one of the documents to view the article.

(continued)

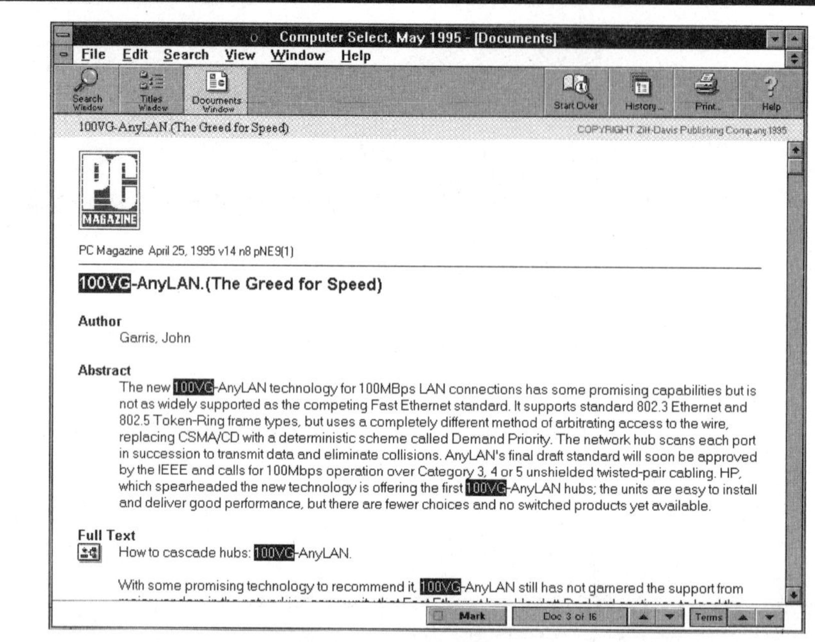

Computer Select, May 1995 - [Documents]

File Edit Search View Window Help

Search Window | Titles Window | Documents Window | Start Over | History... | Print... | Help

100VG-AnyLAN.(The Greed for Speed) COPYRIGHT Ziff-Davis Publishing Company 1995

PC MAGAZINE

PC Magazine April 25, 1995 v14 n8 pNE9(1)

100VG-AnyLAN.(The Greed for Speed)

Author

Garris, John

Abstract

The new 100VG-AnyLAN technology for 100MBps LAN connections has some promising capabilities but is not as widely supported as the competing Fast Ethernet standard. It supports standard 802.3 Ethernet and 802.5 Token-Ring frame types, but uses a completely different method of arbitrating access to the wire, replacing CSMA/CD with a deterministic scheme called Demand Priority. The network hub scans each port in succession to transmit data and eliminate collisions. AnyLAN's final draft standard will soon be approved by the IEEE and calls for 100Mbps operation over Category 3, 4 or 5 unshielded twisted-pair cabling. HP, which spearheaded the new technology is offering the first 100VG-AnyLAN hubs; the units are easy to install and deliver good performance, but there are fewer choices and no switched products yet available.

Full Text

How to cascade hubs: 100VG-AnyLAN.

With some promising technology to recommend it, 100VG-AnyLAN still has not garnered the support from

Mark | Doc 3 of 16 | Terms

The abstract contains enough information, but you're curious about the enclosed diagram. You double-click on its icon, and the graphic appears on your screen.

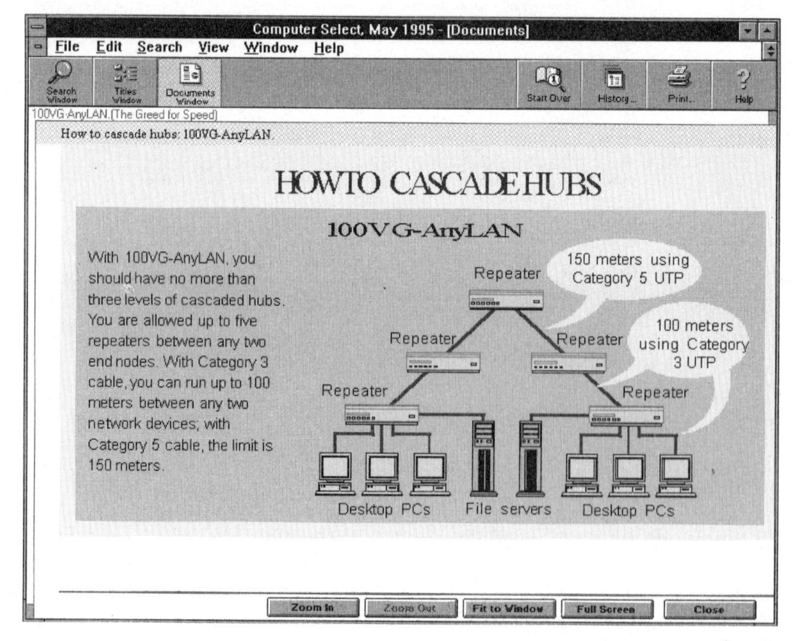

(continued)

You decide that although the 100VG-AnyLAN standard looks feasible for your network, its lack of support makes you too nervous to implement it now.

Information gathering is a vital exercise in the maintenance of good network health and development. Your inherited network should be a dynamic tool that reflects your growing understanding of the technologies available to you and the ways in which they can be made to improve your organization's work flow and business processes. In the next chapter, we return once more to the users who set the goals that shape the business processes—management.

All in the Same Boat: Getting Management on Board

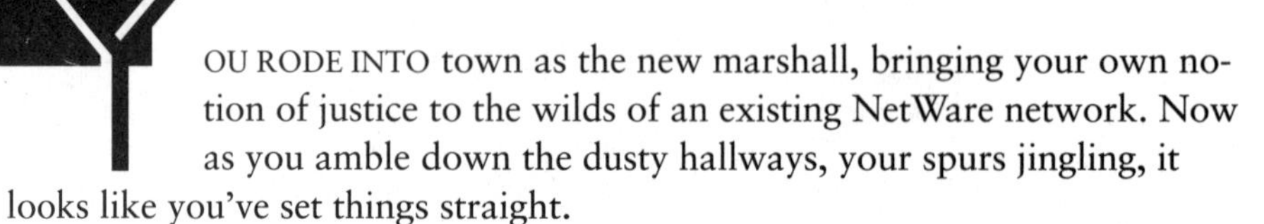

YOU RODE INTO town as the new marshall, bringing your own notion of justice to the wilds of an existing NetWare network. Now as you amble down the dusty hallways, your spurs jingling, it looks like you've set things straight.

Hold up there a second, partner. You're missing just one thing before you can ride off into the sunset. You may be the marshall, but the real law is the justice of the peace. You handle the problems in this here LAN, but you're not the one who determines what happens next.

There really is one more task you need to complete before you're ready to pull off your boots, set your six-shooter down, and have a glass of lemonade. You have to convince the executives that you're doing what needs to be done.

Communicating with executives about the network you administer can be a problem, not just because many high-level managers do not have any appreciable technical background or aptitude. Network operation is an expensive proposition, and you've probably moseyed into your new network demanding enhancements, upgrades, and changes in the way things have been done—all of which take money.

Despite management's tendency to view networking as a strain on the budget and despite the problems you have translating your discussions of technology issues into language executives can understand, the outlook is not all bleak. In fact, if you can find a way to communicate the information you have learned about the ways in which network operations can be improved, you may find that upper management is a major ally rather than an impediment to progress.

Contributing to the Bottom Line

YOUR FIRST TASK when attempting to improve relations with upper management is to placate the bean-counters. Whether these are the financial managers or other executives, it's wise to anticipate some resistance to your plans to spend money.

This phenomenon manifests itself particularly strongly in centralized IS departments that do not have the entrenched history of a heavy metal data center. A distributed network environment is less likely to resist spending money on improving the network, in part because the network management function is distributed among other profit centers.

Since businesses that formerly used mainframe computers have a legacy of large budgets for maintenance and development of large-scale applications and systems, they are also somewhat safer from this attitude.

Regardless of your organization's history and your IS group's structure, however, you can expect pressure to decrease your costs while helping to decrease the operating costs of the other business units.

The solution to this problem is to highlight every cost-saving measure you implement. If you increase available network bandwidth by adding a network switch, estimate the time savings users will experience. If your fault tolerance improvements increase the amount of time the servers are up, don't be shy about reporting the difference.

If you want to go whole hog, install accounting on your NetWare servers, and start billing your users for your services. Actually sending a bill won't be necessary in most cases, but it may be useful for making a point to someone who's a little too focused on the bottom line. Just as you need to see yourself and your network as parts of your organization's production process, management needs to see—sometimes in a tangible way—how the production process involves and relies on you.

Translating Technospeak

ANOTHER PROBLEM NETWORK administrators encounter when attempting to communicate with managers is a language gap. Have you ever been baffled by the slang used by an eight year old? How about a biochemist? If you're trying to explain SAP filtering to a sales executive with little technical interest, you're in for trouble. On the other hand, if you tell the same executive that the servers are broadcasting so much status information that performance is reduced for users of the marketing contact database, you are more likely to have a sympathetic ear when you indicate that you want to purchase NetWare 4.x to reduce this status broadcast information.

The idea, then, is to explain technical concepts in terms of their effects. Follow the lead of the managers you're speaking to: if they use certain technical terms comfortably, follow suit. But do not push the envelope, because you don't want the executives to shut you out. You want them to listen to what you have to say because your message is relevant and important to them.

Tailoring the Message to Your Audience

CONVEYING A RELEVANT and important message is critical. If you aren't convinced that what you're talking about will be interesting and important to the person you're talking to, it will take an impressive act of salesmanship for you to pull it off.

Employ your observational skills to ascertain what issues are important to each of the managers you need to deal with. If they voice pet concerns, make note of it, and use that information to position your own arguments.

For example, if one of the vice presidents at your company is concerned about electronic mail security and privacy issues, be careful to mention mail database access when you are attempting to gain support for funding of a more secure server room. If one of your organization's executives is interested in moving production processes offshore, what better way to sell your plan for remote access enhancements? When you couch your argument in terms that the listener cares about and can hear, you're most of the way to getting what you want.

Exciting Executives

GETTING THE REST of the way to what you want requires a little more effort. If you're hoping to increase the size and power of your network, the best way to accomplish this is by giving upper management reasons to take an interest in your efforts. This approach dovetails nicely with my network administration credo, which instructs you to know what your organization wants to do so that you can help your coworkers make it happen.

If you know what your organization wants to accomplish, you can make your network as effective a tool as possible to reach the corporate goals.

Another Approach: Excuses

Once there was a network administrator who inherited a NetWare network. When she arrived on her first day, she noticed three sealed envelopes on her desk. They were numbered and marked "Open only in case of emergency."

Everything went well for six months when the entire network suddenly crashed. Her manager called her, piping mad. Remembering the envelopes, she pulled out the first one, opened it, and read the message inside. It said, "Blame your predecessor."

Since she couldn't think of another excuse, she went to see her manager and confided, "The previous administrator was completely incompetent. It was just a matter of time before the network collapsed." This seemed to pacify her manager.

(continued)

All went well until another six months passed, and the network crashed again. When she got the angry call from her manager, the administrator turned once again to her stash of envelopes. The second message suggested, "Blame the old equipment."

Thinking this excuse seemed reasonable, she went to her manager's office and said firmly, "We absolutely have to get new equipment; this old network is about to go for good." The manager agreed, a new network was installed, and all went well for six months.

When the next disaster struck, the administrator looked at the third envelope even before her manager called. This message instructed, "Make three envelopes...."

When you are viewed as an enabler, rather than the petty ruler of a fiefdom, you gain the respect of the managers who are driving the corporate policy. As you gain respect, you gain the opportunity to be heard.

We've gone over lots of ground while investigating your inherited NetWare network. By this time, you should feel a sense of understanding and ownership. You know about the network's hardware and software components, its safety, its use, and its management. You're armed with sources of information that can help you identify and choose among the technologies and products being offered and developed. The network is officially yours; you're in the position to repair what goes wrong, expand to meet your organization's growing needs, and change components or designs that need to be updated.

Following a logical approach to taking charge of your network is only the first step. You need to continue to expand your understanding of networking technologies, business objectives, and interpersonal communications. Enjoy the challenges of network management, appreciate the skills of your coworkers, and respect the needs of your users and management. Network administrators who enjoy their jobs and work well with others are valuable beyond belief, so have fun out there, okay?

Netware Command Quick Reference

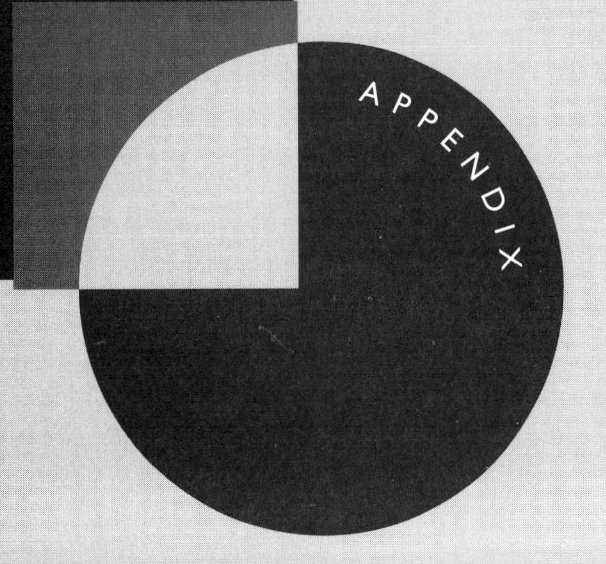

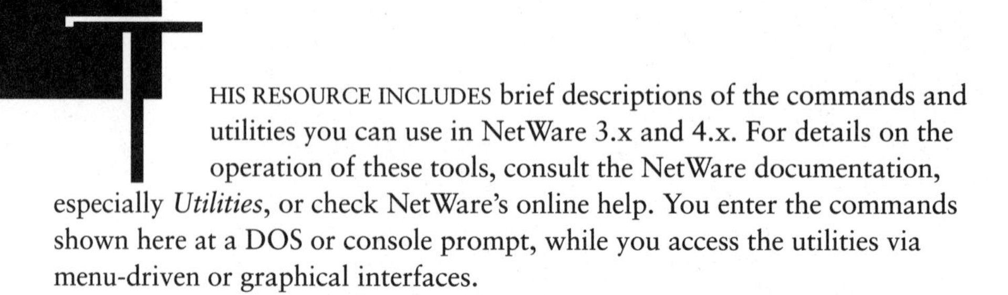

THIS RESOURCE INCLUDES brief descriptions of the commands and utilities you can use in NetWare 3.x and 4.x. For details on the operation of these tools, consult the NetWare documentation, especially *Utilities*, or check NetWare's online help. You enter the commands shown here at a DOS or console prompt, while you access the utilities via menu-driven or graphical interfaces.

Tools You Use in NetWare 3.x and 4.x

ADD NAME SPACE A console command that stores files from Macintosh, OS/2, NFS, or other name spaces. Support for the desired name spaces is added individually to the appropriate volumes.

ATOTAL A DOS command that determines the total accounting services used on a server with accounting installed.

BIND A console command that links server NIC drivers with transport protocols, such as IPX or IP. Each protocol is bound individually to each network board.

BROADCAST A console command that allows users to send a brief message to other users on the network.

CAPTURE A DOS command that directs print jobs to network printers.

CLEAR STATION A console command that disconnects users from the network. It closes open workstation files and severs communications between the server and workstations.

CLS A console command that clears the console display.

COLORPAL A DOS utility that creates, modifies, and removes color palettes used with NetWare menu utilities.

CONFIG A console command that displays file server configuration information.

DISABLE LOGIN A console command that prevents users from logging in or attaching to a file server.

DISMOUNT A console command that makes a network volume unavailable to users.

DISPLAY NETWORKS A console command that lists known IPX network numbers and the time and number of hops required for packets to reach those networks.

DISPLAY SERVERS A console command that lists known file servers.

DOSGEN A DOS command that boots diskless client workstations from files on the network server rather than a local drive.

DOWN A console command that clears server cache buffers, closes files, and updates FAT and DET tables before exiting to DOS or turning off the server power.

EDIT A console utility that creates or edits text files from the file server.

ENABLE LOGIN A console command that allows users to connect to the file server after the DISABLE LOGIN command has been run.

ENABLE TTS A console command that enables NetWare's Transaction Tracking System after it has been disabled.

EXIT A console command that returns the console to the DOS prompt after a server has been brought down. This command can restart a file server if preceded by the REMOVE DOS command.

FILER A DOS utility that manages volumes, directories, and files.

FLAG A DOS command that views or alters the attributes of files in a directory.

INSTALL A console utility that installs NetWare components, manages NetWare partitions, mirroring, and volumes, and creates or edits the NetWare startup files.

LOAD A console command that adds NLMs to the NetWare operating system on a file server.

LOGIN A DOS command that connects to a server using a particular user account.

LOGOUT A DOS command that terminates the connection with one or all of the servers to which a user is currently attached.

MAP A DOS command that views, creates, or changes network drive mappings, search drive mappings, and fake root drive mappings.

MEMORY A console command that displays the amount of server memory addressable by NetWare.

MODULES A console command that displays a list of currently installed NLMs on a file server.

MONITOR A console utility that views file server information.

MOUNT A console command that makes a network volume available to attached users.

NAME A console command that displays a file server's name.

NCOPY A DOS command that copies files between network directories.

NDIR A DOS command that lists files and directories and related information. NDIR supports a variety of filters and sorting options.

NPRINT A DOS command that sends one print job to a network printer.

NVER A DOS command that identifies the version numbers of the file server and client workstation network software.

OFF A console command that clears the console display.

PCONSOLE A DOS utility that configures print servers and queues and displays information about network print jobs.

PRINTCON A DOS utility that creates print options used with CAPTURE, NPRINT, and PCONSOLE.

PRINTDEF A DOS utility that creates a database of print options used by PRINTCON, NPRINT, and CAPTURE.

PROTOCOL A console command that displays protocol information on a file server.

PSC A DOS command that displays information about print servers and controls print server operations.

PSERVER A DOS command and a console utility that establishes network print services.

PURGE A DOS command that frees the file and disk space used by deleted files, permanently removing those files.

RCONSOLE A DOS utility that controls the network file server console from a client workstation.

REGISTER MEMORY A console command that alerts NetWare to server memory above 16MB if the operating system cannot already see it.

REMOVE DOS A console command that eliminates DOS from the server memory. This command prevents NLMs from being loaded via the server floppy drives or DOS partitions.

RENDIR A DOS command that renames a network directory.

RESET ROUTER A console command that recreates the file server's router table.

RIGHTS A DOS command that views effective directory and file rights.

SEARCH A console command that specifies a search path for NLMs and file server .NCF batch files.

SECURE CONSOLE A console command that requires NLMs to be loaded from SYS:SYSTEM, prevents the use of an OS debugger, and limits changes to the server date and time.

SEND A DOS command and a console command that sends messages to users on the network. You can use the DOS version to send a message from a client workstation to network users or groups, and you can use the console version to send a message to one or all network clients.

SERVER A DOS command that starts the NetWare operating system on a file server. SERVER runs from a floppy drive or a DOS partition on the server.

SET A console command that displays and alters operating system parameters, including:

Communications

Memory

File Caching

Directory Caching

File System

Locks

Transaction Tracking

Disk

Miscellaneous

SET TIME A console command that sets the file server date and time.

SETPASS A DOS command that sets a user account password on one or more servers.

SETTTS A DOS command that sets TTS configuration.

SPEED A console command that displays a file server processor speed rating.

SPXCONFIG A console utility that configures SPX on a file server.

SYSTIME A DOS command that views the date and time on any file server to which a user is attached.

TIME A console utility that views the file server date and time.

TRACK OFF A console command that turns off Router Tracking Screen to prevent server and network advertising packets from being displayed.

TRACK ON A console command that activates a new Router Tracking Screen to display server and network advertising packets.

UNBIND A console command that removes a network protocol from a server's NIC driver.

UNLOAD A console command that removes an NLM and returns the memory it occupied to the caching system.

UPS A console utility that links the file server to its UPS.

UPS STATUS A console command that checks a file server's UPS.

UPS TIME A console command that alters the maximum time you want the server to run on UPS power and the estimated recharge time.

VERSION A DOS command that displays the version number of an NLM or of a file server utility.

VOLUMES A console command that views a list of currently mounted network volumes.

VREPAIR A console utility that repairs problems with a network volume.

WHOAMI A DOS command that views information about a user account and the servers to which a user is connected.

WSUPDATE A DOS command that updates files on client workstations by overwriting them with files on the file server.

Tools You Use Only in NetWare 3.x

ACONSOLE A DOS utility that provides remote control of a file server via a modem connection.

ALLOW A DOS command that views, sets, or alters the Inherited Rights Mask of a directory or a file.

ATTACH A DOS command that connects to a file server without executing a login script.

BINDFIX A DOS command that repairs the NetWare file server bindery database.

BINDREST A DOS command that recovers an earlier version of the bindery if BINDFIX fails.

CASTOFF A DOS command that blocks messages from being received at a network client station.

CASTON A DOS command that receives messages after CASTOFF has run.

CHKDIR A DOS command that displays directory information, including the directory space limitations, maximum storage capacity, the current space in use, and the current space available.

CHKVOL A DOS command that displays volume information, including the volume name, its total size, the space currently used, the space used by deleted files, the total space remaining on the volume, and the space available to the user running the command.

DISABLE TTS A console command that manually disables NetWare's TTS on a server.

DSPACE A DOS utility that views and manages file server attachments, limits the space a user can fill on a network volume, and limits the amount of disk space in a directory.

ENDCAP A DOS command that sends printer redirection to a local parallel printer port.

FCONSOLE A DOS utility that broadcasts network messages, views user connection information, and manages server status.

FLAGDIR A DOS command that views or changes directory attributes.

GRANT A DOS command that grants trustee rights for files and directories to users or groups.

LISTDIR A DOS command that displays subdirectories and their IRMs, effective rights, creation dates, and subdirectories.

MAKEUSER A DOS utility that creates and deletes users. Use this command when you want to add or remove many users.

PAUDIT A DOS command that views server accounting records on a system with accounting services installed.

REMOVE A DOS command that deletes a user or group from the trustee list of a file or directory.

REVOKE A DOS command that revokes trustee rights for a file or directory from a user or group.

RPRINTER A DOS command that connects or disconnects remote printers from network print servers.

SALVAGE A DOS utility that lists, recovers, or purges files that have been deleted.

SECURITY A DOS command that checks for security violations on a NetWare file server.

SESSION A DOS utility that manages file server connections and drive mappings, sends network messages, and lists user information.

SLIST A DOS utility that displays a list of file servers that can be seen from a client workstation.

SMODE A DOS command that controls the way programs look for data files on search drives.

SPOOL A console command that creates, changes, or displays print spooler settings.

SYSCON A DOS utility that controls accounting service settings, handles server connections, displays server information, manages user accounts and groups, and allows access to the system login script, error log, intruder detection features, AUTOEXEC.NCF file, and default user accounts.

TLIST A DOS command that displays the trustee list for a file or directory.

USERDEF A DOS utility that creates multiple users with simple login scripts, home directories, login security, account restrictions, disk space limitations, and print job configurations.

USERLIST A DOS command that displays a file server's current users and their connection numbers, login times, network and node addresses, and object types.

VOLINFO A DOS utility that shows information about the volumes on a file server, including volume names, total volume space, free volume space, total number of directory entries allowed, and the number of directory entries available.

Tools You Use Only in NetWare 4.x

ABORT REMIRROR A console command that cancels remirroring of a logical disk partition.

ATCON A console utility that allows monitoring of AppleTalk network segment activity.

AUDITCON A DOS utility that configures auditing of NDS, server, and file events.

BRGCON A console utility that displays bridge configuration information for NetWare Server for OS/2.

CD A console command that controls a CD-ROM disk used as a NetWare volume. This command mounts, lists, renames, and changes media in networked CD-ROM drives.

CDROM A console utility that enables the use of a CD-ROM in a server-attached CD-ROM drive as a read-only network volume. Also available in NetWare 3.12.

CONLOG A console utility that captures console messages generated by NLMs during initialization.

CX A DOS utility that changes a user's context in an NDS tree.

DOMAIN A console utility that creates server memory domains to segment and protect server RAM.

DSMERGE A console utility that merges and renames NDS tree structures.

DSREPAIR A console utility that maintains and repairs the server's NDS database.

FILTCFG A console utility that establishes and configures IPX, TCP/IP, and AppleTalk protocol filters.

HCSS A console command that displays and changes High Capacity Storage System settings.

HELP A console command that shows a list of all console commands, displays the syntax of a command, and provides a description and an example of the use of a command.

INETCFG A console utility that configures IPX, IP and AppleTalk network protocol configurations for internetworking.

INITIALIZE SYSTEM A console command that enables multiprotocol router configuration. This command executes from the AUTOEXEC.NCF file and runs the commands in the NETINFO.CFG file.

IPXCON A console utility that monitors IPX network segments and routers on an internetwork.

IPXPING A console utility that sends an IPX ping request packet to another station on an internetwork to determine whether the node is accessible.

KEYB A console utility that sets the server keyboard to one of the preset national or language definitions.

LANGUAGE A console command that sets NLMs and server commands to use message files for a certain language.

LIST DEVICES A console command that displays information about the server's connected devices.

MAGAZINE A console command that confirms the completion of requests for magazine insertion and removal.

MEDIA A console command that confirms the completion of requests for media insertion and removal.

MIRROR STATUS A console command that displays the status of mirrored logical disk partitions on a file server. Also available in NetWare 3.12.

NCUPDATE A DOS utility that sets a new name context in a NET.CFG file on a client system after a container object has been altered.

NETADMIN A DOS utility that creates NDS objects and manages the NDS tree. Use NETADMIN to view, move, delete, or assign rights to an object.

NETSYNC3 A console utility that allows NetWare 3.x file servers to be managed by NetSync.

NETSYNC4 A console utility that allows a NetWare 4.x file server to manage as many as 12 NetWare 3.x servers using NetSync.

NETUSER A DOS utility that manages user control of print jobs, drive mappings, server attachments, and broadcast messaging.

NLIST A DOS command that displays information about files and directories, as well as NDS objects, including users, groups, volumes, servers, and print queues.

NPATH A DOS command that displays a utility program's file search sequence. NPATH helps identify the source of error messages indicating missing files or incorrect versions.

NPRINTER A console utility that allows a server-attached printer to be accessed by network users.

PARTMGR A DOS utility that manages partitions and replicas, allowing creation and merging of partitions and the addition, modification, removal, and synchronization of partitions in various contexts.

PING A console utility that sends an echo request packet to a specified IP node and acknowledges receipt to confirm that the node is accessible on the network.

PMMON An OS/2 utility that monitors CPU utilization between OS/2 and NetWare Server for OS/2 more accurately than MONITOR.

PUPGRADE A console utility that upgrades NetWare 3.x printer definitions, print job configurations, print servers, and print queues to a NetWare 4.x system.

REINITIALIZE SYSTEM A console command that implements changes to a server's multiprotocol router configuration by executing new or altered commands in the NETINFO.CFG file.

REMAPID A console utility that loads on a NetWare 3.x server to manage passwords under NetSync.

REMIRROR PARTITION A console command that begins remirroring a server's logical disk partition. Also available in NetWare 3.12.

RESTART SERVER A console command that restarts a downed server.

RPL A console utility that allows remote booting of diskless client workstations.

SBACKUP A console utility that backs up and restores file servers, workstations, and services.

SCAN FOR NEW DEVICES A console command that identifies disk hardware added since the server started up.

SCHDELAY A console utility that controls server process priorities and schedules to reduce the load on a server CPU or give precedence to more important tasks.

SERVMAN A console utility that performs server management functions, including altering time synchronization parameters in server batch files and setting IPX/SPX packet parameters.

SET TIME ZONE A console command that displays and configures time zone information on a server.

TCPCON A console utility that displays information and activity about the TCP/IP segments in an internetwork.

TIMESYNC A console utility that controls synchronization of time between servers using NDS databases to prevent replication errors.

TPING A console command that sends an echo request packet to a specified IP node and acknowledges receipt to confirm that the node is accessible on the network.

UIMPORT A DOS command that imports user information from one NDS database into another.

WSUPGRD A DOS command that updates dedicated IPX NIC drivers on client workstations to ODI drivers.

GLOSSARY

ABEND An abnormal end on a NetWare server. This type of system crash occurs when NetWare detects a serious error. It results in the server stopping dead in its tracks; an error message is displayed on the console monitor indicating the type of error that occurred and the process that caused the error.

access method A way of determining which network node may use the communications medium. ARCNet and Token Ring networks use slightly different token-passing access methods, while Ethernet networks use a collision detection access method.

access rights *See* rights.

adapter *See* host adapter.

alias An NDS object that points to another object in a NetWare 4.x directory tree. Aliases can be useful for giving users in one part of the tree access to objects in another part of the tree. A noncontainer resource, such as a printer, or a container, such as an organizational unit, can be aliased.

API An application programming interface is a set of function calls used by one application to control another application. By using an API, a programmer can employ standard functions and messaging understood by an application.

AppleTalk Apple Computer's network architecture uses Ethernet, Token Ring, or Apple's LocalTalk access methods. Although LocalTalk is slow, Macintosh systems using EtherTalk or TokenTalk can communicate at full Ethernet and Token Ring speeds. The AppleTalk protocol follows the OSI model.

AppleTalk zones An AppleTalk internetwork is divided into zones so users can find network objects more easily. Each zone name can be up to 32 characters in length and is maintained with a table of addresses on each router. On a

NetWare network, each NetWare server with AppleTalk nodes performs routing and zone maintenance for its AppleTalk users.

applications server A computer system that runs applications. Systems running NetWare 2.x, 3.x, and 4.x do not make very effective applications servers; these operating systems are designed to provide rapid and secure access to files and network peripherals. UNIX and Windows NT are better suited to the role of applications servers.

ARCNet Called the Attached Resource Computer Network, this local area network design was created by Datapoint Corporation. Its original 2.5 Mbps design is slow by current standards, and despite the introduction of a 20 Mbps version, ARCNet has been eclipsed by Token Ring and Ethernet networks.

ARL The Access Rights List is an enterprisewide list of network users and network resources in Banyan Systems' StreetTalk global naming service. The ARL is replicated between servers to maintain consistent user access across the network.

attach The act of establishing a connection from a user workstation to a file server. ATTACH is a NetWare command that connects a user to a server without severing existing network connections or running login scripts.

ATM Although this acronym also refers to automated teller machines and the Adobe Type Manager font management software package, in the networking context, it refers to Asynchronous Transfer Mode. ATM is a speedy, scalable, and reliable switched network technology that uses small, fixed-length packets.

attributes Properties of NetWare files and directories that provide universal control over the use of the files and directories. Attributes override effective rights when the settings conflict. For example, you can set attributes to prevent files from being copied, deleted, or renamed. You can also hide and purge files and directories by setting the appropriate attributes.

backbone The portion of a network that handles the lion's share of the traffic. An internetwork backbone typically connects the file servers and routers to provide links between LANs. Because backbones carry the most traffic, they typically use the fastest communications equipment and media in a network. A backbone may span a large geographical area or may consist of a single hub connecting several servers.

bandwidth The capacity of data that can be transmitted, often on a communications line, computer bus, or peripheral channel. For example, standard IEEE 802.3 Ethernet's 10 Mbps bandwidth means it can theoretically transmit 10 Mbps. The PCI bus allows 32 bits to be transferred simultaneously, giving it greater bandwidth than the 16-bit ISA bus.

bindery A database of network objects, properties, and property values used in NetWare 3.x networks. The objects in the bindery include users, groups, file servers, print queues, and print servers. The properties of each object are its defining characteristics, such as a user's full name, password, account restrictions, and trustee assignments. The values for each object's properties are stored in the bindery. NetWare 4.x replaces the bindery with NDS but offers bindery emulation mode, which allows backward compatibility to bindery-based applications.

BIOS The basic input/output system is code that facilitates communications between a computer and its I/O components. The BIOS is usually stored in firmware on a computer's motherboard and on some add-in devices such as SCSI host adapters.

blocks Units of data stored on a volume. NetWare defaults to 4KB blocks. Files smaller than the block size still take up the full block size on NetWare 3.x systems because the block is the smallest addressable space on the volume. This means that large numbers of tiny files can occupy much more space than you expect. For example, one thousand 512-byte files don't take up 512,000 bytes on a default NetWare volume, they take up 4,096,000 bytes—4MB! NetWare 4.x includes a feature called block suballocation, which allows small files to share blocks. This suballocation scheme divides each block into 512-byte units.

board An add-in card that fits into a connector on a computer's motherboard and is connected to the system via the expansion bus.

bridge A device that forwards a packet from one network segment to another segment. A bridge looks at the packet's destination address and transmits the data if the packet is headed for the other side.

broadcast If you're talking about data communications, broadcast packets are those sent to all nodes on the network. If you're talking about NetWare utilities, broadcast messages are short missives composed at the server console or client workstation and sent to one or more users or network workstations.

buffer A portion of memory set aside to hold data being processed. Data can be held for quick processing when the processor is ready. In NetWare, communications and caching operations are handled using designated buffers, the size of which are generally configurable at the server console.

bus-mastering A feature of certain computer bus designs that allows devices such as add-in boards, peripherals, or memory to directly communicate without burdening the computer's CPU.

bus topology A physical topology that connects network nodes to a single cable that is terminated at both ends.

cache buffer *See* buffer.

client/server A system architecture in which user workstations, running front-end software and performing at least some of the application execution, make requests of data from servers. File servers specialize in storing, reading from, and writing to centrally located files, while application servers perform some of the application processing. In a client/server system, processing is split between the client stations and the servers.

coaxial cable Also called coax, this cable contains a central conductor, surrounded by an insulated material, which is in turn surrounded by another conductor. The cable is usually covered in another insulator and a protective cover. Coax can carry large amounts of data, and its electromagnetic properties make it less likely to produce or be affected by EMI than twisted-pair cable.

collision This is a fact of life in the world of Ethernet. Collisions occur when two network nodes attempt to use the same data transmission medium at the same time. Devices attempting to use the network at the same time are said to be in contention.

communications protocols Standards for hardware and software systems that manage data transmission between computer systems. In a loose sense, communications protocols range from modem communications specifications such as Zmodem, to network access methods such as Ethernet, and to higher-level communications such as IPX and TCP/IP.

concentrator *See* hub.

container These NetWare 4.x NDS objects organize other objects to logically organize the NDS tree. Container objects include countries, organizations, and organizational units.

context The position of an object in a NetWare 4.x NDS tree. An object can be specified in its context by including the names of the containers above it in the directory tree.

CRC Cyclical redundancy checking is a method of error checking in which an error is detected if a check character is not matched at both ends of a data transmission. The source device determines the check character based on the contents of the data being transmitted and appends the value to the message. The destination device performs the same calculation, compares its result to the appended check character, and requests retransmission if the results do not match.

CSU/DSU Channel service units and digital (or data) service units connect digital communications lines, such as T1 leased lines, to your in-house communications systems. CSU/DSU functions are sometimes found in multiplexers.

DET A Directory Entry Table is maintained for each network volume and contains that volume's directory entries. The DET is maintained in the NetWare server's RAM and allows very fast lookup of directory names.

deterministic network Although this sounds a bit like Calvinist philosophy, it refers to networks in which a node's access to the transmission medium can be guaranteed. Token Ring, FDDI, and ARCNet are deterministic because they use token passing to prevent multiple nodes from attempting to use the same cabling simultaneously.

device driver This software allows the operating system to address and control computer devices such as disk drives and NICs. In the NetWare world, ongoing updates to the drivers for NICs and disk controllers are common, and updating your device drivers can often prevent or solve problems with the corresponding devices.

disk duplexing A fault tolerance scheme in which data is simultaneously written to multiple redundant disk drives connected to multiple redundant disk controllers. Duplexing prevents the failure of a single drive or controller from causing data loss. Support for duplexing is built into NetWare.

disk mirroring A fault tolerance mechanism in which data is simultaneously written to multiple redundant disk drives connected to a single disk controller. Mirroring prevents failure of a single drive from causing data loss, but if the disk controller fails, mirroring fails. Mirroring support is built into NetWare.

disk partition A logical division of disk space. A NetWare file server's network volumes are stored on NetWare partitions; the server may also have DOS or

OS/2 partitions or a system partition that stores configuration information. A NetWare volume can span multiple NetWare partitions.

disk striping This process distributes data onto multiple disk drives to increase performance or improve fault tolerance. Performance is enhanced because multiple drives can be simultaneously reading or writing the data. Fault tolerance is provided when disk striping is coupled with parity checking. RAID systems sometimes use this technique.

DMA Direct Memory Access logic is used on microcomputers to accelerate data transfer between a device such as a disk controller, a NIC, or a sound board and memory. DMA allows the peripheral to directly access system memory, bypassing the CPU to improve throughput.

DNS The Domain Name Service is an addressing method used on the Internet to associate node names and address numbers. A DNS is a distributed database of IP addresses, names, and aliases.

downtime This is usually the bane of a working administrator's existence. Downtime is time in which a network or its components are not functioning and its users cannot work. When a file server is down, users cannot log in or access files on its disks. When a network communication device is down, data cannot travel as it should and may end up being inefficiently routed or even stranded. Scheduled downtime is time you anticipate and use to perform upgrades or other maintenance, while unscheduled downtime is what happens when your server suddenly abends.

driver Software that manages the interaction between a peripheral device and an operating system. Drivers are usually designed to control specific hardware models or devices that conform to particular standards. Operating systems, including network operating systems such as NetWare, typically include drivers for basic or very common devices. Drivers are typically refined and improved to eliminate conflicts with other devices or with the operating system itself.

ECC Error checking and correcting or error correcting code is used in various computer components, particularly RAM, to determine whether an error has occurred, and if it has, to correct the error on the fly.

effective rights These are the directory, file, or object rights that another bindery or NDS entity can actually use on the file, directory, or object. Effective rights to files and directories are calculated by checking trustee assignments, inherited rights from parent directories, group trustee assignments, and security equivalencies. Effective NDS object rights are calculated from profiles, containers, groups, security equivalencies, and those explicitly granted to the object.

EIDE The Enhanced Integrated Drive Electronics interface supports faster data transfer rates than standard IDE drives, can access drives larger than 528MB, and can control four hard disks rather than just two. EIDE interfaces are typically found on PC systems and can also control CD-ROM drives.

EISA The Extended Industry Standard Architecture is a 32-bit bus architecture that can accept EISA or standard ISA boards. The EISA bus inventories the EISA boards it contains, and many of the add-in boards available take advantage of EISA's bus mastering features.

elevator seeking This is a technique used to optimize handling of requests when reading data from hard disks. Elevator seeking performs queued read operations according to the physical location of the data on the disks. The drive heads flow smoothly, reducing wear on the heads and the delay caused by unnecessary head movement.

EMF *See* EMI.

EMI Electromagnetic interference is electromagnetic force that radiates from an electrical device and creates an electrical field that can disrupt other electrical current. For example, a power cable can radiate EMI that may interfere with the twisted pair cable lying across it in a server room.

ENS Banyan's Enterprise Network Services are a suite of networking services, including the StreetTalk network directory services, electronic mail, and network management services. ENS has been split from VINES and is offered on other network operating system platforms.

ESDI The Enhanced Small Device Interface is a disk controller technology with slower data transfer than IDE, EIDE, and SCSI interfaces. ESDI controllers and disks are relatively uncommon today.

enterprisewide network An internetwork that connects an entire organization. This term is generally used to refer to networks even more grandiose than metropolitan area networks (MANs) and wide area networks (WANs); an enterprisewide network generally includes disparate network systems and may span the globe.

Ethernet The most widely used local area network design comes in a variety of configurations. Ethernet supports multiple physical topologies and cabling schemes and several frame types, and it currently offers 10 Mbps or 100 Mbps speeds. Since Ethernet is nondeterministic, it is prone to packet collisions, which increase in number as more nodes become active. Ethernet was originally created by Bob Metcalfe, who named it after the imaginary and invisible substance once thought to conduct light.

EtherTalk *See* AppleTalk.

fake root A drive mapping that points to a subdirectory but acts as a root directory. This is useful when applications need to run from the root directory but you do not wish to place them in the root or do not wish to give access rights at the root level.

fault tolerance *See* SFT.

FAT The File Allocation Table is an index of the blocks in which files can be found. Because files may occupy multiple, noncontiguous disk areas, the FAT is used to keep track of all a file's component parts. Each NetWare volume includes a FAT that is cached into server RAM to accelerate file access.

FDDI The Fiber Distributed Data Interface is a 100 Mbps network that runs primarily over fiber optic cable. A version running over copper, known as Copper Distributed Data Interface (CDDI) also achieves 100 Mbps throughput but at shorter maximum distances. FDDI is a token-passing architecture in which dual counter-rotating rings service the network; if a single ring is severed, network operation can still continue. Nodes can be attached to one ring, as Single Attached Stations (SAS), or to both rings, as Dual Attached Stations (DAS). FDDI is expensive but is a good choice for network backbones.

file caching This technique stores file data in server RAM to improve read and write performance. Cached files are much more rapidly accessed than files stored and accessed on disk.

file server A computer providing shared access to files and peripherals on a network. NetWare is designed to perform best as a file server—managing access to centrally located files and network connected printers—rather than as an applications server. File server hardware generally reflects this function, with emphasis placed on high-speed disk access and large amounts of RAM used for FAT and DET caching.

frame A packet format used to transmit network data. Multiple frame types can be supported on a single network; the most common frames are Ethernet 802.3, Ethernet 802.2, Ethernet II, Ethernet SNAP, Token Ring, and Token Ring SNAP.

frame relay A technology employing packet switching to transmit data at speeds that may exceed 2 Mbps. Frame relay is faster than X.25 because it uses less error detection.

gateway A device or software package that allows communications between networks running different protocols. Gateways are also sometimes used to connect disparate applications.

GFS The grandfather-father-son backup strategy maintains multiple copies of backed up files. The son copy is usually a daily backup of files that have changed since the last father backup. The father is created weekly and is maintained so that in conjunction with a son tape, all files can be restored. The grandfather might be a monthly backup that is retained for long periods.

global naming service A network feature that translates logical object names into physical device addresses. NetWare 4.x uses the NDS global naming service; Sun's UNIX systems use a naming service called NIS.

hop Each server or router that data travels through on a NetWare network is considered a hop. Network routing usually attempts to minimize the number of hops a packet must travel from its source to its destination. Packets are discarded when the maximum number of hops (16 on a NetWare system) is exceeded. Each hop slows the flow of data because each router has to look at the contents of the packet before sending the packet on its way.

host adapter Another name for a SCSI disk controller. Also used to refer to disk coprocessor boards, which include dedicated processors that offload tasks from a computer's CPU.

hot swap In RAID 5 systems, disk drives may be removed and replaced on the fly. This feature, which takes advantage of the disk striping and parity data storage that characterize RAID 5, allows replacement of a failed drive without downtime. Of course, rebuilding the data that was stored on the old drive can be time consuming, but that's the way it goes.

hub A device that amplifies or splits transmission signals for broadcast to additional network workstations. Current usage is loose enough to include such devices as active and passive ARCNet hubs, 10BaseT concentrators, and Token Ring MAUs.

IDE Integrated Drive Electronics disks and controllers are extremely common in standalone PCs and network workstations, and they are also found in network servers, although the more robust SCSI interface is preferred in file servers. IDE drives and controllers are less expensive than SCSI drives and controllers, but Enhanced IDE (EIDE) is required for addressing drives larger than 510MB. EIDE controllers can address four devices, twice as many as standard IDE, and EIDE allows double the transfer rate of the older design.

Inherited Rights Filter *See* IRM.

Internet An enormous internetwork based on the TCP/IP protocol that connects government, university, and business computers around the world. Originally designed for the Department of Defense and until recently used primarily by the academic world, the Internet is now being used by many businesses and individuals to share data. And when somebody figures out a way to make money on the Net, look out.

internetwork Two or more separate networks connected by a router—often a NetWare file server with multiple NICs. This type of server can act as a multiprotocol router.

I/O port The computer memory location used by a particular device to communicate with the CPU. The I/O port is one of the settings that may need to be specified for an add-in device such as a serial board or a NIC.

IP address A node's TCP/IP physical address is a 32-bit value that identifies the node's network and its network station. The address is divided into four bytes, separated by periods.

IPX The Internet packet exchange protocol is a Novell-designed protocol used to route data on a network. Although IPX is well suited to LAN communications, TCP/IP is regarded as a better protocol for wide area networking.

IPX internal network number A number uniquely identifying a NetWare server. The number is in hexadecimal format and can be one to eight digits long.

IPX network number A number that uniquely identifies a transmission medium segment (usually a cable system). This hexadecimal number can be one to eight digits long.

IRF See IRM.

IRM The Inherited Rights Mask is a list of rights that control how access flows from one directory to another. Only the Supervisor trustee right and rights designated in a directory's IRM are inherited from parent directories. In NetWare 4.x networks, the Inherited Rights Filter (IRF) controls the flow of rights from parent directories and container objects to files, directories, and objects.

IRQ The interrupt request is a PC hardware interrupt that signals the microprocessor that a computer device or peripheral needs CPU attention.

ISA bus The Industry Standard Architecture bus design is commonly found in PC systems. The ISA bus can address 8-bit or 16-bit add-in boards and is much slower than newer designs such as EISA and PCI buses.

IS Information systems departments generally include computer development and support operations and computer programming staff. *See also* MIS.

ISDN The Integrated Services Digital Network standard defines a communications method that can transmit data, voice, and video. The most common form of ISDN is the Basic Rate Interface (BRI), a 144 Kbps implementation. Primary Rate Interface (PRI) offers 1.54 Mbps bandwidth. Both forms use a dedicated communications channel for control data.

IT Information technology includes the gamut of computer and communications equipment and software managed by IS departments. IT forms the infrastructure upon which your organization creates, manipulates, and delivers its data.

KAPP File server named after former Cal quarterback and head coach Joe Kapp, the only player ever to appear in the Super Bowl, Grey Cup, and Rose Bowl.

kernel The essential portion of an operating system that provides the basic services vital to the system's operation. The microkernel is the portion of the operating system that is used to control the hardware; it is a hardware-specific part of the kernel.

LAN A local area network is a computer network in a limited area or a department of an organization. Although in a strict sense, a LAN includes only one network number, small internetworks or multiserver networks are often referred to as LANs.

local bus A connection between a computer's processor, peripherals, and memory that runs at the full speed of the processor rather than a more constricted bus width. PCI and VL-bus are common local bus architectures.

LocalTalk *See* AppleTalk.

LSL The Link Support Layer is part of the ODI specification and handles the interaction between NIC drivers and communications protocols running on the NICs. The LSL can handle multiple protocols on a single NIC.

MAN A metropolitan area network spans an organization's sites in a single city. A MAN is bigger than a breadbox. It is also larger than a LAN, but it's smaller in geographical area than a WAN.

map The process of designating a drive letter on a workstation to point to a directory on a NetWare volume. MAP is a NetWare command that can establish, remove, or redefine drive mappings, including fake roots and search drives.

MAU Multistation access units are the hub devices used in Token Ring networks. Although these devices used to be called MSAUs, they are now usually referred to as MAUs, especially since people stopped referring to Ethernet media access units and started calling them hubs.

MCA The Micro Channel Architecture is a bus design created by IBM. It uses 32-bit communications, provides automatic configuration from information stored on Micro Channel boards, and offers high data transfer rates and busmastering. However, it was introduced at a time when compatibility with ISA boards was important, and it carried a price premium, so it never became popular. IBM called it the MCA bus until the Music Corporation of America (MCA) found out and put a stop to that moniker, so it's now referred to as the Micro Channel bus.

Micro Channel *See* MCA.

MIS A Management Information Systems department is sometimes distinguished from an IS organization when the IS group handles systems and software and the MIS group handles data processing. MIS and IS are often used interchangeably, and arguing about the difference seems a waste of time, doesn't it?

MLID A Multiple Link Interface Driver is a NIC driver used with the ODI network specification. The MLID controls transmission and receipt of data from the network; it adds and removes the frame headers of outgoing and incoming message packets.

MSAU *See* MAU.

MSL A mirrored server link is the high-speed connection that runs between the primary and secondary server in an SFT III mirrored server system. This umbilical cord handles the synchronization of the servers.

multiserver network A network with a single network number that has multiple file servers connected is called a multiserver network. Internetworks include multiple network numbers.

mux A multiplexer is a communications device that allows a single communications line to carry multiple signals.

name space An NLM loaded to support non-DOS files on a NetWare volume. NetWare supports DOS files by default, but OS/2, UNIX, and Macintosh files can also be stored on NetWare volumes if the appropriate name space modules are added on the server.

NCP The NetWare Core Protocol is the portion of the network operating system that handles requests from network stations. Workstation requests to create and eliminate connections, perform file operations, print, or alter the NDS directory are handled by NCP.

NDIS The Network Driver Interface Specification is a device driver design developed by Microsoft and 3Com and used in Vines, Windows NT, and LAN Manager. It is supported by NetWare.

NDS The NetWare Directory Services is a database of network resources and access information that is distributed across an entire NetWare 4.x network and is replicated to ensure consistent access and security. The NDS stores network services and treats them as objects with properties that define relationships and control access. These objects are divided into organizations and arranged in a hierarchical tree. NDS replaces the NetWare bindery.

NetBEUI The NetBIOS Extended User Interface is an enhanced version of the NetBIOS driver. NetBEUI provides network communications services at the transport level and is used in Windows NT, Windows for Workgroups, and other network operating systems.

NetBIOS A network transport protocol used largely by IBM. NetBIOS is not routable, so it can cause routing loops and other problems on larger networks. It is best suited to its designed role in support of peer-to-peer applications.

NetWare Requester The NetWare client software for OS/2 and DOS. This software allows client workstations to connect to the network and can even provide data access to OS/2 application servers without a NetWare server connection.

NetWire Novell's online presence on CompuServe (`GO NETWIRE`) and the WWW (`http://www.novell.com`) is called NetWire. Product information, updated files, and problem/resolution information can be found at both sites.

NFS The Network File System is a file system that allows data sharing across protocol, operating system, and hardware boundaries. Used almost universally in the UNIX world, NFS provides distributed file and peripheral access.

NIC A network interface card is a board in a client workstation or server that allows communication between the machine and the network. NICs are also known as network boards and network adapters.

NIS The Network Information Service manages network resource locations. NIS is used widely in the UNIX world to provide lookup services for network resources that are linked by TCP/IP and shared via NFS.

NLM A NetWare Loadable Module is a program that is linked to the NetWare operating system while it is running but that can be loaded and unloaded from the server's memory while the server is running. Disk and NIC drivers, name space modules, utilities, and applications are all NLMs.

NLSP NetWare Link Services Protocol is an IPX routing protocol that distributes routing information, including network numbers, media types, and routing costs, between routers on a network. NLSP creates a logical network map at each router.

node number Each NIC is assigned an identification number that uniquely identifies that NIC on the network. Ethernet NICs use node numbers assigned by the manufacturer; these numbers are allotted so that no two boards have the same number. ARCNet and Token Ring NICs allow node numbers to be altered. Node numbers are particularly important in ARCNet networks, where the token is passed according to the NIC numbers.

nondeterministic network This is the flip side of the determinism characteristic in ARCNet and Token Ring networks. Nondeterministic networks—those using Ethernet, for example—cannot ensure that only one node is transmitting at one time, and in high-traffic networks, collisions are quite common.

NOS A Network Operating System is the software that manages network resources and requests for network services. The NOS may be a peer network operating system (PNOS), in which each station acts as a client workstation and as a server, requesting services from other stations and servicing requests from other clients. True NOS software runs on a dedicated file server.

ODI The Open Datalink Interface is a specification for network drivers that couples unique NIC drivers with standard network protocol software. Separating the protocol stacks from the device drivers increases modularity and allows multiple protocols to run on the same hardware simultaneously.

OSI model The Open Systems Interconnection standard for data communications defines a seven-layer structure in which each layer performs a distinct function. Although few network protocols strictly adhere to the OSI model, the structure is useful for understanding the communications process and comparing different protocol architectures.

packet A packet is a package of data transmitted over a network. When network nodes send data across the network, their NICs create the data packets, which include headers used for instructing network nodes on how to handle the packet. If the data that is to be sent at one time cannot fit in a single packet, the network message is divided into several packets, which are reassembled at the destination node.

packet burst A NetWare protocol that sends related groups of packets to increase data transfer. Although standard IPX transmissions require an acknowledgment of the receipt of each packet, Packet Burst allows multiple packets to be sent before receipt is acknowledged.

partition *See* disk partition.

PCI bus The Peripheral Component Interconnect bus is an Intel-developed bus technology that connects peripherals to a computer's microprocessor via high-speed logic. PCI offers very high throughput, automatic configuration, and bus-mastering.

PCMCIA The Personal Computer Memory Card International Association's PC Card add-in modules, which are more commonly referred to as PCMCIA cards, are small expansion devices that are primarily used in portable computers. These devices are self-configuring and are often memory, modems, NICs, or hard disks. Some PCs include PC Card ports.

PNOS *See* NOS.

print queue A network directory in which print jobs are stored while waiting to be serviced by a print server. Users direct their print jobs to a queue through a process called capturing. Print jobs directed to a NetWare print queue are stored temporarily in a network directory and are fed to the printer by the print server.

print server An NLM, workstation, or dedicated device that controls the flow of print jobs from print queues to printers.

protocol A protocol is a standard way of communicating, especially on a network. Communications protocols used on NetWare client workstations include IPX, TCP/IP, and AppleTalk.

queue operators NetWare users who can control the queue to edit other users' print jobs, delete print jobs, modify the queue status, and reorder jobs.

RAID Redundant array of inexpensive disks are groups of physical disk drives logically grouped to create a single logical device. These arrays can be used to improve performance or enhance system fault tolerance.

remote control This software allows you to connect to a remote computer and take over its functions. The connection is usually established via modem. Remote control software is often used to perform remote management functions or access network data from a remote location.

remote node This software allows you to connect to your network using a phone line. By calling a network-connected modem from a system running the network client software, you can attach to the network as though your system had a local network connection. Performance is ploddingly slow, especially when you run executable files that are not local.

repeater A device that boosts communications data signals for long distance communications or to connect two similar networks. 10BaseT hubs act as repeaters.

Requester *See* NetWare Requester.

rights Properties of files and directories that control the users and groups that can gain access and determine the extent of access allowed.

ring topology A physical network structure in which the nodes are connected in a circle. Token Ring networks are physically structured in a star topology, but their logical structure follows the ring design, with the token being passed in a circle from node to node.

RIP The Routing Information Protocol allows NetWare routers on an internetwork to maintain a table that allows data to be transmitted by the fastest route available. RIP broadcast packets are broadcast periodically to keep the tables updated, and when changes in the internetwork are detected, additional broadcasts are made.

router A device that determines the best route for the packets that cross its path. The router examines the packet's destination address and uses its routing table to calculate the most expedient route. NetWare servers can act as multiprotocol routers.

SAP The Service Advertising Protocol is used by NetWare servers to broadcast their addresses and services. This information populates a router table containing server information.

SCSI The Small Computer Systems Interface is one of the most popular peripheral interface standards. A SCSI host adapter can access up to seven peripherals (usually disk drives, tape drives, or CD-ROM drives). Apple Macintosh and several common UNIX systems provide built-in SCSI support, while DOS systems must load additional device drivers to address SCSI devices.

shielded twisted pair *See* twisted pair.

SFT System Fault Tolerance provides hardware and software redundancy to reduce the risk of data loss in the event of a device failure.

SMP Symmetric multiprocessing uses multiple processors sharing system memory, disk, and network functions to improve performance. Any of the processors in the SMP system can execute the next operating system call that comes up.

SNA IBM's System Network Architecture is a proprietary networking system for connecting IBM mainframes to local area networks.

sneakernet This access method involves copying files to a diskette or other portable media and walking it over to a colleague's machine. I find that Converse provides the best throughput.

SNMP The Simple Network Management Protocol defines network management data formats to standardize network information collection. Compliance with the SNMP standard allows management of network services and devices using SNMP management systems.

SNYDER File server named after former Cal head football coach Bruce Snyder, who led the Golden Bears to a 10-2 record and a 37-13 victory over Clemson in the Citrus Bowl.

SPX Sequenced Packet Exchange is an enhancement to the IPX protocol that adds packet delivery verification. SPX attempts retransmissions when it identifies delivery failures.

star topology A physical network layout in which the network nodes are connected to a central computer system or hub. This configuration provides some overall fault tolerance because a single failed spoke usually does not affect any of the neighboring nodes.

switching This technology is rapidly becoming popular, especially on bandwidth-starved Ethernet networks. An Ethernet switch provides the entire 10 Mbps bandwidth to one connection for a brief period, then cycles through the rest of the connections, providing full bandwidth to each in turn.

TCP/IP The Transmission Control Protocol/Internet Protocol is a suite of communications protocols designed for Internet networking. Protocols in the suite include Telnet, File Transfer Protocol, Simple Mail Transfer Protocol, TCP, RIP, and IP.

termination Ending a bus topology or device chain with a terminator (terminating resistor) that eliminates signals that reach the end of bus or chain. Commonly used with SCSI devices and bus-based Ethernet networks.

THEDER File server named after former Cal head football coach Roger Theder, who coached the 1979 team to a 7–5 record and an appearance in the Garden State Bowl.

token passing This access method transmits a frame to workstations on the network. Since these nodes cannot communicate except by using the token, outgoing messages are included in empty frames. Frames containing data are checked as they pass each station so the recipient can claim the data and the frame can be cleared.

Token Ring An IBM network design that features a physical star topology in which the hub (called a MAU) passes tokens in a ring among the connected computers.

TokenTalk *See* AppleTalk.

topology The physical arrangement of network cables, nodes, and connections. Although hybrid forms exist, the star, ring, and bus topologies are the most common.

Tower of Hanoi A backup tape management scheme similar to the GFS method. Unlike the GFS method, which uses a single grandfather and father tape, the Tower of Hanoi adds multiple fathers. By including more intermediate-level tapes, this method retains data longer but uses more tapes.

TTS NetWare's Transaction Tracking System backs out of incomplete transactions that could result in database file corruption if the server goes down. The NetWare server returns the data to the state it was in just before the failure.

twisted pair These insulated wires come in shielded and unshielded forms. Twisted pair wires are thin, insulated wires that are twisted to reduce interference. Shielded Twisted Pair (STP) is less common than Unshielded Twisted Pair (UTP), but the addition of shielding greatly reduces electromagnetic interference.

UPS Uninterruptible power supplies provide power to connected devices in case of power failure. Online UPS systems are always active, so there is no lag between the failure of power from the wall and the supply of power from the UPS battery. UPS monitoring software can notify you when power failures occur and can even shut a server down in an orderly fashion.

UTP *See* twisted pair.

VAP A Value Added Process is an add-in program for NetWare 2.x servers. Although VAPs are similar to NLMs, you should upgrade your NetWare 2.x systems and eliminate your VAPs if possible.

VESA bus *See* VL-bus.

VL-bus The Video Electronics Standards Association's local bus architecture that connects the CPU directly to the peripheral expansion bus to provide high performance for up to three devices. Although the VL-bus standard is still under development, PCI is generally considered a better future technology.

VLMs Virtual Loadable Modules are components of the latest NetWare client software for DOS and Windows. This modular client software allows easier expansion and upgrading than previous designs.

volume A fixed amount of disk space, composed of one or more disk segments on one or more hard disks. Volumes are the highest level of division in NetWare's file system and can be logically divided into subdirectories.

WAN Wide area networks are internetworks that connect LANs across wide geographical areas. WANs are often connected via high-speed digital communications lines, but they can also consist of LANs tied together with modem connections.

WWW The World Wide Web is a virtual network running on the Internet. WWW sites typically contain graphics, text, and hot links to other network sites with logically related information. The software packages used to look at these sites are called Web browsers.

X.25 A standard defining communications between a packet switching network and a network station. The X.25 standard uses check sum error checking and extensive acknowledgment that enhance reliability but limit performance.

10Base5 Ethernet Thick Ethernet runs on thick coaxial cable at 10 Mbps. Network nodes are connected to the coax backbone via transceivers that connect to a NIC's AUI port and are tapped into the coaxial cable itself.

10Base2 Ethernet Thin Ethernet runs over thin coaxial cable and connects network nodes via BNC connectors. Like 10Base5, 10Base2 runs at 10 Mbps maximum. It is also referred to as ThinNet or CheaperNet.

10BaseT Ethernet running at 10 Mbps over twisted pair cabling, which makes it less expensive than 10Base2 and 10Base5 cables. It also uses a star topology, which has inherent fault tolerance features not found in the coax-based bus topologies.

100BaseTX An implementation of the 100 Mbps 100BaseT Ethernet technology that uses two-pair Category 5 cabling.

100BaseT The family of 100 Mbps Ethernet running over copper twisted pair wiring. This implementation of Fast Ethernet has the advantage of being similar to 10BaseT and has been more widely accepted than 100VG-AnyLAN.

100VG-AnyLAN A Fast Ethernet implementation running at 100 Mbps that uses a different access method than 10BaseT to reduce network collisions. Despite this difference, 100VG is intended to be compatible with both Ethernet and Token Ring frame types and networks.

Index

Note to the reader:

Main entries are in **bold. Boldfaced** numbers indicate pages where you will find the principal discussion of a topic or the definition of a term. *Italic* numbers indicate pages where topics are illustrated in figures.

Numbers and Symbols

A

B

C

E

G

H

S

U

V

FULL TEXT ON CD.

This dynamic update to *Novell's Complete Encyclopedia of Networking* expands upon the original with a more comprehensive collection of data for users of every type of network. *The Encyclopedia* brings you in-depth analyses of hardware, software, competitive networking topologies, and network operating systems. You'll also find details on cabling, interface cards, shells, applications, standards, protocols, and more. The companion CD contains the complete text of *The Encyclopedia*, including graphics and tables, in a format that allows for detailed data searches.

ISBN 1829-1
1,400 pages

Available soon wherever computer books are sold.

Installing the Software from the Companion CD-ROM

The software included on the companion CD-ROM must be installed before you can use it. Computer Select and the network utilities can be installed using the following procedures:

Installing Computer Select Trial Edition

From DOS:

1. Put the CD-ROM in your computer's CD-ROM drive.
2. From any non-CD-ROM drive letter, enter `n:CS`, where `n:` is the CD-ROM drive letter. Computer Select displays a license agreement, installs software to your hard disk, and starts its DOS version.

From Windows:

1. Put the CD-ROM in your computer's CD-ROM drive.
2. Start Windows, and select **File...Run.**
3. Enter `n:SETUPW`, where `n:` is the CD-ROM drive letter. The Setup program displays license information and prompts you for a destination for installed files. It creates a Computer Library group in Windows with a **Computer Select** icon.
4. Double-click the **Computer Select** icon to start the trial edition software.